International Policy Institutions

Around the
Pacific Rim

A Directory of Resources in East Asia, Australasia, and the Americas

compiled by Ramón Bahamonde
with a preface by Abraham F. Lowenthal
and an introduction by Charles E. Morrison

LYNNE
RIENNER
PUBLISHERS

BOULDER
LONDON

Published in the United States of America in 1998 by
Lynne Rienner Publishers, Inc.
1800 30th Street, Boulder, Colorado 80301

and in the United Kingdom by
Lynne Rienner Publishers, Inc.
3 Henrietta Street, Covent Garden, London WC2E 8LU

ISBN: 1-55587-795-8

Library of Congress Cataloging-in-Publication Data
A record for this publication is available from the Library of Congress.

British Cataloguing in Publication Data
A Cataloguing in Publication record for this book
is available from the British Library.

Printed and bound in the United States of America

The paper used in this publication meets the requirements
of the American National Standard for Permanence of
Paper for Printed Library Materials Z39.48-1984.

5 4 3 2 1

Contents

Detailed Table of Contents   vii

Preface, *Abraham F. Lowenthal*   xv

Acknowledgments   xvii

Introduction, *Charles E. Morrison*   xix

The Directory
    Asia   1
    Australia and New Zealand   115
    Canada   135
    Latin America   167
    Western United States   221

Index by Institution   307

Index by Head of Institution   313

Detailed Table of Contents

Preface, *Abraham F. Lowenthal,* xv
Acknowledgments, xvii
Introduction, *Charles E. Morrison,* xix

ASIA

China

Academy of Macroeconomic Research of the State Planning Commission, 3
Asia Institute, 4
China Center for International Studies, 5
China Institute for International Strategic Studies, 6
China Institute of Contemporary International Relations, 7
China Institute of International Studies, 8
Chinese Academy of Social Sciences
    Institute of Asia-Pacific Studies, 9
    Institute of Finance and Trade Economics, 10
    Institute of Industrial Economics, 11
    Institute of Japanese Studies, 12
    Institute of Latin American Studies, 13
    Institute of World Economics and Politics, 14
Chinese People's Institute of Foreign Affairs, 15
Development Research Center of the State Council, 16
Foundation for International and Strategic Studies, 17
Fudan University
    Center for American Studies, 18
    Center for Japanese Studies, 19
    Department of International Politics, 20
Peking University, School of International Relations, 21
Shanghai Academy of Social Sciences
    Institute of Asia and Pacific Studies, 22
    Institute of European and Asian Studies, 23
Shanghai Center of International Studies, 24
Shanghai Institute for International Studies, 25

Hong Kong

The Better Hong Kong Foundation, 26
Chinese University of Hong Kong
    Centre for Environmental Studies, 27
    Hong Kong Institute of Asia-Pacific Studies, 28
City University of Hong Kong, Contemporary China Research Centre, 29
The Hong Kong Centre for Economic Research, 30
Lingnan College, Hong Kong Institute of Business Studies, 31
University of Hong Kong
    Centre of Asian Studies, 32
    Centre of Urban Planning and Environmental Management, 33
Vision 2047 Foundation, 34

Indonesia

Center for Information and Development Studies, 35
Center for Policy and Implementation Studies, 36
Center for Strategic and International Studies, 37
Indonesian Institute of Sciences, Center for Political and Regional Studies, 38
Institute for Economic and Social Research, Education and Information, 39

Japan

Asia Pacific Association of Japan (*Asia Taiheiyo Kenkyukai*), 40
Association for Promotion of International Cooperation (*Kokusai Kyoryoku Suishin Kyokai*), 41
Foundation for Advanced Information and Research (*Kenkyu Joho Kikin*), 42
Institute for International Policy Studies (*Sekai Heiwa Kenkyujo*), 43
Institute of Developing Economies (*Ajia Keizai Kenkyusho*), 44
The International Center for the Study of East Asian Development, Kitakyushu (*Kokusai Higashi-Asia Kenkyu Center*), 45
International Development Center of Japan (*Kokusai Kaihatsu Center*), 46
International House of Japan (*Kokusai Bunka Kaikan*), 47
International University of Japan, Center for Japan-United States Relations (*Kokusai Daigaku Nichibei Kankei Kenkyujo*), 48
Japan Center for Economic Research (*Nihon Keizai Kenkyu Center*), 49
Japan Center for International Exchange (*Nihon Kokusai Koryu Center*), 50
Japan Economic Foundation (*Kokusai Keizai Koryu Zaidan*), 51
The Japan Forum on International Relations (*Nihon Kokusai Forum*), 52
Japan Institute of International Affairs (*Nihon Kokusai Mondai Kenkyujo*), 53
Keidanren (Japan Federation of Economic Organizations), 54
Kyoto University, Center for Southeast Asian Studies (*Kyoto Daigaku Tonan-Asia Kenkyu Center*), 55
National Institute for Defense Studies (*Bouei Kenkyujo*), 56
National Institute for Research Advancement (*Sohgo Kenkyu Kaihatsu Kikoh*), 57
Nomura Research Institute (*Nomura Sohgo Kenkyujo*), 58
Research Institute for Peace and Security (*Heiwa Anzen Hosho Kenkyujo*), 59
Seikei University, Center for Asian and Pacific Studies (*Seikei Daigaku Asia Taiheiyo Kenkyu Center*), 60
Sophia University, Institute of International Relations for Advanced Studies on Peace and Development in Asia (*Johchi Daigaku Kokusai Kankei Kenkyujo*), 61
Tokyo Club Foundation for Global Studies (*Tokyo Kokusai Kenkyu Club*), 62
The United Nations University *(Kokusai Rengoh Daigaku)*, 63
University of Tokyo, Institute of Oriental Culture (*Tokyo Daigaku Toyo Bunka Kenkyujo*), 64

Malaysia

Asian Institute for Development Communication, 65
Asian Strategy & Leadership Institute, 66
Institute of Strategic and International Studies, 67
Malaysian Institute of Economic Research, 68
Malaysian Strategic Research Centre, 69

Philippines

Center for Research and Communication Foundation, 70
Institute for Strategic and Development Studies, 71
Philippine Institute for Development Studies, 72
Washington SyCip Policy Forum, Asian Institute of Management, 73

Singapore

Institute of East Asian Political Economy, 74
The Institute of Policy Studies, 75

Institute of Southeast Asian Studies, 76
Singapore Institute of International Affairs, 77

South Korea

Institute for Global Economics, 78
The Institute of Foreign Affairs and National Security, 79
Kim Dae-jung Peace Foundation for the Asia-Pacific Region, 80
Korea Development Institute, 81
Korea Economic Research Institute, 82
Korea Institute for Industrial Economics and Trade, 83
Korea Institute for International Economic Policy, 84
Korea Institute for National Unification, 85
Korea University
    Asiatic Research Center, 86
    Ilmin International Relations Institute, 87
Kyung Hee University, Institute of Asia-Pacific Studies, 88
Kyungnam University, Institute for Far Eastern Studies, 89
Pacific Asia Society, 90
The Research Institute for International Affairs, 91
The Sejong Institute, 92
Seoul Forum for International Affairs, 93
Yonsei University, Institute of East and West Studies, 94

Taiwan

Academia Sinica
    Institute of Economics, 95
    Institute of European and American Studies, 96
    Sun Yat-Sen Institute for Social Sciences and Philosophy, 97
Chinese Council of Advanced Policy Studies, 98
Chung-Hua Institution for Economic Research, 99
Institute for National Policy Research, 100
National Chengchi University, Institute of International Relations, 101
Taiwan Institute of Economic Research, 102

Thailand

Chulalongkorn University
    Center for International Economics, 103
    Institute of Asian Studies, 104
    Institute of Security and International Studies, 105
Thailand Development Research Institute, 106

Vietnam

Center for Environmental Research, Education, and Development, 107
Institute for Economic Research of Ho Chi Minh City, 108
Institute for International Relations, 109
National Center for Social Sciences and Humanities
    Center for Japanese Studies, 110
    Center for North America Studies, 111
    Institute for Southeast Asian Studies, 112
Vietnam Asia-Pacific Economic Center, 113

AUSTRALIA AND NEW ZEALAND

Australia

Australian Institute of International Affairs, 117

Australian National University, Research School of Pacific and Asian Studies
    Australia-Japan Research Centre, 118
    Contemporary China Centre, 119
    Department of International Relations, 120
    National Centre for Development Studies, 121
    Strategic and Defence Studies Centre, 122
Griffith University, Centre for the Study of Australia-Asia Relations, 123
Macquarie University, Asia-Pacific Research Institute, 124
Murdoch University, Asia Research Centre on Social, Political and Economic Change, 125
University of Adelaide, Centre for Asian Studies, 126
University of Sydney, Research Institute for Asia and the Pacific, 127
University of Wollongong, Centre for Research Policy, 128

New Zealand

Asia 2000 Foundation of New Zealand, 129
Massey University, New Zealand Centre for Japanese Studies, 130
New Zealand Institute of Economic Research, 131
Victoria University of Wellington
    Centre for Strategic Studies, 132
    Institute of Policy Studies, 133
    New Zealand Institute of International Affairs, 134

CANADA

Asia Pacific Foundation of Canada, 137
British Columbia Chamber of Commerce, 138
Business Council on National Issues, 139
C.D. Howe Institute, 140
Canada-ASEAN Centre, 141
The Canadian Consortium on Asia Pacific Security, 142
Canadian Council for International Co-operation, 143
Canadian Council for International Peace and Security, 144
Canadian Foundation for the Americas/Fondation Canadienne pour les Amériques, 145
Canadian Institute of International Affairs, 146
Canadian Institute of Strategic Studies, 147
Carleton University, Centre for Trade Policy and Law, 148
Centre for Asia-Pacific Initiatives, 149
The Conference Board of Canada, 150
The Fraser Institute, 151
Joint Centre for Asia Pacific Studies, 152
Laval University, Groupe d'études et de recherche sur l'Asie contemporaine, 153
Niagara Institute of International Affairs (A Division of The Conference Board of
    Canada), 154
North-South Institute, 155
Queen's University, The Centre for Canada-Asia Business Relations, 156
Simon Fraser University
    Centre for Policy Research on Science & Technology, 157
    David Lam Centre for International Communication, 158
Université de Montréal, Centre d'études de l'Asie de l'Est, 159
Université du Québec á Montréal and Concordia University, Joint Centre for Asia-Pacific
    Communication Research/Centre conjoint de Recherche en Communication sur
    l'Asie Pacifique, 160
University of British Columbia
    Centre for Asian Legal Studies, 161
    Institute for Asian Research, 162
    Institute for International Relations, 163
York University
    Centre for Research on Latin America & the Caribbean, 164
    York Centre for International and Security Studies, 165

LATIN AMERICA

Argentina

Centro de Investigaciones Europeo-Latinoamericanas, 169
Consejo Argentino para las Relaciones Internacionales, 170
Facultad Latinoamericana de Ciencias Sociales, Área de Relaciones Internacionales, 171
Fundación de Investigaciones Económicas Latinoamericanas, 172
Instituto de Relaciones Internacionales de Asia-Pacífico, 173
Instituto para la Integración de América Latina y el Caribe, 174
Universidad de Buenos Aires, Facultad de Ciencias Sociales, 175

Brazil

Centro de Estudos Estratégicos, 176
Instituto de Estudos Econômicos, Sociais e Políticos de São Paulo, 177
Instituto de Estudos Políticos e Sociais, 178
Instituto Universitario de Pesquisas do Rio de Janeiro, 179
Federation of Industries of the State of São Paulo, 180
Fundação Getúlio Vargas, 181
Pontifícia Universidade Católica do Rio de Janeiro, Instituto de Relações
        Internacionais, 182
Universidade de São Paulo, Núcleo de Pesquisa em Relações Internacionais, 183
University of Brasília, Instituto de Ciência Política e Relações Internacionais,
        Departmento do Relações Internacionais, 184

Chile

Centro de Estudios del Desarrollo, 185
Centro de Estudios Públicos, 186
Comisión Económica para América Latina y el Caribe, 187
Comisión Sudamericana de Paz, 188
Corporación de Investigaciones Económicas para Latinoamérica, 189
Fundación Chilena del Pacífico, 190
Libertad y Desarrollo, 191
Universidad de Chile
        Centro de Economia Internacional y Desarrollo, 192
        Instituto de Estudios Internacionales, 193
Universidad Gabriela Mistral, Instituto de Estudios del Pacifico, 194

Colombia

Fundación para la Educación Superior y el Desarrollo, 195
Universidad de los Andes
        Centro de Estudios Asiáticos, 196
        Centro de Estudios Internacionales, 197
Universidad Externado de Colombia, Facultad de Finanzas, Gobierno y Relaciones
        Internacionales, 198
Universidad Nacional de Colombia, Instituto de Estudios Políticos y Relaciones
        Internacionales, 199

Ecuador

Corporación de Estudios para el Desarrollo, 200

Mexico

Centro de Estudios Monetarios Latinoamericanos, 201
Centro de Investigación para el Desarrollo, 202

Centro de Investigación y Docencia Económicas, 203
Centro de Investigaciones sobre América del Norte, 204
El Colegio de la Frontera Norte, 205
El Colegio de México, 206
Universidad de Colima, Centro Universitario de Estudios e Investigaciones sobre la
    Cuenca del Pacífico, 207
Universidad de Guadalajara, Departamento de Estudios del Pacífico, 208
Universidad Nacional Autónoma de México, Centro de Relaciones Internacionales, 209

Peru

Centro de Estudios y Promoción del Desarrollo, 210
Centro de Investigación de la Universidad del Pacífico, 211
Centro Peruano de Estudios Internacionales, 212
Comisión Andina de Juristas, 213
Grupo APOYO, 214
Grupo de Análisis para el Desarrollo, 215
Instituto de Estudios Peruanos, 216
Instituto Libertad y Democracia, 217

Venezuela

Instituto Venezolano de Estudios Sociales y Políticos, 218
Sistema Económico Latinoamericano, 219

WESTERN UNITED STATES

American Graduate School of International Management/Thunderbird, Center for
    International Business Education and Research, 223
The Asia Foundation, 224
The Asia Society/California Center, 225
Brigham Young University/University of Utah, Center for International Business
    Education and Research, 226
Center for Continuing Study of the California Economy, 227
Center for the New West, 228
Claremont Graduate School, Program in Politics and Policy, 229
Claremont McKenna College, Keck Center for International and Strategic Studies, 230
The Commonwealth Club of California, 231
Discovery Institute, 232
East-West Center, 233
Economic Development Corporation of Los Angeles County, 234
Federal Reserve Bank of San Francisco, Center for Pacific Basin Monetary and Economic
    Studies, 235
The Hoover Institution, 236
Human Rights Watch/California, 237
Institute for Contemporary Studies, 238
Institute of the Americas, 239
Japan Policy Research Institute, 240
Japanese American Citizens League, 241
Leadership Education for Asian Pacifics, Inc., 242
Los Angeles Urban League, 243
The Mansfield Center for Pacific Affairs, 244
Mexican-American Legal Defense and Educational Fund, 245
Monterey Institute of International Studies, 246
National Association of Japan-America Societies, Japan-America Society of Southern
    California, 247
The National Bureau of Asian Research, 248
National Center for APEC, 249
Nautilus Institute for Security and Sustainable Development, 250
The North America Institute, 251

Pacific Basin Economic Council, 252
The Pacific Basin Institute, 253
Pacific Council on International Policy, 254
Pacific Forum CSIS, 255
Pacific Institute for Women's Health, 256
Public Policy Institute of California, 257
RAND, 258
Rice University, The James A. Baker III Institute for Public Policy, 259
San Diego State University, Center for International Business Education and Research,
    260
Southern California Association of Governments, 261
Southwest Voter Research Institute, 262
Stanford University
    Asia/Pacific Research Center, 263
    Center for East Asian Studies, 264
    Center for International Security and Arms Control, 265
    Center for Latin American Studies, 266
    North America Forum, 267
Texas A&M University, Center for International Business Studies, 268
The Tomás Rivera Policy Institute, 269
Town Hall Los Angeles, 270
United States-Mexico Border Progress Foundation, 271
University of California, Berkeley
    Berkeley APEC Study Center, 272
    Berkeley Roundtable on the International Economy, 273
    Institute of East Asian Studies, 274
    Institute of International Studies, 275
University of California, Irvine, Global Peace and Conflict Studies, 276
University of California, Los Angeles
    Asian American Studies Center, 277
    Center for International Business Education and Research, 278
    Center for International Relations, 279
    Center for Pacific Rim Studies, 280
    North American Integration and Development Center, 281
University of California, San Diego
    Center for U.S.-Mexican Studies, 282
    Institute on Global Conflict and Cooperation, 283
University of Colorado, Institute for International Business, 284
University of Hawaii at Manoa
    APEC Study Center (in cooperation with the East-West Center), 285
    Center for International Business Education and Research, 286
    Pacific Asian Management Institute, 287
    School of Hawaiian, Asian and Pacific Studies, 288
University of New Mexico, New Mexico U.S.-Japan Center, 290
University of Oregon, Center for Asian and Pacific Studies, 291
University of San Francisco, Center for the Pacific Rim, 292
University of Southern California
    Center for International Studies, 293
    The Center for Multiethnic and Transnational Studies, 294
    East Asian Studies Center, 295
    International Business Education and Research Program, 296
    Southern California Studies Center, 297
University of Washington
    APEC Study Center, 298
    Center for International Business Education and Research, 299
Washington Council on International Trade, 300
World Affairs Councils, 301
World Trade Center Association, 305

Preface

Abraham F. Lowenthal

I am pleased to present one of the first publications of the new Pacific Council on International Policy: this unique directory of Pacific Rim institutions on international policy, profiling in concise detail some 289 institutions around the Pacific Basin that are key resources for understanding political, economic, and social issues in this vast region, and that are particularly relevant to international policy concerns.

The Pacific Council on International Policy, founded in 1995, is one such institution. It has been launched in the conviction that leaders in many sectors cannot remain provincial when economic, social, demographic, political, technological, and cultural issues are so relentlessly global. Established in cooperation with the Council on Foreign Relations (New York) and based in Los Angeles, the Pacific Council is grounded in the western region of the United States, where international policy institutions have been lacking, even though international ties—particularly with Asia, Latin America, and Canada—have been burgeoning. The Pacific Council seeks to help leaders from many sectors in the U.S. West—in business, labor, politics, government, nongovernmental organizations, academia, and the media—to improve their own understanding of key global trends, network more effectively with counterpart institutions, and contribute to illuminating and resolving shared policy concerns.

As part of pursuing this ambitious mission, we at the Pacific Council sought to inform ourselves about other organizations in the western region of the United States and around the Pacific Rim that are relevant to our mission. We found, however, that it is not easy to identify which institutions are relevant nor to obtain much information about their aims, activities, constituencies, and products, precisely because such institutions have been proliferating in recent years. Because the very notion of the Pacific Rim has been more of a mental construct than a political reality, no comprehensive source of information exists about the range of institutions with which we hope to build connections.

That is the origin and purpose of this directory. We do not claim to have compiled a fully comprehensive guide—and indeed we invite submission of additional profiles to be included in an updated and more complete edition. We are particularly conscious that we have not covered Southeast Asia and Oceania in as much depth as other regions and we aim to do better next time. Nevertheless, we believe that this publication is the most complete, accurate, and informative source available in any language to introduce interested parties to the international policy networks and institutions around the Pacific Rim.

Rather than extend my remarks about these institutions in general, we have invited Charles E. Morrison, director of the U.S. Consortium of APEC Study Centers and an experienced Pacific Rim policy analyst, to provide a substantive introduction, commenting on the rise of international policy institutions around the Pacific Rim and on their current and potential significance. I invite the attention of readers to this thoughtful, well informed, and stimulating essay, itself a contribution to the building of policy networks.

It remains for me to express the Pacific Council's appreciation to a number of individuals and institutions without which this project could not have been completed. Ramón Bahamonde played the major coordinating and drafting role on the project, and he is appropriately credited as the book's author. Mr. Bahamonde managed a complex information-gathering, analytical, and drafting process with intelligence, skill, diplomatic tact, and perseverance.

Many others assisted at various stages with the collection of data and rewriting, checking, and editing the profiles: Andrew Oros, now a Ph.D. candidate at Columbia University; David Hsu, now a Ph.D. candidate at MIT's Sloan School of Management; Mika Chambers, a graduate of Harvard's John F. Kennedy School of Government; graduate students at the University of Southern California's School of International Relations, including Albert Cimadamore, Heather Day, Feng Xu, and especially Mohammed Hafez, who supervised the final stages of the publication process; Timothy Nelson of the Pacific Council's staff; and Linda C. Lowenthal, who edited most of the profiles.

Paul Irwin and his colleagues at the Asia Pacific Foundation of Canada took the leading role in preparing the profiles on Canadian institutions, and Manfred Wilhelmy and Marcela Ugalde of the Fundación Chilena del Pacífico in Chile played a similar role in developing profiles for institutes in that country.

A large number of colleagues in many countries were consulted in the process of identifying the organizations that should be included. I will not list them all here, but we thank all who helped us prepare the directory.

Special mention should be made of the important role of the Japan Center for International Exchange (JCIE), led by Mr. Tadashi Yamamoto, in building Asian networks of policy institutions and compiling useful background information on many centers. We are grateful to JCIE, and to Mr. Yamamoto and Mr. Makito Noda personally, for sharing important materials with us and providing useful advice and encouragement.

Finally, we express our appreciation to those who have contributed the resources necessary to prepare and distribute this directory. We received specific grants for this project from the Ford Foundation and from the Freeman Foundation, and we also drew upon general support from the Carnegie Corporation of New York; for distribution costs, we rely on support made available especially for this purpose by the Bank of Montreal, Coutts & Co., The Japan Times, and Payden & Rygel.

I have personally enjoyed and learned a great deal from this project, which should enable the Pacific Council to facilitate transnational communication around the Pacific Rim. I hope and believe that it will be immensely helpful to others.

Acknowledgments

The Pacific Council on International Policy thanks the following organizations
for their support provided to assure distribution of this publication:

The Japan Times

Payden&Rygel

Introduction:
The Rise of International Policy Institutions

Charles E. Morrison

This directory of *International Policy Institutions Around the Pacific Rim* has been developed in the belief that there is a significant need for a guide to the rich nongovernmental organizational resources on both sides of the Pacific Ocean on issues of international economics, politics, and society. Two important assumptions underlie this effort. First, the organizations we call international policy institutions already have a vital impact on the region's international relations, and this impact will continue to grow, with global implications. Second, the highly dynamic and private sector–led integrative processes around the Pacific Rim will continue to throw up new challenges and opportunities for the societies of the region. Effective collaboration among the international policy institutions of this region is essential in order to identify these trends, challenges, and opportunities; analyze them well; and suggest practical public policy responses.

THE EXPANDING ROLE OF INTERNATIONAL POLICY INSTITUTIONS

International policy institutions are a new phenomenon in international relations. They are a very diverse group, but have some common features. All are concerned with issues of policy import in the region's international relations; all seek to promote greater international understanding and awareness of the issues they deal with; all are open to various forms of international collaboration; and all stand outside the administrative structure of governments. Collectively they embody a gold mine of intellectual resources that can be addressed to the principal international challenges facing the region.

As individual institutions, however, they vary widely. Some have large in-house research or educational programs, while others are brokers or network organizations, drawing upon talent from many other institutions. Some emphasize advanced research, while others mainly promote policy dialogue or public understanding of policy issues. Some specialize in a region, a part of a region, or on a topical area such as the environment, and others are broadly focused. Some are engaged in public advocacy, while others seek to be neutral brokers, fostering debate without taking an institutional position. Some are associated with larger organizations, such as universities, while others are independent.

Despite or because of this diversity, international policy institutions are increasingly significant and dynamic actors in the international relations of the Pacific Rim. The growth in the number of such institutions is associated with the great forces reshaping international society in general, but especially that of the Pacific. These include the rapid economic growth rates; the dramatically increased international movements of goods, capital, and people; the globalization of business organization and activity; the democratization and pluralization of domestic societies; and the revolution in transport and communications.

These forces are creating a more complex, robust international civil society. In the process they are establishing new and indispensable roles for nongovernmental policy institutions. Many governments traditionally regarded foreign policy as the special and almost exclusive province of the bureaucracy and a small elite closely connected with but formally outside the government. Today's new issues, however, require a breadth and flexibility that is all but impossible for bureaucracies to achieve. Moreover, as local communities are intimately connected with and affected by international society, the multiple forms of engagement cannot possibly be carried out through governmental mechanisms alone, much less through foreign ministries.

Governments increasingly recognize the value of nongovernmental policy organizations as sources of analysis and innovative policy ideas, as well as links with the private sector, local communities, and intellectual talent abroad. Even those East Asian governments most reluctant to engage genuinely private institutions in matters of public policy concern have established government-sponsored policy institutions outside the formal ambit of the government administrative bureaucracy, expressly to promote more flexible thinking and to engage in the collaborative exploration of international policy issues with counterparts from abroad.

The main functions of international policy institutes can be summed up as follows:

- They provide venues away from the day-to-day working environment for the development of more creative and long-term policy strategies. International policy institutes may do contract work for government agencies. More often, however, they may engage in "track two" projects that seek to establish new policy directions.
- They serve as avenues in which private citizens can influence public policy-making through the development of policy ideas or through policy advocacy. Policy institutes are frequently a bridge between local communities and national governments or international agencies.
- Virtually all policy institutes are engaged in public education of one form or another. Their efforts frequently take a different form than the foreign policy statements provided by government, in that many policy institutes encourage debate among competing perspectives rather than disseminate information on policies that have been already decided upon by government.

There is no more striking example of the increased role of nongovernmental institutions in the Pacific Rim than the notion of a "Pacific Community" and the establishment of intergovernmental institutions to promote that community. The idea that the nations around the Pacific Rim might have common interests and could derive benefit from international cooperation was first suggested only about thirty years ago. It continued to percolate among committed individuals in nongovernmental networks for years before becoming acceptable to governments. Thus, both the Asia Pacific Economic Cooperation (APEC) process and its counterpart security dialogue, the ASEAN Regional Forum (ARF), owe their genesis to proposals emerging from networks of international policy institutions. Several institutions, the Pacific Economic Cooperation Council, the Pacific Basin Economic Council, and the PAFTAD (Pacific Free Trade and Development) group of economists share credit for APEC, while the ASEAN Institutes for Strategic and International Studies originated the ARF proposal. Not coincidentally, APEC and ARF discussions are mirrored by parallel "track two" processes sponsored by networks of private, nonprofit organizations and designed to filter ideas into government or intergovernmental tracks. As a result, a close and relatively symbiotic relationship has developed between governmental and nongovernmental processes in the development of multilateral political and economic cooperation in the Pacific.

THE WESTWARD EXPANSION OF POLICY INSTITUTIONS

Had we mapped international policy institutions sixty years ago, we would have found a few isolated dots mainly placed in the great political and commercial capitals of the Western industrial world. The first wave of private institution-building took place in the early part of the twentieth century in anticipation of or following World War I. The Council on Foreign Relations, the Carnegie Endowment for Peace, and the Foreign Policy Association, all in the United States, as well as the Canadian Institute of International Affairs and the Royal Institute of International Affairs (Chatham House) belong to this generation. It was natural that these institutions, mainly although not exclusively focused on issues of war and peace, should be located in the major cities of the Western world and concerned primarily with intra-European and transatlantic relations.

A map of thirty years ago would show many more institutions. The Great Depression, World War II, the Cold War, and the development challenges in the newly independent countries of the "South" provided the stimuli for a second, more robust wave of institution-building. These new institutions, however, were still clustered in the major capitals of the Western world. The networks among them connected these capitals with a stray line or two going off in the direction of Japan or perhaps Brazil. By the 1970s, Japan had emerged as the second largest economy in the noncommunist world, but nonprofit, private, policy-oriented institutions remained remarkably underdeveloped there.

In the past ten to fifteen years, the empty areas of the map have been rapidly filled in. Institution-building is occurring at a dramatic pace outside Western Europe and North America. As this directory shows, virtually every country in the Pacific Rim region has established at least one major center focused on international economic policy and another on politics and security. The larger institutions usually have governmental or university affiliations. Moreover, in many countries dozens of other organizations have been created, often to deal with more specialized topics and frequently with precarious financial and limited human resources. Although the growth of international policy institutes outside the Western world is impressive compared with the past, truly independent institutions find their resources stretched very thinly indeed, sharply limiting their ability to engage in meaningful collaborative activities with developed country counterparts. In many countries, truly independent policy institutions remain chronically underfunded or precariously dependent upon a single, talented individual.

A parallel process is the growing density of policy-oriented institutions outside the capital cities. Increasing lines of collaboration connect them, moreover, with other national and international institutions. The western parts of the United States and Canada are leading the way. Some important international policy research and educational institutions have flourished in the North American West for decades, such as RAND, the Hoover Institution, and the area studies and foreign policy centers associated with the great public and private universities along the Pacific Coast from Vancouver to San Diego. Western North America was also the natural host for U.S. and Canadian government programs devoted to developing their links with Asia. These have included the Asia Foundation and the East-West Center, both created by the U.S. government, and the newer Asia Pacific Foundation of Canada.

In recent years, there has been a proliferation of new institutions in the North American West, some engaged in advanced research at university institutes or think-tanks, others principally devoted to public education, and still others working with particular communities or specialized issue areas. This explosion reflects the region's awareness that global issues are vital to its economy and society, and the desire for the region's people to play a more effective role in their governments' foreign policies.

THE NEED FOR A SURVEY

Both these trends—the institutional explosion in developing Pacific Rim countries and its counterpart in the North American West—underscore the tremendous potential for increasing networking and collaboration among the new international policy networks. This is particularly true of the contacts among institutions in developing Latin America and developing Asia.

The directory's origins lie in the desire of the newly created Pacific Council on International Policy to identify counterparts and potential collaborators. The Pacific Council discovered that, despite the many policy institutes and policy-oriented projects and activities existing in the region, no one had attempted to map them. The Japan Center for International Exchange (JCIE) had probably done the most extensive survey work, initially collaborating with Japan's National Institute for Research Advancement to monitor think-tank activities in Europe and North America. More recently JCIE prepared an extensive overview of emerging civil society in Asia and the Pacific, including the development of international policy institutions, and it is now expanding upon its previous institutional surveys to include developing Asia and Oceania. This directory has drawn extensively on JCIE's work.

The Pacific Council has also benefited from a number of other pioneering efforts to monitor the intellectual resources of the region. The Seattle-based National Bureau of Asian Research publishes *AccessAsia,* which includes profiles of many individual scholars working on Asia and the Pacific. The London-based International Institute of Strategic Studies provides a listing of security-oriented organizations in the region and the world.

Other more specialized directories exist. But there is no other general survey of the international policy institutes of Asia, Australasia, North America, and Latin America. Identifying these institutions, making judgments about which to include, and acquiring the needed information is no simple task. We can only regard the directory as a work in progress, and surely it will always be a work in progress as civil society continues to grow more robust and more globalized. We hope, however, that the directory will be an indispensable first point of reference for individuals and organizations seeking to tap into the vast knowledge base of the Pacific Rim.

ASIA

Academy of Macroeconomic Research of the State Planning Commission

Background and objectives: The Academy of Macroeconomic Research was established in 1988 as the Economic Research Center and given its present name in 1995. As a research institution under the direct leadership of the State Planning Commission, the Academy conducts research on major issues arising from China's economic reform, analyzes the economic development experiences of other countries to learn from their example, and advises the government on macroeconomic policy decisions.

Programs: The Academy's nine research institutes focus on general economics, investment, industrial development, energy, transportation, land development and regional economics, human resources development, markets and prices, and foreign economic relations.

The Department of Comprehensive Research analyzes the major issues facing China and undertakes urgent tasks assigned by the State Planning Commission. Recent research projects have focused on the eighth five-year plan and the ten-year plan, the basic structure of socialist market economy, and the macrocontrol of the Chinese economy.

The Academy also directs the China Macroeconomic Society, the China Industrial Economy and Technology Research Federation, the China Society of Fixed Assets Investment and Construction, the China Price Society, and the China Society of Human Resources Development, whose main function is to organize and coordinate related research all over the country.

Publications: The Academy publishes, in Chinese, the bimonthly journal *China Techno-Economics* and four monthly journals entitled *China Investment and Construction, China Prices, Comprehensive Transport,* and *China Energy.*

Funding sources: The Academy is funded by the Chinese government.

Staffing: The Academy has more than 360 full-time researchers, including 250 senior research fellows, and about 180 administrative/support staff members.

Head of the institution: Mr. She Jianming, President

Contact officer: Mr. Shi Kang, Chief, Secretariat

The Academy of Macroeconomic Research of the State Planning Commission
38 South Yuetan Street
Sanlihe
Beijing, 100824
CHINA
Tel: (86-10) 6850-1707
Fax: (86-10) 6850-1708

Asia Institute

Background and objectives: The Asia Institute is a nonprofit, non-government research institution established in 1988 to study economic, political, and social developments in Asia-Pacific countries and advise government agencies and businesses on public policy matters.

Programs: Most of the Institute's research focuses on Shanghai, where it is based; the Yangtze River delta; the role of these areas in the Asia-Pacific economy; and the development experiences of Asia-Pacific countries. Recent research projects have addressed mechanisms in Asia-Pacific economic cooperation, the role of Shanghai in Asia-Pacific economic cooperation, and Shanghai's potential as an international financial center.

The Institute sponsors national and international symposiums on such topics as economic development and China's industrial policy (1996) and infrastructure development and financing in China (1996).

The Institute also promotes international exchange with foreign counterparts, hosting visiting scholars from such institutions as the Korean Institute for Industrial Economics and Trade and the Institute of East Asia Politics and Economy in Singapore.

Publications: The Institute publishes in Chinese the weekly magazine *Asian Trends*, the *Quarterly Report*, and *New Asia*, a collection of papers released at irregular intervals. Recent Chinese-language books include *The Handbook of China's Finance and Investment* (1996), *Southeast Asia on a New Starting Point* (1995), *Exchange Rate Reform in China* (1993), *On International Competition* (1992), and *The Current International Capital Market* (1992).

Funding sources: The Institute is funded by income from contract research and consulting services, and by grants from international organizations including the Ford Foundation.

Staffing: The Institute has five full-time and thirteen part-time researchers and three administrative assistants.

Head of the institution: Dr. Chen Qiwei, President

Contact officer: Mr. Tian Zhongqing, Vice President

Asia Institute
396 Pan Yu Road, 4F, Shanghai, 200052
CHINA
Tel: (86-21) 6281-0656
Fax: (86-21) 6281-4409

China Center for International Studies

Background and objectives: The China Center for International Studies (CCIS), founded in 1982, is a research and consulting institution that analyzes the major international issues affecting China, develops policy recommendations for government agencies, and promotes mutual understanding and cooperation between China and other countries through academic exchanges.

Programs: CCIS conducts research in the areas of international politics and security, economic development, and science and technology, with a regional focus on the Asia-Pacific. It has an annual bilateral dialogue on security issues with the Strategic and Defense Centre of the Australian National University. It also hosts international conferences, symposiums, and seminars on topics ranging from the emerging post-Cold War security system in the Asia-Pacific to economic development in China.

Publications: The Center publishes the *CCIS International Review* in Chinese and, intermittently, in English. Recent articles include "The United Nations at the Turn of the Century,"

"Questions in U.S. Readjustment of External Strategy," and "Explorations for a More Secure South Asia."

Funding sources: CCIS is funded by the Chinese government.

Staffing: The Center has twenty-two full-time researchers, including five Senior Research Fellows, supported by twelve administrative staff members. Some of its researchers are former ambassadors.

Head of the institution: Amb. Li Luye, Director-General

Contact officer: Feng Huiyun, Secretary

China Center for International Studies
22 Xi An Men Avenue, P.O. Box 1744
Beijing, 100017
CHINA
Tel: (86-10) 6309-7083
Fax: (86-10) 6309-5802

China Institute for International Strategic Studies

Background and objectives: The China Institute for International Strategic Studies, established in 1979 as the Beijing Institute for International Strategic Studies and given its present name in 1992, is a non-government research institution that investigates international security, economic, and political issues.

Programs: The Institute conducts research on international strategy, regional security, and China's relations with the United States and Japan in order to advise Chinese decision makers on matters of public policy.

The Institute offers consulting services and undertakes the task of preparing research papers for government agencies, the military, and other national security institutions and enterprises. It also organizes academic exchanges and sponsors seminars, bilateral and multilateral symposiums, and international conferences on issues in Asia-Pacific security and Sino-American relations.

Publications: The Institute publishes the quarterly journal *International Strategic Studies* in Chinese and English.

Funding sources: The Institute is funded by subsidies from the Chinese government and military, income from consulting services, and individual contributions from China and abroad.

Staffing: The Institute has approximately 100 full-time researchers—including active and retired officers, diplomats, and scholars specializing in international strategic issues—and ten administrative assistants.

Head of the institution: Gen. Xu Xin, Chairman

Contact officer: Gen. Mu Huimin, Secretary General

China Institute for International Strategic Studies
P.O. Box 9812
No. 6 Hua Yan Bei Li
Xiao Guan Road, Chao Yang District (not for mail)
Beijing, 100029
CHINA
Tel: (86-10) 6201-6943
Fax: (86-10) 6202-1048

China Institute of Contemporary International Relations

Background and objectives: The China Institute of Contemporary International Relations (CICIR), formally established in 1980, is a research institution dedicated to the study of international affairs and the elaboration of policy proposals for the Chinese government.

Programs: The Institute conducts research on both thematic issues, such as global strategic patterns and trends in world politics and economics, and issues specific to particular regions or countries. Recent projects have focused on the worldwide implications of Russia's presidential election and on issues in Sino-Japanese relations.

The Institute maintains contacts with major international research institutions—including the Sigur Center at George Washington University in the United States, the Asian Forum in Japan, the Institute for Far-East Studies in Russia, and the Sejong Institute in South Korea—and sponsors international conferences on such topics as Asia-Pacific security and Sino-ASEAN relations.

The Institute also offers M.A. and Ph.D. degrees in International Relations.

Publications: CICIR publishes *Contemporary International Relations,* a monthly journal in both English and Chinese. Recent Chinese-language books include *China and Her Neighbors: Prospects for the Twenty-First Century* (1995), *Major Events in Sino-US Relations since 1979* (1995), and *Japan at the Turn of the Century* (1995).

Funding sources: The Institute is funded by the Chinese government.

Staffing: CICIR has more than 300 researchers, including fifty research professors, supported by an administrative staff of 100 people.

Head of the institution: Prof. Shen Qurong, President

Contact officer: Mr. Liu Liping, Director, Division of International Exchanges

**China Institute of Contemporary International Relations
A-2 Wanshousi, Haidian, Beijing, 100081
CHINA
Tel: (86-10) 6841-8640
Fax: (86-10) 6841-8641**

China Institute of International Studies

Background and objectives: The China Institute of International Studies (CIIS) was founded in 1956 as the Institute of International Relations and took its present name in 1987. Although it operates under the auspices of the Ministry of Foreign Affairs, CIIS sets its own research agenda, which focuses on strategic issues in international politics and economics. Its research findings are submitted to government agencies and institutions for policy-making purposes.

Programs: The Institute conducts comprehensive studies of international politics and economics, as well as regional and country studies of North America, Latin America, Eastern Europe, Central Asia and Russia, and the Asia-Pacific region. The Institute also sponsors conferences, seminars, and workshops, such as the 4th Plenary meeting of the Northeast Asia Cooperation Dialogue, and promotes scholarly exchanges with foreign research institutions.

Publications: CIIS publishes *International Studies,* a quarterly journal in Chinese with English abstracts. The English edition of *International Studies,* featuring selected articles from the Chinese-language journal, is published at irregular intervals.

Funding sources: The Institute is funded by the Chinese Ministry of Foreign Affairs.

Staffing: CIIS has a total staff of approximately 100, of whom about seventy are engaged in research. Some of its researchers are experienced foreign-service diplomats.

Head of the institution: Amb. Chengxu Yang, President

China Institute of International Studies
3 Toutiao, Taijichang, Beijing, 100005
CHINA
Tel: (86-10) 6513-2225
Fax: (86-10) 6512-3744

Chinese Academy of Social Sciences

Institute of Asia-Pacific Studies

Background and objectives: The Institute of Asia-Pacific Studies (IAPS) at the Chinese Academy of Social Sciences was established in 1988 to promote a better understanding of the Asia-Pacific region and to advise the Chinese government on issues related to the region.

Programs: IAPS's six research departments focus on Asia-Pacific international relations, society, and culture and the politics and economics of Northeast, Southeast, and South Asia. Recent research programs have addressed economic cooperation in the Asia-Pacific region, including regional and sub-regional organizations such as APEC and ASEAN; economic development in newly industrializing countries and regions; political systems, parties, and social structures characteristic of the region; and Asian-Pacific security and China's relations with its neighbors.

IAPS work regularly with the APEC Policy Research Center; the Center for Australian, New Zealand and South Pacific Studies; and the Center for Korean Studies, which are under the exclusive management of the Institute.

IAPS also sponsors or co-sponsors international seminars and symposiums once or twice a year to discuss such topics as international relations between China, Japan, and the United States and economic cooperation among the Asia-Pacific countries.

Publications: IAPS publishes, in Chinese, the bimonthly journal *Contemporary Asia-Pacific Studies*. Recent Chinese-language books include *Nurturing Asia-Pacific Cooperation* (1996), *Asia-Pacific Economy: Toward the 21st Century* (1995), *Economic Development in Thailand* (1995), and *A Comparative Study of Economic Development between China and India* (1990).

Funding sources: IAPS is largely funded by the Chinese government. Domestic and foreign private foundations also provide grants for special projects.

Staffing: IAPS consists of sixty-one researchers, including nine research professors and twenty-three associated research professors, supported by five library staff members and five administrative assistants.

Head of the institution: Prof. Zhang Yunling, Director

Contact officer: Ms. Liu Yajun, Deputy Head, Academic and Exchange Department

---

Institute of Asia-Pacific Studies, CASS
3 Zhang Zizhong Lu, Dong Cheng District, Beijing, 100007
CHINA
Tel: (86-10) 6406-3042
Fax: (86-10) 6410-8641
e-mail • aprccass@public3.bta.net.cn

Chinese Academy of Social Sciences

Institute of Finance and Trade Economics

Background and objectives: The Institute of Finance and Trade Economics (IFTE), established in 1978, is a research institution under the administration of the Chinese Academy of Social Sciences. Dedicated to the study of finance and commerce, the Institute addresses both theoretical and practical issues in Chinese economic development and reform, provides macroeconomic policy recommendations for the State Council and other government agencies, and provides consulting services to local governments, financial institutions, and enterprises on matters such as regional economic development, corporate restructuring, and marketing strategies.

Programs: IFTE consists of six research departments that concentrate respectively on finance, domestic commerce, urban economics, foreign economic relations and trade, costs and prices, and service and tourism.

Recent projects have addressed relations between price reform and market growth, the cultivation and standardization of the Chinese securities market, the resumption of China's contractual member status in GATT/WTO and its impact on the Chinese market and domestic prices, and the opening of Chinese border regions to the outside world. Some of these projects are designated by the central government under the five-year plan or sponsored by the State Social Sciences Foundation.

The Institute also offers M.A. and Ph.D. programs in international trade, public finance, and money and banking.

Publications: IFTE publishes, in Chinese, the monthly journals *Finance and Trade Economics* and *Securities Research.* Chinese-language books include *Financial System Reform and Fiscal Policy* (1989), *Contemporary Chinese Economy* (1988), and *Study on Some Issues in the Economic System Reform* (1985).

Funding sources: IFTE is funded by the Chinese government.

Staffing: IFTE has seventy-seven full-time researchers, including thirty-eight senior research fellows, and twenty-one administrative assistants.

Head of the institution: Prof. Yang Shengming, Director

Contact officer: Mr. Shen Jinjian, Staff Member

Institute of Finance and Trade Economics, CASS
2 Yuetan Beixiaojie, Beijing, 100836
CHINA
Tel: (86-10) 6858-2445
Fax: (86-10) 6858-2440

Chinese Academy of Social Sciences

Institute of Industrial Economics

Background and objectives: The Institute of Industrial Economics (IIE), founded in 1978 at the Chinese Academy of Social Sciences, is a research institution dedicated to the study of China's industrial development and the reform of its industrial and enterprise systems. It provides theoretical analysis, addresses practical issues in the establishment of China's market economy, and advises local governments and businesses on regional economic development and management.

Programs: IIE has six research departments specializing in industrial development, industrial investment and marketing, enterprise ownership, business management, regional economies, and small and medium-sized businesses. Recent projects have addressed such topics as China's outward-oriented enterprises, China's industrial policy, and the experiences of other countries in reducing the adverse impact of joining the WTO.

The Institute sends its researchers abroad to conduct field research; hosts visiting scholars from countries including the United States and Japan; and organizes international conferences and seminars such as the "China-Japan Economic Conference" (1988, 1991, 1994) and the 19th Pacific Trade and Development Conference (1991).

IIE also offers M.A. and Ph.D. programs in industrial and business economics.

Publications: The Institute publishes, in Chinese, the monthly journal *China's Industrial Economics* and the monthly magazine *Economic Management*. Chinese-language books include *The Chinese Economy: Readjustment, Reform, and Development* (1996), *On Enterprise Management with China's Style* (1985), and *China's Economic Structure* (1981).

Funding sources: IIE is funded by the Chinese government.

Staffing: The Institute has a total of seventy full-time researchers and forty-seven administrative staff members.

Head of the institution: Prof. Chen Jiagui, Director

Contact officer: Ms. Yi Ding, Deputy Head, Section of Research Work Organization

Institute of Industrial Economics, CASS
No. 2 Fuwai Yuetan Beixiaojie, Xicheng District
Beijing, 100836
CHINA
Tel: (86-10) 6585-3728
Fax: (86-10) 6858-2679
e-mail • dingyi@sun.ihep.ac.cn

Chinese Academy of Social Sciences

Institute of Japanese Studies

Background and objectives: The Institute of Japanese Studies was established in 1981 at the Chinese Academy of Social Sciences to pursue wide-ranging research on Japan, provide policy analysis, and promote mutual understanding and friendship between China and Japan.

Programs: The Institute's four research departments concentrate on Japan's political institutions, political parties, and defense; its economic system and industrial structure; its foreign policy and foreign economic relations, especially with the Asia-Pacific countries; and its social structure, society, and culture.

Recent projects have addressed the Japanese economy after World War II, trends in Sino-Japanese relations, and contemporary political thought in Japan.

The Institute maintains contact with more than thirty institutions in Japan and other countries, exchanges publications with its foreign counterparts, receives foreign visiting scholars, and sponsors (jointly with Japanese research institutions and corporations) international symposiums on such topics as Sino-Japanese relations and enterprise management.

Publications: Together with the Chinese Society of Japanese Studies, the Institute co-edits the journal *Japanese Studies,* a bimonthly published in Chinese. Its recent books, most of which are published in Chinese, include *A Comparative Study of Circulation Trade between China and Japan* (1996), *Japan: Toward a Political Power* (1994), *An Introduction to Japanese Politics* (1994), and *Problems, Solutions, and Lessons of Japan's Economic Development* (1993).

Funding sources: The Institute is funded mainly by the Chinese government. Some special projects are funded by grants and donations from private foundations and organizations, such as the Japan Foundation.

Staffing: IJS consists of thirty-five full-time researchers, including eight senior research fellows, and fourteen full-time administrative assistants.

Head of the institution: Prof. Zhang Yunling, Director

Contact officer: Ms. Guo Ying, Head, Academic and Exchange Department

Institute of Japanese Studies, CASS
3 Zhang Zizhong Lu, Dong Cheng District, Beijing, 100007
CHINA
Tel: (86-10) 6406-3042
Fax: (86-10) 6401-4022
e-mail • aprccass@public3.bta.net.cn

Chinese Academy of Social Sciences

Institute of Latin American Studies

Background and objectives: The Institute of Latin American Studies (ILAS) was established in 1961 and came under the administration of the Chinese Academy of Social Sciences in 1981. As the only Chinese institution for comprehensive research on Latin America, ILAS advises the government and businesses and educates the public on Latin American affairs.

Programs: The Institute's four research divisions focus on Latin American economics; politics, history, and international relations; society and culture; and country studies. Recent research projects have addressed economic reform in Latin America, development models in Latin America and Asia, and economic integration in the Western Hemisphere.

Since the 1980s, the Institute has sponsored or co-sponsored national and international conferences on topics such as economic adjustment in Latin American countries, the politics of openness in Latin America, U.S.-Latin American relations, and Latin America in the 1990s. It has hosted short-term visiting Latin Americanists, government officials, and former statesmen from around the world, including several former presidents of the Latin American Studies Association of the United States. It has also sent researchers to Latin America and the Caribbean to conduct field research.

Publications: ILAS publishes *Latin American Review,* a Chinese-language bimonthly journal, and *Selected Articles from Latin American Review,* a semiannual publication in both Spanish and English. Recent Chinese-language books include *A*

Study of Latin American Development Models (1996), *Political Stability and Modernization in Mexico* (1996), *NAFTA: An Approach to North-South Cooperation* (1996), *On Latin American External Debt* (1994), *Economic Development and Inflation: Theory and Practice in Latin America* (1992), and *A Concise History of Chinese-Latin American Relations* (1989).

Funding sources: ILAS is funded by the Chinese government.

Staffing: ILAS has fifty-six full-time researchers, including thirty-two senior research fellows, and fourteen administrative assistants.

Notes: The Chinese Association of Latin American Studies, a nationwide organization that coordinates Latin American studies in China, is now under ILAS's administration.

Head of the institution: Prof. Su Zhenxing, Director

Contact officer: Prof. Hai Jinying, Chief of Research Organization

Institute of Latin American Studies
P.O. Box 1113, 3 Zhangzizhong Lu
Beijing, 100007
CHINA
Tel: (86-10) 6401-4009 / 6401-4013
Fax: (86-10) 6401-4011

Chinese Academy of Social Sciences

Institute of World Economics and Politics

Background and objectives: The Institute of World Economics and Politics (IWEP) is a research institution affiliated with the Chinese Academy of Social Sciences. Established in 1981 by merging the former Institute of World Economy and Institute of World Politics, the Institute undertakes comprehensive research on world economics and politics, addresses the practical and theoretical issues arising from China's economic reform, and analyzes the lessons that other countries have learned in the pursuit of economic and foreign policy.

Programs: IWEP's areas of research cover international economic theory, development economics, environmental economics, comparative economics, international finance, European economic history, and international political economy.

Recent research projects have focused on comparative studies of inflation control, financial reform and economic development in developing countries, and the industrialization of agriculture.

In collaboration with MIT's Sloan School of Management and the London School of Economics, IWEP has co-sponsored major international symposiums on China-U.S. economic relations and on socioeconomic issues in China and Britain.

Publications: IWEP publishes, in Chinese, the monthly journal *World Economics and Politics,* the monthly journal *World Economy,* the bimonthly journal *International Economic Review,* the annual *Analyzing and Forecasting World Economic Situations,* and *The Almanac of World Economy.* The Institute also publishes, in English, the bimonthly journal *World Economy and China.* Recent Chinese-language books include *The World Heading into the Twenty-First Century* (1996), *Economic Relations among Major Western Countries* (1996), and *New Patterns in the World Economy and International Security* (1996).

Funding sources: IWEP is funded by the Chinese government.

Staffing: IWEP has 145 full-time researchers supported by ten administrative staff members.

Head of the institution: Prof. Gu Yuanyang, Director

Contact officer: Ms. Hu Facheng, Chief, Department of Research Planning and Cooperation

Institute of World Economics and Politics, CASS
5 Jianguomennei Dajie, Beijing, 100732
CHINA
Tel: (86-10) 6512-6105 / 6513-7744
Fax: (86-10) 6512-6105
e-mail • guyy@sun.ihep.ac.cn

Chinese People's Institute of Foreign Affairs

Background and objectives: The Chinese People's Institute of Foreign Affairs (CPIFA) was founded in 1949 to promote international exchanges, facilitate people-to-people contacts, and foster mutual understanding between China and other countries. CPIFA is headquartered in Beijing, with chapters in other major Chinese cities.

Programs: CPIFA hosts foreign guests from more than 100 countries, including former heads of state, leaders of political parties, and famous statesmen, diplomats, or scholars in international studies.

CPIFA also sponsors international forums and seminars on such issues as international relations after the Cold War, Sino-U.S. relations, Sino-German relations, economic cooperation between China and Thailand, and China's relations with South Korea. CPIFA's research activities have centered around the topics discussed in these events.

Publications: CPIFA publishes, in English, the quarterly *Foreign Affairs Journal.*

Funding sources: CPIFA is funded by the Chinese government.

Staffing: CPIFA has eight senior officers and about 100 administrative staff members. CPIFA also has more than 170 Council members, some of whom are activists in international affairs, senior diplomats, and well-known scholars in international studies.

Head of the institution: Amb. Liu Shuqing, President

Contact officer: Ms. Sun Aqing, Deputy Secretary-General

Chinese People's Institute of Foreign Affairs
71 Nanchizi Street, Beijing, 100006
CHINA
Tel: (86-10) 6513-1826
Fax: (86-10) 6513-1831

Development Research Center of the State Council

Background and objectives: The Development Research Center of the State Council (DRC), established in 1981, is a research and consulting institution that analyzes macroeconomic policies and provides policy proposals for the State Council on issues concerning China's economic and social development.

Programs: DRC consists of eight research departments and five research institutes covering such fields as economic development and reform, economic forecasting, macro regulation, property rights relations and the management of state-owned enterprises, rural development, theory and practice of socialist market economy, foreign economic relations, international cooperation, international technological and economic studies, and world development (with a focus on the United States and Western European countries).

DRC has been involved in the government's major decision-making processes, including the formulation of state five-year plans. It has also conducted research projects sponsored by the United Nations Development Program (UNDP), the World Bank, the Asian Development Bank, the Ford Foundation, and the Rockefeller Foundation on such topics as economic development policy and planning.

Under the "China and the World in the Nineties" program, it has organized or sponsored a series of major international seminars and conferences on topics ranging from economic development and environmental protection to the performance of state-owned enterprises.

Publications: DRC publishes, in Chinese, the *China Economic Yearbook,* the bimonthly *Management World Magazine,* and *China Economic Times,* an economic newspaper published three times a week. Recent Chinese-language book series include *China Development Studies* (1996) and *Economic Situation and the Prospects of China* (1995-1996).

Funding sources: DRC is funded primarily by the Ministry of Finance of the PRC. It also receives financial support, on a project basis, from external sources including UNDP, the World Bank, the Asian Development Bank, and the Ford Foundation.

Staffing: DRC has in its Beijing headquarters a total of 160 researchers, many of whom are senior economists, supported by forty administrative staff members.

Notes: DRC is a ministry-level research institution. All its senior administrators occupy the rank of minister or vice minister.

Head of the institution: Appointment pending

Contact officer: Mr. Lan Weiban, Division Chief, International Department

Development Research Center of the State Council of PRC
22 Xianmen Street, Beijing, 100017
CHINA
Tel: (86-10) 6309-9162 (International Department)
Fax: (86-10) 6601-3530
e-mail • lanwb@drc.go.cn.net
URL • http:// drc.go.cn.net

Foundation for International and Strategic Studies

Background and objectives: The Foundation for International and Strategic Studies (FISS), established in 1989, is a non-governmental, nonprofit organization that fosters international and strategic studies, facilitates domestic and international exchanges, and promotes national awareness of world events and strategic issues.

Programs: FISS organizes and supports research on international politics, economics, military affairs, science and technology, and culture. Recent projects have addressed future power relations in East Asia, the history and development of Sino-Japanese relations, China's mid- and long-term strategies for reunification with Taiwan, and the cultural, religious, and social dimensions of the issues of Xinjiang and Tibet.

FISS has sponsored domestic and international seminars, forums, and symposiums on such topics as the international and strategic thinking of the PRC's founders, future developments in China's Special Economic Zones, and the PRC's non-proliferation policy.

FISS has also hosted foreign visiting scholars, subsidized Chinese scholars pursuing post-doctoral studies or conducting field research abroad, and offered consulting services to concerned parties.

Publications: Recent Chinese-language books published by FISS include *China's Foreign Relations during the War of Resistance against Japan* (1995), *Could Taiwan Win Independence?* (1994), and *How to Confront Beijing in the Post-Cold War Era—A Case Study of MFN Debate and the Evolution of Washington's China Policy* (forthcoming).

Funding sources: FISS is funded by contributions from domestic enterprises, financial institutions, civilian organizations, and individuals; donations and grants from foreign foundations, financial institutions, and academic organizations; and income from the fund's value increases.

Staffing: The Foundation has ten senior administrators, all of whom are former high-ranking government officials, diplomats, or scholars, and about twenty support staff members.

Head of the institution: Appointment pending

Contact officers:

Mr. Zhang Tuosheng, Director, Department of Research

Mr. Wu Baiyi, Deputy Director, Department of Research

Foundation for International and Strategic Studies
No. 40 Dong Tangzi Hutong, Dongdan
Beijing, 100005
CHINA
Tel: (86-10) 6513-0944
Fax: (86-10) 6513-0943

Fudan University

Center for American Studies

Background and objectives: The Center for American Studies (CAS) at Fudan University, established in 1985 with the support and approval of the State Educational Commission, is one of the key institutions for American studies in China. It promotes research; trains Chinese students in the analytical and language skills necessary for a better understanding of the United States; and provides policy consulting services to the public and private sectors.

Programs: The Center's multidisciplinary research areas include U.S. politics and diplomacy, with emphasis on political institutions, foreign policy, and Sino-U.S. relations; U.S. economic policy and Sino-U.S. economic relations; arms control and regional security, with a focus on U.S. defense policy, nuclear arms control and disarmament, and nuclear nonproliferation; and American society and culture.

In conjunction with the Department of International Politics, CAS offers M.A. programs in arms control, regional security, and American Studies. CAS also encourages academic exchanges and sponsors research workshops, independently or jointly with counterpart institutions. Past events have included the 1994, 1995, and 1996 Sino-U.S. Summer Workshops on International Security and the 1996 Summer Workshop on the Fundamentals of American Law.

Publications: Articles published by CAS staff members include "A Vertical-and-Horizontal Perspective on Sino-U.S. Relations" (1996), "China and Nuclear Non-Proliferation" (1996), "China as a Cooperative Power" (1996), "China: Building Peace on Its Borders" (1996), and "The American Middle Class" (1996).

Funding sources: CAS is funded by University budget allocation.

Staffing: CAS consists of more than twenty staff members, about ten of whom work on a full-time basis as administrators or as researchers with the rank of professor, associate professor, or lecturer. The Center's director, deputy director, and resident researchers are experts in their respective fields who work for CAS on a part-time basis.

Head of the institution: Prof. Xie Xide, President

Contact officer: Ms. Lu Huifang, Executive Officer

Center for American Studies
Fudan University
220 Han Dan Road, Shanghai, 200433
CHINA
Tel: (86-10) 6549-2222 ext. 2269
Fax: (86-10) 6548-8949
e-mail • xdxie@fudan.ihep.ac.cn

Fudan University

Center for Japanese Studies

Background and objectives: The Center for Japanese Studies at Fudan University was established in 1990 to conduct in-depth research on Japan, to analyze Japan's modernization experience and draw lessons for China's own development, and to promote mutual understanding between the two countries.

Programs: The Center's three research divisions focus on the study of Japan's economy, politics, and culture. Recent research has addressed postwar Japan's prices, enterprise system, industrial policy, social security system, finance, and experience in privatizing state-owned enterprises.

The proposed research projects for the period 1996-2000 will expand on those topics to examine postwar Japanese economic relations with other Asian countries, the role of Japanese culture in modernization, and the internationalization of Japanese culture.

The Center has established exchange relations with the Institute of Social Sciences at Tokyo University, Waseda University, and Keio University. It has also organized international conferences on topics such as price change and price policy in postwar Japan, the vitality of Japanese enterprises, and changes in the postwar Japanese financial system.

Publications: The Center publishes, in Chinese, the biannual journal *Japanese Studies* and a paper series featuring articles presented to international conferences. Recent Chinese-language books include *Fast-Growing Economies in the Asia-Pacific Region* (1996) and *Japan's Social Security System after World War II* (1996).

Funding sources: The Center is funded by University budget allocation as well as contract research.

Staffing: The Center has ten full-time researchers, twenty part-time researchers drawn from other departments at Fudan, and three administrative assistants.

Head of the institution: Prof. Zheng Lizhi, Director

Contact officer: Prof. Meng Xiangsheng, Deputy Director

Center for Japanese Studies
Fudan University
220 Han Dan Road, Shanghai, 200433
CHINA
Tel: (86-21) 6549-2888
Fax: (86-21) 6549-2888

Fudan University

Department of International Politics

Background and objectives: The Department of International Politics at Fudan University, established in 1964, is a teaching and research institution on international relations. It aims to train future professionals, promote quality research in international affairs, and provide analyses for public policies on matters of concern to China.

Programs: The Department has recently expanded its teaching and research areas from European and American studies to include security studies, with emphasis on the Asia-Pacific region. Recent research projects have focused on China's international environment at the turn of the century, postwar U.S.-Japanese relations, Japanese foreign policy, American human rights diplomacy, and China's relations with the Korean peninsula.

The International Relations and Global Studies program—conducted in collaboration with the Center for American Studies, the Center for Japanese Studies, the Center for Korean Studies, and the Institute of World Economy at Fudan—is part of China's 2110 Project, jointly established by the State Education Commission, the State Planning Commission, and the Ministry of Finance to address such issues as globalization and regionalism, international security, and the role of the international environment in China's economic development.

The Department offers M.A. and Ph.D. programs in comparative politics, North-South economic relations, Asia-Pacific international relations, and international conflict and cooperation.

The Department also maintains international exchanges with a number of foreign universities and research institutions, and it sponsors international conferences on topics such as globalization and regional security in Northeast Asia.

Publications: The Department publishes the Chinese-language *Chinese Political Science Association Newsletter* three times a year. Recent books in Chinese published by faculty members include *U.S. National Security Policy* (1996), *Nuclear Proliferation: Danger and Prevention* (1995), *A Study of North-South Economic Relations* (1994), *War and Morality* (1992), and *An Introduction to Contemporary International Relations* (forthcoming).

Funding sources: Apart from its regular University budget allocation, the Department also receives funds for special projects from the State Education Commission, China's National Social Sciences Fund, the Shanghai Social Sciences Fund, and the Education Commission of Shanghai.

Staffing: The Department has fifty-four full-time faculty members, including thirteen professors and fourteen associated professors, supported by an administrative staff of eight people.

Heads of the institution:
Prof. Cao Peilin, Chairman

Prof. Yu Zhengliang, Executive Vice-Chairman

Contact officer: Dr. Ren Xiao, Secretary, International Program

---

Department of International Politics
Fudan University
220 Han Dan Road, Shanghai, 200443
CHINA
Tel: (86-21) 6549-2222 ext. 2322
Fax: (86-21) 6549-0653
e-mail • xiaoren@fudan.ihep.ac.cn

Peking University

School of International Relations

Background and objectives: The School of International Relations at Peking University, formerly the Department of International Politics, was established in 1996 to train students in analytical skills, foreign-language competence, public relations, and world affairs. It also undertakes research on international relations.

Programs: The School consists of the Departments of International Politics, Diplomacy and Foreign Affairs Management, and International Communication and Cultural Exchange, and the Institutes of International Relations and World Socialism. Recent research projects have addressed East Asian development models, Sino-Japanese relations, and challenges facing the United Nations.

The School conducts exchanges with counterpart institutions in the United States, Germany, Japan, South Korea, and Hong Kong and organizes and sponsors national and international conferences on such topics as China and the world as they head into the 21st century and theory of international politics with Chinese characteristics.

The School also offers M.A. and Ph.D. programs in international politics; international communications; and Hong Kong, Taiwan, and Macao affairs.

Publications: The School publishes, in Chinese, the quarterly journal *Studies in International Politics*. Recent Chinese-language books include *Inter-Cultural Exchange* (1996), *Challenges Facing the United Nations* (1995), and *The International Society in Transition* (1994).

Funding sources: The School is funded by University budget allocation.

Staffing: The School has a total of fifty faculty members, including fourteen professors and eighteen associate professors, supported by twelve administrative assistants.

Head of the institution: Prof. Liang Shoude, Director

Contact officer: Prof. Wu Zuxin, Head, Office of Foreign Affairs

School of International Relations
Peking University
Beijing, 100871
CHINA
Tel: (86-10) 6275-1631 / 6275-1637
Fax: (86-10) 6275-1639
e-mail • pghua@pku.edu.cn

Shanghai Academy of Social Sciences

Institute of Asia and Pacific Studies

Background and objectives: The Institute of Asia and Pacific Studies (IAPS) is a research institution under the administration of the Shanghai Academy of Social Sciences. Founded in 1990, IAPS tracks developments in the Asia-Pacific region in order to inform government policy.

Programs: IAPS conducts research on international relations, regional security, and the foreign policies and development strategies of Asia-Pacific countries. Recent projects have addressed economic cooperation in the Asia-Pacific region, China's relations with ASEAN countries, Northeast Asian security, Japan's security strategy, and the prospect for peaceful reunification between China and Taiwan.

IAPS sponsors workshops on topics such as the Korean peninsular situation and changes in Taiwan's policy toward China.

Publications: The Institute publishes, in Chinese, the bimonthly journal *Asia and Pacific Forum.* Recent Chinese-language books include *Asia-Pacific Economic Cooperation and China's Strategy toward the Region* (1996).

Funding sources: IAPS is primarily funded by the Shanghai municipal government. Additional funding for special projects comes from government agencies and China's Social Development Fund.

Staffing: IAPS consists of thirteen researchers, including seven full or associate professors, supported by three administrative assistants.

Head of the institution: Prof. Zhou Jianming, Director

Contact officer: Prof. Zhou Jianming

**Institute of Asia and Pacific Studies, SASS
7/622 Huai Hai Zhong Lu, Shanghai, 200020
CHINA
Tel: (86-21) 6327-1170
Fax: (86-21) 6327-8384
e-mail • jmzhou@fudan.ihep.ac.cn**

Shanghai Academy of Social Sciences

Institute of European and Asian Studies

Background and objectives: The Institute of European and Asian Studies (IEAS), established in 1992 within the Shanghai Academy of Social Sciences by merging the former Institute of U.S.S.R. and East European Studies and Institute of World History, is a research institution for the comprehensive study of countries in the Euro-Asian continent and Northeast Asia. In addition to its academic research, it provides policy advice to government agencies.

Programs: IEAS conducts research on the economics, politics, international relations, history, culture, and religion of Russia, Central and Eastern Europe, the Middle East, Central Asia, and Northeast Asia, especially Mongolia, Japan, and South Korea. Recent research projects have focused on ethnic conflicts in Europe and Asia and economic reform in China, Russia, and Eastern European countries.

The Institute also exchanges scholars with foreign institutions and organizes and sponsors conferences on such topics as the crisis in Korean peninsular and Northeast Asian security, Russia's policy toward East Asia, and Euro-Asian and East Asian economic cooperation.

Publications: The Institute publishes, in Chinese, the bimonthly journal *Euro-Asian Perspective.* Among the recent books published by the Institute are *China and the Middle East, 1949-1995* (1996), *On Worldwide Nationalism after the Cold War* (1995), and *Russians in Shanghai* (1994).

Funding sources: IEAS is funded by the Shanghai municipal government.

Staffing: The Institute has nine researchers and one administrative officer.

Head of the institution: Prof. Pan Guang, Director

Contact officer: Prof. Pan Guang

Institute of European and Asian Studies, SASS
7/622 Huai Hai Zhong Lu Road, Suite 352
Shanghai, 200020
CHINA
Tel: (86-21) 6327-1170 ext. 2352
Fax: (86-21) 6375-1446
e-mail • guangpan@fudan.ihep.ac.cn

Shanghai Center of International Studies

Background and objectives: The Shanghai Center of International Studies (SCIS), founded in 1985 by the Shanghai municipal government, is a research and advisory institution that addresses the major economic, political, and technological issues facing Shanghai and provides policy-relevant information on countries and regions of interest to government agencies. In 1988, the Center came under the administration of the Shanghai Academy of Social Sciences.

Programs: SCIS has a regional and country focus on the United States, Japan, and Southeast Asia. Recent research projects have addressed ways to increase exports from Shanghai, economic cooperation in the Asia-Pacific region, and the future of Sino-U.S. relations.

The Center organizes and sponsors international conferences on such topics as Sino-Japanese relations and Asia-Pacific cooperation, trends in Sino-American relations, and elements of instability along China's borders. It also maintains international exchanges with institutions including the Fairbank Center for East Asian Research at Harvard University, the Center for International Security and Arms Control at Stanford University, and the Asia Center of the Japan Foundation.

Publications: SCIS publishes, in Chinese, the journal *International Affairs* (at irregular intervals) and the biweekly *Bulletin of International Issues*. Recent books include *Open Door Policy in Asia, Africa, and Latin America* (1993) and *Contemporary International Crises* (1990).

Funding sources: The Center is funded by the Shanghai municipal government.

Staffing: SCIS has a staff of one secretary-general, two deputy secretaries-general, one chief administrative officer, and one assistant chief administrative officer. Dr. Wang Daohan, former mayor of Shanghai, is the Center's Honorary President.

Head of the institution: Prof. Pan Guang, Secretary-General

Contact officer: Shen Guohua, Assistant Chief Administrative Officer

Shanghai Center of International Studies
33 Zhongshan Dong Yi Lu, Suite 601
Shanghai, 200002
CHINA
Tel: (86-21) 6321-0156
Fax: (86-21) 6375-1446
e-mail • guangpan@fudan.ihep.ac.cn

Shanghai Institute for International Studies

Background and objectives: Shanghai Institute for International Studies (SIIS), founded in 1960 by the Shanghai municipal government, conducts research and advises government agencies on issues in politics, economics, security, and society.

Programs: SIIS has five research departments that focus on the United States, Europe, Japan, the Asia-Pacific, international security, and energy and environmental issues. Recent projects have addressed Asia-Pacific economic cooperation with China, maritime issues and Asia-Pacific security, and China's security relations with the Asia-Pacific countries.

International seminars have addressed such topics as Northeast Asian economic cooperation, the role of China and Japan in East Asian multilateral security mechanisms, and Russia's changing economic system and foreign policy.

The Institute has also established academic exchange relations with more than 100 research institutions in over thirty countries, including the Brookings Institution, the Pacific Forum (CSIS) of the United States, Japan's National Institute for Research Advancement, and the Association of International Relations in Singapore.

Publications: SIIS publishes in Chinese the annual *Survey of International Affairs,* the quarterly journal *International Review,* and the biweekly magazine *World Outlook.*

In English, it publishes the *SIIS Journal,* a collection of papers on international policy issues released at irregular intervals.

Chinese-language books published by SIIS include *Post Cold War America* (1993), *Economic Cooperation in the Asia-Pacific Region and Sino-Japanese Relations* (1989), and *Prospects for Asia-Pacific Development and China's Modernization* (1985).

Funding sources: SIIS receives funding from the Shanghai Municipal Government.

Staffing: The Institute has more than eighty full-time researchers, including some twenty Senior Research Fellows, supported by an administrative staff of approximately twenty-five people.

Heads of the institution:
Dr. Chen Peiyao, President

Prof. Zhu Majie, Vice President

Contact officer: Mr. Zhang Xingyan, Director, Department of Academic Affairs

Shanghai Institute for International Studies
No. 1 Lane 845, Julu Road, Shanghai, 200040
CHINA
Tel: (86-21) 6247-1148
Fax: (86-21) 6247-2272

The Better Hong Kong Foundation

Background and objectives: The Better Hong Kong Foundation is a privately-funded, nonprofit, nonpartisan organization established in 1995 by some of Hong Kong's leading business people. It aims to enhance local and international business confidence in Hong Kong in the face of the transition of sovereignty to China in July 1997.

Programs: The Foundation stages local and international events; addresses local and international social, political, and economic concerns; and facilitates communications with senior Chinese leaders in mainland China. In collaboration with the Hong Kong Trade Development Council, the Foundation organized the Hong Kong Economic Development Conference in April 1996 to address the continuing role of Hong Kong as an international financial, trading, shipping and civil aviation, and communication center.

Publications: The Foundation publishes an English newsletter entitled *Perception and Reality,* as well as conference proceedings.

Funding sources: The Foundation's activities are financed by its trustees, who are leading Hong Kong business people.

Staffing: The Foundation consists of a board of trustees, an advisory council, and an executive committee. Day-to-day work is conducted by a full-time secretariat of ten staff members.

Head of the institution: Ms. Leonie Ki, Chief Executive

Contact officer: Ms. Leonie Ki

The Better Hong Kong Foundation
Room 1301, 13/F Jubilee Centre
18 Fenwick Street, Wanchai
HONG KONG
Tel: (852) 2861-2622
Fax: (852) 2861-3361
e-mail • bhkf@bhkf.org.hk
URL • http://www.bhkf.org

Chinese University of Hong Kong

Centre for Environmental Studies

Background and objectives: The Centre for Environmental Studies (CUCES) at the Chinese University of Hong Kong was established in 1990 to promote interdisciplinary environmental research within the University and to tackle the complex environmental problems of the modern world. To this end, it collaborates with other research institutions, the Hong Kong government, and local interest groups.

Programs: CUCES's research programs cover waste analysis and treatment, including the analysis of different kinds of pollution (solid, liquid, air, and noise); environmental health and hygiene, including environmentally induced health hazards and hygienic problems; environmental monitoring and decision support systems, particularly those using innovative technology, remote sensing, and biological indicators to detect environmental changes and assess the environmental capacities of water bodies and airsheds; and environmental education, policy, and law in different countries, with an eye toward formulating effective environmental policy in Hong Kong.

The Centre offers consulting and analytical services by contract to the public and private sectors. Its clients include the Environmental Protection Department of the Hong Kong government, the Royal Hong Kong Jockey Club, Shell Hong Kong Limited, and the Tsuen Wan District Board.

Publications: The Centre publishes in English the *CUCES Newsletter.*

Funding sources: CUCES is funded by private endowment, income from contract research and projects, and research grants from the Croucher Foundation, Research Grants Council, and the Hong Kong government.

Staffing: CUCES is composed of one director, one associate director, and four program directors, supported by an administrative staff of four people.

Head of the institution: Prof. Yee Leung, Director

Contact officer: Prof. Yee Leung

**Centre for Environmental Studies
Chinese University of Hong Kong
Shatin, N.T.
HONG KONG
Tel: (852) 2609-6643
Fax: (852) 2603-5174
e-mail • cuces@cuhk.edu.hk
URL • http://www.cuces.cuhk.hk**

Chinese University of Hong Kong

Hong Kong Institute of Asia-Pacific Studies

Background and objectives: The Hong Kong Institute of Asia-Pacific Studies (HKIAPS) was established in 1990 at the Chinese University of Hong Kong to promote and coordinate interdisciplinary research on social, political, and economic developments in the region and to link faculty members with overseas scholars of Asia-Pacific studies.

Programs: The Institute offers comprehensive research programs in South China studies, gender studies, Hong Kong and Asia-Pacific economies, Japan and Asia-Pacific development, urban and regional development in Pacific Asia, economic reform and development in China, and the political and social development of Hong Kong. Recent research topics range from comparative political economy in Japan, Taiwan, and China to violence against women in Chinese society.

Outside parties sometimes commission studies and surveys from Institute researchers, and major international organizations such as the World Bank and the Asian Development Bank have undertaken short-term projects with the Institute.

HKIAPS also organizes, independently or with counterpart institutions, seminars, workshops, and conferences such as the 1994 International Conference on Violence Against Women. The Institute has established many links with international research organizations and actively conducts collaborative projects with Yale University, the University of Toronto, and Osaka International University.

Publications: HKIAPS, jointly with Osaka International University, publishes the quarterly *Asian Economic Journal* for the East Asian Economic Association.

The Institute also publishes the *Research Monograph Series* and *Occasional Paper Series*, featuring the results of its in-house research, and the *USC Seminar Series,* which includes selected research papers presented at the Universities Service Center seminars.

Recent books include *Productivity, Efficiency and Reform in China's Economy* (1995), *Inequalities and Development: Social Stratification in Chinese Societies* (1994), and *The New International Order in East Asia* (1993).

Funding sources: HKIAPS's daily operation is funded by the University. Individual research activities are funded by private donations and grants.

Staffing: Apart from the two directors, HKIAPS has three full-time research officers taking care of its functional services (external liaison, publication, and documentation), eight research assistants, and eight secretarial and clerical staff members.

Notes: HKIAPS set up a telephone survey research laboratory in 1995.

Head of the institution: Dr. Yeung Yue-man, Director

Contact officer: Dr. Timothy Wong, Research Officer

Hong Kong Institute of Asia-Pacific Studies
Chinese University of Hong Kong
Shatin, N.T.
HONG KONG
Tel: (852) 2609-8780
Fax: (852) 2603-5215
e-mail • hkiaps@cuhk.edu.hk
URL • http://www.hku.cas

City University of Hong Kong

Contemporary China Research Centre

Background and objectives: The Contemporary China Research Centre at the City University of Hong Kong was established in 1993 to support studies on contemporary China and to provide research and consulting service to the University community and the public.

Programs: The Centre undertakes research in the areas of economics, politics, law, society, education, linguistics, and culture. Recent projects have addressed China's economic reform and development, efficiency in the use of financial resources, state-society relations, legal development and the property market, patterns of urbanization, and the rehabilitation of the disabled.

The Centre runs regular seminars to discuss its research and sponsors workshops and conferences on such topics as the development of the Pearl River Delta region and the social welfare of southern China. It also receives visiting scholars from counterpart institutions, including Peking University, Columbia University, and Murdoch University in Australia, to deliver talks on issues of common interest.

Publications: The Centre publishes, in Chinese, the *Hong Kong Journal of Social Sciences,* a biannual featuring articles on socioeconomic and political issues in China, Taiwan, Hong Kong, and the Asia-Pacific region. The *CCRC News* keeps members and others informed of the Centre's recent activities. Recent books include *Economic and Social Development in South China* (1996), *Capitalist Welfare Development in Communist China: The Experience of Southern China* (1996), and *China in the Post-Deng Era* (forthcoming).

Funding sources: The Centre is funded mainly by the City University of Hong Kong.

Staffing: The Centre has approximately fifty researchers who hold teaching positions in tertiary institutions in Hong Kong, and two research assistants.

Head of the institution: Prof. Joseph Y. S. Cheng, Head

Contact officer: Prof. Joseph Y. S. Cheng

Contemporary China Research Centre
City University of Hong Kong
Tat Chee Avenue, Kowloon
HONG KONG
Tel: (852) 2788-7327
Fax: (852) 2788-7328
e-mail • rcccrc@cityu.edu.hk

The Hong Kong Centre for Economic Research

Background and objectives: The Hong Kong Centre for Economic Research (HKCER), established in 1987, is an independent, nonprofit educational and research institution within the School of Economics at the University of Hong Kong. It aims to analyze the economic problems facing Hong Kong and enhance public understanding of economic issues.

Programs: The Centre focuses on the areas of macroeconomic stability, banking and finance, and industry. Its recent Hong Kong Economic Policy Studies Project included thirty-two studies on topics ranging from institutional framework and development to housing and property.

The Centre holds monthly lunch seminars, featuring such notable lecturers as economists Milton Friedman and Ronald McKinnon. It also organizes and sponsors conferences on topics such as telecommunication and the integration of China, and conducts joint research with the University of Hong Kong and the Business and Professionals Federation of Hong Kong on demand for private residential housing as well as inflation in Hong Kong.

Publications: The Centre publishes *HKCER Letters*, a bimonthly periodical featuring commentaries on public policy issues and transcripts of its monthly lunch seminars. The Centre also publishes policy research monographs; recent titles include *The China Miracle: Development Strategy and Economic Reform* (1995), *Health Care in Hong Kong: An Economic Policy Assessment* (1992), and *International Telecommunications in Hong Kong: The Case for Liberalization* (1991).

Funding sources: The Centre is funded by donations from individuals, foundations, and corporations, and by the sale of its publications.

Staffing: The Centre has forty part-time researchers supported by five administrative assistants.

Head of the institution: Professor Y. C. Richard Wong, Director

Contact officer: Prof. Y. C. Richard Wong

The Hong Kong Centre for Economic Research
School of Economics
The University of Hong Kong
Pokfulam Road
HONG KONG
Tel: (852) 2547-8313
Fax: (852) 2548-6319
e-mail • hkcer@econ.hku.hk

Lingnan College

Hong Kong Institute of Business Studies

Background and objectives: The Hong Kong Institute of Business Studies (HKIBS), based at Lingnan College, offers research support to business faculty members and promotes exchanges with local and international counterparts. Established in 1991 as the Centre for International Business Studies, it adopted its present name in 1996, after it was merged with the Centre for Entrepreneurial Studies.

Programs: HKIBS conducts research in the areas of Chinese business studies, Chinese management in Hong Kong and Southeast Asia, and entrepreneurial studies. Recent research projects have addressed Chinese management, accounting and finance in Asia, and service industries in the Asia-Pacific region. HKIBS offers training workshops on international business and economic management to senior Chinese officials and international business students participating in exchange programs. It has also organized the 1995 International Conference on Global Business in Transition (jointly with City University of Hong Kong) and the first and second South China International Business Symposium (1994 and 1996), in collaboration with the University of Macau and Lingnan College in Zhongshan University of China.

Publications: HKIBS publishes a working paper series featuring articles on management studies, marketing and international business, accounting, and computer studies.

Funding sources: HKIBS is funded by the College through an annual grant from the Hong Kong government.

Staffing: HKIBS consists of one director, one associate director, one secretary, one assistant research officer, and three research assistants.

Head of the institution: Prof. Nyaw Mee-kau, Director

Contact officers:
Ms. Fan Yun-kam Katy, Secretary

Ms. Aouda Tse, Assistant Research Officer

Hong Kong Institute of Business Studies
Lingnan College
Fu Tei, Tuen Mum, N.T.
HONG KONG
Tel: (852) 2616-8373
Fax: (852) 2572-4171
e-mail • hkibs@ln.edu.hk
URL • http://www.ln.edu.hk

University of Hong Kong

Centre of Asian Studies

Background and objectives: The Centre of Asian Studies (CAS), established in 1967 within the University of Hong Kong, coordinates Asian studies at the University, provides research facilities for scholars undertaking doctoral and post-doctoral work in related fields, and promotes research on Asia more generally.

Programs: The Centre's areas of interest are China, Southeast Asia, and Hong Kong, with a substantive focus on politics, society, culture, international relations, business, and information technology. Recent research projects have addressed socioeconomic change in China and its impact on other Asian countries, the history of Chinese-Cantonese music, the history of the Stock Exchange of Hong Kong, and the sociopolitical dimensions of new information technology in Asia.

The Centre's current research seminar series on contemporary China, traditional China, South and Southeast Asia, and Hong Kong cover such topics as Chinese perceptions of Sino-American relations, the politics of China's cultural revolution, India-China relations, and the democratization movement in Hong Kong.

Publications: CAS publishes, in Chinese and English, the biannual *Journal of Oriental Studies,* which covers a wide range of topics concerning China, Japan, Korea, and Southeast Asia; an occasional paper and monograph series; and a research guide and bibliography series. Recent books include *Social Change and Educational Development in Mainland China, Taiwan, and Hong Kong* (in English, 1995), *Culture and Society in Hong Kong* (in Chinese with three papers in English, 1995), and *Papers and Proceedings of the International Seminar on Aesthetics of Chinese Music* (in Chinese, 1995).

Funding sources: The Centre is funded by the University grants commission and by grants from outside sources, including the Japan Foundation-Asia Center, the Stock Exchange of Hong Kong, the Stephen Hui Foundation, the Hang Seng Bank Fund, and the Hong Kong Telecom Foundation. Smaller grants are made by individuals and organizations in support of special research projects and conferences.

Staffing: CAS consists of one director, one assistant to the director, four research officers, and eleven secretarial staff members.

Head of the institution: Dr. Wong Siu-lun, Director

Contact officer: Ms. Coonoor Kripalani-Thadani, Assistant to the Director

Centre of Asian Studies
University of Hong Kong
Pokfulam Road
HONG KONG
Tel: (852) 2859-2460
Fax: (852) 2559-5884
e-mail • casgen@hkucc.hku.hk
URL • http://www.hku.cas

University of Hong Kong

Centre of Urban Planning and Environmental Management

Background and objectives: The Centre of Urban Planning and Environmental Management, originally established in 1980 and given its present name in 1991 to reflect its changing areas of concentration, is a teaching and research institution that coordinates academic programs and facilitates interdisciplinary urban and environmental research within the University of Hong Kong.

Programs: The Centre offers M.S. programs in urban planning, environmental management, and housing management. It also provides research training leading to the degrees of M.Phil. and Ph.D. Recent research projects by faculty members at the Centre have examined metropolitan development in Beijing and Guangzhou, urban housing reform in China, and comparative urban planning in Asia's newly industrializing economies.

The Centre also has academic exchange programs with China and does consulting work for the public and private sectors in Hong Kong and for international agencies.

Publications: The Centre publishes, in English, the biannual *Asian Journal of Environmental Management*. Recent English-language books include *Clearing the Air: Vehicular Emission Policy in Hong Kong* (1995), *The Emerging New Order in Natural Gas* (1995), and *Microeconomic Analytics: A Vade Mecum for Students Reading Modern Economics* (1995).

Funding sources: The Centre is funded by University budget allocation, income from contract research, and grants from a number of funding agencies, such as the Hong Kong Research Grants Council and the Urban and Environmental Studies Trust Fund.

Staffing: The Centre has a total of eight full-time readers and lecturers, eleven part-time lecturers, one research officer, one executive officer, one technician, and five secretarial or clerical staff members.

Head of the institution: Dr. Peter Hills, Director

Contact officer: Dr. Peter Hills

Centre of Urban Planning and Environmental Management
University of Hong Kong
Pokfulam Road
HONG KONG
Tel: (852) 2859-2721
Fax: (852) 2559-0468
e-mail • phills@hkucc.hku.hk
URL • http://www.hku.hk/cupem

Vision 2047 Foundation

Background and objectives: The Vision 2047 Foundation, established in 1989, is a nonprofit, privately funded membership organization that aims to promote a better understanding of Hong Kong around the world.

Programs: The Foundation organizes meetings with decision makers and opinion leaders in Hong Kong and from overseas; maintains contact with senior officials of Hong Kong and the Xinhua News Agency; sends members to the United States, China, and Europe to exchange views with government leaders on issues of concern to Hong Kong; and sponsors programs for U.S. congressional personnel and journalists to increase their knowledge and broaden their perspectives on Hong Kong.

The Foundation provides financial support for international conferences on topics such as law and China's external economic relations. Its most recent research project focuses on Hong Kong's competitiveness.

Publications: The Foundation has published slides and videos to accompany its study of Hong Kong's competitiveness. A book version of the study was published in 1997 by the Oxford University Press.

Funding sources: The Foundation is funded by membership subscriptions and individual donations. Specific projects also receive funds from special donations.

Staffing: In addition to its members, the Foundation consists of one associate director and one administrative assistant. The Board of Directors consists of ten members, headed by Chairman Sir Roger Lobo.

Contact officer: Ms. Kelley Loper, Associate Director

Vision 2047 Foundation
28th Floor, Inchcape Insurance Tower
3 Lockhart Road, Wanchai
HONG KONG
Tel: (852) 2861-1186
Fax: (852) 2804-2970
e-mail • vfound@asiaonline.net
URL • http://www.tdc.org.hk

Center for Information and Development Studies

Background and objectives: The Center for Information and Development Studies (CIDES), established in 1993, is an independent nonprofit research organization that promotes Indonesia's self-reliance and sustainable development. It seeks to study development models and develop strategies to increase the quality of human resources, enhance cooperation among developing countries, stimulate efforts to increase national growth and equality, and secure Indonesian regional autonomy.

Programs: CIDES conducts research on human resources, industrial relocation, foreign aid, electoral systems, education, law, political parties, and economic development. It also organizes international, regional, and national workshops and conferences on these issues and organizes dialogues where academics, politicians, and NGO activists discuss political and economic development, foreign policy, culture, the environment, and human rights.

The Center operates such community development projects as the development of the Indonesian economy through the application of agricultural technology.

Publications: CIDES publishes a biweekly news analysis titled *Fokus;* a bimonthly news analysis titled *Sintesis;* the quarterly *Afkar,* featuring the Center's research findings; and the yearly *Profil Indonesia,* presenting the views of Indonesia's opinion makers.

The Center also publishes working papers, reports, and books, including *Development for People: Integrating Growth and Equity* (1996), *Unity in Diversity: A New Challenge toward a Better World* (1996), *Economic, Social and Ecological Implications of Industrial Relocation* (1995), *Democratization Trends in Southeast Asia* (1994), and *Human Resources Development within the Framework of International Partnership* (1994).

Funding sources: CIDES's activities are supported by donations, project contracts, subscription income, the UNDP, and international foundations.

Staffing: CIDES has twenty-five full-time and ten part-time researchers, and twenty administrative and support staff members.

Notes: CIDES serves as a data collecting and processing center to provide accurate information on all aspects of development in Indonesia.

Head of the institution: Mr. Adi Sasono, Chairman

Contact officer: Mr. Moh Jumhur Hidayat, Executive Director

Center for Information and Development Studies
Jl. Kebon Sirih No. 85, Jakarta, 10340
INDONESIA
Tel: (62-21) 390-8988
Fax: (62-21) 390-8990
e-mail • webmaster@cides.or.id
URL • http://www.cides.or.id

Center for Policy and Implementation Studies

Background and objectives: The Center for Policy and Implementation Studies (CPIS) was established in 1986 to improve Indonesia's quality of life by analyzing development policies and programs from both macro and micro perspectives.

Programs: CPIS's researchers, who have backgrounds in such disciplines as economics, anthropology, sociology, public policy, agriculture, and urban planning, study issues that include Indonesia's economic and social issues, industrial policy, development, agriculture, and environment.

CPIS represents Indonesia at the Asia Forum conducted by the Tokyo Club Foundation for Global Studies. It also acts as the contact point for Indonesia's relations with the Organization for Economic Co-Operation and Development (OECD).

Publications: CPIS publishes *Monografi Kajian CPIS* (CPIS monograph series) twice a year, *Monitoring dan Analisis* (monitoring and analysis) four times a year, and the quarterly report *Indonesian Economy*, all in Indonesian.

Funding sources: CPIS is funded by the Department of Finance.

Staffing: CPIS has thirty-three researchers, seven consultants, and eighteen administrative assistants.

Head of the institution: Dr. Djunaedi Hadisumaro, Director

Contact officer: Dr. Imron Husin, Associate Director for Program

Center for Policy and Implementation Studies
Jl. Medan Merdeka Selatan No.13
Jakarta, 10110
P.O. Box 1520, Jakarta 10115
INDONESIA
Tel: (62-21) 380-0295
Fax: (62-21) 380-6210
e-mail • cpisnet@idola.net.id

Center for Strategic and International Studies

Background and objectives: The Center for Strategic and International Studies (CSIS), established in 1971, is a private, nonprofit research institution that undertakes policy studies in domestic and international affairs, and promotes academic exchanges with international counterparts.

Programs: CSIS's four research departments focus on international, economic, political, and sociocultural affairs. Recent studies have addressed such issues as Asia-Pacific regional security and the world order, the implications of the changing international environment for Indonesia's foreign policy and diplomacy, the future direction of Asia-Pacific economic cooperation and the role of APEC, and the political economy of deregulation, liberalization, and privatization in Indonesia.

The Center also sponsors and organizes a series of public lectures, seminars, and international conferences on such topics as Asia-Pacific economic cooperation and interdependence.

Publications: CSIS publishes *The Indonesian Quarterly,* a journal in English featuring articles on Indonesian and Southeast Asian affairs, and *Analysis CSIS,* a bimonthly journal in Indonesian.

The Center also prints and distributes the *Bulletin of Indonesian Economic Studies* for the Indonesia Project at the Australian National University.

Recent English books published by researchers at the Center include *APEC: Where Do We Go from Here* (1995), *The Challenge of Conventional Arms Proliferation in Southeast Asia* (1995), and *Indonesian Perspectives on APEC and Regional Cooperation in the Asia-Pacific* (1995).

Funding sources: CSIS is funded by donations from the private sector in Indonesia and by its own endowment.

Staffing: CSIS has a total of 129 staff members, of whom fifty-five are full-time researchers, fifty are administrative staff, and twenty-four are services staff.

Notes: CSIS initiated the creation of the Indonesian National Committee for Pacific Economic Cooperation (INCPEC), which is a member committee of Pacific Economic Cooperation Conference (PECC). It is also a founding member of the ASEAN Institute for Strategic and International Studies, and provides secretarial support for the organization.

Heads of the institution:
Dr. Daoed Joesoef, Chairman

Dr. Jusuf Wanandi, Chair of the Supervisory Board

Contact officer: Dr. Mari Pangestu, Executive Director

Center for Strategic and International Studies
Jalan Tanah Abang III, 23-27, Jakarta, 10160
INDONESIA
Tel: (62-21) 380-9637
Fax: (62-21) 380-9641
e-mail • csis@inovasi.comincpec@global.net.id
URL • http://www.inovasi.com/csis

Indonesian Institute of Sciences
Center for Political and Regional Studies
Pusat Penelitian dan Pengembangan Politik dan Kewilayahan, Lembaga Ilma Pengetahuan Indonesia

Background and objectives: The Center for Political and Regional Studies (PPW-LIPI), founded in 1987 as a government research center, aims to contribute to Indonesia's national development through empirical research in the fields of domestic and international politics. The Center provides input to Indonesia's decision makers and formulates domestic and foreign policy alternatives.

Programs: On behalf of the government, PPW-LIPI conducts research in the area of political thought, public policy, comparative politics, local and national administration, international relations, and regional studies. Some of the most notable research projects include studies on the general elections and the political parties of Indonesia, the industrialization of eastern Indonesia, political development in the Middle East, and political, economic, and security issues in the Asia-Pacific.

The Center regularly organizes internal seminars and once a year holds a major national conference focusing on topical political issues, both national and international.

Publications: PPW-LIPI publishes a series of research reports every year, most of which are drawn from the interim findings of three-to-five-year projects. Recent publications include: *AFTA Indonesian Manufacturers' Response, Indonesia and APEC, The Maastricht Treaty: European Economic and Monetary Union, The Political Economy of the Middle East: The Oil Factor,* and *East ASEAN Growth Triangle.* PPW recently started publication of a biannual political journal, *Studia Politika,* in conjunction with the Insan Politika Foundation.

Funding sources: As a state-owned research institution, the Center is funded by the government. Individual or groups of researchers may obtain project sponsorship from other local or international sources.

Staffing: The Center has thirty-nine full-time researchers and twenty-five administrative staff.

Notes: Besides government funded research, researchers pursue their own specialized areas of interests and publish their works separately.

Head of the institution: Dr. Mochtar Pabottingi, Director

Contact officer: Dr. Dewi Fortuna Anwar, Head, Regional and International Affairs Division

Center for Political and Regional Studies
Indonesian Institute of Science
(PPW-LIPI)
Widya Graha, Jl. Jendral Gatot Subroto, No. 10
Jakarta, 12190
INDONESIA
Tel: (62-21) 525-1542
Fax: (62-21) 520-7188

Institute for Economic and Social Research, Education and Information
Lembaga Penelitian, Pendidikan dan Penerangan Ekonomi dan Sosial (LP3ES)

Background and objectives: The Institute for Economic and Social Research, Education and Information (LP3ES), established in 1971, is a private, autonomous, nonprofit organization that strives to promote economic and social research, improve public knowledge and understanding of development problems facing Indonesia, and facilitate exchanges with national and international counterparts.

Programs: LP3ES conducts research on a wide variety of economic and social issues, including small-scale entrepreneurship and management, economic and community development, land and water resources management, and democracy and human rights.

Some representative programs include the Small-Scale Irrigation Project, the Action Program of Jakarta Sewerage and Sanitation Project, the Cirebon Community and Participation Program, the Urban Informal Sector Policy and Community Action Program, Community Participation Programs through Development of Local Media, Community and Economic Development Programs through Pesantren, Human Rights Promotion Programs among Pesantren and NGOs, and Income Improvement Programs among Female Workers in Agriculture.

With support from government and funding agencies, LP3ES also sponsors seminars, workshops, and other forums to bring together researchers, policy makers, and development experts for discussion of such development issues as water management, small-scale industry development, military and civilian roles in politics, and government research policy.

Publications: LP3ES has published a monthly journal, *Prisma,* since 1971. It contains articles on economic, political, social, and cultural issues. The Institute is also a well-known academic publisher of books by Indonesian and foreign authors.

Funding sources: LP3ES is funded by donations and grants from international and local foundations, as well as foreign and national development agencies. Foreign contributors include Friedrich Naumann Stiftung, the United States Agency for International Development, the Ford Foundation, the Asia Foundation, the Swiss Development Cooperation, and the Toyota Foundation. Local partners include the Ministries of Public Works, Industry and Trade, Home Affairs, Cooperatives, and a number of private institutions.

Staffing: LP3ES has thirty full-time researchers and ninety field workers, supported by an administrative staff of thirty people.

Head of the institution: Mr. Ismid Hadad, Chairman

Contact officer: Mr. Rustam Ibrahim, Director

Institute for Economic and Social Research, Education and Information
(LP3ES)
Jl. S. Parman 81, Jakarta, 11420
INDONESIA
Tel: (62-21) 567-4211
Fax: (62-21) 568-3785
e-mail • lp3es@nusa.or.id

Asia Pacific Association of Japan

Asia Taiheiyo Kenkyukai

Background and objectives: The Asia Pacific Association of Japan (APAJ), established in 1974 in close collaboration with the United Nations Association of the United States of America (UNA-USA), analyzes global political and economic trends to promote Japan's economic growth, engages in collaborative research with foreign research institutes, and conducts policy studies on the Asia-Pacific region and Japan-U.S. relations.

Programs: APAJ pursues research and organizes international symposiums on topics ranging from regional crisis management and the role of the United Nations to Asian security and developments in the Korean peninsula. Its research results are presented as policy recommendations to high-ranking government officials.

The APA Forum, a monthly lecture meeting, convenes politicians, businessmen, and scholars to exchange views on such issues as Russia after the presidential election, ASEAN, and the recent development of China's military. Recent international speakers at the Forum include Professor G. Curtis of Columbia University, Professor Kent Calder of Princeton University, Dr. Sergei Rogov of the Russian Academy of Sciences, and Mr. Sam Rainsy, Cambodian Minister of Economics and Finance.

Publications: APAJ publishes its research results and other information in the form of APA Forum transcripts and the irregularly published *APA News* and *APA Report*.

Funding sources: APAJ's activities are supported by membership dues from more than seventy member corporations, as well as by donations from associations.

Staffing: APAJ has two part-time researchers, supported by three administrative assistants.

Head of the institution: Mr. Toshiaki Ogasawara, President

Contact officer: Mr. Masaru Tanimoto, General Manager

Asia Pacific Association of Japan
3-14-5 Shibaura, Minato-ku, Tokyo, 108
JAPAN
Tel: (81-3) 3457-1570
Fax: (81-3) 3457-1574

Association for Promotion of International Cooperation

Kokusai Kyoryoku Suishin Kyokai

Background and objectives: The Association for Promotion of International Cooperation (APIC) was created in 1975 as a non-profit foundation under the direction of the Ministry of Foreign Affairs. Its primary function is to help the government and the private sector cooperate in promoting the development of recipient countries.

Programs: APIC conducts research on developing country issues, disseminates information on Japan's Official Development Assistance (ODA), and carries out a variety of projects to promote a better understanding of developing countries throughout Japan. These include seminars and symposiums, such as the annual international symposium "Messages from Asia," to promote dialogue among government officials, business leaders, and the public on matters related to international cooperation and development.

The Plaza for International Cooperation, which APIC opened in 1993, supports ODA- and NGO-related activities and provides citizens with easy access to data on such activities. APIC also analyzes the results of country-by-country surveys on economic cooperation with Japan and the suitability for receiving aid.

Publications: APIC publishes the monthly *Plaza for International Cooperation* (in Japanese). Other publications include *Japan's ODA Annual Report*, *A Guide to Japan's Aid* (both in Japanese and in English), and a *Guide to Participating in Economic Cooperation*.

Funding sources: APIC's major financial sources are both internally generated and from government subsidies, and membership dues.

Staffing: APIC has eleven researchers and fourteen administrative assistants.

Head of the institution: Mr. Yoshio Okawara, President

Contact officer: Mr. Hiroyuki Yanagitsubo, Executive Director

Association for Promotion of International Cooperation
5-2-32 Minami Azabu, Minato-ku, Tokyo, 106
JAPAN
Tel: (81-3) 5423-0571
Fax: (81-3) 5423-0576
e-mail • apic1@gol.com
URL • http://www.apic.or.jp

Foundation for Advanced Information and Research

Kenkyu Joho Kikin

Background and objectives: The Foundation for Advanced Information and Research (FAIR) was established in 1985 with the cooperation of the Institute of Fiscal and Monetary Policy, the Ministry of Finance, and other domestic and foreign parties. FAIR aims to enhance foreign understanding of Japan through the dissemination of information on Japanese society; conduct research on various countries and regions; and promote U.S.-Europe-Japan cooperation in the development of the Pacific Basin area. In 1992, the Institute of Global Financial Studies (IGFS) was established as an affiliated institution to facilitate joint international research and technical assistance. FAIR includes over seventy corporate members and over 270 individual associate members from around the world.

Programs: FAIR conducts research in the fields of economics, international relations, and technology; promotes international exchanges of researchers, businessmen, and policy makers; and sponsors international symposia and joint study programs with foreign universities and research organizations.

Through the FAIR-Fujitsu Library Program, organizations in foreign countries can apply to obtain information and updated publications on Japan both in Japanese and in foreign languages.

Publications: FAIR disseminates information through the publication of books (in English and Japanese) and the quarterly *FAIR Report* (in Japanese). Recent publications include the multi-volume *FAIR Fact Series* and *Science and Technology: A Message from Japan* (1993).

Funding sources: FAIR is primarily funded by its domestic corporate members.

Staffing: FAIR has nine full-time researchers and eighteen administrative staff.

Head of the institution: Mr. Jiro Saito, President

Contact officer: Ms. Chie Ikarashi, Secretariat

FAIR
Toranomon NN Bldg., 1-21-17 Toranomon, Minato-ku
Tokyo, 105
JAPAN
Tel: (81-3) 3503-0231
Fax: (81-3) 3503-0236
e-mail • KYF00553@niftyserve.or.jp.FAIR@jp.
         interramp.com

Institute for International Policy Studies

Sekai Heiwa Kenkyujo

Background and objectives: The Institute for International Policy Studies (IIPS), formerly the International Institute for Global Peace, was established in 1988 as an independent, non-profit institute to examine global security, economic, and environmental issues. Former Japanese prime minister Yasuhiro Nakasone is chairman of the IIPS, and Ambassador Yoshio Okawara is the president and executive director.

Programs: The Institute conducts policy-oriented research on topics which include the future prospects for the world economy, the post-Cold War security challenges for Japan and Europe, post-Cold War cooperative denuclearization and plutonium issues, and Asian-Pacific economic and security issues.

IIPS also promotes and co-sponsors domestic and international symposiums, conferences, and roundtable discussions where local and foreign experts from academia, government, and research organizations are invited to speak on topics ranging from security issues of the Asia-Pacific region to prospects for integrating Russia into the Pacific Rim economy. Distinguished speakers have included former Soviet president Mikhail Gorbachev and former U.S. secretary of state Henry Kissinger.

Publications: The Institute publishes the biannual *Asia-Pacific Review* (in English). The results of research and conference activities are disseminated through the *IIPS News* (both in English and in Japanese), *IIPS Policy Papers*, and occasional conference reports. Recent publications in English include *Security in Asia: Roles and Tasks for Japan and the United States* (1996); *Future Prospects for the World Economic System: Conference Report* (1996); *The New Russia and Asia 1991-1995: Conclusions from the "New Russia/CIS in Asia" Project* (1996); *Fifty Years after Hiroshima: A Half-Century of Nuclear Energy and Beyond* (1995); *Russia and the Central Asian Republics in East Asia: The New Era* (1995); *Assessing Japan's Security Risks: Ballistic Missile Dangers and Countermeasures* (1995).

Funding sources: The Institute's activities are funded through investments, membership contributions, and research contracts.

Staffing: IIPS has a staff of fourteen researchers (eleven full-time, two part-time, and one visiting), supported by thirteen administrative assistants.

Head of the institution: Dr. Seizaburo Sato, Research Director

Contact officer: Mr. Tetsuo Toda, Administrative Director

Institute for International Policy Studies
Sumitomo Hanzomon Building, 7F
3-16 Hayabusa-cho, Chiyoda-ku
Tokyo, 102
JAPAN
Tel: (81-3) 3222-0711
Fax: (81-3) 3222-0710
e-mail • iips@gol.com

Institute of Developing Economies

Ajia Keizai Kenkyusho

Background and objectives: The Institute of Developing Economies (IDE), founded in 1958 as a nonprofit research organization and later reorganized into a quasi-governmental body, is dedicated to the study of social, political, and economic issues that affect developing countries. Its goal is to promote closer economic cooperation between Japan and the developing nations.

Programs: The Institute's research draws on the cooperation of outside specialists from developing countries themselves in the areas of socioeconomic development and statistical analysis of developing economies in Asia, the Middle East, Africa, Latin America, and Eastern Europe.

A total of 395 research fellows from fifty-four developing countries have participated in the Visiting Research Fellows Program and 522 IDE researchers have conducted field surveys in sixty-five countries under the auspices of the Institute's Overseas Research Program.

IDE also compiles statistical data on production, population, and trade in developing economies, in collaboration with governmental and research institutes in 130 countries.

The IDE Advanced School was established in 1990 to offer a post-graduate diploma course, a Master's course and a Ph.D. course in development studies for Japanese students, and a diploma course for government officials from developing countries.

Publications: IDE publishes eight periodicals, including *The Developing Economies* (quarterly in English) and *Ajia Keizai* (monthly in Japanese); *Occasional Papers Series; IDE Symposium Proceedings; International Joint Research Project Series;* and *Statistical Data Series* (all in English). The Institute has also published about 1,000 research reports in Japanese.

Funding sources: Most of IDE's activities are subsidized by the government.

Staffing: The Institute has 150 researchers (including thirty-four stationed overseas) and 104 administrative and support personnel.

Note: The IDE library has arrangements with 690 foreign libraries, research institutes, universities, government organizations, and banks for the exchange of books and other research materials. Also, about 150 newspaper titles from developing countries, dating from 1959, are held on microfilm.

Head of the institution: Mr. Katsuhisa Yamada, President

Contact officer: Mr. Toshiaki Hayashi, Director, Public Relations Department

Institute of Developing Economies
42 Ichigaya-Hommura-cho, Shinjuku-ku, Tokyo, 162
JAPAN
Tel: (81-3) 3353-4231
Fax: (81-3) 3226-8475
Telex: AJIKEN J32473
Cable: AJIKEN Tokyo
e-mail • infor@ide.go.jp
URL • http://www.ide.go.jp

The International Center for the Study of East Asian Development, Kitakyushu

Kokusai Higashi-Asia Kenkyu Center

Background and objectives: The International Center for the study of East Asian Development (ICSEAD), jointly founded in 1989 by the City of Kitakyushu and the University of Pennsylvania, conducts interdisciplinary and empirical studies on the economic and social problems facing East Asia in order to contribute to regional development.

Programs: ICSEAD conducts research on such topics as the international division of labor and inter-industry cooperation, the growth of the megalopolis, and strategic development in East Asia. The Center also holds seminars, symposiums, and study meetings to exchange opinions and to present the results of its research activities.

ICSEAD exchanges academic personnel and research materials with various institutes specializing in East Asian socioeconomic issues, such as the Korea Development Institute, the Korea Institute for Industrial Economics and Trade, and the Philippine Institute for Development Studies.

Publications: ICSEAD has published for six years the quarterly *ICSEAD News* to promote its activities and the quarterly *East Asian Economic Perspectives* to provide updates on regional issues. In June 1996, the Center initiated a new annual series, *A Viewpoint of East Asia from Kitakyushu* (in Japanese with an English summary of all papers included).

Results of research projects are published as working papers and books. Recent publications include *Environmental Problems in China* (1995), and *Verification for the Pan-Yellow Sea Zone* (1995) (both in Japanese).

Funding sources: The Center is supported mainly by subsidy from Kitakyushu City.

Staffing: The Center has six full-time researchers and three visiting scholars, supported by eleven administrative workers.

Head of the institution: Dr. Kenzo Tanaka, Chairman, Board of Trustees

Contact officers:
Dr. Shinichi Ichimura, Director

Mr. Hiroshi Yano, Secretary General

The International Center for the Study of East Asian Development, Kitakyushu
11-4 Otemachi, Kokurakita-ku, Kitakyushu, 803
JAPAN
Tel: (81-93) 583-6202
Fax: (81-93) 583-6576
e-mail • yano@icsead.or.jp

International Development Center of Japan

Kokusai Kaihatsu Center

Background and objectives: The International Development Center of Japan (IDCJ), founded in 1971, was the first Japanese think tank specializing in institutional and economic development and assistance. IDCJ is a training institute, a policy and planning consultant to Japanese ministries and international organizations, and a research center. It works closely with industry, government, and academia to promote international development and cooperation.

Programs: IDCJ's Human Resources Development program offers courses for overseas participants on topics such as development policies and economics, technology management, and Japanese industry and trade policies. It also offers courses for Japanese participants on project identification and evaluation, overseas business management, and language and cultural orientation.

IDCJ's Policy-making, Planning, and Study projects, commissioned by various Japanese ministries and international organizations, focus on economic policy, regional planning, and aid evaluation and management in specific countries or sectors.

Research and Development activities include an in-house program of theoretical and applied study on topics such as development economics and assistance methodology.

Publications: IDCJ publishes several periodicals, including *IDCJ Forum* and a working paper series. Other recent publications include *The Impact of ODA on Central Asian Republics* (1995) and *Technology Diffusion, Productivity, Employment, and Phase Shifts in Developing Economies* (1994).

Funding sources: IDCJ's activities are supported by endowments from the Japan Keirin Association, the Japan Shipbuilding Industry Foundation, and the industrial and construction sectors. Additional revenues are derived from research commissioned by ministries and agencies.

Staffing: IDCJ has thirty-six full-time researchers, supported by an administrative staff of twenty-nine.

Head of the institution: Mr. Saburo Kawai, Chairperson

Contact officer: Dr. Norimichi Toyomane, Ph.D., Director, Planning and Research Division

International Development Center of Japan
Kyofuku Bldg., 9-11, Tomioka 2-chome, Koto-ku
Tokyo, 135
JAPAN
Tel: (81-3) 3630-6911
Fax: (81-3) 3630-8120

International House of Japan

Kokusai Bunka Kaikan

Background and objectives: The International House of Japan (IHouse) is a private, nonprofit organization established in 1952 to promote cultural exchange and international cooperation. Its membership represents more than fifty nationalities.

Programs: IHouse sponsors international exchange programs for intellectual and opinion leaders, scholars, and artists. It also organizes research projects in cooperation with overseas institutions such as the Japan Society, the Aspen Institute, the Asia Society, the Chinese Academy of Social Sciences, the Reischauer Institute for Japanese Studies, Harvard University, and the India International Centre; arranges seminars, conferences, and study groups; provides fellowships and scholarships; and assists in major research projects.

IHouse maintains a 20,000-volume library of English-language books, particularly social science and humanities titles that focus on Japan.

Publications: A quarterly newsletter, the *IHJ Bulletin* (*Kaiho* is the Japanese sister publication), features articles, book reviews, and a list of upcoming activities. Occasional publications also appear in Japanese on a variety of topics. Recent publications include *Bound to Lead? Domestic Challenge and the Capacity for International Leadership in Japan and the United States* (1995) and *Arms Control and Non-Proliferation after the Cold War* (1995).

Funding sources: Support for the IHouse's ongoing program of activities is provided by its more than 5,000 individual and 500 corporate members, as well as by foundation grants.

Staffing: IHouse has an administrative staff of eighty.

Notes: IHouse's purpose-built building features sixty-one rooms for overnight guests, five seminar rooms, a lecture hall for 130 people, and an impressive Japanese garden.

Head of institution: Prof. Motoo Kaji, Chairman

Contact officer: Mr. Mikio Kato, Executive Director

International House of Japan
5-11-16, Roppongi, Minato-ku
Tokyo, 106
JAPAN
Tel: (81-3) 3470-3211
Fax: (81-3) 3470-3170
e-mail • J90165@sinet.ad.jp

International University of Japan
Center for Japan-United States Relations

Kokusai Daigaku Nichibei Kankei Kenkyujo

Background and objectives: The Center for Japan-U.S. Relations, founded in 1985 at the International University of Japan, examines Japan-U.S. interactions and their implications for the Asia-Pacific region. The Center has worked to develop new methods of data collection on, and analysis of, the history and structure of Japan-U.S. relations.

Programs: The Center supports original research on political, economic, and strategic relations between Japan and the U.S. Recent projects have examined conflict and cooperation among Japan, China, and the U.S. in the Asia-Pacific region and compared the political systems of Japan, the U.S., and Europe in the post-Cold War era.

The Center also sponsors lectures, seminars, and the monthly "Japan-U.S. Research Roundtable," where faculty and students discuss their ongoing research.

Publications: The Center publishes *Outlook*, a semiannual periodical in Japanese that offers diverse perspectives on Japan-U.S. relations. It also publishes occasional papers, working papers, and its students contribute to the annual *Report on Japan-U.S. Relations* (produced with the Paul H. Nitze School of Advanced International Studies at Johns Hopkins University). Recent publications include *The United States and Japan in 1996—Redefining the Partnership* (1996) and *The Meaning of the Seattle APEC Meetings* (1994).

Funding sources: The Center's research is funded largely by grants from foundations and government ministries, including the Japan Foundation Center for Global Partnership, Suntory Foundation, and the Ministry of Education. Additional funding is provided by the International University of Japan.

Staffing: The Center has a staff of thirteen part-time research fellows from various universities, supported by two administrative assistants.

Head of the institution: Dr. George R. Packard, Visiting President

Contact officer: Dr. Tomohito Shinoda, Research Fellow

Center for Japan-U.S. Relations
International University of Japan
Yamato-machi, Minami Uonuma-gun
Niigata, 949-72
JAPAN
Tel: (81-257) 79-1112
Fax: (81-257) 79-4442
e-mail • ori@iuj.ac.jp
URL • http://www.iuj.ac.JP/research

Japan Center for Economic Research

Nihon Keizai Kenkyu Center

Background and objectives: The Japan Center for Economic Research is a private, nonprofit organization established in 1963 under the auspices of the Nihon Keizai Shinbun, Inc. The Center is dedicated to developing Japan's economy and assisting corporate management by providing economic data and trend analysis. It has more than 370 corporate members, most of which are banks and large firms, and 320 individual members, who are economists in business, academia, and government.

Programs: In addition to its economic research and forecasting, JCER conducts economic study courses, seminars, lectures, and symposia in which leading experts from academia, business, and government are invited to discuss financial subjects, macroeconomics analysis, and economic forecasting.

JCER also conducts joint research with counterpart institutions such as the National Bureau of Economic Research, provides study facilities to a limited number of researchers from abroad, and trains young scholars in advanced economics and research.

Publications: The Center publishes the biweekly *JCER Bulletin* (in Japanese) and the quarterly *JCER Report* (in English), as well as short- to long-term Japanese economic forecasts in both English and Japanese. Other publications include the *JCER Economic Journal*, the *JCER Paper Series*, and research reports that feature the Center's occasional studies.

Funding sources: The Center is funded by fees and donations from its members, income from training economists, and contract research.

Staffing: The Center has fifteen full-time and six part-time researchers, all of whom are economists, supported by twenty-nine administrative assistants.

Notes: The Center maintains a close link with the *Nihon Keizai Shinbun* (*Nikkei*), Japan's leading financial newspaper, which sponsors researchers at the Center and provides it with information. JCER also maintains an office in Osaka.

Head of the institution: Dr. Yutaka Kosai, President

Contact officer: Mr. Yoshiki Ikeda, Executive Secretary

Japan Center for Economic Research
Nikkei Kayabacho Building
2-6-1, Nihombashi Kayabacho
Chuo-ku, Tokyo, 103
JAPAN
Tel: (81-3) 3639-2801
Fax: (81-3) 3639-2839

Japan Center for International Exchange

Nihon Kokusai Koryu Center

Background and objectives: The Japan Center for International Exchange (JCIE) was founded in 1970 as an independent, non-profit, nonpartisan organization dedicated to strengthening Japan's role in international affairs. JCIE aims to broaden the debate on Japan's international responsibilities through international and cross-regional programs of exchange, research, and discussion. The Center creates opportunities for informed policy discussion but does not take policy positions.

Programs: JCIE combines research and policy dialogue in such programs as the Shimoda Conferences, which bring together prominent figures from the U.S., Japan, and other Asian countries to discuss Asia-Pacific issues; the ASEAN-Japan Dialogue Program, which examines the ASEAN-Japan relationship in a broader regional context; and the Korea-Japan Intellectual Exchange Program, a joint study and conference series on domestic and bilateral issues.

Recent policy research programs include Japan's Asian Identity, a study of Japan's position and role in Asia-Pacific in terms of economics, history, and security and foreign relations; and Japan's International Agenda, a study of Japan's "civilian power" and its role in the international community.

JCIE occasionally conducts joint public policy studies with such institutions as the American Assembly, the Institute of Southeast Asian Studies of Singapore, the Winrock International Institute for Agricultural Development, the Institute on Global Conflict and Cooperation at the University of California, and the Brookings Institution.

JCIE also sponsors exchange programs to facilitate mutual understanding among policy makers and organizes study programs for foreign institutions seeking to understand Japanese policy-making processes. Such programs include the U.S.-Japan Parliamentary Exchange Program, the U.S.-Japan Young Political Leaders Exchange Program, the Brookings/JCIE Japan-U.S. Partnership Forum, and the Israel-Japan Intellectual Exchange Program.

The Center promotes grassroots international activities through such exchanges as the U.S.-Japan Women's Dialogue, and the U.S.-Japan Agricultural Community Leaders Exchange.

JCIE also serves as the Japanese secretariat for private bilateral forums such as the UK-Japan 2000 Group, the Japanese-German Dialogue Forum, and the Korea-Japan Forum.

Finally, JCIE encourages private philanthropy in Japan and in Asia's developing countries through such efforts as the Asian Community Trust.

Publications: JCIE publishes an English-language quarterly newsletter, *The Civil Society Monitor,* which provides up-to-date information on Japan's civil society. Recent books include *Emerging Civil Society in the Asia Pacific Community* (1996), co-published by JCIE and the Institute of Southeast Asian Studies in Singapore; *The Role of Non-State Actors in International Affairs* (1995); and *Japan and the United States in the Asia Pacific: The Challenges for Japan in Asia* (1995).

Funding sources: JCIE is funded by private foundation grants, corporate contributions, and research contracts.

Staffing: JCIE has twenty-seven full-time and three part-time staff members.

Head of the institution: Mr. Tadashi Yamamoto, President

Contact officer: Ms. Hideko Katsumata, Executive Secretary

Japan Center for International Exchange
4-9-17 Minami Azabu, Minato-ku , Tokyo, 106
JAPAN
Tel: (81-3) 3446-7781
Fax: (81-3) 3443-7580
e-mail • admin@jcie.or.jp
URL • http://www.jcie.or.jp

Japan Economic Foundation

Kokusai Keizai Koryu Zaidan

Background and objectives: The Japan Economic Foundation (JEF), established in 1981, is an independent nonprofit organization whose aim is to foster deeper mutual understanding between Japan and the rest of the world through the exchange of leading business, media, and government figures. JEF seeks to bridge those communication gaps that prevent opinion leaders in different countries from truly understanding each other and thereby to promote improved understanding of Japan's economy, industry, trade, and economic policies and to help to strengthen the international free trade system.

Programs: The Foundation sponsors visits by Japanese economic policy makers and business executives to Europe, North America, Australia, Southeast Asia, and the Middle East; invites from overseas leading economic policy makers and business executives to Japan to become acquainted with Japanese opinion leaders in the fields of politics, economics, industry, academia, and journalism; publishes information on Japan's economic, industrial, and trade policies, and produces video films; and sponsors research on trade, industry, and economics in other countries.

JEF also organizes forums and seminars such as the JEF-Aspen U.S.-Japan Council Meeting, Anglo-Japanese High Technology Industry Forum, and Global Contribution Seminar.

Publications: JEF publishes the bimonthly *Journal of Japanese Trade & Industry.*

Funding sources: JEF is funded by its own endowment and through a subsidy from the Ministry of International Trade and Industry.

Staffing: JEF has fourteen administrative staff and sponsors outside research rather than employing its own researchers.

Head of the institution: Mr. Minoru Masuda, Chairman

Contact officer: Mr. Aichy Tamori, Executive Managing Director

Japan Economic Foundation
2-2-2 Uchisaiwai-cho, Chiyoda-ku, Tokyo, 100
JAPAN
Tel: (81-3) 3580-9291
Fax: (81-3) 3501-6674
e-mail • jef@po.jah.or.jp
URL • http://www.jef.or.jp

The Japan Forum on International Relations

Nihon Kokusai Forum

Background and objectives: The Japan Forum on International Relations (JFIR), established in 1987, is an independent nonprofit membership organization dedicated to the study of Japanese foreign policy and international relations. Founded by a group of business, academic, political, and media leaders, the Forum conducts policy research on international affairs and disseminates its findings domestically and internationally. The Forum takes no institutional position on issues of foreign policy, but encourages its members to propose their own alternatives.

Programs: The Forum's research addresses such issues as U.S.-Japanese economic conflicts, the future of China and its implications for Asian security, and the international monetary and trade systems. When the findings are complete, the results are presented to the Prime Minister and made public at a press conference.

JFIR also conducts monthly roundtable discussions on international political and socioeconomic issues with senior officials from Japanese government ministries and agencies.

In addition, the Forum promotes "International Exchange Seminars" with leading intellectuals, businessmen, journalists, and government officials from foreign countries.

Publications: JFIR's English-language publications include the *Annual Report* and the occasional *Japan Forum Paper Series*. The forum also publishes periodicals in Japanese at quarterly, annual, and five-year intervals. Recent books in English include *The WTO System and Japan* (1996), *The Perspective of Security Regimes in the Asia-Pacific Region* (1996), *Peace and Order in the 21st Century* (1996), *Perspective of International Security Framework in the 21st Century: Global and Regional* (1996), and *"ASIATOM": A New Framework for Nuclear Cooperation in the Asia-Pacific Region* (1996).

Funding sources: The Forum is funded primarily by corporate, associate, and individual membership dues. It also receives income from its ¥200 million endowment and additional contributions.

Staffing: The Forum has eight researchers and an administrative staff of five.

Head of the institution: Mr. Kenichi Ito, President

Contact officer: Mr. Hironori Saito, Chief of Research Programs

The Japan Forum on International Relations, Inc.
2-17-12, Akasaka, Minato-ku, Tokyo, 107
JAPAN
Tel: (81-3) 3584-2190
Fax: (81-3) 3589-5120
e-mail • jfir@mars.dtinet.or.jp

Japan Institute of International Affairs

Nihon Kokusai Mondai Kenkyujo

Background and objectives: The Japan Institute of International Affairs (JIIA), established in 1959, is a private, nonprofit research organization specializing in the study of international issues. The Institute helps formulate Japan's foreign policy and maintains close ties with the Ministry of Foreign Affairs. Its goals include advancing scientific study of international politics, economics, and law; promoting international exchanges; and disseminating research findings.

Programs: The Institute conducts research, from the perspective of Japan's national security, on the political, social, and economic issues facing the former Soviet Union, North America, and Asia-Pacific.

JIIA also co-sponsors annual conferences with counterpart institutions such as the China Institute of International Studies and the Korean Institute of Foreign Affairs and National Security.

In addition, the Institute serves as the national secretariat for the Pacific Economic Cooperation Conference, whose membership includes nineteen nations and regions in Asia-Pacific.

Publications: JIIA publishes in English the semiannual *Japan Review of International Affairs*, the annual *White Papers of Japan*, and the *Pacific Cooperation Newsletter*. In Japanese, JIIA publishes the monthly *Kokusai Mondai* (International Affairs) and the annual *Kokusai Nenpo*. Representative publications include *Twenty Years of ASEAN: Its Survival and Development* (1988) and *Indochina in Transition—Confrontation or Co-Prosperity* (1989).

Funding sources: The JIIA's main sources of revenue are government subsidies, donations from foundations, membership dues, and income from the sale of publications.

Staffing: Information not provided.

Head of the institution: Amb. Nobuo Matsunaga, Director

Japan Institute of International Affairs
Toranomon Mitsui Building
3-8-1, Kasumigaseki, Chiyoda-ku
Tokyo, 100
JAPAN
Tel: (81-3) 3503-7744
Fax: (81-3) 3503-6707

Keidanren (Japan Federation of Economic Organizations)

Background and objectives: Keidanren is a private, nonprofit membership organization representing virtually all branches of economic activity in Japan. Founded in 1946, Keidanren has become a nationwide body with more than 100 member associations and approximately 1,000 corporate members, many of which are leading Japanese enterprises. Its primary purpose is to provide a forum for the study and discussion of problems facing Japanese industries and businesses.

Programs: Keidanren holds meetings throughout Japan on topics ranging from taxation and administrative reform to the promotion of space development. Its policy recommendations and proposals are submitted to the Japanese government and other influential bodies. Keidanren administers twenty-nine policy-making committees, chaired by executives from Japan's largest firms, and twenty-one bilateral and regional relations committees, linking Japan with other countries.

Together with the Japanese government, Keidanren sponsors the Japan International Development Organization, which promotes foreign-currency-generating projects in developing countries; the Japan International Training Cooperation Organization, which facilitates the training of foreign workers at Japanese companies; and the Foundation for Advanced Studies on International Development, which trains Japanese personnel in economic assistance and development.

Publications: Keidanren publishes a monthly Japanese information magazine, *Monthly Keidanren*, and research papers (mainly in Japanese) on topics as diverse as tax reform, new business opportunities, and environmental policy.

Funding sources: Keidanren is funded entirely by membership dues and other contributions from its members.

Staffing: Keidanren has 197 full-time staff including researchers.

Notes: Keidanren's research papers, policy recommendations, and speech drafts by executive members are available, in English, on the Internet.

Heads of the institution:
Mr. Masaya Miyoshi, President & Director General

Mr. Shoichiro Toyoda, Chairman

Contact officer: Mr. Hideaki Tanaka, Manager, Public Affairs Group

Keidanren
1-9-4, Otemachi, Chiyoda-ku
Tokyo, 100
JAPAN
Tel: (81-3) 3279-1411
Fax: (81-3) 5255-6231
URL • http://www.keidanren.or.jp

Kyoto University
Center for Southeast Asian Studies

Kyoto Daigaku Tonan-Asia Kenkyu Center

Background and objectives: The Center for Southeast Asian Studies (CSEAS), formally established in 1963, pursues global, interdisciplinary, cooperative research on Southeast Asia and its surrounding countries.

Programs: CSEAS is dedicated to "integrated studies," which encompasses not only the humanities and social sciences—particularly history, anthropology, and political science—but also the natural sciences of Southeast Asia.

The Research Department of CSEAS has five divisions: Ecological Studies (with natural environment and biological environment sections), Socio-Cultural Studies (including population studies, social dynamics, and cultural dynamics), Integrative Processes (including political culture, political dynamics, and regional integration), Development Studies (including rural development, development planning, and economic development), and Human Environment (including production environment, tropical environment, and life environment).

The Research Department has sections for both Japanese and foreign visiting scholars. CSEAS focuses on five-year joint research projects that emphasize fieldwork, interdisciplinary team membership, and the participation of Southeast Asian researchers. Past projects resulted in studies such as "An Integrated Study on the Formation of the Southeast Asian World" (1980-1984), "A Civilization-Oriented Integrated Study on the Formation and Evolution of the Southeast Asian World" (1985-1989), and "An Integrated Study on Indigenous Logic and the Development Structure of the Southeast Asian World" (1990-1995).

Several other projects have been carried out with grants from the Ministry of Education, Science, and Culture, including a "Global Area Studies" project that involves 130 specialists nationwide, with CSEAS as its core institution. CSEAS organizes seminars, forums, and symposia for participants inside and outside Kyoto University.

Publications: The Center's quarterly journal, *Southeast Asian Studies,* publishes important research findings on Southeast Asia from within and outside CSEAS. The Center also publishes two series of monographs on Southeast Asian studies, one in Japanese and one in English.

Funding sources: The activities of CSEAS are funded by the Ministry of Education.

Staffing: The Center has twenty-seven full-time and three part-time research staff, with eight full-time and twenty-one part-time administrative staff.

Notes: CSEAS has overseas liaison offices in Bangkok, Thailand, and Jakarta, Indonesia, which facilitate fieldwork in Southeast Asia.

Head of the institution: Dr. Prof. Yoshihiro Tsubouchi, Director

Contact officer: Ms. Yoko Taki, Staff at International Office

Center for Southeast Asian Studies
Kyoto University
46 Shimoadachi-cho, Yoshida, Sakyo-ku, Kyoto, 606-01
JAPAN
Tel: (81-75) 753-7300
Fax: (81-75) 753-7350
e-mail • director@cseas.kyoto-u.ac.jp
int!@cseas.kyoto-u.ac.jp
editorial@cseas.kyoto-u.ac.jp
URL • http://www.cseas.kyoto-u.ac.jp

National Institute for Defense Studies

Bouei Kenkyujo

Background and objectives: The National Institute for Defense Studies (NIDS), formerly the National Defense College, was founded in 1952 to provide specialized research on national security issues and to assist in the formulation of national defense policy. NIDS is the highest-level resource for strategic research and education in the Japanese Defense Agency. The Institute conducts basic research on the management and control of the three self-defense forces; educates selected senior officials of the self-defense forces and the government on the problems of national defense; and maintains an official military history of Japan.

Programs: The Institute conducts research on Japan's national security and defense policies; international affairs in North America and Western Europe, the former Soviet Union and Eastern Europe, and the Asia-Pacific region; and military history. In addition, NIDS organizes annual seminars and symposiums where domestic and foreign scholars exchange their research. Since 1994, the Institute has held the annual *Asia-Pacific Security Seminar,* attended by uniformed officers of major and lieutenant colonel rank.

NIDS also conducts courses in economics, science, international affairs, and national security for military officers and government officials of equivalent seniority.

The Institute maintains a significant library of books, maps, and archival materials, particularly on military history.

Publications: The Institute issues occasional papers entitled "Defense Studies" and publishes, in Japanese, the annual *Asian Strategic Review* (an English version is available). The Institute's War History Office has published a 102-volume study entitled *The Official War History of World War II in the Asia-Pacific Region.*

Funding sources: The Institute is funded directly by the Japanese government.

Staffing: The Institute has a staff of eighty full-time researchers, supported by ninety administrative assistants.

Head of the institution: Mr. Hirotsugu Ohta, President

Contact officer: Ms. Kagami Funada, Planning and Coordination Office

National Institute for Defense Studies
2-2-1, Nakameguro, Meguro-ku
Tokyo, 153
JAPAN
Tel: (81-3) 3713-5912
Fax: (81-3) 3713-6149
e-mail • planning@nids.go.jp
URL • http://www.jda.go.jp

National Institute for Research Advancement

Sohgo Kenkyu Kaihatsu Kikoh

Background and objectives: The National Institute for Research Advancement (NIRA) was established in 1974, on the initiative of leading figures from the industrial, academic, and labor communities, to conduct independent research on the complex issues facing contemporary Japanese and international society.

Programs: NIRA conducts research on political, economic, international, social, and technological issues. Recent topics range from the social and economic conditions of East Asia to educational policies in Japan.

NIRA also participates in international and domestic research exchanges and organizes conferences and symposia on such topics as Northeast Asian cooperation and Arab-Japanese dialogue.

NIRA sponsors research grants and awards, such as the Tohata Commemorative Award for Policy Research. Its recently founded Center for Policy Research Information (Saburo Okita Memorial Library) disseminates information on the policy research activities of the world's leading think tanks.

Publications: The Institute publishes, in English and in Japanese, the *NIRA Output Series,* the monthly *NIRA Policy Research*, and the quarterly *NIRA Review*. Recent publications include *NIRA's World Directories of Think Tanks* (1996), *The*

History of U.S.-Japan Relations (1995), and *Globalization of Economy and the Law* (1994).

Funding sources: NIRA is funded through an endowment of capital contributions and donations from the public and private sectors.

Staffing: NIRA has forty-six researchers, supported by an administrative staff of forty-eight.

Heads of the institution:
Mr. Takashi Ishihara, Chairman

Mr. Shinyasu Hoshiono, President

Contact officer: Mr. Hajime Ishida, Director, Center for Policy Research Information

National Institute for Research Advancement
4-20-3 Ebisu, Shibuya-ku, Tokyo, 150
JAPAN
Tel: (81-3) 5448-1700
Fax: (81-3) 5448-1743
e-mail • cpri@nira.go.jp
URL • http://www.nira.go.jp

Nomura Research Institute

Nomura Sohgo Kenkyujo

Background and objectives: Nomura Research Institute (NRI), Japan's first think tank, was founded in 1965. NRI is a very large and broad-based institution. Its mission is to equip corporations, governments, and society to prosper in the new information age. There is a strong focus on the use of information technology in formulating solutions for its clients. NRI undertakes research, consulting, and information technology system integration.

Programs: NRI analyzes economic, financial, industrial, social, regional, and consumer trends to assist governments and other public institutions with policy planning and to advise corporate management on strategy.

NRI's policy research deals with such issues as deregulation and market opening; policy coordination among developed nations in the areas of macroeconomics, finance, trade, and national security; and the economic strategies of developing nations in Asia and elsewhere.

Economic and investment research focuses on dynamic analysis and economic forecasting, financial and securities markets, industrial and corporate analysis from a securities investment perspective, and corporate financial and management strategies.

Social and regional research addresses all the issues and problems facing individuals and society, including national land planning, urban development, energy and the environment, the formation of local and urban communities, and health, medicine, and welfare. NRI also analyzes market trends for a broad range of technologies and products.

Publications: Based on its analysis, NRI publishes policy proposals, short-term and semi-long-term macroeconomic forecasts, and corporate profits forecasts. NRI's quarterly publication *Creating Intellectual Assets* deals with a broad range of economic, political, technological, and social trends. It also publishes books on advanced social systems, corporate strategies, and government systems. Publications in 1996 include "Industrial Development Strategy for Asian Countries," "The Outlook for the Cyber Society," "Stock Investment Style in the New Era of Asset Management," and "The Japanese Economy in the Post-Deflation Period" (all in Japanese).

Funding sources: NRI's income is generated from research and consulting contracts with both public and private clients.

Staffing: NRI employs approximately 2,500 personnel. Among them, approximately 440 are researchers, including financial analysts and economists; 120 are management and system consultants; 1,500 are system engineers; and 140 are administrative staff.

Notes: In collaboration with the Tokyo Club Foundation for Global Studies, NRI promotes joint research on the stable development of the global economy through a network of think tanks from the U.S., UK, Germany, France, Korea, Taiwan, Hong Kong, the Philippines, Thailand, Malaysia, Singapore, Indonesia, and China.

Head of the institution: Mr. Shozo Hashimoto, President

Contact officer: Mr. Naohiko Araki, Senior Manager, Corporate Communications Department

Nomura Research Institute
1-10-1, Nihonbashi, Chuo-ku, Tokyo, 103
JAPAN
Tel: (81-3) 5255-1800
Fax: (81-3) 5255-9312
e-mail • kouhou@nri.co.jp
URL • http://www.nri.co.jp

Research Institute for Peace and Security

Heiwa Anzen Hosho Kenkyujo

Background and objectives: The Research Institute for Peace and Security (RIPS), established in 1978, is an independent research center that aims to inform public policy, increase public awareness of security issues, and promote international understanding of Japan through publications and international exchanges.

Programs: RIPS conducts research on topics ranging from technology and security to Russian foreign policy toward Asia; holds regular study seminars; and organizes international conferences on political, economic, and security issues.

RIPS recently co-organized the Japan-U.S. Joint Studies on the Korean Peninsula, which assessed the North Korean economic, political, and security situation and the prospects for unification. It is also co-organizing two upcoming conferences: "Trilateral Security Cooperation in East Asia: Japan, U.S. and China," which will discuss the relationship between economic development and security, and "Revitalizing the Japan-U.S. Alliance," which will discuss issues related to U.S. military bases in Okinawa, the change of U.S. base structure and its impact on the alliance, and Japan-U.S. coordination for Western Pacific security.

The Institute's Strategic Studies Fellowship Program sponsors individual researchers in the area of international security and arms control.

Publications: The Institute's major publication, *Asian Security* (*Ajia no Anzen Hosho*), is an annual report published in both English and Japanese. It also issues the *RIPS Special Reports Series*, a monthly newsletter, and occasional pamphlets.

Representative publications include *UN Peacekeeping: Japanese and American Perspectives* (1995), *Vietnam Joins the World: American and Japanese Perspectives* (1995), and *Perspectives on Security Studies* (1988).

Funding sources: RIPS activities are funded primarily through individual and corporate sponsorship. Research projects are commissioned by grants from several foundations—including the Sasakawa Peace Foundation, the U.S.-Japan Foundation, and the Center for Global Partnership of the Japan Foundation—as well as the Defense Agency, the Ministry of Foreign Affairs, and other Japanese government ministries.

Staffing: The Institute's projects are conducted by over a dozen research associates, most of whom are university professors, supported by five to eight in-house staff members.

Head of the institution: Mr. Takuma Yamamoto, Chairman

Contact officer: Lt. Gen. (Ret.) Hiroyasu Eguchi, Director and General Secretary

Research Institute for Peace and Security
Roppongi Denki Building 8F
6-1-20 Roppongi, Minato-ku
Tokyo, 106
JAPAN
Tel: (81-3) 3401-2230
Fax: (81-3) 3478-3105

Seikei University
Center for Asian and Pacific Studies

Seikei Daigaku Asia Taiheiyo Kenkyu Center

Background and objectives: The Center for Asian and Pacific Studies (CAPS) was established at Seikei University in 1981 to promote communication and cooperation between scholars from the Asia-Pacific region on the political, technological, and environmental challenges facing Pacific Rim countries. The Center encourages collaborative research between students of economics, applied and natural sciences, sociology, and political science; facilitates exchanges between experts from different countries; and publishes research and information on the Asia-Pacific region.

Programs: The Center's research focuses on issues of industrialization and structural change in the Asia-Pacific region. CAPS also sponsors international symposiums, conferences, and seminars on topics ranging from the future of democracy in Asia and Europe to enterprise reform in formerly socialist economies. CAPS maintains a collection of studies on Asian-Pacific issues in history, sociology, and international relations.

Publications: CAPS's main publication is the semiannual *Review of Asian and Pacific Studies*, issued in English and Japanese. The Center also publishes an annual report, a quarterly newsletter, and a discussion paper series in both English and Japanese. Recent publications include *Industrial Transformation in China and Russia: Enterprise Reform and Transition to the Market* (1996), *East Asian Economies: Transformation and Challenges* (1995), and *The Future of Democracy: Asia and Europe* (1993).

Funding sources: The Center's activities are fully funded by Seikei University.

Staffing: The Center is staffed by four research fellows chosen from three faculties (economics, humanities, and law), supported by three administrative assistants.

Head of the institution: Dr. Chikara Komura, Director

Contact officer: Mr. Tokuji Sugaya, Chief Administrator

Center for Asian and Pacific Studies
Seikei University
3-3-1, Kichijoji-Kitamachi
Musashino-shi, Tokyo, 180
JAPAN
Tel: (81-4) 2237-3549
Fax: (81-4) 2237-3866

Sophia University
Institute of International Relations for Advanced Studies on Peace and Development in Asia
Johchi Daigaku Kokusai Kankei Kenkyujo

Background and objectives: The Institute of International Relations for Advanced Studies on Peace and Development in Asia (IIR) is a nonprofit research organization that was established in 1969 at Sophia University to address the issues raised by the social, economic, and political transformations taking place worldwide. IIR's interdisciplinary staff of social scientists conducts research on a wide range of topics in international and comparative studies.

Programs: IIR research projects address diverse topics such as domestic change and the international system and Japan-USSR relations in the post-Cold War era. IIR also participates in symposiums, the International Sociological Association's meetings on "Power Shifts and Value Changes in the Post-Cold War World," and study groups which examine such issues as law and society, comparative voting behavior and political participation, and Japan's domestic politics and international environment in the early 1940s.

Publications: The Institute publishes the semiannual *Journal of International Studies (Kokusaigaku Ronshu)*, which carries articles, survey reports, research notes, review articles, and book reviews in English and Japanese. IIR also publishes books and an occasional *Research Papers Series*. Recent book titles include

Changing Risks and the Japanese Employment System (1996), *Political Generations in Post World War II Japan—With Some Comparisons to the Case of Germany* (1995), and *New International Studies: Change and Order* (1995).

Funding sources: The Institute's activities are funded by Sophia University.

Staffing: IIR has eleven full-time professors and two full-time assistants, supported by an administrative staff of three.

Head of the institution: Prof. Masatsugu Naya, Director

Contact officer: Prof. Hisashi Takahashi, Member of the Institute

---

The Institute of International Relations for Advanced Studies on Peace and Development in Asia
Sophia University
7-1 Kioi-cho, Chiyoda-ku, Tokyo, 102
JAPAN
Tel: (81-3) 3238-3561
Fax: (81-3) 3238-3592
e-mail • kokusai@hoffman.cc.sophia.ac.jp

Tokyo Club Foundation for Global Studies

Tokyo Kokusai Kenkyu Club

Background and objectives: The Tokyo Club Foundation for Global Studies is a private, nonprofit organization established in 1987 to promote research and dialogue on international trends in industry, trade, and the capital markets. The Tokyo Club gathers wisdom from the world's leading research organizations and scholars to produce creative proposals for solving global problems, and then makes its findings available to the public.

Programs: The Foundation selects research topics related to the stable growth of the world economy and assigns these projects, with funding, to institutions and individual scholars around the world.

Recent projects include "United States Economic Policy in Asia," conducted by the Brookings Institution; "The Policy of the European Union towards the Countries of Central and Eastern Europe," conducted by the Institut für Wirtschaftsforschung; "Regionalization within Globalization: Nations' and Firms' Perspectives," conducted by the Institut Français des Relations Internationales; "Globalization, Productivity Growth in Manufacturing and U.K. Labour Markets," conducted by the Royal Institute of International Affairs; and "A Yen Bloc in Asia: An Integrative Approach" and "Security Guarantees and the Role of Japan in the Asia-Pacific Region," conducted by the Nomura Research Institute.

The Foundation also arranges symposiums such as the Tokyo Forum and Asia Forum, focusing on the management of the world economy.

Publications: The Foundation publishes the annual periodicals *Tokyo Club Papers* and *Asia Club Papers*. It also publishes the minutes of "Asia Forum."

Funding sources: The activities of the Tokyo Club Foundation are funded by the Nomura Securities Co., Ltd.

Staffing: The Club's secretariat has two full-time staff members. The Club does not have its own research staff.

Notes: The Tokyo Club Foundation is associated with five think tanks in the developed countries: The Brookings Institution (U.S.), Institut für Wirtschaftsforschung (Germany), Institut Français des Relations Internationales (France), the Royal Institute of International Affairs (UK), and Nomura Research Institute (Japan). It is also associated with eight think tanks in Asia: the Centre of Asian Pacific Studies (Hong Kong), the Center for Policy and Implementation Studies (Indonesia), the Korea Development Institute (Korea), the Institute of Strategic and International Studies (Malaysia), the Institute for Economic Policy Research (Philippines), the Institute of Southeast Asian Studies (Singapore), the Chung-Hua Institution for Economic Research (Taiwan), and the Thailand Development Research Institute (Thailand).

Head of the institution: Mr. Shozo Hashimoto, President

Contact officer: Mr. Masao Kudo, Secretary General

Tokyo Club Foundation for Global Studies
1-10-1 Nihonbashi, Chuo-ku, Tokyo, 103
JAPAN
Tel: (81-3) 5255-1818
Fax: (81-3) 5255-9314

The United Nations University

Kokusai Rengoh Daigaku

Background and objectives: The United Nations University (UNU) was established in 1975 to promote goodwill by bringing together the world's leading scholars. The UNU's activities are carried out through its own network of research and training centers and through worldwide networks of associated and cooperating institutions, scholars, and scientists.

Programs: UNU examines such issues as the evolving role of the United Nations, conflict resolution, cultural identity, governance, growth and sustainable development, ecosystem and environmental management, socioeconomic implications of new technology, and population dynamics.

The University's post-graduate programs support and train young scholars and scientists from developing countries to promote self-reliant development and strengthen institutional capacity in developing countries. It offers fellowships in such areas as natural resources and the environment, advances in sciences and technology, and population dynamics and human welfare.

Publications: UNU publishes brochures such as *Work in Progress* and *UNU Nexions,* which report on ongoing research and activities within the University's academic networks. It also publishes the quarterly *Food and Nutrition Bulletin,* which deals with all aspects of global malnutrition, and books. Recent titles include *The United Nations System: The Policies of Member States* (1995); *State, Society, and the UN System: Changing Perspectives on Multilateralism* (1995); and *Hydropolitics Along the Jordan River: Scarce Water and Its Impact on the Arab-Israeli Conflict* (1995).

Funding sources: The activities of the UNU are supported entirely by voluntary contributions from governments and foundations. The University receives no funding from the regular budget of the United Nations.

Staffing: The UNU has some 165 full- and part-time employees worldwide, including research and research support staff. In addition, the University engages some 750 to 1,000 scholars annually for specific assignments.

Head of the institution: Prof. Heitor Gurgulino de Souza, Rector

Contact officer: Mr. Max Bond, Council & External Relations Officer

The United Nations University
5-53-70, Jingumae, Shibuya-ku, Tokyo, 150
JAPAN
Tel: (81-3) 3499-2811
Fax: (81-3) 3499-2828
e-mail • mbox@hq.unu.edu
URL • http://www.unu.edu

University of Tokyo
Institute of Oriental Culture

Tokyo Daigaku Toyo Bunka Kenkyujo

Background and objectives: The Institute of Oriental Culture, University of Tokyo, established in 1941, is one of the most distinguished centers of Asian studies in Japan. The Institute places emphasis on interdisciplinary and regional studies. The research staff is composed of specialists in humanities and social sciences, including history, literature, religious studies, art, archaeology, political science, law, economics, human geography, and cultural anthropology.

Programs: The Institute is comprised of Pan Asian studies, East Asian studies, South Asian studies (including Southeast Asia), and West Asian studies (including Central Asia and Egypt).

The research done at the Institute, which emphasizes analysis of documentary materials and field surveys, is conducted in close contact with scholars in related fields, both in Japan and in the different regions of Asia. Each faculty member of the Institute carries out individual research in his/her own research area, in addition to joint research programs.

The Institute also undertakes long-term projects that examine such issues as the Islamic challenge, an investigation of the political, social, and economic changes in the Islamic world; and social change in China, a study of the dramatic transformations taking place in China, with special emphasis on the effects on the rest of Asia.

The Institute has agreements for joint research and exchange of source materials with the Center of Asian Studies at the University of Hong Kong, the Faculty of Economics and Business Administration of the Kasetsart University, Thailand, and Fudan University, Shanghai, China.

The Institute also holds international conferences such as "Asia in the 21st Century: Toward a New Framework of Asian Studies," which considered the research focuses and perspectives for Asian studies in the coming century.

Publications: The Institute publishes *The Memoirs of the Institute of Oriental Culture* in Japanese three times a year, containing scholarly articles by the research staff of the Institute and its affiliated members; and the annual *Oriental Culture* in Japanese, with each issue devoted to a specific subject. The Institute also publishes many monographs, catalogues, and expedition reports.

Funding sources: The Institute is funded by the University of Tokyo, the Ministry of Education, and other sources.

Staffing: The Institute has thirty-four research fellows.

Notes: The Institute's faculty members also teach in various graduate schools at the University of Tokyo. The Institute's library specializes in Asian studies and contains over 510,000 books and 5,400 periodicals. The Institute also houses the Documentation Center for Asian Studies, which collates many Asian databases.

Head of the institution: Prof. Takeshi Hamashita, Director

Contact officer: Mr. Katsushi Chiba, Administrative Director

Institute of Oriental Culture
University of Tokyo
7-3-1 Hongo, Bunkyo-ku, Tokyo, 113
JAPAN
Tel: (81-3) 3812-2111 ext. 5833
Fax: (81-3) 5684-5964
e-mail • shomu@ioc.u-tokyo.ac.jp
URL • http://www.ioc.u-tokyo.ac.jp

Asian Institute for Development Communication

Background and objectives: The Asian Institute for Development Communication (AIDCOM) was established in 1986 as a regional, nonprofit, non-government organization aimed at enhancing the skills of media communication management in economic, cultural, health, population, social, environmental, and other development efforts. AIDCOM provides communication support to any development agency—governmental or non-governmental, national, regional or international.

Programs: AIDCOM develops projects for communication workers in the fields of economics, health, population, cultural and social development, women in development, environmental issues, and family planning.

AIDCOM also organizes meetings, conferences, seminars, and workshops related to communication support systems and to the management of communication development programs; provides a platform for journalists and media personnel by organizing workshops and seminars to promote freedom of information and expression; provides consultancy and advisory services in media communication design, and monitoring of development programs; and develops training packages for initiating and enhancing community participation, especially in the area of development communication projects.

The development programs with which AIDCOM deals address issues like juvenile delinquency, drug addiction, the environment, human rights, women's status, population issues, urban/rural poverty, and consumerism.

Several of its research projects were commissioned by UNESCO and UNHCR, including studies on the flow of foreign television material into Asia, the watchdog role of media in Malaysia and Thailand, and the media and information needs of refugees.

Publications: AIDCOM publishes *The Journal of Development Communication* twice a year. Recent books include *Human Rights and the Media* (1996) and *Malaysian Women: Creating Their Political Awareness* (1993).

Funding sources: AIDCOM is supported by such international organizations as the Konrad Adenauer Foundation and the Friedrich Naumann Foundation of Germany, the Canadian International Development Agency, the Asia Foundation, the Netherlands Organization for International Development Cooperation, and the Australia International Development Assistance, as well as the United Nations agencies UNESCO, ESCAP, UNHCR, UNFPA, and UNDP. It also raises funds through publications, training courses, and workshops for media and the corporate sector.

Staffing: AIDCOM has five full-time and ten part-time researchers, supported by five administrative staff members.

Head of the institution: Ydhg Dato'Haji Mazlan Nordin, Chairman

Contact officer: Mr. Khairul Bashar, Executive Director

Asian Institute for Development Communication (AIDCOM)
6th Floor, APDC Building
Persiaran Duta, 50480 Kuala Lumpur
MALAYSIA
Tel: (60-3) 651-0558
Fax: (60-3) 651-3785
e-mail • devcom@pc.jaring.my

Asian Strategy & Leadership Institute

Background and objectives: The Asian Strategy & Leadership Institute (ASLI), established in 1993, is an independent, non-profit organization that promotes strategic thinking and leadership through its conference and training activities.

Programs: Among the many conference programs ASLI has organized are the First Pacific Rim Business Collaboration Symposium, the Global Capital Market Forum, the International Education Conference, the First Malaysia-China Forum, and the International Conference on the Indonesia-Malaysia-Thailand Growth Triangle.

ASLI is also engaged in a series of management training programs on corporate culture, marketing strategies, and strategic management.

Publications: ASLI publishes the quarterly *ASLI Review,* which analyzes key current issues and trends affecting Malaysia.

ASLI has co-published *Penang into the 21st Century* (1994) and *Pacific Rim in the 21st Century* (1995). The Institute also has produced a corporate video series entitled *Profiles of Excellence,* which contains in-depth interviews with Malaysian leaders in government and business on such issues as business strategy, entrepreneurial development, international operations, and human resource management and development.

Funding sources: ASLI's activities are funded by corporate sponsorship.

Staffing: ASLI has twenty-seven full-time staff plus a network of associates.

Notes: The head of ASLI is the son of Dr. Mahathir, the Malaysian Prime Minister.

Head of the institution: Mr. Mirzan Mahathir, President

Contact officer: Mr. Michael Yeoh, Director/Executive Vice-President

Asian Strategy & Leadership Institute
Menara SungeiWay, Jalan Lagun Timur, 46150 Petaling Jaya, Selangor Darul Ehsan
MALAYSIA
Tel: (60-3) 735-2811
Fax: (60-3) 736-4048

Institute of Strategic and International Studies

Background and objectives: The Institute of Strategic and International Studies (ISIS), established in 1983, is an autonomous, nonprofit organization dedicated to the study of strategic and policy issues directly relevant to Malaysia's national interests. The Institute's main objectives are to promote informed discussions on important national and global issues; provide a forum for experts to exchange views and research in a free and conducive environment; and disseminate policy-relevant information.

Programs: The Institute conducts problem-oriented studies and applied research on international affairs, defense, national and international economics, science and technology, and energy, natural resources, and the environment. Recent research topics ranged from economic integration and cooperation in Pacific Asia to managing industrial transition in Malaysia.

In 1991, ISIS established the Center for Japan Studies to undertake specialized research on Japan and the Center for Environmental Studies to enhance research and understanding of environmental issues.

The Institute also sponsors and organizes seminars and conferences, independently and with counterpart institutions such as the ASEAN Institutions of Strategic and International Studies, Japan Institute of International Affairs, and the Canadian International Development Agency.

ISIS also hosts scholars, researchers, and occasionally graduate students from around the world.

Publications: ISIS actively publishes books on a variety of political, economic, and social issues.

Recent titles include *The Emerging Regional Security Architecture in the Asia Pacific Region* (1996), *Economic Integration and Economic Cooperation in Pacific Asia* (1994),

and *Environment and Development: Changing Concerns and Approaches* (1993).

The Institute also publishes in English and Malaysian the *World Affairs Lecture* series, comprising the lectures of world leaders who participated in ISIS conferences; the *Issue Papers* and *Opinion* series, featuring the views of experts on a wide range of topics; the *Research Notes* series, containing the research of ISIS staff; the *ASEAN Series* and *Pacific Papers;* and the *TV Forum* series, including the transcripts of ISIS televised meetings.

Funding sources: The Institute was initially funded by a government grant. Today it is financially self-sustaining by means of an "endowment fund" and contributions.

Staffing: ISIS has thirty-eight researchers, drawn from the business and public sectors as well as academia, supported by fifty-one administrative staff.

Notes: The Institute serves as the secretariat for the Malaysian Business Council.

Head of the institution: Dato' Dr. Noordin Sopiee, Director General

Contact officer: Mr. Valentine Siva, Director of Public Affairs

Institute of Strategic and International Studies
1 Pesiaran Sultan Salahuddin
P.O. Box 12424, 50778 Kuala Lumpur
MALAYSIA
Tel: (60-3) 293-9366
Fax: (60-3) 293-9430
e-mail • infser@isis.po.my

Malaysian Institute of Economic Research

Background and objectives: The Malaysian Institute of Economic Research (MIER), established in 1985, is an independent, nonprofit organization that studies the economic, financial, and business issues facing the country; provides advice on macroeconomic management and future economic perspectives; and serves as a bridge between the government and the private sector.

Programs: MIER maintains three research units: the Economic Policy Research Division, the Macroeconomic and Forecasting Bureau, and the Bureau for Malaysian Enterprise.

Recent research has focused on Malaysia's industrial master plan and economic development plan, the impact of sales and service taxes on price levels, management of state-owned enterprises, health scenarios and health-care economics, sustainable energy development toward the year 2020, and federal-state fiscal relations. Many of these projects are commissioned by government ministries.

MIER also conducts quarterly surveys of business conditions and consumer sentiment and sponsors national and international conferences, such as the National Outlook Conference (1995); the Conference on Health-Care Planning and Development, co-sponsored by the Friedrich Naumann Foundation of Germany (1995); and the Malaysian Econometric Conference (1995).

Publications: MIER publishes, in English, the quarterly *Survey of Business Conditions, Survey of Consumer Sentiments,* and *Economic Indicators;* the *Malaysian Economic Outlook,* released twice a year in June and December, with supplements in March and September; a *Discussion Paper Series,* issued occasionally to report ongoing research and findings of completed projects; and the quarterly *MIER News.*

Recent books and monographs published by MIER's researchers include *Health Care Planning and Development* (1996), *Malaysia's Economic Development, Policy and Reform* (1996), and *For a Greener Future, Ecological Aspects: The Public and the Business Perspectives* (1995).

Funding sources: MIER's activities are funded by income from an endowment fund established with contributions from private corporations and the government. The Institute also receives technical assistance from the Canadian International Development Agency (CIDA).

Staffing: MIER has twenty-three researchers (six of them part-time), supported by twelve administrative assistants.

Heads of the institution:
Tan Sri Dato' Haji Basir bin Ismail, Chairman

Dr. Sulaiman bin Mahbob, Executive Director

Contact officer: Mr. Lee Kim Bian, Assistant Director

Malaysian Institute of Economic Research
9th Floor, Block C
Bangunan Bank Negara Malaysia
P.O. Box 12160, Jalan Kuching, 50768 Kuala Lumpur
MALAYSIA
Tel: (60-3) 292-6188 / 292-6496
Fax: (60-3) 292-6163
e-mail • kblee@mier.po.my

Malaysian Strategic Research Centre

Background and objectives: The Malaysian Strategic Research Centre (MSRC) is an independent, nonprofit organization established in 1993 to advance understanding of Malaysia's domestic and international activities and their ramifications for the Asia-Pacific region and the world.

Programs: MSRC sponsors conferences, seminars, and forums, including the Current Affairs Forum and the Face to Face series, on topics such as the new frontiers of the Malaysian economy; organizes study groups on strategic issues to inform participants of current developments and make policy recommendations to the government; and provides legislative support services for the Malaysian Parliament to enhance the knowledge of its members. The Centre also conducts the Corporate Associate Program, designed to give individuals in the business sector access to all of the Centre's activities.

Publications: The Centre publishes, in English, the semi-annual *AGENDA*, containing articles on politics, security, economics, business, and society. In Malay, the Centre publishes the semi-annual *Bulletin MSRC*, which reports on the Centre's activities; the *MSRC's Distinguished Lecture Series;* and the *MSRC Current Affairs Forum.*

Funding sources: The Centre is funded primarily by contributions from private corporations, foundations, and individuals. Support for the Centre's research projects comes mainly from local and international foundations and individual corporations.

Staffing: The Centre is staffed by six researchers, supported by ten research and administrative assistants.

Head of the institution: Mr. Abdul Razak Abdullah Baginda, Executive Director

Contact officer: Ms. Khairina Awang, Coordinator, Research Unit

Malaysian Strategic Research Centre
10th Floor, Bangunan Getah Asli
148 Jalan Ampang, 50450 Kuala Lumpur
MALAYSIA
Tel: (60-3) 263-6086 / 263-6089
Fax: (60-3) 263-6087
e-mail • cap@msrc.po.my

Center for Research and Communication Foundation

Background and objectives: The Center for Research and Communication Foundation, founded in 1967, is a private voluntary organization specializing in research and professional training in economics, business, education, and international relations. It aims to mold an informed, competent, and socially responsible private sector and contribute to the development and security of the Philippines.

Programs: CRC conducts regular economic and sociopolitical briefings, occasional conferences and seminars, as well as a number of planning and training workshops on topics ranging from tariff liberalization to deregulation of the civil aviation industry to comprehensive tax reform.

The Foundation also runs a fellows program that brings together distinguished persons from government and the private sector to share their experience and insights with the public.

Research is conducted within the Institute for International and Strategic Studies (IISS), a project of the Foundation. Research topics cover international trade and investment policies, security issues, and regional cooperation.

IISS also serves as the secretariat for the Asia Pacific Economic Cooperation Business Advisory Council and consults business, diplomatic offices, and government on both domestic and regional political and security matters.

Publications: The Foundation publishes the monthly *Philippine Political Monitor*, which features political trends and developments in the Philippines, and the monthly *Economic Policy Papers*, which analyzes economic policy alternatives.

Recent book publications include *China and ASEAN: Business and Cooperation Opportunities in Expanding Trade and Investment Linkages* (1996), *Philippine-German Economic Relations in the Context of Asian and European Regionalism* (1996), and *Facing the Asia-Pacific Challenge* (1995).

Funding sources: The Foundation is funded by grants and voluntary contributions from individuals and institutions in the private sector. Additional income is derived from contract research and briefings as well as sale of publications.

Staffing: The Foundation has seven full-time researchers and one administrative assistant.

Head of the institution: Mr. Enrique Esteban, President

Contact officer: Dr. Julius Caesar Parreñas, Director, IISS

Center for Research and Communication Foundation, Inc.
Unit 202, Gabriel Condominium III
San Miguel Avenue, Pasig City, 1605
PHILIPPINES
Tel: (63-2) 634-2831 / 631-1284
Fax: (63-2) 633-6741 / 634-4273
e-mail • jcp@mnl.sequel.net

Institute for Strategic and Development Studies

Background and objectives: The Institute for Strategic and Development Studies (ISDS), founded in 1991, is an independent, nonprofit research and training organization whose officers and fellows are faculty members of the University of the Philippines. It aims to contribute to regional cooperation and development by mobilizing specialists in the fields of international relations, policy studies, and countryside development.

Programs: The Institute mainly conducts policy-oriented research within three core programs: Strategic and International Studies Program, Government Performance and Democratic Governance Program, and Local Resources Development Program. Recent research topics range from a study monitoring the implementation of devolution of powers to an assessment of legislative performance of the 8th and 9th Philippine Congress.

ISDS also conducts national and international roundtable discussions to generate and disseminate quality information on international, regional, and local issues such as regional security, human rights, and the South China Sea disputes.

The Institute provides research and training fellowships for graduate and undergraduate students whose research interests are related to the Institute's programs. It also maintains a multidisciplinary and multisectoral Council of Fellows composed of academics, ambassadors, foreign service officers, and media and business people.

Publications: The Institute publishes *ISDS News and Views*, an occasional newsletter on its international and national activities, and *Salin Lakas* (Empowerment), a quarterly magazine on local governance and development.

Funding sources: The Institute receives funding from international foundations and local non-governmental organizations such as the Asia Foundation, Ford Foundation, Konrad Adenauer Foundation, and Green Forum. Additional funding is provided by government agencies such as the National Security Council, Armed Forces of the Philippines, and Local Government Academy.

Staffing: The Institute usually hosts twenty to thirty full-time researchers, mostly professors in political science, public administration, and economics, supported by eight administrative staff.

Head of the institution: Dr. Carolina G. Hernandez, President

Contact officer: Prof. Malaya C. Ronas, Director for International Affairs

Institute for Strategic and Development Studies
Commonwealth Avenue, Quezon City, 1101
PHILIPPINES
Tel: (63-2) 927-3894
Fax: (63-2) 924-4774
e-mail • isdsphil@mnl.sequel.net

Philippine Institute for Development Studies

Background and objectives: The Philippine Institute for Development Studies (PIDS), established in 1977, is a non-stock, nonprofit government research institution engaged in long-term, policy-oriented research on social and economic development. Its aim is to provide rigorous analyses of socioeconomic problems and support the formulation of policies for sustained social and economic development in the Philippines.

Programs: The Institute conducts studies in the areas of macroeconomic policies; trade, industry, and international economic relations; agriculture and rural development; natural resources and environmental management; human resources and social development; energy and infrastructure development; and science and technology policies.

Recent research projects range from an assessment of development incentives and impact of structural adjustment on the agricultural and rural sectors to studies on health care financing reforms.

PIDS also conducts an outreach program whereby senior staff provide technical advice and support to key policy-makers upon request. In addition, it organizes and sponsors seminars, conferences, and roundtable discussions on topics such as issues and prospects in the Philippine sugar industry and food and agricultural policy challenges in Asia-Pacific.

The Institute is also the lead agency and secretariat of the Philippine APEC Study Centers Network, a consortium of learning and research institutions in the Philippines that address APEC-related topics.

Publications: PIDS publishes a bimonthly newsletter, *Development Research News*, a semiannual periodical, *Journal of Philippine Development*, the *Research Paper Series*, *Executive Memo Series*, *Policy Notes*, and books.

Representative publications include the two-volume study *Catching Up with Asia's Tigers* (1995 & 1996), *Essays in Social Science and Development* (1995), *Breaking Away from the Fiscal Bind: Reforming the Fiscal System* (1994), and *Poverty, Growth and the Fiscal Crisis* (1993).

Funding sources: PIDS is supported by a Philippine government endowment fund, supplementary appropriations from the annual budget, project funding from government agencies, and funds from the international donor community.

Staffing: The Institute has thirteen research fellows and twelve research associates, supported by sixty-two administrative staff.

Head of the institution: Dr. Ponciano S. Intal, Jr., President

Contact officer: Ms. Jennifer P. T. Liguton, Director for Research Information

Philippine Institute for Development Studies
NEDA sa Makati Building
106 Amorsolo St., Legaspi Village
Makati City, 1229
PHILIPPINES
Tel: (63-2) 893-9578 / 893-5705
Fax: (63-2) 893-9589 / 816-1091
e-mail • jliguton@pidsnet.pids.gov.ph
URL • http://www.pids.gov.ph

Washington SyCip Policy Forum

Asian Institute of Management

Background and objectives: The Policy Forum, founded in 1994 at the Asian Institute of Management (AIM), is a private, nonpartisan leadership forum intended to facilitate dialogue among Filipino cabinet members, congressional committee chairpersons, public sector agency directors, and chief executive officers and entrepreneurs from the private sector on issues of public policy and welfare. Its aim is to produce mutual trust between multiple stakeholders and generate creative solutions to the Philippines' problems.

Programs: The Forum mainly organizes multi-sectoral roundtable discussions between representatives of disparate constituencies to address such issues as export growth, environmental policy, human rights, regional security, and media expansion. The Forum also conducts policy-oriented research and issue surveys to promote informed roundtable discussions. It maintains "action desks" that identify key issues and establish discussion agendas in the areas of Politics and Governance, Competitiveness, and Sustainable Development.

The Forum also conducts seminars, provides sectoral briefings, and consults with the government at the national (Department of Environmental & Natural Resources) and at the local (City of Makati) levels.

Publications: The Forum publishes working papers, conference documentation, and policy case studies and monographs. Recent publications include *A Tale of Two Districts: The Citizen as Customer in Makati City* (1996) and *Governance for Maritime Competitiveness: Notes on Policy Reforms in the Philippines* (1996).

Funding sources: The Forum is funded by the Washington SyCip Endowment Fund and international donor agencies such as the Asia Foundation. Additional income is derived from AIM, and industry associations fund individual projects and conferences.

Staffing: Five AIM faculty members are assigned to the Forum, with another five or six drawn from the faculty pool for particular projects. The support staff consists of a dozen research and conference assistants.

Head of the institution: Dr. Francisco L. Roman, Executive Director

Contact officer: Ms. Pam de la Paz, Liaison Officer

Washington SyCip Policy Forum
Asian Institute of Management
Lopez, Inc. Hall, 4/F AIM Center for Continuing Executive
    Education
Benavides Corner, Trasierra Street
Legaspi Village, Mekati City, Metro Manila
PHILIPPINES
Tel: (63-2) 892-4011
Fax: (63-2) 894-1406
e-mail • pf@aim.edu.ph
URL • http://www.netserve.aim.ph

Institute of East Asian Political Economy

Background and objectives: The Institute of East Asian Political Economy (IEAPE), established in 1983, is a nonprofit research organization focusing on contemporary East Asian societies and their modernization processes. IEAPE is committed to empirical and policy-oriented research of the political and economic developments in the People's Republic of China, particularly its attempt at economic reforms and modernization since 1979.

Programs: Research at the Institute is carried out by China specialists who are trained in economics, political science, sociology, and law. Research subjects include reforms of Chinese state-owned enterprises, township organization and structure, town and village enterprises, China's special economic zones, Beijing-Provincial relations, and foreign investment in China.

Publications: The Institute's publications in Chinese and in English are in the form of internal study papers for restricted circulation. Plans are underway to publish some of these papers for sale and wider distribution.

Funding sources: Private funding from local contributors.

Staffing: The Institute has fifteen full-time researchers and five visiting fellows, six administrative workers, and a staff of ten in the library and resource center.

Head of the Institution: Prof. Wang Gung Wu, Chairman

Contact officer: Mrs. Jeanie Toong, Assistant Director, Administration

The Institute of East Asian Political Economy
Block AS5, Level 4
Arts and Social Sciences Faculty
National University of Singapore
10 Kent Ridge Crescent
SINGAPORE 119260
Tel: (65) 779-1037
Fax: (65) 779-3409

The Institute of Policy Studies

Background and objectives: The Institute of Policy Studies (IPS), established in 1987, is a public policy think-tank that aims to promote interest in and studies of the major issues of concern to Singapore. It seeks to facilitate dialogue between government, business, opinion makers, and scholars in Singapore and promote understanding between Singapore, the region, and the world.

Programs: The Institute primarily conducts policy-oriented studies covering such topics as management of ethnic relations, "regionalization," demographic policy and trends, health economics, and international economic, political, and security relations. Recent research projects include "The United States and East Asia: Conflict and Cooperation" and "Projection of the National Health Expenditure in Singapore: The Effect of Aging Population and Policy Implications."

IPS also organizes local and international conferences, often in cooperation with other research organizations such as Japan's National Institute for Research Advancement and the Center for Strategic and International Studies of the United States.

In addition, IPS organizes events featuring such speakers as Kim Young Sam, President of South Korea, James D. Wolfensohn, President of the World Bank, and executive briefings for its corporate associates.

Publications: The Institute publishes the *IPS Report Series,* which includes commissioned as well as unsolicited papers that are "think" pieces on social, economic, and political issues affecting Singapore. It also publishes the *IPS Regional Speakers Series,* containing speeches from its Regional Speakers Programme; the *IPS Occasional Paper Series;* and *The Singapore Year in Review Series.*

Recent publications include *The United States and East Asia: Conflict and Cooperation* (1995); *Environment and the City: Sharing Singapore's Experience and Future Challenges* (1995); *Overseas Investment: The Experience of Singapore's Manufacturing Companies* (1994); *The Management of Ethnic Relations in Public Housing Estates* (1993); and *Heritage and Contemporary Values* (1993).

Funding sources: The Institute's activities are funded by corporate associates, private foundations, and the government.

Staffing: The Institute employs eight full-time researchers supported by six administrative staff.

Heads of the institution:
Prof. Tommy Thong-Bee Koh, Director

Dr. Lee Tsao Yuan, Deputy Director

Contact officer: Ms. Shirley Lim, Administrative Manager

The Institute of Policy Studies
Hon Sui Sen Memorial Library Bldg.
Kent Ridge Drive
SINGAPORE 119260
Tel: (65) 779-2633
Fax: (65) 777-0700
e-mail • ips@technet.sg
URL • http://pacweb.net.sg/ips1

Institute of Southeast Asian Studies

Background and objectives: The Institute of Southeast Asian Studies (ISEAS), founded in 1968, is an autonomous regional research center for scholars and specialists concerned with modern Southeast Asia and its wider geostrategic and economic environment. Its aims are to research the multifaceted problems of stability and security, economic development, and political, social, and cultural change; enhance public awareness of the region; and provide policy alternatives to the varied problems confronting Southeast Asia.

Programs: ISEAS conducts studies under four broad research programs: Regional Economic Studies, Regional Strategic and Political Studies, Regional Social and Cultural Studies, and the Indochina Program. Recent research projects range from the deepening and widening of ASEAN in the post-Cold War era to democratization in East and Southeast Asia.

The Institute also has an active program of public lectures, conferences, seminars, and workshops, organized independently or in collaboration with other research institutions.

ISEAS has a substantial library, open to visiting scholars upon approval, and is particularly strong in international relations, security, and economic studies concerning Southeast Asia.

Publications: ISEAS publishes the triannual *ASEAN Economic Bulletin*, the quarterly *Contemporary Southeast Asia*, the semiannual *Sojourn: Social Issues in Southeast Asia*, and two annuals on the region, *Southeast Asian Affairs* and *Regional Outlook,* all in English.

In addition, the Institute publishes an average of forty new titles annually and a monthly broadsheet, *Trends*, which is distributed by Singapore's *Business Times* newspaper and syndicated to the *Jakarta Post* and *Bangkok Post*.

Recent publications include *Australia, Asia and the New Regionalism* (1996), *Emerging Civil Society in the Asia-Pacific Community* (1996), *ASEAN in the WTO: Challenges and Responses* (1996), and *The New Wave of Foreign Direct Investment in Asia* (1995).

Funding sources: The Institute is funded through an annual government grant and donations from private foundations, organizations, agencies, and individuals.

Staffing: The Institute has about twenty-five full-time researchers, about ten editors and librarians, and about thirty administrative support staff. It also has about 100 visiting researchers.

Notes: ISEAS is the APEC National Study Centre for Singapore and the academic contact for the Indian Ocean Rim Initiative.

Head of the institution: Prof. Chia Siow Yue, Director

Contact officer: Prof. Chia Siow Yue, Director

Institute of Southeast Asian Studies
Heng Mui Keng Terrace, Pasir Panjang
SINGAPORE 119596
Tel: (65) 778-0955
Fax: (65) 778-1735
e-mail • admin@iseas.ac.sg
URL • http://www.iseas.ac.sg

Singapore Institute of International Affairs

Background and objectives: The Singapore Institute of International Affairs (SIIA), established in 1961, is a membership organization with the objective of promoting public interest in the economic, political, and security challenges facing the Asia-Pacific region; facilitating contacts between Singaporean and international policy and opinion makers; and providing information to its members through publications and meetings.

Programs: The Institute organizes seminars, workshops, and conferences on topics ranging from the development of financial markets to East Asian security. SIIA also coordinates the participation of Singapore in regional non-governmental organizations including the ASEAN-Institute of Strategic and International Studies (ASEAN-ISIS), Pacific Economic Cooperation Council (PECC), and the Council for Security Cooperation in the Asia Pacific (CSCAP).

SIIA is the founding member of ASEAN-ISIS and serves as the Secretariat for the National Committees of PECC and CSCAP.

Publications: SIIA carries out a modest publication program of papers presented at conferences and seminars as well as research work undertaken by members.

Funding sources: The Institute's activities are funded by private donations.

Staffing: The Institute has two administrative staff.

Head of the institution: Mr. Kwa Chong Guan, Chairman

Contact officer: Ms. Betty Chin, Deputy Director

Singapore Institute of International Affairs
6 Nassim Road, SINGAPORE 258373
Tel: (65) 734-9600
Fax: (65) 733-6217
e-mail • siia@pacific.net.sg

Institute for Global Economics

Background and objectives: The Institute for Global Economics (IGE), established in 1993, is a private, nonprofit institute that provides a forum for Korean and international leaders in academia, government, business, and journalism to discuss global economic issues and their implications for Korea. IGE seeks to propose economic strategies and policies that will help Korea's public and private sectors adapt to the rapidly changing global economic and technological environment.

Programs: IGE conducts policy research on topics ranging from Asian-Pacific economic cooperation in the post-Uruguay Round era to the relationship between the environment and trade.

The Institute also organizes the Distinguished Lecture Forum and the Seoul Global Trade Forum; sponsors the annual International Next Generation Leaders Forum and co-hosts the annual meeting of the Korea-U.S. 21st Century Council; and promotes international exchanges and joint research projects with premier research institutes around the globe, such as the Institute for International Economics in Washington, D.C.

Publications: The Institute publishes an occasional bulletin in Korean, *Global Economic Horizon*, mostly written by research fellows. Other recent publications include *The Multilateral Trading and Financial System: Challenges Ahead* (1996), *Korea-U.S. Cooperation in the New World Order* (1995), and *Newly Launched WTO and Options for Korea* (1995).

Funding sources: The Institute's activities are funded by annual fees from its corporate and individual members, including most of the major corporations and financial institutions in Korea.

Staffing: The Institute has a staff of four full-time and eleven part-time senior researchers, supported by five administrative assistants.

Head of the institution: Dr. Il SaKong, Chairman & CEO

Contact officer: Taehyun Ha, Director of Planning & Coordination

Institute for Global Economics
2505 Korea World Trade Center
159 Samsung-dong, Kangnam-ku, Seoul, 135-729
SOUTH KOREA
Tel: (82-2) 551-3334 / 551-3337
Fax: (82-2) 551-3339
e-mail • genet@chollian.dacom.co.kr

The Institute of Foreign Affairs and National Security

Background and objectives: The Institute of Foreign Affairs and National Security (IFANS) was established in 1963 as an affiliate of the Ministry of Foreign Affairs. IFANS is the largest research and training institute of its kind in the nation, playing the role of "a think-tank for foreign policy decision-makers" and a training ground for diplomats. IFANS performs both policy-related research and education/training.

Programs: IFANS conducts research on foreign affairs and national security; prepares policy recommendations on foreign policy and national security issues; hosts conferences and seminars with experts at home and abroad on international affairs as well as foreign policy and national security issues; and promotes exchanges and joint research with counterpart institutions at home and abroad.

Research is conducted by faculty professors and senior foreign service officers with special emphasis placed on the study and development of mid- and long-term foreign policy alternatives for Korean government decision makers.

The Institute also closely monitors major current affairs and provides analysis in its occasional papers. Its education programs provide professional training for foreign service officers; offer in-house and overseas training in foreign languages; and organize overseas training in specialized studies for mid-career foreign service officers.

Publications: IFANS publishes *Annual Forecasts for International Affairs* (in Korean), *Weekly Analysis on Current International Affairs* (in Korean), the bimonthly *IFANS Review* (in English), and intermittently a *Proceedings Issue of International Conferences* (in Korean and in English), the most recent of which is "Peace Regime-Building on the Korean Peninsula and the Roles of Regional Powers." Other reports include policy recommendation papers on major foreign affairs and national security issues; articles by returning ambassadors; and studies on mid- and long-term foreign policy issues.

Funding sources: IFANS is funded by the Korean government.

Staffing: IFANS has about forty full-time researchers including sixteen research professors, and about forty administrative staff.

Notes: IFANS is strongly involved in the Northeast Asia Cooperation Dialogue (NEACD) process, initiated by the Institute of Global Conflict and Cooperation, University of California, San Diego.

Head of the institution: Amb. Suk-Kyu Kim, Chancellor

Contact officer: Mr. Jai-Hyon Yoo, Director, Planning and Research Division

The Institute of Foreign Affairs and National Security
1376-2 Socho 2-dong, Socho-ku, Seoul, 137-072
SOUTH KOREA
Tel: (82-2) 571-1020
Fax: (82-2) 571-1019
e-mail • mofa1@bora.dacom.co.kr

Kim Dae-jung Peace Foundation for the Asia-Pacific Region

Background and objectives: The Kim Dae-jung Peace Foundation (KPF), founded in 1994 by opposition party leader and former presidential candidate Kim Dae-jung, is a nonprofit public-interest institution based in Seoul. Its priorities are reunifying the Korean peninsula, democratizing the Asian region, and studying major issues bearing on world peace.

Programs: The Foundation focuses on the issues of Korean reunification, comparative democratization, and security cooperation in Northeast Asia. Research topics range from nuclear proliferation to comparative approaches to reunification.

KPF also operates an information bank to collect and manage research data and to disseminate its findings to domestic and international research institutions. In addition, the Foundation sponsors conferences, seminars, and roundtable discussions and has established links with international research institutions such as the Peace Research Institute in Oslo, the Gorbachev Foundation, and the Research Institute on Asia-Pacific in Australia.

Publications: The Foundation publishes the *KPF Newsletter*, which contains a monthly update of KPF activities. It also issues policy papers and plans to publish a scholarly journal.

Funding sources: The Foundation is funded by an endowment from Dr. and Mrs. Kim Dae-jung and by the KPF Supporters' Association.

Staffing: The Foundation has ten full-time research fellows, three full-time researchers, and two specialists on Russia and China, supported by an administrative staff of three.

Notes: Overseas advisors include former Soviet president Mikhail Gorbachev, former Philippine president Corazon Aquino, and former German foreign minister Hans-Dietrich Genscher.

Head of the institution: Dr. Kim Dae-jung, Chairman

Contact officer: Mr. Lim Dong-won, Vice Chairman & Secretary General

Kim Dae-jung Peace Foundation for the Asia-Pacific Region
Aryung Bldg, Suite 701
506-20, Changchun-Dong
Seodaemun-ku, Seoul
SOUTH KOREA
Tel: (82-2) 322-2491
Fax: (82-2) 322-0295
e-mail • pefa@chollian.dacom.co.kr

KDJ Peace Foundation—USA
Head: Dr. Lee Young-jak
Tel: (1-301) 231-5143

Korea Development Institute

Background and objectives: The Korea Development Institute (KDI), founded in 1971 by the Korean government, is an autonomous, policy-oriented economic research organization. It aims to provide expert analysis and advice on all aspects of long- and short-term government policies in areas ranging from domestic economic options to international trade and investment.

Programs: KDI conducts research in the areas of macroeconomics management; financial systems; law and economics; industry, trade, and labor; public finance and social development; regional development and the environment; and the North Korean economy. Recent topics include institutional reform of the financial industry, the global economy and economic integration, and economic regulation of environmental contamination.

The Institute's *International Development Exchange Program* offers senior policy forums to promote understanding of Korea's economic development, and its management training courses broaden the knowledge of mid-level practitioners on substantive and technical issues.

KDI also offers consulting services to developing countries, hosts a limited number of experts from developing countries for individual policy research projects, and conducts joint research with counterpart institutions abroad.

Publications: KDI publishes, in Korean, the quarterly *KDI Journal of Economic Policy* and *KDI Economic Outlook.* It also publishes books, research monographs, and working and seminar papers. Recent titles include *Manufacturing Productivity and Its Changing Structure: 1967-93* (1996), *Industrial Support Policy:* *International Norms and Domestic Practices* (1995), and *A Review of Competition Policy: U.S., Japan, and Germany* (1994).

Funding sources: KDI's activities are funded mainly by the Korean government.

Staffing: The Institute employs fifty-three full-time Ph.D. research fellows, 100 research assistants, and an administrative staff of 105.

Notes: In 1991, KDI incorporated the Center for Economic Education, which provides training in economics to civil servants, entrepreneurs, managers, and teachers.

Head of the institution: Dr. Dong-Se Cha, President

Contact officer: Dr. Bongsung Oum, Director, Office of Research Planning and Coordination

Korea Development Institute
207-41, Chongnyangni-dong, Tongdaemun-gu
P.O. Box 113, Chongnyang
Seoul
SOUTH KOREA
Tel: (82-2) 958-4114
Fax: (82-2) 961-5092
e-mail • kdi-guide@kdiux.kdi.re.kr
URL • http://kdiux.kdi.re.kr

Korea Economic Research Institute

Background and objectives: The Korea Economic Research Institute (KERI) was established in 1981 as a private research organization with the aim of formulating practical policy recommendations on Korea's economy and industry. KERI seeks to promote national progress within a free market economy through practical policy recommendations based on thorough research and analysis of the economy.

Programs: KERI's research is divided into the Macroeconomic Studies Office, which forecasts macroeconomic developments and recommends policy adjustments; the Financial Studies Office, which examines corporate and international finance, financial market structures, and tax systems; the Industrial Studies Office, which evaluates industrial policies and technological developments for large firms; the Center for Regulation Studies, which focuses on governmental regulation policy and regulatory law; and the Special Project Studies Office, which recommends on national economic strategy.

Each office conducts conferences, seminars, and symposiums such as the World Economic Outlook and Korean Conference, the International Symposium on the Free Market, and the Symposium on a Blueprint for Better Local Government. KERI also serves as a data resource for business enterprises.

Publications: KERI publishes in Korean two quarterlies, *KERI Macroeconomic Analysis and Forecast* and *Journal of Regulation Studies*. In English, the Institute publishes the *KERI Economic Quarterly*. Recent publications include the "World Economic Outlook and Korea's Economy," "The Analysis of the Business Failure Prediction Model," "A Viewpoint of Financial Institutions on Financial Opening," "International Comparison of Financial Systems," "Corporate Governance in Korea," and "Analysis of Thirty Big Business Groups in Korea for 1995" (all published in 1995).

Funding sources: The Institute is primarily funded by its corporate members.

Staffing: The Institute has thirty-six full-time researchers supported by twenty administrative staff.

Head of the institution: Mr. Suck-Rai Cho, Chairman

Contact officer: N/A

Korea Economic Research Institute
FKI Building, 28-1 Yoido-Dong, Yeongdungpo-ku
Seoul, 150-756
SOUTH KOREA
Tel: (82-2) 3771-0001
Fax: (82-2) 785-0270 / 785-0271
e-mail • keri@red.kfke.re.kr.

Korea Institute for Industrial Economics and Trade

Background and objectives: The Korea Institute for Industrial Economics and Trade (KIET), established in 1976, is an autonomous nonprofit research institute that aims to analyze domestic and global economic trends and to advise the Korean government and the private sector on industrial, trade, and commercial policies. KIET seeks to establish international economic networks and devise effective strategies for the private and public sectors to meet the challenges of a changing world economy.

Programs: The Institute conducts policy studies of industrial structure and technology, finance, and trade; analyzes major industrial markets from light to hi-tech industries; monitors and forecasts economic trends; and consults the private and public sectors on the feasibility of specific business opportunities and management strategies.

KIET also has a regional and country focus on current economic and business issues, with particular emphasis on Japan's role in Asia.

The Institute hosts more than forty symposia annually to discuss industrial and trade issues and presents its results to the government. It also implements many cooperative programs with overseas economic research institutions.

Publications: KIET publishes many monographs, papers, and three periodicals in Korean with some translated into English. Recent publications include *A New Trade Industrial Policy in the Globalization of Korea* (1996); *Competition Policies, Trade and Foreign Direct Investment in the Asia-Pacific Region* (1996); and *Trade and Environment: Choice between Harmony and Conflict* (1995).

Funding sources: KIET's activities are funded by the Korean government.

Staffing: KIET has 146 full-time researchers supported by an administrative staff of thirty-eight.

Head of the institution: Dr. Kyu Uck Lee, President

Contact officer: Ok-Yoon, Senior Researcher

Korea Institute for Industrial Economics and Trade
Cheong Ryang P.O. Box 205, Seoul
SOUTH KOREA
Tel: (82-2) 962-6211 / 962-6218
Fax: (82-2) 963-8540 / 969-8540
e-mail • oyahm@kiet.re.kr
URL • http://kiet.re.kr

Korea Institute for International Economic Policy

Background and objectives: The Korea Institute for International Economic Policy (KIEP) is an autonomous, non-profit research institute established by the Korean government in August 1989 to provide a practical academic perspective on international economic policy issues. The Institute monitors and analyzes world economic trends; makes policy recommendations to the Korean government on international economic relations; consults with industry on international economic opportunities; and publishes research findings for the use of the government, business, and the general public.

Programs: KIEP conducts research in the areas of international economics, trade and investment, economic cooperation, and regional and area studies. In addition, KIEP holds domestic and international conferences, on topics ranging from globalization of the world economy to technological cooperation in the Pacific Rim.

KIEP also funds and organizes public programs and seminars to foster bilateral and multilateral cooperation between Korea and countries of other regions.

Publications: KIEP disseminates its research findings in books, seminar proceedings, working papers, and issue reports. It publishes the biweekly *International Economic Issues* and the semiweekly *International Economic Information*. Other recent publications include *A Proposal for the North Pacific Technology Community* (1996); *Toward Liberalization of International Direct Investment in Korea* (1996); *Korea in the New World Economic Order* (1995); *Strategic Partnership and Globalization of Technological Development* (1994); and *Internationalization of the Korean Economy* (1994).

Funding sources: The Institute's activities are funded by the Korean government.

Staffing: KIEP employs thirty-five full-time researchers, supported by an administrative staff of 100.

Notes: KIEP funds the Korea Economic Institute in Washington, D.C., and facilitates the Secretariat of the Korea National Committee for the Pacific Economic Cooperation. The Korean government designated KIEP as the APEC National Study Center (ANSC) in January 1994.

Head of the institution: Dr. Jang Hee Yoo, President

Contact officer: Dr. Bak Soo Kim, Chief Administrative Officer

Korea Institute for International Economic Policy
P.O. Box 235, Socho
Seoul, 135-619
SOUTH KOREA
Tel: (82-2) 3460-1114
Fax: (82-2) 3460-1122
e-mail • admin@kiep.kiep.go.kr
URL • http://www.kiep.go.kr

Korea Institute for National Unification

Background and objectives: The Korea Institute for National Unification (KINU), established in 1991, is a nonprofit, public policy research organization dedicated to the study of issues related to the unification of the Korean peninsula. The Institute aims to play a key role in formulating unification policy options and providing timely recommendations for the government of the Republic of Korea.

Programs: The Institute conducts interdisciplinary research—combining politics, defense, economics, technology, and diplomacy—to examine medium- and long-term issues of Korean unification. Recent studies address questions of human rights violations in North Korea, inter-Korean bilateral and multilateral cooperation in nuclear power, and North Korean economic reforms.

The Institute also convenes a series of conferences to help individuals in government, academia, media, and business exchange views on security- and unification-related issues.

KINU holds joint workshops with counterpart institutions in the U.S., Japan, China, Russia, and Germany on an annual basis. The Institute also hosts a guest speaker series featuring eminent policy makers, scholars, and journalists.

Publications: The Institute publishes the annual *Korean Journal of National Unification* (in English), the biannual *Korean Journal of Unification Studies* (in Korean), and the *KINU Newsletter*. It also publishes books, monographs, policy studies, "Current Issue Papers," and seminar and workshop proceedings.

Representative publications include *A Study on the Power Elite of the Kim Jong-il Regime* (1995), *A Comparative Study on the Negotiating Strategy of North and South Korea* (1994), and *North Korea's Economic Opening Policy: Present and Future* (1994).

Funding Sources: Activities of the Institute are fully financed by the government of the Republic of Korea.

Staffing: The Institute's research staff includes forty-five Ph.D.s, fourteen research associates, and four research assistants in the field of political science, law, economics, management, history, and sociology. Thirty-five administrators conduct the day-to-day activities of the Institute.

Head of the institution: Dr. Se Hyun Jeong, President

Contact officer: Dr. Ho-Yeol P. Yoo, Director, Planning & Budget

Korea Institute for National Unification
C.P.O. Box 8232
Seoul 100-392
SOUTH KOREA
Tel: (82-2) 232-4725 / 234-9113
Fax: (82-2) 232-3291
e-mail • ku.rinu.or.kr
URL • http://www.unikorea.go.kr

Korea University

Asiatic Research Center

Background and objectives: The Asiatic Research Center (ARC), established in 1957, is a nonprofit research institute dedicated to advancing scholarly research on modern and contemporary Asian affairs and enhancing public understanding of Asia's social, political, and economic realities.

Programs: ARC conducts research on historical, political, social, demographic, and ecological topics, with a country-study focus on North Korea, Japan, and China. Recent projects include a comparative analysis of political thought in Korea and other Asian countries, a study of industrialization and scientific-technological developments in Asia, and an examination of contemporary Japanese social, political, and economic history.

ARC holds regular seminars and conferences on topics chosen from the projects currently in progress, featuring specialists from home and abroad. It also conducts joint projects with institutions, both domestic and international, that share common research interests, such as the Chinese Association for Korean Studies in Taiwan and the Japan-Korea Cultural Foundation.

Publications: The Center publishes the biannual *Journal of Asiatic Studies* and other publications covering most countries in the Asian region. Other publications comprise diplomatic documents of the late Yi dynasty, studies on communist countries, social science studies of Korea, studies on Japan, and reports of international conferences, etc.

Funding sources: The Center's activities are financed by Korea University, international and domestic foundations and corporations, and gifts from individuals. It now draws its main support from the Japan-Korea Cultural Foundation, the Japan Foundation, the Korea Research Foundation, and the Korean Ministry of Education.

Staffing: Research at ARC is conducted by forty-nine part-time Ph.D. research fellows and sixteen research assistants, supported by an administrative staff of seven.

Head of the institution: Dr. Choi Sang-Yong, Director

Contact officer: Mr. Choi Kwang-Pil, Chief Executive Secretary

Asiatic Research Center
Korea University
1 Anam-Dong, Seoul, 136-701
SOUTH KOREA
Tel: (82-2) 922-4117
Fax: (82-2) 924-9132
e-mail • ia1775@kuccnx.korea.ac.kr
URL • http://www.korea.as.kr

Korea University

Ilmin International Relations Institute

Background and objectives: The Ilmin International Relations Institute (IRI), established in 1995, is a nonprofit research organization researching political, economic, and social issues and recommending appropriate responses to national, regional, and international challenges.

Programs: IRI conducts research on such global issues as international trade and economic affairs, environmental and resource problems, and information and mass media issues. The Institute also has a regional focus on such issues as tensions in the Korean peninsula, politics among Asian and Pacific Rim nations, current affairs in America and Europe, and political conflicts in Africa and the Middle East.

Educational programs are offered to students, businessmen, and government officials. IRI also coordinates international conferences, distinguished lecture series, and policy workshops on such topics as "The United Nations: The Next Fifty Years" and "Consolidating Democracy in South Korea."

Publications: The Institute publishes the quarterly *I.R.I. Review* in Korean as well as research monographs and occasional paper series. Recent publications include *The United Nations: The Next Fifty Years* (1996); *The New International System: Regional and Global Dimensions* (1996); and *Korea in a Changing World* (1995).

Funding sources: IRI's activities are funded by Hyundai Heavy Industries and the Dong-Ah Ilbo.

Staffing: The Institute has four full-time researchers supported by two administrative staff.

Head of the institution: Prof. Han Sung-Joo, Director

Contact officer: Mr. Richard Kim, Administrative Assistant

Ilmin International Relations Institute
Korea University
Inchon Memorial Bldg., Korea University
1 Anam-dong, Sungbuk-ku
Seoul 136-701
SOUTH KOREA
Tel: (82-2) 923-2416
Fax: (82-2) 927-5165
e-mail • iriku@chollian.dacom.co.kr

Kyung Hee University

Institute of Asia-Pacific Studies

Background and objectives: The Institute of Asia-Pacific Studies (IAPS), founded in 1992 at Kyung Hee University, is a nonprofit research institute that promotes regional cooperation in political, economic, and cultural affairs; analyzes the issues and problems facing the Asia-Pacific region; provides policy recommendations to Korea's political leaders; and trains students, government officials, and entrepreneurs in market economics.

Programs: The Institute's recent research projects include an analysis of South Korea's tax system, economic cooperation between Korea and Australia, and Confucianism in Korean society.

IAPS also offers an annual market economy training program, where Chinese government officials in the Liaoning province are trained in industrial policy, banking, foreign investment, and governmental control over private business.

In addition, IAPS plans, sponsors, and participates in international conferences on topics ranging from comparative unification of Germany and Korea to the future of Northeast Asia in the 21st century.

The Institute also holds a series of forums where scholars and government officials are invited to speak about current issues and problems facing Pacific Rim countries. Recent forums have addressed the prospects of cooperation between India and the Republic of Korea and between Vietnam and the Republic of Korea.

Publications: IAPS publishes books, monographs, proceedings, working papers, and periodicals in both Korean and English. Its major publication is the annual periodical *Asia-Pacific Studies* (in English and Korean), featuring the Institute's research findings along with articles by foreign scholars and IAPS research fellows. Representative publications include *The Role and Prospects of China, Japan, and Korea in the Process of the APEC Building* (1995); *Studies on East Asia Countries with Special Reference to Korea, China and Mongolia* (1993); and *A Search for Cooperation among the Countries in Northeast Asia* (1990).

Funding sources: The Institute is funded by a subsidy from Kyung Hee University, research contracts, and donations from the advisory board.

Staffing: IAPS has a staff of twenty-eight full-time research fellows from the fields of law, geography, economics, political science, and history. The Institute is supported by an administrative staff of six.

Head of the institution: Dr. Chungwon Choue, Chairman

Contact officer: Dr. Dal Hyun Kim, President

Institute of Asia-Pacific Studies
Kyung Hee University at Suwon Campus
1 Seocheon-Ri, Kihung-Eup, Yongin-Gun
Kyungki-Do, 449-701
SOUTH KOREA
Tel: (82-331) 280-2147 / 280-2148
Fax: (82-331) 285-6344

Kyungnam University

Institute for Far Eastern Studies

Background and objectives: The Institute for Far Eastern Studies (IFES) was established in 1972 as a nonprofit social science research organization to promote regional cooperation and the unification of Korea through scholarly research on Northeast Asian and international affairs.

Programs: The Institute pursues research on North Korea, national unification issues, international and security affairs concerning Korea, and the international relations of East Asia. Recent projects have addressed peace regimes on the Korean peninsula, the negotiation strategies of North Korea, and the new East Asian order in the Asia-Pacific era.

The Institute's Research Grant Program is open to all Korean scholars with an interest in inter-Korean relations, unification issues, the international relations and security affairs of Korea, and the Northeast Asian international environment.

IFES also holds domestic and international conferences on such issues as Korean unification strategies for the 21st century and the U.S.-ROK alliance. Since 1975, the Institute has sponsored an annual Korean Unification Seminar to deal with the complex issues and strategies surrounding peaceful unification.

Publications: IFES publishes the *Asian Perspective* (in English) and *Korea and World Politics* (in Korean) biannually, *The Journal of Northeast Asian Studies* (in Korean) annually, and the *Index of Social Sciences Research* (both in Korean and in English) monthly. Recent monographs include *The U.S.-ROK Alliance* (1996) in English, *Negotiation Strategies of the Two Koreas* (1996) in Korean, and *Culture and Development in a New Era and a Transforming World* (1994) in English.

Funding sources: IFES's activities are funded by the Kyungnam University and private donations.

Staffing: The Institute has sixteen researchers (twelve full-time and four part-time) supported by fourteen administrative assistants.

Head of the institution: Dr. Tae-Hwan Kwak, Executive Director

Contact officer: Dr. Su-Hoon Lee, Director for International Relations, Professor of Sociology

The Institute for Far Eastern Studies
Kyungnam University
28-42 Samchung-dong, Chongro-ku, Seoul 110-230
SOUTH KOREA
Tel: (82-2) 3700-0700
Fax: (82-2) 3700-0707
e-mail • ifes@soback.kornet.nm.kr

Pacific Asia Society

Background and objectives: The Pacific Asia Society (PAS) was established in 1994 as a nonprofit, private organization whose membership includes prominent leaders from all sectors of Korean society. Its main objective is to enhance understanding, friendship, and cooperation among countries in Asia, Oceania, and North America.

Programs: The Society organizes, sponsors, assists, and participates in a variety of social and cultural programs. In its personnel exchange program, outstanding civil leaders, scholars, professionals, and artists are invited to Korea from overseas, while their Korean counterparts receive support for their participation in seminars, conferences, and research held abroad.

PAS also organizes and sponsors international conferences, seminars, and forums such as the "Dragon Valley Dialogues" that feature a mix of business and political figures, as well as scholars who influence decision making.

Under its academic program, PAS conducts research to identify and analyze relevant issues in the Pacific Asian region.

In its cultural exchange program, PAS sponsors performances and exhibitions in Korea and abroad to introduce Korean culture to foreign countries and foreign cultures to Korean people.

Under its youth program, PAS organizes youth exchanges, youth forums, workshops, and educational activities among young workers and students in the Asia-Pacific region.

Publications: The Society currently publishes the monthly *The Pacific Asia Society Newsletter* in English and the quarterly magazine *Next*. PAS also publishes research papers and reports, as well as seminar and conference proceedings. PAS plans to publish books and periodicals in the future.

Funding sources: The Pacific Asia Society operates through generous support from foundations, corporations, and contributions from its membership of several hundred private citizens. Among its notable supporters are the Daewoo Group, Korea Foundation, and Korea International Cooperation Agency.

Staffing: The Society has a small core of management and administrative staff.

Notes: The Society is in the process of creating the Pacific Asia Network, an association of Pacific Asia organizations who address common issues arising from changes in the political, economic, and social environment of the Asia-Pacific region.

Head of the institution: Mr. Kim Sang-Chul, Chairman

Contact officer: Mr. Lee Chul-Ho, Executive Secretary

The Pacific Asia Society
637 Yoksam-dong, Kangnam-ku
Seoul 135-080
SOUTH KOREA
Tel: (82-2) 563-4123
Fax: (82-2) 563-4126

The Research Institute for International Affairs

Background and objectives: The Research Institute for International Affairs (RIIA) is an independent, nonprofit research organization incorporated in 1977 to develop foreign policy alternatives and to inform Korean policy makers and scholars on international relations, economics, and military affairs.

Programs: The Institute conducts policy research on national security and international affairs, with special emphasis on regional understanding. Research topics range from the Clinton administration's Asia policy to the WTO and its impact on Korean policy.

RIIA also monitors international political, economic, and military affairs and participates in conferences and research exchanges with scholars and institutions around the world, including the RAND Corporation, the International Institute for Strategic Studies, the Japan Institute of International Affairs, and the Korean Political Science Association. The Institute's annual domestic and international conferences on Northeast Asian affairs address the region's security environment in the 1990s.

Publications: RIIA publishes the quarterly *Policy Studies* in Korean, the biannual *Journal of East Asian Affairs* in English, and the yearly *Northeast Asian Security Environment* in Korean.

Funding sources: RIIA's activities are funded by its board of directors and by research contracts.

Staffing: Information not available due to current staff changes.

Head of the institution: Mr. Kyu Woong Hwang, Director

Contact officer: Chunghoon Min, Academic Exchange

The Research Institute for International Affairs
143-40 Samsung-dong, Kangnam-gu, Seoul
SOUTH KOREA
Tel: (82-2) 565-3557
Fax: (82-2) 565-3558

The Sejong Institute

Background and objectives: The Sejong Institute is a private research organization dedicated to studying Korea's domestic and international affairs. Formally established in 1986, the Institute conducts research on a wide range of political, economic, and social issues affecting Korea and the world at large. As a fully self-funded organization, it can make independent and objective policy assessments and recommendations.

Programs: The Institute divides its research into five programs: the Area Studies Program, which emphasizes basic research and policy alternatives related to the evolution of domestic and foreign policy in the Asia-Pacific region; the Foreign Policy and Security Studies Program, which undertakes research on such topics as global and regional security, regional confidence building measures and arms control, alliance management needs, and defense spending trends; the International Political Economy Studies Program, which focuses on global and regional economic trends, trade conflicts, multilateral trade negotiations, regional economic integration and cooperation, and Korea's longer-term development strategy; the Inter-Korean Relations Studies Program, which examines the domestic affairs and unification policies of South and North Korea and the international environment surrounding the Korean peninsula; and the Policy Studies Program, which undertakes special projects to help formulate Korea's national strategy.

The Institute's Academic Exchange Program promotes extended on-site research through the exchange of personnel with other research and/or academic institutions at home and abroad.

The Institute also organizes international conferences and symposiums, such as the National Strategy and Science Symposium (1996) and the National Security and Globalization Symposium (1996).

Publications: The Institute publishes the biannual *Kukka Chollyak* (the Journal of National Strategy Studies) in Korean. Recent books include *Korea's National Strategy toward the 21st Century* (1996, in Korean); *Changes in Russia's Security and Strategic Environment: Issues and Prospects* (1996, in Korean); and *Korea's Economic Diplomacy* (1995, in English). Recent monographs include *Castro's Future* (1996, in Korean); *Russia's Conventional Weapons Export after the Cold War* (1995, in Korean); and *Globalization and Japan's Political Reformation* (1995, in Korean).

Funding sources: Sejong Institute is supported entirely by its own endowment.

Staffing: Sejong Institute has twenty-four full-time research fellows, four visiting fellows, and thirty-four administrative assistants.

Head of the institution: Dr. Hahn, Bae Ho, President

Contact officer: Dr. Han, Taejoon, Director, Foreign Policy and Security Studies Program

The Sejong Institute
C.P.O. Box 8102, Seoul
SOUTH KOREA
Tel: (82-2) 233-9351
Fax: (82-2) 233-8832
e-mail • dopa@sun.sejongi.re.kr

Seoul Forum for International Affairs

Background and objectives: The Seoul Forum for International Affairs, established in 1986, is a private, nonpartisan membership association that aims to promote a better understanding of Korea and disseminate authoritative findings on the global and regional issues of importance to the country. Its members include leading figures from universities, research institutes, business, law, government, and the press.

Programs: The Seoul Forum promotes a distinguished speaker series with speakers such as Dr. James Tobin, Professor of Economics at Yale University, and Mr. James Lilley, U.S. Ambassador to Korea; bilateral forums with countries of particular importance to Korea such as the U.S.; and multinational conferences on topics ranging from security cooperation in Asia-Pacific to prospects for Korean unification.

The Forum also conducts joint policy studies with fellow institutions such as the East-West Center and acts as a secretariat to public affairs groups, such as the Korea-Japan 21st Century Committee and the Korea-U.K. Forum for the Future.

Publications: The Forum publishes the quarterly *Seoul-Forum Newsletter* (in English), along with books, monographs, and conference reports. Recent publications include *Success or Sellout?* *The U.S.-North Korean Nuclear Accord* (1995), *Inter-Korean Relations and Prospects of Korean Unification* (1993), and *Korea-Japan Relationship in the 21st Century* (1990).

Funding sources: The Seoul Forum is financed by membership dues and contributions from individuals, foundations, and corporations.

Staffing: The Forum has nine researchers and five administrative staff members.

Head of the institution: Mr. Kyung-Won Kim, President

Contact officer: Mr. Park Soon-chun, Administrative Assistant

Seoul Forum for International Affairs
Asiana Bldg., 5th Floor
Hoehyun-dong 2-ka, Chung-ku
Seoul, 100-022
SOUTH KOREA
Tel: (82-2) 755-4568
Fax: (82-2) 755-4417

Yonsei University

Institute of East and West Studies

Background and objectives: The Institute of East and West Studies, founded in 1972 at Yonsei University, researches the key political, economic, and technological issues confronting East Asia. It seeks to promote regional and country-specific studies; articulate the significant challenges facing Korea in the political, security, and economic arenas; build institutional ties with other research institutions and organizations around the globe; and facilitate cultural exchange between East and West.

Programs: The Institute undertakes major research on topics ranging from the reform of East European countries to the prospects of cooperation between South and North Korea. It is comprised of eight semi-independent research centers including the Centers for Canadian, European, Russian, North Korean, and Southeast Asian Studies, and eight departments including Korean, Chinese, Japanese, American, and Latin American Studies.

In addition, the Institute conducts functional research programs in the areas of resources and energy, philanthropy, and Asian-Pacific cooperation.

Each year the Institute organizes over a dozen international conferences and approximately sixty seminars bringing together Korean and foreign scholars and officials.

Publications: The Institute publishes in English the biannual *Journal of East and West Studies* and the *East and West Series* monograph. In Korean, the Institute publishes the biannual *Korean Journal of Canadian Studies* and the *Dongso Yon'gu (East-West Studies)*. The Institute also publishes in English and Korean a quarterly newsletter, *Networker*, and selected findings from seminars and conferences are published in the Institute's *Occasional Paper Series*. Recent book publications include *German Unification and Its Lessons for Korea* (1996); *Marine Policy, Maritime Security and Ocean Diplomacy in the Asia-Pacific* (1995); and *Economic Integration Strategies in East Asia and Europe* (1995).

Funding sources: The Institute receives financial support from the Yonsei University Research Funds, endowments from local and international companies, the Ministry of Education, the Asia-Pacific Philanthropy Consortium, and foundations such as the Rockefeller Brothers Fund, the Asia Foundation, the Sasakawa Peace Foundation, and the Samsung Welfare Foundation.

Staffing: As of 1995, seventy-six Yonsei University faculty members have participated in research projects at the Institute, supported by more than twenty graduate school students and research assistants.

Notes: Recently, the Institute created the Sea Lanes of Communication Center, the Northeast Asia Development Center, and the Asia-Pacific Philanthropy Consortium Information Center.

Head of the institution: Dr. Ku-Hyun Jung, Director

Contact officer: Mr. Yim Kyung-Soo, Manager

Institute of East and West Studies
Yonsei University
134 Shinchon-dong, Seodaemoon-Gu
Seoul 120-749
SOUTH KOREA
Tel: (82-2) 361-3507 / 361-3509
Fax: (82-2) 393-9027
e-mail • iews@bubble.yonsei.ac.kr
URL • http://ellie.yonsei.ac.kr/iews

Academia Sinica

Institute of Economics

Background and objectives: The Institute of Economics at Academia Sinica was established in 1970, after eight years of preparation, to conduct scientific research in economics, to analyze the economic development problems and related policy issues confronting Taiwan, and to coordinate research activities all over Taiwan.

Programs: The Institute's four research divisions cover the areas of general economics, economic theory, mathematical economics, and econometrics; industrial economics, agricultural economics, welfare economics, regional economics, environmental economics, and natural resources; domestic and international macroeconomics; and economic history, economic development, labor and demography economics, and empirical studies.

Recent projects have focused on labor migration and human resources in Asia, the new international agricultural order and Taiwanese agriculture, tariff issues, exchange rate systems and economic stabilization, and business groups and trade in East Asia.

The Institute has also organized and sponsored workshops, symposiums, and conferences, such as the International Conference on Asian Population History (1996) and the International Conference on Growth and Development in Asia-Pacific Economies (1996).

Publications: The Institute publishes the quarterly journal *Academia Economic Papers* (with articles in Chinese or English) and the policy-oriented biannual journal *Taiwan Economic Forecast and Policy* (in Chinese), as well as conference proceedings and discussion papers. Recent English-language books include *The Economics of Pollution Control in the Asia Pacific* (1996) and *Sediment of Time* (forthcoming).

Funding sources: The operating budget of the Institute is provided by the government. Some research projects are funded by grants from such agencies as the National Science Council, the Environment Protection Agency, the Health Administration Agency, and the Council of Agriculture.

Staffing: The Institute has twenty-one research fellows, sixteen associate research fellows, nine assistant research fellows, two research assistants, fifteen project research assistants, and eight administrative/support staff members.

Head of the institution: Dr. Sheng-Cheng Hu, Director

Contact officer: Dr. Tsu-tan Fu, Deputy Director

Institute of Economics
Academia Sinica
Nankang, Taipei, Taiwan
REPUBLIC OF CHINA
Tel: (886-2) 782-2791 / 789-9761
Fax: (886-2) 785-3946 / 782-2019
e-mail • #admin@ieas.econ.sinica.edu.tw
URL • http://www.sinica.edu.tw/econ

Academia Sinica

Institute of European and American Studies

Background and objectives: The Institute of European and American Studies at Academia Sinica, which grew out of the Institute of American Studies in 1991, is an academic institution in social sciences and humanities that studies, promotes, and coordinates research on the United States and European countries.

Programs: The Institute's research divisions of humanities, social and economic studies, and legal and political studies offer areas of concentration in American literature, philosophy, and history; American social structure and economic growth; American politics, law, and diplomacy; and European politics and law.

Recent projects have studied Sino-American relations, the European Union Integration and EU-ROC relations, and resource allocation policies in Taiwan and the United States.

The Institute has also hosted visiting scholars from abroad and has sponsored national and international conferences on such topics as social structure and social change (May 1995), Sino-American relations in the 1990s (March 1995), EC integration and EC-ROC (Republic of China) relations (April 1994), social and economic aspects of international migration (June 1993), and electoral systems in the U.S. and Europe (April 1993).

Publications: The Institute publishes, both in Chinese and English, *EurAmerica,* a quarterly journal on European and American studies. Its recent Chinese- and English-language monographs and paper collections include *European Social Theory* (1996), *Civil Service System: A National Comparison* (1996), *Urban Development and Problems* (1995), *The Nature of Policy Studies* (1994), and *U.S. Foreign Policy and Crisis Management* (1993).

Funding sources: The Institute receives financial support from the Office of the President of the Republic of China.

Staffing: The Institute has thirty-eight full-time researchers—including fifteen research fellows and twelve associate research fellows; seven part-time researchers; and three research fellows by correspondence, supported by fifteen research assistants and five secretarial and clerical staff members.

Head of the institution: Dr. Jia-You Sheu, Director

Contact officer: Dr. Cheng-yi Lin, Deputy Director

Institute of European and American Studies
Academia Sinica
130 Yen-chiu-yuan Road, Section 2,
Taipei, Taiwan
REPUBLIC OF CHINA
Tel: (886-2) 789-9390
Fax: (886-2) 785-1787
e-mail • jysheu@eanovell.ea.sinica.edu.tw

Academia Sinica

Sun Yat-Sen Institute for Social Sciences and Philosophy

Background and objectives: The Sun Yat-Sen Institute for Social Sciences and Philosophy at Academia Sinica was established in 1981 as a national research institution to encourage interdisciplinary studies on social, political, economic, and cultural change in accordance with Dr. Sun Yat-sen's ideas of constitutional democracy, national construction, and people's livelihood.

Programs: ISSP's five research sections concentrate on history and philosophy, social research, political science, economics, and juristic sciences. Recent research topics range from an analysis of overseas Chinese to political democracy and income distribution in Taiwan. Some of these research projects have been sponsored by the National Science Council.

ISSP also sponsors seminars, symposiums, and cross-institutional conferences on such topics as the history of China's maritime development, capitalism in Taiwan, and economic growth and income distribution in East Asia.

Publications: ISSP publishes, in Chinese, the biannual *Journal of Social Sciences and Philosophy*. Recent Chinese-language books include *Demographic Transition, Health Care, and Social Security* (1996), *Political Community* (1995), and *Theory of Democracy: Classical and Modern* (1995).

Funding sources: ISSP is funded by the Taiwanese government.

Staffing: ISSP has forty-seven full-time researchers, including thirty-four research fellows, and seven part-time adjunct research members, supported by six administrative staff members.

Head of the institution: Dr. Yun-peng Chu, Director

Contact officer: Ms. Yen Chen, Assistant to the Director

Sun Yat-Sen Institute for Social Sciences and Philosophy
Academia Sinica
Nankang, Taipei 11529, Taiwan
REPUBLIC OF CHINA
Tel: (886-2) 782-1693
Fax: (886-2) 785-4160
e-mail • ypchu@ssp.sinica.edu.tw
URL • http://www.sinica.tw/ipps

Chinese Council of Advanced Policy Studies

Background and objectives: The Chinese Council of Advanced Policy Studies (CAPS) is an independent public policy research institution established in 1992 to analyze emerging Asia-Pacific security issues and inform government decision makers of its findings.

Programs: CAPS conducts research on international politics, military strategy, and defense economics. Recent research projects have addressed Taiwan Strait security, the PRC's military modernization and its impact on Asia-Pacific security, and arms control and arms proliferation in the Asia-Pacific region.

In collaboration with international research institutions, including the International Institute of Strategic Studies (London), *China Quarterly,* the RAND Corporation, the Atlantic Council (Washington, D.C.), and the Strategic and Defense Studies Center at the Australian National University, CAPS has sponsored international conferences on such issues as China and Southeast Asian security (1996), the People's Liberation Army (PLA) at the century's end (1995), and the PLA's role in the new world order (1992).

Publications: CAPS has published, in English, the *Yearbook on PLA Affairs* (1987, 1988-89, 1990-91, and 1992-93) and *CAPS Papers,* an occasional paper series featuring articles on the PLA, China's defense industry, and regional security. Its recent English-language books include *The Chinese Economic Reform:*

The Impact on Security (1996) and *Chinese Regionalism: The Security Dimension* (1994).

Funding sources: CAPS is funded by individual and corporate membership dues and project funds.

Staffing: CAPS has fifteen adjunct researchers and four support staff members.

Head of the institution: Dr. Richard H. Yang, Chairman

Contact officer: Mr. Andrew N. D. Yang, Secretary General

The Chinese Council of Advanced Policy Studies (CAPS)
Taipei Office:
4F, 259, Section 1, Dun-hua South Road
Taipei, Taiwan
REPUBLIC OF CHINA
Tel: (886-2) 702-0153 / 702-0154
Fax: (886-2) 702-0157

Kaohsiung Office:
6F, 253, Chung-cheng Fourth Road
Kaohsiung, Taiwan
REPUBLIC OF CHINA
Tel: (886-7) 216-0151
Fax: (886-7) 216-0152

Chung-Hua Institution for Economic Research

Background and objectives: Chung-Hua Institution for Economic Research is a nonprofit and autonomous research organ established in 1981 to advise Taiwan's policy makers on national and international economic issues. The Institute seeks to advance Taiwan's economic progress and strengthen its international ties through cooperation with other research organizations around the world.

Programs: The Institute conducts research in the areas of mainland China, international economics, domestic economics, energy and the environment, and economic forecasting. Recent research topics range from the price structure in Taiwan to the impact of joining the WTO on Taiwanese industries.

The Institute also convenes international and domestic conferences; organizes an economic lecture series, featuring Nobel laureates such as Milton Friedman; and provides support services to local and international institutions.

Publications: The Institute publishes, in Chinese, the bimonthly *Economic Outlook*, the *Modern Economic Studies Series*, *Economic Papers*, and *Position Papers* featuring the Institute's research findings. In English, the Institute publishes a bimonthly newsletter, the *Discussion Paper Series*, the *Occasional Paper Series*, the *Economic Monograph Series*, and the *Mainland China Economic Series*. Recent publications include *Changing*

Employment Relations in Asian Pacific Countries (1996), *Globalization, Regionalization, and Taiwan's Economy* (1995), and *Confucianism and Economic Development* (1995).

Funding sources: The Institute is largely funded by an endowment totaling approximately 1.4 billion New Taiwan dollars, made up of donations from the government and leading business organizations. Investments and research contracts constitute other sources of income.

Staffing: The Institute employs seventy-five full-time researchers, supported by forty-nine administrative staff members.

Head of the institution: Dr. Chao-cheng Mai, President

Contact officer: Dr. Hong Hwang, Vice President

Chung-Hua Institution for Economic Research
75 Chang-Hsing St, Taipei, Taiwan, 106
REPUBLIC OF CHINA
Tel: (886-2) 735-6006
Fax: (886-2) 733-0030
e-mail • hhwang@rs930.cier.edu.tw

Institute for National Policy Research

Background and objectives: The Institute for National Policy Research (INPR), established in 1989, is a private, nonprofit public policy research organization affiliated with the Chang Yung-fa Foundation. The nonpartisan Institute aims to advance democracy and a liberal economic system in Taiwan and contribute to its political and economic well-being.

Programs: INPR conducts research on major policy issues, with special emphasis on social welfare, democratic institutions, defense policy, and mainland affairs. Recent research topics range from the restructuring of the executive branch in Taiwan to Taiwan's role in international economic organizations.

The Institute occasionally undertakes contract research for the government and collaborates with counterpart institutions on major research projects.

INPR also organizes and participates in international conferences, seminars, and symposiums and sponsors international exchanges with leading institutions such as the Brookings Institution, the Council on Foreign Relations, the American Enterprise Institute, and the National Endowment for Democracy.

Publications: The Institute publishes, in Chinese, the biweekly *National Policy Dynamic Analysis*, featuring articles on the effect of Taiwan's democratization on the mainland, Taiwan's education reform, and cross-strait relations. Representative publications include *The Predicament of Modernization in East Asia* (1995), *The Asian Regional Economy: Growing Linkages, Global Implications* (1993), and *Crafting Democracy in Taiwan* (1992).

Funding sources: The Institute is fully financed by the Chang Yung-fa Foundation.

Staffing: The Institute employs nineteen researchers, ten of whom work on a part-time basis, and eighteen administrative assistants.

Head of the institution: Dr. Hung-mao Tien, President

Contact officer: Yun-han Chu, Director of Programs

Institute for National Policy Research
5F, 111 Sung-Chiang Road, Taipei, Taiwan
REPUBLIC OF CHINA
Tel: (886-2) 509-9181 ext. 6
Fax: (886-2) 509-2949
e-mail • inprpd@ms8.hinet.net

National Chengchi University

Institute of International Relations

Background and objectives: The Institute of International Relations (IIR) was established in 1953 as a private research organization dedicated to the study of Chinese communist affairs to assist Taiwanese policy makers with their relations with mainland China. By 1975, the Institute had become formally affiliated with the National Chengchi University and expanded its research focus to include the many regions of the world. IIR plans to intensify its research on Southeast Asia as part of an effort to develop Taiwan's regional ties.

Programs: The Institute mainly conducts research of the political and economic relations of Europe, Africa, and Pacific Rim countries and has an extensive focus on the social, political, and economic affairs of mainland China. Recent research projects range from China toward the year 2000 to Taiwanese investment in mainland China.

IIR also co-sponsors international conferences and exchanges with counterpart institutions such as the American Enterprise Institute for Public Policy Research, the Asia Open Forum of Japan, and the Chinese Academy of Social Sciences.

The Institute has an extensive library of books, journals, and newspapers in many languages, particularly strong in international affairs and mainland China studies.

Publications: IIR publishes *Issues & Studies* (monthly in English, Chinese, and Japanese, and quarterly in Spanish and French), the monthly *Mainland China Studies* (in Chinese), *Europe and America Monthly* (in Chinese), and the *East Asia Quarterly* (in Chinese). The Institute has published more than 150 books, including such recent titles as *Divided Nations: The Experience of Germany, Korea, and China* (1995), *Cultural Harmonization and Regional Development* (1995), and *The Asia-Pacific and Europe in the Post-Cold War Era* (1995).

Funding sources: The Institute is funded by the University.

Staffing: IIR has 102 full-time researchers supported by forty-six administrative staff members.

Head of the institution: Dr. Yu-ming Shaw, Director

Contact officer: Dr. Yu-ming Shaw

Institute of International Relations
National Chengchi University
64, Wan Shou Road, Wen Shan 11625
Taipei, Taiwan
REPUBLIC OF CHINA
Tel: (886-2) 939-4921
Fax: (886-2) 234-4919
e-mail • ymshaw@cc.nccu.edu.tw
URL • http://www.iir.nccu.edu.tw

Taiwan Institute of Economic Research

Background and objectives: The Taiwan Institute of Economic Research (TIER), established in 1976, is a government-chartered research institution that studies domestic and foreign macroeconomics and industrial economics, provides consulting services to the government and businesses, and promotes Taiwan's economic development.

Programs: TIER comprises seven research divisions specializing in domestic macroeconomics, transportation economics, financial and economic laws, and the service industry; the manufacturing industry and small- and medium-sized enterprises; machine, electrical engineering, and electronic information industries; agriculture and petrochemical, textile, and real-estate industries; energy and environmental economics; finance and international and mainland China economics; and industrial economic advice and information processing.

Recent research projects have studied environmental impact evaluation regulations in Japan and the ROC, Japan's export insurance and its impact on export borrowing insurance, and development strategies for Taiwan's manufacturing industry.

In addition to occasional financial and economic symposiums and seminars, TIER holds economic forecast and trend seminars twice a year to exchange ideas among scholars and inform the public of its research results. TIER also houses the Secretariat of the Pacific Economic Cooperation Council (PECC) and is a member of the Pacific Trade and Development Conference (PAFTAD), an international academic organization that holds a conference every eighteen months.

Publications: TIER publishes, in Chinese, *Daily Forecasts of Interests and Exchange Rates; The International Economic Trends Weekly Report; Taiwan Economic Research Monthly; Monthly Reportcard on Main Economic Indicators; Japan's Industrial Policy Monthly; Energy Monthly; The Rural Sentiment,* a monthly periodical that reports on nuclear power generation and community activities at the sites of nuclear power plants; *ROC Industrial Year Book;* and *Annual Survey on Economic Trends and Forecast.* TIER has also been commissioned by the Secretariat of the Chinese Taipei Committee of the Pacific Basin Economic Council (PBEC) to publish annual reports on PBEC's primary activities.

Funding sources: TIER derives most of its funds from research contracts.

Staffing: TIER has more than 100 full-time researchers, supported by twenty-five research assistants and forty-six administrative staff members. Some eighteen local and foreign scholars are also employed as advisors on a contractual basis.

Head of the institution: Dr. Rong-I Wu, President

Contact officer: Mr. Jason Liu, Administrative Officer, Department of International Affairs

Taiwan Institute of Economic Research
7th Floor, 16-8, Tehwei Street, Taipei, Taiwan
REPUBLIC OF CHINA
Tel: (886-2) 586-5000 ext. 712
Fax: (886-2) 594-6528 / 594-6317
e-mail • mail.tier.org.tw
URL • http://www.tier.org.tw

Chulalongkorn University

Center for International Economics

Background and objectives: The Center for International Economics (CIE), established in 1993, is a research and training institution affiliated with the Faculty of Economics at Chulalongkorn University. It aims to meet the needs of business and government by producing qualified economists and researchers and advancing research on important economic issues.

Programs: The Center conducts policy-oriented research on such topics as ASEAN in a changing international economy, technology transfer, and privatization, free trade, and economic integration in Asia-Pacific. Research projects are often conducted in collaboration with government agencies and international institutions such as the Ministry of Commerce, Ministry of Finance, ASEAN, and APEC.

CIE also confers an M.A. degree in international economics and finance; promotes international exchanges for both professors and graduate students; and regularly organizes conferences and seminars in international economics.

Publications: The Center publishes in Thai books, monographs, articles, and occasional papers, featuring CIE's research findings.

Recent publications include *Regional Integration in the Asian-Pacific Region and Its Implications for Europe* (1995); *Implications of AFTA for ASEAN and Non-ASEAN Countries* (1995); and *Towards a New Vision: Thailand and the World* (1994).

Funding sources: The Center is funded through research contracts with government agencies such as the Ministry of Commerce, Ministry of Finance, and National Economic and Social Development Board. Additional funding comes from consultancy with local and foreign firms.

Staffing: The Center's researchers are mainly professors at the Faculty of Economics. They are supported by ten administrative staff.

Head of the institution: Dr. Suthiphand Chirathivat, Director

Contact officer: Ms. Irini Lemou-Maniati, Program Coordinator

Center for International Economics
Faculty of Economics
Chulalongkorn University
Phya Thai Rd., Bangkok 10330
THAILAND
Tel: (66-2) 218-6295
Fax: (66-2) 218-6295 / 251-3967
e-mail • cie@netserv.chula.ac.th

Chulalongkorn University

Institute of Asian Studies

Background and objectives: The Institute of Asian Studies (IAS), established in 1967 at Chulalongkorn University, is an interdisciplinary research and service organization with the aim to advance academic research in the field of Asian Studies and promote understanding of and between Thailand and the rest of Asia.

Programs: The Institute conducts interdisciplinary research projects mainly confined to the Asian region. Recent research includes a comparative analysis of the role of mass media in politics, trade and investment in Indochina and Myanmar, and an empirical study of the economic foreign policy of ASEAN countries in the 1990s.

IAS also offers consultative and informational services on Asian affairs to students, entrepreneurs, and government officials.

In addition, the Institute organizes regular lectures and panel discussions, seminars, and conferences at national, regional, and international levels to facilitate the exchange of ideas between Asian experts.

IAS also conducts an annual training program on Asian and Japanese studies for teachers in secondary schools throughout Thailand to upgrade knowledge of Asian countries.

The Institute established the *Data Bank on Asian Countries*, to collect and disseminate information on Asia, and the *Asian Research Centre for Migration*, to study migration problems in Asia.

Publications: IAS publishes in Thai the *Journal of Asian Review* and the annual *Asia Yearbook*. In English, IAS publishes the annual *Asian Review*.

The Institute also publishes occasional and research papers. Recent publications include *The United States, the Mekong Committee, and Thailand: A Study of American Multilateral and Bilateral Assistance to North-East Thailand since the 1950s* (1995), *Rupture and Return: Repatriation, Displacement and Reintegration in Battambang Province, Cambodia* (1995), and *Border Trade* (1994).

Funding sources: IAS is partially funded by the Thai government and Chulalongkorn University. Additional funds come from international as well as domestic public and private sources in the form of research grants, support for specific programs, and co-sponsorship of activities.

Staffing: The Institute has a staff of seventeen researchers and research assistants supported by twenty administrative assistants.

Head of the institution: Dr. Withaya Sucharithanarugse, Director

Contact officer: Mrs. Charunee Lakthong, Secretary

Institute of Asian Studies
7th Floor, Prajadhipok-Rambhai
Barni Building
Chulalongkorn University, Phyathai Rd.
Bangkok 10330
THAILAND
Tel: (66-2) 251-5199 / 218-7460 / 218-7468
Fax: (66-2) 255-1124
e-mail • withaya@chulkn.car.chula.ac.th

Chulalongkorn University

Institute of Security and International Studies

Background and objectives: The Institute of Security and International Studies (ISIS) was founded in 1981 at Chulalongkorn University to conduct independent research and disseminate knowledge on international and security issues. The Institute seeks to identify policy options for Thai governmental agencies and enhance public awareness and understanding of strategic and international challenges, particularly those affecting Thailand and Southeast Asia.

Programs: The primary function of ISIS is to promote research on crucial political, military, and socioeconomic issues affecting the security of Thailand and Southeast Asia. Recent research projects included studies on Thai defense and foreign policies and the impact of environmental problems on national security.

ISIS also organizes seminars and workshops at the national and international levels, many arranged in cooperation with other institutions such as the Institute of Southeast Asian Studies in Singapore, Indonesia's Centre of Strategic and International Studies, and the International Institute for Strategic Studies in London.

In addition, ISIS conducts public lectures and panel discussions in Thai and English and welcomes foreign scholars as visiting researchers. It also co-sponsors an internship program with the School of Advanced International Studies at Johns Hopkins University and with other universities in the United States and Europe.

Publications: The Institute publishes Thai-language textbooks on international relations and politics of Southeast Asia, as well as books and monographs on various aspects of Thai defense and foreign policies.

English-language volumes include conference proceedings, completed research reports, and the "ISIS Papers" on Southeast Asia security issues by leading domestic and international scholars.

Funding sources: ISIS is funded mainly by grants from major international philanthropic organizations such as the Ford Foundation, the Asia Foundation, and the Rockefeller Foundation. Additional funds are provided on a project by project basis by Chulalongkorn University and the Thai government.

Staffing: The Institute has four full-time researchers, supported by five administrative staff.

Notes: In 1988, ISIS joined with other Southeast Asian institutions to form the ASEAN Institutes of Strategic and International Studies, an association with the aim to provide an arena for discussing security cooperation.

In 1993, ISIS became a founding member of the Council on Security Cooperation in the Asia Pacific, which was established to provide a basis for confidence building and security cooperation among Asian-Pacific countries.

Head of the institution: Dr. Kusuma Snitwongse, Chairperson

Contact officer: Dr. Suchit Bunbongkam, Acting Director

**Institute of Security and International Studies
5th Floor, Prajadhipok-Rambhaibarni Building
Chulalongkorn University
Bangkok 10330
THAILAND
Tel: (66-2) 253-2686 / 218-7433
Fax: (66-2) 254-0119
e-mail • isis@chulkn.car.chula.ac.th**

Thailand Development Research Institute

Background and objectives: The Thailand Development Research Institute (TDRI), founded in 1984, is a nonprofit, nongovernmental foundation that aims to conduct policy research, create a research network linking institutions and individuals engaged in policy research, and provide policy options for sustaining social and economic development in Thailand.

Programs: The Institute conducts studies within six research programs: Human Resources and Social Development, International Economic Relations, Macroeconomic Policy, Natural Resources and Environment, Science and Technology Development, and Sectoral Economics. Research projects cover such topics as industrialization and the environment, public-sector reform, macroeconomic development, and international cooperation.

TDRI also conducts "master plan" studies for governmental agencies such as the Communication Authority of Thailand, Ministry of Industry, Ministry of Transport and Communications, and the Tourism Authority of Thailand.

The Institute sponsors and participates in international seminars and holds an annual year-end conference to disseminate results of its major research projects to the public.

Publications: The Institute publishes the *TDRI Monographs*, the *TDRI Quarterly Review*, and the *TDRI Economic Information Kit*. Recent publications include *Thailand's Perspective on Foreign Loans* (1995); *Women in Development: Enhancing the Status of Rural Women in Northern Thailand* (1995); and *Natural Resources Management in Mainland Southeast Asia* (1995).

The Institute also offers the *TDRI Information Service,* which allows subscribers to have access to publications via Internet web site http://203.149.0.33.

Funding sources: TDRI received start-up funding from the Canadian International Development Agency. Presently, it is funded through research projects, interest from its own endowment fund, and donations.

Staffing: The Institute has seventy-one full-time and seventeen part-time researchers, supported by twenty-nine administrative staff.

Heads of the institution:
H.E. Mr. Anand Panyarachun, Chairman of the Council of Trustees and Board of Directors

Dr. Chalongphob Sussangkarn, President

Contact officer: Ms. Ryratana Suwanraks, Editor

Thailand Development Research Institute
565 Soi Ramkhamhaeng 39 (Thepleela 1)
Ramkhamhaeng Road, Wangthonglang, Bangkapi
Bangkok 10310
THAILAND
Tel: (66-2) 718-5460
Fax: (66-2) 718-5461 / 718-5462
e-mail • publications@leelal.tdri.or.th
URL • http://www.info.tdri.or.th

Center for Environmental Research, Education, and Development

Background and objectives: The Center for Environmental Research, Education, and Development (CERED) is an independent, non-government organization sponsored by the Vietnam Union of Science and Technology Association. Established in 1991 to analyze strategies for balancing environmental conservation with socioeconomic development, CERED seeks to establish an international research network in the field of environmental studies, advise policy makers on environmental issues, and raise the environmental awareness of the general public.

Programs: CERED's recent research covers such topics as the effects of global environmental change, including changes in climate, sea levels, and land usage; ecological diversity in mangrove forests, coastal zones, and wetlands; environmental impact assessment for health and agriculture; and the relationship between environmental protection and economic development.

In collaboration with the University of East Anglia in the United Kingdom, the University of Waikato in New Zealand, and the University of Hanoi, CERED facilitates training for Vietnamese scientists and policy makers on environmental issues, and is currently studying adaptive strategies for coping with typhoon threats in the Red River delta.

CERED also organizes international conferences and workshops, including the OECD-Development Center/CERED workshop on environmental management in the face of rapid industrialization (1993) and the UN Environmental Program/CERED conference on the impact of climate change and sea level rise (1991).

Publications: Among CERED's publications are "Environmental Surveys of Seven Provinces/Cities in Vietnam" (1994), "Environmental Problems and Management Challenges in Vietnam" (1993), "Global Warming and Vietnam: A Policy-Makers' Guide" (1993), and "The Potential Socio-Economic Effects of Climate Change on Vietnam," a report to be published by the UN Environmental Program.

Funding sources: CERED's operating costs and research activities are funded by research contracts and by contributions from domestic and international organizations, including the Asian Development Bank.

Staffing: CERED has fifteen researchers and five administrative assistants.

Head of the institution: Dr. Nguyen Huu Ninh, Chairman

Contact officer: Ms. Ngo Cam Thanh, International Desk

Center for Environmental Research, Education, and Development
A01, K40 Giang Vo, Hanoi
VIETNAM
Tel: (84-4) 8515-213
Fax: (84-4) 8515-213
e-mail • cered@netnam.org.vn

Institute for Economic Research of Ho Chi Minh City

Background and objectives: The Institute for Economic Research of Ho Chi Minh City (IER) was founded in 1976 as the Division for Economic Regionalization of Ho Chi Minh City and given its present name in 1988. As a research institution under the People's Committee of Ho Chi Minh City and directed by the Committee's chairman, IER studies regional socioeconomic issues of concern to the Committee, provides consulting services for the public and private sectors, and organizes training courses on managerial skill improvement for entrepreneurs.

Programs: IER's five departments specialize in management studies; socioeconomic infrastructure studies; natural resources, environment, and regional economics; information and computer science; and administration and finance.

Recent research has addressed such issues as long-term socioeconomic development planning for Ho Chi Minh City through the year 2010, economic reform and development, and administrative reform of local government agencies.

In cooperation with international organizations and foreign institutions, such as the United Nations Development Program (UNDP), the United Nations Fund for Population Activities (UNFPA), and the Hanns Seidel Foundation, IER sponsors conferences, seminars, workshops, and joint research programs on topics ranging from social development in the context of market-oriented economic reform to international finance and investment.

Publications: In cooperation with the Ministry of Trade, IER publishes *Market,* a daily Vietnamese-language newsletter listing price changes for imports and exports in the domestic and international markets. IER has also published a number of articles, research reports, and books, including *Development Experience of Singapore* (1996).

Funding sources: IER is funded by the Vietnamese government. Financial support for special research projects comes from international organizations, including UNDP and UNFPA.

Staffing: IER has seventy researchers and twenty support staff members.

Head of the institution: Mr. Bach Van Bay, Director

Contact officer: Mr. Pham Xuan Ai, Deputy Director

The Institute for Economic Research of Ho Chi Minh City
175 Hai Ba Trung Street, Dist. 3
Ho Chi Minh City
VIETNAM
Tel: (84-8) 8295-405
Fax: (84-8) 8243-896
e-mail • ier@netnam2.org.vn

Institute for International Relations

Background and objectives: The Institute for International Relations (IIR) was created in 1987 when the Council of Ministers of Vietnam decided to merge the former School of Diplomacy and Institute of International Relations, established respectively in 1959 and 1977. In addition to serving as a think tank for the Ministry of Foreign Affairs and other ministries concerned with international issues, IIR is the country's only institution for training diplomats and foreign service officers.

Programs: IIR encompasses research divisions of Northeast Asian Studies, Southeast Asian Studies, and European-American Studies, as well as a School of Foreign Affairs. Recent research has focused on such topics as major trends in the world and the Asia-Pacific; security issues in the South China Sea; the emerging triangular relationship among the United States, Japan, and China; and the relations between the United States and China in the 21st century.

IIR has hosted bilateral meetings with a number of foreign counterpart institutions, including the Japan Institute of Foreign Affairs, the Australian Institute of Strategic and Defense Studies, and the China Institute of Contemporary International Relations, to discuss the issues of regional security, economic development, and international cooperation.

It has also coordinated the participation of Vietnam in the ASEAN Institute of Strategic and International Studies.

The School of Foreign Affairs offers B.A. studies in international relations and other short-term training programs for government officials.

Publications: IIR publishes the bimonthly *Journal on International Studies* in Vietnamese and a biannual journal under the same name in English. Recent Vietnamese-language books include *ASEAN in the 21st Century: Opportunities and Challenges* (1996), *Multinational Corporations and Developing Countries* (1996), and *Vietnam-Japan Relations* (1994).

Funding sources: IIR is funded by the Vietnamese government.

Staffing: IIR has twenty-five researchers and thirty-two lecturers, supported by twenty administrative assistants.

Head of the institution: Amb. Dao Huy Ngoc, Director General

Contact officer: Mr. Le Linh Lan, Chief, Bureau for International Cooperation and Administration

Institute for International Relations
Lang Thuong, Dong Da, Hanoi
VIETNAM
Tel: (84-4) 8343-543
Fax: (84-4) 8343-543

National Center for Social Sciences and Humanities

Center for Japanese Studies

Background and objectives: The Center for Japanese Studies (CJS) is a research institution affiliated with the National Center for Social Sciences and Humanities of Vietnam. Established in 1993, CJS conducts research, promotes public education on Japan, and coordinates Japanese studies at the national level.

Programs: The Center's six research departments focus on Vietnamese-Japanese relations and on the economy, politics and society, history, culture, and linguistics of Japan. Recent and prospective research projects have addressed Japanese administrative reform, Japan's experiences in promoting private investment and reforming state-owned enterprises, changes in Japan's social structure in the postwar period, and Vietnam-Japan relations in the post-Cold War era.

Publications: CJS publishes *Japanese Studies Review,* a quarterly journal covering issues ranging from Japan's socioeconomic development to its external relations.

Recent books in Vietnamese include *The Japanese Administrative Reform* (1995), *A Comparison of Administrative Reform between Japan, China, and Vietnam* (1995), and *Research on the Japanese Social Welfare System* (forthcoming).

Funding sources: CJS is funded mainly by the Vietnamese government. Other sources of funding include research grants and donations from Japanese foundations, such as the Toyota Foundation and the Sumitomo Foundation.

Staffing: CJS has twenty-six full-time researchers and six administrative assistants.

Head of the institution: Dr. Duong Phu Hiep, Director

Contact officer: Dr. Pham Quy Long, Assistant Director on Training and External Relations

Center for Japanese Studies
National Center for Social Sciences and Humanities
H1, TTKHXH, Kim Ma Thuong Street
Cong Vi, Badinh District, Hanoi
VIETNAM
Tel: (84-4) 8325-178
Fax: (84-4) 8326-653

National Center for Social Sciences and Humanities

Center for North America Studies

Background and objectives: The Center for North America Studies (CNAS), a research institution within the National Center for Social Sciences and Humanities, was established in 1993 to promote interdisciplinary research on the United States and North America, inform government agencies on related policy issues, and help promote public understanding of the United States and North America.

Programs: CNAS's research areas cover politics, economics, history, and culture, with emphasis on North American international relations, NAFTA, and Asia-Pacific international relations. Recent research has focused on such topics as the U.S. economy in the 1990s, industrialization in the Republic of Korea, U.S.-Japanese relations in the 1990s, and U.S. relations with Asia-Pacific countries.

CNAS has also established exchanges with the Yale China Association, Georgetown University, Johns Hopkins University, and the University of Denver. Together with these counterpart institutions, the Center has organized seminars on American culture and politics and U.S.-Vietnamese relations.

Publications: CNAS publishes (in Vietnamese) *Americas Today,* a bimonthly journal featuring articles by its own members and overseas authors, and *North-America Today,* a monthly bulletin aimed at the general public.

Recent Vietnamese-language books include *1000 U.S. Largest Corporations* (1996), *U.S.-Japanese Relations in the Post-Cold War Period* (1995), and *Prospects for the U.S. Economy* (1994).

Funding sources: CNAS is funded by the Vietnamese government and by income derived from research contracts with domestic and foreign organizations, including NGOs.

Staffing: CNAS has twenty full-time researchers, five administrative staff members, and more than 100 members by correspondence in academia, government agencies, and civilian organizations.

Head of the institution: Dr. Do Loc Diep, Director

Contact officer: Dr. Nguyen Thiet Son, Deputy Director

Center for North America Studies
National Center for Social Sciences and Humanities
234 Thaiha Street, Dong Da District
Hanoi
VIETNAM
Tel: (84-4) 8534-912
Fax: (84-4) 8534-955

National Center for Social Sciences and Humanities

Institute for Southeast Asian Studies

Background and objectives: The Institute for Southeast Asian Studies (ISEAS) at the National Center for Social Sciences and Humanities was established in 1973 to pursue comprehensive research on Southeast Asian countries, provide policy analysis for the government, and coordinate Southeast Asian studies all over Vietnam.

Programs: ISEAS's eight research centers study the economics, politics, history, and culture of Southeast Asia, with a subregional and country focus on Laos, Cambodia, Thailand, the insular countries, India, and Australia.

Recent research programs have concentrated on ethnic groups and religions in Southeast Asian countries, cultural contacts between the East and the West, the environment and behavior of Southeast Asian peoples, economic cooperation among ASEAN countries, and Vietnam's relations with other Southeast Asian countries.

ISEAS has also exchanged scholars and publications with research institutions in the United States, China, Russia, France, and Japan. With these foreign counterparts, it has sponsored joint conferences, seminars, and symposiums on such topics as overseas Chinese in Vietnam, Vietnam-Thailand relations, and relations between Vietnam and Southeast Asian countries.

Publications: ISEAS publishes (in Vietnamese) *SEA Studies,* a quarterly journal featuring research articles on Southeast Asia, and *Vietnam & Southeast Asia Today,* a monthly magazine oriented more toward the general public.

Recent Vietnamese-language books include *The Ethnic Chinese and Economic Development in Vietnam and Singapore* (1993), *Singapore: Thirty Years of Development* (1995), and *Vietnam and ASEAN* (1996).

Funding sources: ISEAS is funded by the Vietnamese government.

Staffing: ISEAS has fifty-three researchers, including thirty professors, and ten administrative staff members.

Head of the institution: Dr. Pham Duc Thanh, Director

Contact officer: Mr. Nguyen Huy Thanh, Head, Administrative and Executive Department

The Institute for Southeast Asian Studies
National Center for Social Sciences and Humanities
27 Tran Xuan Soan Street, Hanoi
VIETNAM
Tel: (84-4) 8261-628 / 8261-629
Fax: (84-4) 8259-071 / 8245-966
e-mail • pdthanh@iseas.ac.vn / chong@iseas.ac.vn

Vietnam Asia-Pacific Economic Center

Background and objectives: The Vietnam Asia-Pacific Economic Center (VAPEC) is a non-governmental, nonprofit membership institution established in 1993 to analyze socioeconomic development in Asia-Pacific countries and inform the development of national economic policies and business strategies. VAPEC is headquartered in Hanoi, with four branch centers in major Vietnamese cities and one office in Tokyo.

Programs: VAPEC collects information on Asia-Pacific economic issues; conducts research on economic theories, growth models, and the development experiences of Asia-Pacific economies; and explores options for economic cooperation between Vietnam and other Asia-Pacific countries.

Recent research projects have addressed Vietnam and APEC, Vietnam in the process of joining WTO, government-enterprise relations in the transition to a market economy, and the lessons that Vietnam might draw from the development experiences of other Southeast Asian countries.

VAPEC also sponsors seminars and training courses on such topics as economic development in Vietnam and the Asia-Pacific region, financial policy in macroeconomic management, strategies for regional development in industrialization, and economic development in cooperative and non-state owned enterprises in Central Vietnam.

Publications: VAPEC publishes, in Vietnamese and English, *Asia-Pacific Economic Review,* a quarterly journal featuring articles on economic issues in Asia-Pacific countries and Vietnam's integration in the region.

Recent Vietnamese-language books include *Vietnam and Asia-Pacific Countries: Present and Prospective Relations* (1996), *Prospects for Vietnam's Industrialization* (1996), *Japan's Foreign Direct Investment and Interdependence in Asia* (1996), and *Challenges to Development in the Asia-Pacific* (1995).

Funding sources: VAPEC is funded by donations and grants from foundations, organizations, and individuals, and by fees from contract research. VAPEC has also received financial assistance from Japan in the establishment and initial operation of its Tokyo office.

Staffing: VAPEC has forty researchers supported by ten administrative assistants.

Head of the institution: Mr. Vu Quang Tuyen, President

Contact officer: Dr. Le Van Sang, Vice-President, Director, Hanoi Branch Center

Vietnam Asia-Pacific Economic Center
234 Thai Ha, Trung Liet, Dong Da
Hanoi
VIETNAM
Tel: (84-4) 8534-304
Fax: (84-4) 8534-955
e-mail • inevn@netnam.org.vn

AUSTRALIA AND NEW ZEALAND

Australian Institute of International Affairs (AIIA)

Background and objectives: The Australian Institute of International Affairs (AIIA) is a non-governmental and nonpartisan organization established in 1933 to encourage greater awareness of foreign policy matters bearing on Australia's place in the world. AIIA is a membership organization for politicians, foreign diplomats, scholars, business representatives, journalists, students, and others with professional interest in foreign policy. Headquartered in Canberra, the Institute has branches in Sydney, Melbourne, Brisbane, Townsville, Perth, Adelaide, and Hobart.

Programs: The Institute arranges regular lectures, workshops, and discussions for its members on matters ranging from traditional issues of diplomacy, trade, and military security to more recent concerns such as environmental security, foreign aid, and telecommunications issues.

AIIA organizes an annual national conference such as the 1995 "Australia and India" conference and 1996 "United States-Australia Relationship" conference, featuring senior politicians and academics. The Institute also participates in second-track diplomacy discussions as a member of the Australian National Committee for the Council for Security Cooperation in Asia and the Pacific and conducts a public outreach program to engage the interest of Australian high school students in international relations.

Publications: AIIA publishes the triannual *Australian Journal of International Affairs*, featuring research on international political, social, economic, and legal issues with emphasis on the Asia-Pacific region. The Institute also publishes a regular survey of Australian foreign policy entitled *World Affairs*. Recent volumes in this series include *Indonesia: Dealing with a Neighbor* (1996) and *Diplomacy in the Market Place* (1992)

Funding sources: Individual branches are funded through their membership dues and, in some cases, through corporate sponsorship. At the national level, AIIA is funded by the commonwealth government, rental income from AIIA's national headquarters in Canberra, corporate sponsorship, royalty income, and contributions from the branches.

Staffing: The national and regional offices have a small core of management staff and administrative support, which includes volunteers.

Head of the institution: Mr. Richard Searby QC, National President

Contact officer: Dr. Lesley Jackman, Executive Director

Australian Institute of International Affairs
Stephen House, 32 Thesiger Court
Deakin ACT 2600
AUSTRALIA
Tel: (61-6) 282-2133
Fax: (61-6) 285-2334
e-mail • ceo@aiia.as.au
URL • http://www.aiia.asrr.au

Australian National University

Research School of Pacific and Asian Studies, Australia-Japan Research Centre

Background and objectives: The Australia-Japan Research Centre, established in 1980, aims to foster expertise in the economic, political, and social issues central to Australian and Japanese interests in the Asia-Pacific economy and contribute to public policy making.

Programs: The Centre sponsors a steady stream of researchers with interest in the social, political, and economic challenges facing the Asia-Pacific region. Recent research topics included Australian and regional trade blocs, Japanese corporate strategies, and Japanese and Australian labor market reform.

The Centre organizes lectures, seminars, and conferences involving representatives of academia, government, and industry from around the region. It also hosts the secretariats of the Pacific Trade and Development Conference Series, the Australian Pacific Economic Cooperation Committee, and the Pacific Economic Cooperation Council's Minerals and Energy Forum.

In addition, the Centre collaborates on research activities and training programs with major institutions throughout the Asia-Pacific such as the Centre for Strategic and International Studies (Indonesia), Japan's Nomura Research Institute, and the Chinese Academy of Social Sciences.

Publications: The Centre publishes the *Asia Pacific Economics and Politics* book series and the *Pacific Economic Papers*. The results of ongoing research and colloquia are also disseminated through a series of special reports.

Recent publications include *Japanese Firms, Finance and Markets* (1996), *Changing Global Comparative Advantage: Evidence from Asia and the Pacific* (1996), and *Environment and Development in the Pacific: Problems and Policy Options* (1996).

Funding sources: A Centre endowment fund was established in 1981 with the support of the Japanese government and private business organizations. Annual funding comes from the Australian and Japanese governments and Australian industry. Additional income is derived from commissioned projects.

Staffing: The Centre has six full-time and two part-time researchers supported by seven administrative staff.

Head of the institution: Prof. Peter Drysdale, Executive Director

Contact officer: Margitta Acker, Centre Administrator

Australia-Japan Research Centre
Research School of Pacific and Asian Studies
Australian National University
Canberra, ACT 0200
AUSTRALIA
Tel: (61-6) 249-3780
Fax: (61-6) 249-0767
e-mail • ajrcgen@ajrc.anu.edu.au
URL • http://coombs.anu.edu.
au/SpecialProj/AJRC/ajrcpage.html

Australian National University

Research School of Pacific and Asian Studies, Contemporary China Centre

Background and objectives: The Contemporary China Centre, established in 1970, is concerned with multidisciplinary scholarly analysis of post-1949 China, Hong Kong, and Taiwan.

Programs: The Centre conducts research in the areas of Chinese economics, modern political and legal structures, and the social ramifications of political and economic change in China, Hong Kong, and Taiwan. Recent research topics include an examination of rural-to-urban migration patterns in China, Hong Kong's retrocession to China, and small businesses in Taiwan.

The Centre also houses the Transformation of Communist Systems Project, which brings specialists on Eastern Europe together with specialists on China and Vietnam in collaborative research.

Publications: The Centre publishes *The China Journal*, a semi-annual periodical covering contemporary social, economic, and political developments in China, Hong Kong, and Taiwan. It also publishes the *Contemporary China Papers* series, featuring such titles as *Chinese Nationalism* (1996); *Directory of Officials and Organizations in China* (1994); and *Using the Past to Serve the Present: Historiography and Politics in Contemporary China* (1993). The Centre's Transformation of Communist Systems Project publishes a separate book series, including such recent titles as *China after Socialism: In the Footsteps of Eastern Europe or East Asia?* (1996) and *The Development of Civil Society in Communist Systems* (1993).

Funding sources: The Centre is largely funded by the Australian National University. Its projects receive additional funding from outside foundations.

Staffing: The Centre has four full-time academic staff and hosts approximately fifteen other researchers, including Ph.D. students.

Head of the institution: Dr. Jonathan Unger, Director

Contact officer: Mrs. Heli Petryk, Administrator

Contemporary China Centre
Coombs Annex, 9 Liversidge Street
Research School of Pacific and Asian Studies
Australian National University
Canberra, ACT 0200
AUSTRALIA
Tel: (61-6) 249-4157
Fax: (61-6) 257-3642
e-mail • unger@coombs.anu.edu.au
URL • http://online.anu.edu.au/ RSPAS/ccc/journal.htm

Australian National University

Research School of Pacific and Asian Studies, Department of International Relations

Background and objectives: The Department of International Relations, founded in 1951, is an academic and research institution dedicated to the study of international political, security, and economic issues. Its aim is to produce qualified scholars of international relations and prepare its students for a professional career in diplomacy, civil service, teaching, journalism, or business.

Programs: The Department conducts research in the areas of global politics, international relations of the Asian-Pacific region, Australian foreign and defense policies, and international political economy. Research topics cover international history and theory, strategic and peace studies, international law, and Asia-Pacific regional security and economics.

The Department confers an M.A. degree and Graduate Diploma in International Relations and a Ph.D. degree through the ANU's Graduate Program in Political Science and International Relations. It also organizes conferences, seminars, and workshops, independently or with counterpart organizations, on such topics as "Cooperating for Peace" and "International Relations in Australia in the 1990s."

Publications: The Department of International Relations *Bulletin* is published three times a year to update readers on forthcoming conferences and events.

The Department also publishes working papers and, in conjunction with Allen & Unwin, the *Studies in World Affairs* monograph series. In addition, it houses the Australian Foreign Policy Publications Programme, which produces the *Australian Foreign Policy Papers*.

Recent publications include *Presumptive Engagement: Australia's Asia-Pacific Security Policy in the 1990s* (1996), *Discourses of Danger and Dread Frontiers: Australian Defense and Security Thinking after the Cold War* (1996), and *The New Agenda for Global Security: Cooperating for Peace and Beyond* (1995).

Funding sources: The Department is primarily funded by the Australian National University. Additional funding is derived from foundation support and research grants.

Staffing: The Department has seven full-time and fifteen part-time (Ph.D.) researchers, supported by five administrative staff.

Head of the institution: Prof. Andrew Mack, Director

Contact officer: Ms. Amy Chen, Departmental Administrator

Department of International Relations
Research School of Pacific and Asian Studies
Australian National University
Canberra, ACT 0200
AUSTRALIA
Tel: (61-6) 249-2166
Fax: (61-6) 279-8010
e-mail • ir.rspas@coombs.anu.edu.au
URL • http://coombs.anu.edu.au/
        Depts/RSPAS/PS-IR/ir-home.htm

Australian National University

Research School of Pacific and Asian Studies, National Centre for Development Studies

Background and objectives: The National Centre for Development Studies (NCDS), established in 1975, is a postgraduate training and research body based in the Economics Division of the Research School of Pacific and Asian Studies. Its aim is to provide an Australian focus for the study and evaluation of aid and development issues with particular emphasis on East Asia and the South Pacific.

Programs: The Centre provides graduate training and conducts policy-oriented research on economics of development, environmental management, and development administration. Recent research projects addressed governance and development in Pacific Island countries, impacts of APEC's trade liberalization regime, transitional economies and reform, and the process of building indigenous institutions to facilitate development.

NCDS also sponsors conferences, workshops, and seminars, bringing together academics, government policy makers, donor agencies, and business to address topics ranging from environmental management and community development to public sector reform, fiscal equity, and intergovernmental relations.

Publications: The Centre publishes semiannually the *Pacific Economic Bulletin* and *Asian-Pacific Economic Literature*. NCDS also publishes the *Pacific Policy Papers* and the *Pacific Research Monographs*. A *Trade and Development* book series is published in association with Cambridge University Press. Recent titles include *Building a Modern Financial System* (1996); *Sustaining Export-Oriented Development: Ideas from East Asia* (1995); and *The Third Revolution in the Chinese Countryside* (1995).

Funding sources: The Centre's activities are funded by grants from AusAid, fees from its graduate program, research contracts from national and international organizations, and contributions from the Australian National University.

Staffing: The Centre has thirty researchers and research assistants supported by twenty-five administrative staff.

Notes: In 1995, the North Australia Research Unit, which investigates the relationships between the historical, cultural, political, and physical landscapes of northern Australia and its people, was made part of the Centre.

Head of the institution: Prof. Ron Duncan, Executive Director

National Centre for Development Studies
Research School of Pacific and Asian Studies
Australian National University
Canberra, ACT 0200
AUSTRALIA
Tel: (61-6) 249-4705
Fax: (61-6) 257-2886
e-mail • ronald.duncan@anu.edu.au
URL • http://ncdsnet.anu.edu.au

Australian National University

Research School of Pacific and Asian Studies, Strategic and Defence Studies Centre

Background and objectives: The Strategic and Defence Studies Centre, established in 1966, is dedicated to the study of the military, political, economic, environmental, and technological challenges facing Australia's strategic planners. It aims to illuminate policy options and formulate strategic and defense policy.

Programs: The Centre's research is not limited to the control and application of military force but also addresses economic, scientific, and technological aspects of strategic developments as well as the peaceful settlement of disputes. Recent studies investigate the problems of security and confidence building in Asia-Pacific, arms proliferation and arms control, and new security issues such as environment, immigration, and transnational crime in the region.

The Centre regularly organizes seminars and conferences and its staff frequently advise and train government officials in the Departments of Defence and Foreign Affairs and Trade.

The Centre also confers a graduate diploma and a Master's degree in strategic studies.

Publications: The Centre publishes the *Canberra Papers on Strategy and Defence* and the *SDSC Working Papers*, which contains more than two dozen studies a year on strategic and defense issues. Recent publications include *Calming the Waters: Initiatives for Asia Pacific Maritime Cooperation* (1996), *Transforming the Tatmadaw: The Burmese Armed Forces since 1988* (1996), *Planning a Defence Force without a Threat* (1996);

and *India Looks East: An Emerging Power and Its Asia-Pacific Neighbours* (1995).

Funding sources: The Centre is funded by the Australian National University, Department of Defence and Employment, and from education and training fees.

Staffing: The Centre has eight full-time researchers, supported by four administrative staff.

Notes: The Centre provides the Secretariat for the Australian Committee of the Council for Security Cooperation in the Asia Pacific.

Head of the institution: Prof. Paul Dibb, Director

Contact officer: Ms. Susan Gerrard, Centre Administrator

Strategic and Defence Studies Centre
Research School of Pacific and Asian Studies
Australian National University
Canberra, ACT 0200
AUSTRALIA
Tel: (61-6) 243-8555
Fax: (61-6) 248-0816
e-mail • sgerrard@coombs.anu.edu.au
**URL • http://coombs.anu.edu.au/~sgerrard/SDSC/
index.htm**

Griffith University

Centre for the Study of Australia-Asia Relations

Background and objectives: The Centre for the Study of Australia-Asia Relations, established in 1978, is an allied Centre within the Faculty of Asian and International Studies at Griffith University. It aims to develop a wider understanding of Australia's relations with Asia among policy makers, scholars, business people, and the community.

Programs: The Centre conducts research covering Australia's political, economic, and strategic relations with Asia from a historical and contemporary perspective. Research projects range from an examination of the importance of strategic culture in determining the security policies of Asian states to a comparative study of output, productivity, and purchasing power between Australia and other Asian countries.

The Centre organizes conferences and workshops, bringing together academics, journalists, and politicians on issues such as Asia-Pacific economic cooperation and Australian foreign policy in the post-Cold War era.

In addition, the Centre conducts the Asia-Pacific Business Training Program, a series of workshops that provide application-oriented training for businesses seeking entry into the Asian markets. The Centre also offers commercial research, consulting, and international marketing services to industry and government.

Publications: The Centre publishes three monograph series— the *Australia-Asia Papers*, *Australians in Asia*, and the *COPPAA* series—as well as occasional books and reports. Recent publications include *Security Policy in the Asia-Pacific: A US Strategy for a New Century* (1996), *From Coup to Coup: Diplomatic Experiences in Five Asian Countries* (1996), *China's Manufacturing Performance from an Australian Perspective, 1980-1991* (1996), and *Manufacturing Sector Output and Productivity in Indonesia: An Australian Comparative Perspective, 1975-1990* (1995).

Funding sources: The Centre receives financial support from the Faculty of Asian and International Studies, Department of Foreign Affairs and Trade, and other granting institutions in Australia and overseas.

Staffing: The Centre has one full-time and one part-time researcher as well as five administrative staff.

Head of the institution: Assoc. Prof. Russell Trood

Contact officer: Ms. Louise Goodsell, Executive Assistant to the Director

Centre for the Study of Australia-Asia Relations
Faculty of Asian and International Studies
Griffith University
Nathan Campus, Nathan Qld 4111
AUSTRALIA
Tel: (61-7) 3875-7916
Fax: (61-7) 3875-7956
e-mail • csaar@ais.gu.edu.au

Macquarie University

Asia-Pacific Research Institute

Background and objectives: The Asia-Pacific Research Institute at Macquarie University (APRIM) was established in 1992 to enhance greater understanding of the Asia-Pacific region and foster business links between Asia and the world by conducting academic and entrepreneurial projects, education programs, intellectual exchanges, and consulting services.

Programs: APRIM undertakes extensive research on issues of concern to the Asia-Pacific region such as labor market analysis, environmental accounting, internationalization of small and medium-sized businesses, and poverty alleviation. The Institute also offers a range of educational training programs in the areas of international trade and industry; banking and finance law; environmental, economic, and development policy; and public sector management.

APRIM is appointed by the government as the Australian Lead Institution for the Network of Economic Development Management (NEDM) within the APEC Human Resource Development (HRD) Working Group. It is responsible for coordinating and leading Australia's participation in NEDM's projects and activities as well as briefing Australian delegates attending APEC HRD meetings.

The Institute also provides assistance to UNESCO's Asia-Pacific Higher Education Network (APHEN), which is working on the establishment of an electronic network of higher education institutions across the region.

In addition, APRIM is working with the United Nations Trade Point Development Centre (UNTPDC) to facilitate global trade transactions electronically through an interconnected electronic network that has been established in over 170 countries.

Recently, APRIM was appointed as the Specialist Focal Point for Australia-Environmental Economics in the Network for Environmental Training at Tertiary Level in Asia and the Pacific (NETTLAP), a UN Environmental Programme project.

Publications: APRIM's recent publications include *Collaborative Policy-Related Research for the APEC Region Labour Market* (1996), *APEC Labour Market Information Statistical Database* (1996), *Environmental Problems and Sustainable Development: Environmental Accounting and Macroeconomics* (1995), and *Survey on Skill Development in Intercultural Teaching of International Studies* (1995).

Funding sources: The Institute receives overseas funding from the APEC Central Fund and UNESCO. Domestic funding comes from Federal Departments of Employment, Education, Training and Youth Affairs (DEETYA); Environment, Sports and Territories (DEST); Australian Agency for International Development (AusAID); Australian Vice-Chancellors' Committee (AVCC); and commercial activities.

Staffing: The Institute has three full-time and five part-time researchers, supported by three administrative staff.

Head of the institution: Dr. Richard Braddock, Director

Contact officer: Mr. Truong Nguyen, Executive Assistant to the Director

Asia-Pacific Research Institute
Graduate School of Management
Macquarie University
Sydney NSW 2109
AUSTRALIA
Tel: (61-2) 9850-9929
Fax: (61-2) 9850-9926
e-mail • aprim@mq.edu.au
URL • http://www.gsm.mq.edu.au/aprim/aprim.html

Murdoch University

Asia Research Centre on Social, Political and Economic Change

Background and objectives: The Asia Research Centre on Social, Political and Economic Change at Murdoch University was established in 1991 as a Special Research Centre of the Federal Australian Research Council. Its mission is to assess the impact of the emerging middle classes upon the social, economic, and political environment of the Asia-Pacific region and analyze the process of Australian and Western engagement with the region.

Programs: The Centre focuses partly on the impact of the "new rich" on the economic and political institutions of the Asia Pacific region. Recent studies range from an analysis of political opposition in East and Southeast Asia to the emergence of a new Indonesian business class in the post-oil era to a survey of household consumption in China.

The Centre also conducts consultancy work for government and business. In 1995, the Centre undertook a study of agribusiness opportunities in Sumatra and East Java, and was awarded a consultancy to study Asian literacy in the vocational and technical education sector.

The Centre actively sponsors and participates in public lectures, workshops, seminars, and conferences featuring leading academics, opinion makers, government officials, and entrepreneurs from around the world. It also supports graduate students at the M.A. and Ph.D. levels and hosts a stream of visiting scholars working in areas related to political, social, and economic change in Asia.

Publications: The Centre publishes working and policy papers, conference proceedings, and the quarterly newsletter *Asiaview*. Book publications include *Pathways to Asia: The Politics of Engagement* (1996), *Political Oppositions in Industrializing Asia* (1996), *The New Rich in Asia: Mobile Phones, McDonald's and Middle Class Revolution* (1995), and *The Press in New Order Indonesia* (1994).

Funding sources: The Centre is funded by a grant from the Australian Research Council, Murdoch University, and income from consultancies, publication sales, and private donations.

Staffing: The Centre has six full-time and two part-time researchers and a range of research fellows involved in over twenty projects. Six administrative and professional staff support the activities of the Centre.

Head of the institution: Prof. Richard Robison, Director

Business and government relations: Mrs. Cisca Spencer, Deputy Director

Contact officer: Mrs. Del Blakeway, Executive Officer

Asia Research Centre on Social, Political and Economic Change
Murdoch University
Murdoch, Western Australia, 6150
AUSTRALIA
Tel: (61-9) 360-2846
Fax: (61-9) 310-4944
e-mail • blakeway@sunarc.murdoch.edu.au
URL • http://www.hum.murdoch.edu.au/arc

University of Adelaide

Centre for Asian Studies

Background and objectives: The Centre for Asian Studies, established in 1975, is a nonprofit, interdisciplinary institute dedicated to research and teaching in the areas of Chinese and Japanese studies. It seeks to produce qualified scholars with language proficiency and research skills for the study of Asian history, culture, economics, and politics.

Programs: The Centre conducts studies of historical and contemporary social, cultural, political, and economic development of China and Japan. It offers a three-year sequence of Japanese, Chinese, and Vietnamese languages along with social science courses in areas such as the politics and economy of modern China and Japan, relations between Australia and Asia-Pacific, and Korean industrial sociology. Recent research covers Japan's postwar foreign policy, rural industrialization in China, and democratization and economic growth in the Asia region.

The Centre also consults government and private organizations on matters ranging from marketing strategies in China and Japan to issues of labor relations.

The Centre is active in organizing national and international seminars and conferences on such topics as political democracy and economic growth in the Asia region.

Publications: The Centre publishes monographs, journal articles, and reports featuring its in-house research. Recent publications include *Distant Asian Neighbors: Japan and South Asia* (1996), *Japan's Internationalization of the Grassroots Level* (1996), and *Rural Enterprises in China* (1994).

Funding sources: The Centre is funded by the Australian government, research grants from national and international organizations such as the World Bank and Japan Foundation, and overseas student fees.

Staffing: The Centre has eighteen full-time research and teaching staff supported by two administrative assistants.

Head of the institution: Prof. P.C. Jain, Director

Centre for Asian Studies
University of Adelaide
Adelaide, South Australia 5005
AUSTRALIA
Tel: (61-8) 8303-5815
Fax: (61-8) 8303-4388
e-mail • lowndes@arts.adelaide.edu.au
URL • http://chomsky.arts.adelaide.
edu.au/AsianStudies/Index.htm

University of Sydney

Research Institute for Asia and the Pacific

Background and objectives: The Research Institute for Asia and the Pacific, established in 1987, is a nonprofit, membership organization with the aim to assist Australian business to operate effectively in the Asia-Pacific region and to enhance Australian-Asian corporate, government, and academic collaboration. It seeks to provide relevant and current research by highly qualified Asia-Pacific specialists and equip organizations and individuals with practical skills and knowledge to succeed in business in the Asia-Pacific region.

Programs: The Institute conducts policy-relevant research with emphasis in sociocultural and environmental issues, human resource development and management, and international political economy. Recent research projects include an analysis of cross-cultural technology transfer, a study of natural resource management for the Mekong Basin, and an examination of urban services in South Pacific island states.

RIAP is the Australian Lead Institution for the Business Management Network-Human Resource Development Working Group of the Asia Pacific Economic Cooperation Forum, where it organizes research projects such as the Human Resources for Sustainable Development project.

The Institute also conducts public lectures, roundtable discussions, and confidential luncheon briefings on topics ranging from the status of women in Korea to business opportunities in Hong Kong for Australians.

Publications: The Institute publishes occasional papers and research papers. Representative titles include *Cultural, Social and Institutional Influences on Saving: Asia Viewed from Australia* (1996), *Australia's Asia Pacific Journey* (1993), and *Multilateral Partnership for ASEAN Security* (1993).

Funding sources: The Institute's funding is derived from its APEC-related research activities, individual and corporate membership fees, and sale of its publications.

Staffing: The Institute has two full-time researchers supported by University of Sydney consultant researchers and five administrative staff.

Head of the institution: Dr. Rikki Kersten, Director

Contact officer: Mr. Leslie Williams, APEC Research Manager

Research Institute for Asia and the Pacific
University of Sydney
Level 9 Shaw House, 49 York Street
Sydney, NSW, 2000
AUSTRALIA
Tel: (61-2) 9290-3233
Fax: (61-2) 9262-4819
e-mail • L.Williams@riap.biz.usyd.edu.au
URL • http://www.biz.usyd.edu.au/~riap/intro.htm

University of Wollongong

Centre for Research Policy

Background and objectives: The Centre for Research Policy, established in 1991, is a nonprofit institute dedicated to research and development in the structure, organization, and management of science, innovation, and research policy. It aims to enhance understanding of the links between science, technological innovation, and socioeconomic development and promote collaborative research and development projects in Australia and the Asia-Pacific region.

Programs: The Centre research projects investigate science policy, technology, culture, and industrial innovation. Projects are intended to produce short-term practical results that are linked with current policy concerns of the research community and decision makers. Research topics cover issues such as human resource development for effective technological transfer, organizational structures for the management of science, and international science and technology research linkages.

The Centre also offers consultancy and local and international training services in the areas of research management, technology, and science.

The Centre is Australia's Focal Point for the UNESCO-based Science and Technology Policy Asian Network (STEPAN) and is the Australian Lead Institution for the APEC Human Resource Development for Industry Technologies network.

In addition, the Centre offers Master's and Ph.D. programs in research policy, cross-cultural management, and international science and technology policy. It also organizes seminars and workshops on the management of technology, innovation, and science policy and has an active visiting fellows program, many of whom come from Britain, China, Korea, and Japan.

Publications: The Centre publishes research reports and findings in a variety of periodicals including the *Asian Studies Review*, *Journal of Industry Studies*, and *International Journal of Technology Management*. Recent publications include "Regional Empowerment in the New Global Science and Technology Order" (1995) and "Technology and Innovation Networks in the People's Republic of China" (1995).

Funding sources: The Centre is financially supported by the University of Wollongong, the Australian government, UNESCO, AusAID, and other national governments.

Staffing: The Centre has six full-time and two part-time researchers, supported by two administrative staff.

Head of the institution: Dr. Tim Turpin, Director

Contact officer: Mrs. Priscilla Kendall, Office Administrator

The Centre for Research Policy
University of Wollongong
Northfields Avenue, Wollongong, NSW, 2522
AUSTRALIA
Tel: (61) 42-213256
Fax: (61) 42-213257
e-mail • CRP@uow.edu.au
URL • http://www.uow.edu.au/crp/crp.htm

Asia 2000 Foundation of New Zealand

Background and objectives: Asia 2000 was founded in 1994 as an independent trust with charitable status to promote a major reorientation of New Zealand towards Asia by the year 2000. It aims to develop New Zealanders' knowledge and understanding of the countries and peoples of Asia; help New Zealanders develop the right skills to work effectively with their Asian counterparts; and build New Zealand's links with Asia.

Programs: Asia 2000 conducts four major programs. In its *Business Programme*, the Foundation helps the business sector develop greater understanding of the Asian market through fellowships, research grants, and support for workshops and conferences. In its *Education Programme*, Asia 2000 promotes the teaching of Asian studies in New Zealand as well as supports educational links with Asia by way of higher-education exchange programs, professional development grants, and scholarships such as the APEC and Rewi Alley Scholarships. In its *Media and Culture Programme*, the Foundation supports coverage of Asia in the New Zealand media by providing media travel awards, media exchanges, and media seminars and briefings. In its *Public Affairs Programme*, Asia 2000 promotes greater knowledge of Asia by conducting commissioned research on attitudes and opinions towards Asia and by organizing speaking engagements in main and secondary centers.

Publications: The Foundation publishes the bimonthly *Asia 2000 Foundation Review*, containing news and information about Asia and New Zealand.

Funding sources: The Foundation is funded by government grants, donations from the private sector, and interest receivable.

Staffing: Information not provided.

Head of the institution: Hon. Philip Burdon, Chairman

Contact officer: Mr. Phillip Gibson, Executive Director

Asia 2000 Foundation of New Zealand
Level 7, AMP House, Featherston Street
Wellington P.O. Box 10-144
NEW ZEALAND
Tel: (64-4) 471-2320
Fax: (64-4) 471-2330
e-mail • Asia2000@Asia2000.tradenz.co.nz
URL • http://www.asia2000.org.nz

Massey University

New Zealand Centre for Japanese Studies

Background and objectives: The New Zealand Centre for Japanese Studies at Massey University was established in 1987 to encourage New Zealanders to learn more about Japan, to mobilize existing resources for the benefit of all those interested in international affairs, and to advance the field of Japanese studies.

Programs: The Centre promotes awareness of New Zealand-Japanese relations in teaching institutions (both tertiary and secondary), the business community, the media, and the general public; helps New Zealand universities develop Japanese studies courses in history, politics, economics, science, technology, agriculture, business administration, music, and the arts; and administers several outside scholarships for New Zealanders to study in Japan or in New Zealand.

The Centre focuses especially on high-level post-graduate research, which may be sponsored or commissioned by interested parties.

Publications: The Centre publishes working papers and booklets on New Zealand-Japanese relations and the development of Japanese studies in New Zealand. A monthly newsletter covers current issues, forthcoming visits and exchanges, scholarships and appointments, new publications, and general information of interest to the academic and business communities.

Funding sources: The Centre's activities are funded primarily by Massey University and foundations including the Japan Foundation and the Sasakawa Foundation.

Staffing: The Centre has a director and an executive officer, with facilities for visiting or resident fellows.

Head of the institution: Dr. Roger Peren, Director

Contact officer: Appointment pending

New Zealand Centre for Japanese Studies
Massey University
Private Bag 11-222, Palmerston North
NEW ZEALAND
Tel: (64-6) 350-5473
Fax: (64-6) 350-5626
e-mail • nzcjs@massey.ac.nz

New Zealand Institute of Economic Research

Background and objectives: The New Zealand Institute of Economic Research (NZIER), established in 1958, is a nonprofit membership organization that provides research reports, economic advice, and economic forecasting services for its members.

Programs: NZIER develops quarterly economic forecasts by analyzing inflation, monetary conditions, wage tracks, prices, trade flows, exchange rates, investment, consumption, savings, international conditions, and fiscal policy. Based on these data, it publishes annual five-year forecasts for all the production sectors of the economy, and it provides monthly updates on economic development and other matters of business interest.

NZIER's quarterly survey of business opinion samples manufacturers, builders, architects, merchants, and the service sector to assess the general business situation, the labor market, the constraints on production, investment plans, costs, and prices.

The Institute also holds seminars to brief its members on economic forecasts, arranges lectures by distinguished speakers, and undertakes contract research for firms, private sector associations, and government bodies.

Publications: The Institute publishes *Quarterly Predictions, Quarterly Survey of Business Opinion, Industry Outlook*, and *Update*. Latest research monographs include *Full Employment: Whence It Came and Where It Went* (1996), *A Season of Excellence? An Overview of New Zealand Enterprise in the Nineties* (1996), and *In Defence of the Open Economy: A Personal Retrospective* (1996).

Funding sources: NZIER is funded by membership subscriptions and income from contract research.

Staffing: NZIER houses fourteen researchers and four administrative/support staff members.

Notes: The Institute confers the NZIER/Qantas Economics Award for significant contributions in applied economic research or economic policy making affecting New Zealand.

Head of the institution: Ms. Kerrin M. Vautier, Chairman

Contact officer: Dr. John Yeabsley, Director

New Zealand Institute of Economic Research
P.O. Box 3479, Wellington
NEW ZEALAND
Tel: (64-4) 472-1880
Fax: (64-4) 472-1211
e-mail • econ@nzier.org.nz
URL • http:// www.nbr.co.nz

Victoria University of Wellington

Centre for Strategic Studies

Background and objectives: The Centre for Strategic Studies (CSS) at Victoria University of Wellington was established in 1993 to provide a focal point for research and discussion on Asia-Pacific security from a New Zealand perspective.

Programs: The Centre conducts research on national security and defense, conflict resolution, and arms control and disarmament. It also examines the strategic implications of political, economic, social, and industrial issues such as human rights, the environment, and sustainable development.

Recent research projects include Asian security and regional security arrangements (especially ASEAN), Japan and the Asia-Pacific region, and post-Cold War international relations.

The Centre coordinates New Zealand's representation at the Working Groups of the Council for Security Cooperation in the Asia Pacific (CSCAP) and articulates its perspective in the biannual CSCAP Steering Committee.

Publications: CSS publishes a working paper series, featuring "work in progress" by scholars studying security issues.

The Centre also publishes, in book form, the proceedings of CSCAP Comprehensive Security Working Group Conferences held in Wellington and the results of specially commissioned work on security issues.

A quarterly bulletin describes the Centre's current activities and its involvement in CSCAP.

Recent books include *Unresolved Futures: Comprehensive Security in the Asia-Pacific Defense Arrangements* (1995) and *Maritime Futures: New Zealand and Its Strategic Maritime Environment* (1995).

Funding sources: CSS is funded by the Ministry of Defence, the New Zealand Defence Force, the Ministry of Foreign Affairs and Trade, and the Asia 2000 Foundation.

Staffing: CCS consists of three researchers and two administrative assistants.

Notes: The Centre regularly contributes "op ed" pieces for national newspapers and opinions for TV and radio news.

Head of the institution: Mr. Terence O'Brien, Director

Contact officer: Mr. David Dickens, Deputy Director

Centre for Strategic Studies
Victoria University
P.O. Box 600, Wellington
NEW ZEALAND
Tel: (64-4) 495-5434
Fax: (64-4) 496-5437
e-mail • css@matai.vuw.ac.nz
URL • http://www.vuw.ac.na/css

Victoria University of Wellington

Institute of Policy Studies

Background and objectives: The Institute of Policy Studies (IPS) was established in 1983 within the Victoria University of Wellington to coordinate international studies and promote the discussion of public policy issues considered important to New Zealand.

Programs: IPS conducts research on political, social, and economic issues; business and industrial policy; science and technology; communications; security and defense; environment; and foreign relations.

Recent topics include the trade policies of Japan, China, NAFTA countries, and the Pacific Island Forum countries; a comparison of policy developments in Australia and New Zealand; and parliamentary processes and electoral reform in New Zealand.

In collaboration with the State Services Commission, the Institute conducts policy seminars and symposiums for senior public service managers. Since 1993, two semi-autonomous research centers have functioned within the Institute. The Centre for Strategic Studies, funded by the Ministry of Foreign Affairs and Trade, the Ministry of Defence, and the NZ Defence Force, monitors the activities of a network of strategic studies institutions in the Asia-Pacific region. The Health Services Research Centre promotes and publicizes independent research on issues such as mental health, asthma, health service priority setting and technology assessment, primary health care evaluation, social services in the health system, and health care economics.

Publications: The Institute publishes the quarterly *IPS Newsletter.* Recent books include *New Zealanders of Asian Origin* (1996), *Income Distribution in New Zealand* (1996), *Social Assessment and Central Government* (1995), and *Reconciling Trade and the Environment Issues for New Zealand* (1995).

Funding sources: In addition to a grant from the Victoria University, IPS receives funds from both the public and private sectors in the form of project grants or fellowships.

Staffing: IPS consists of one director and three administrative officers.

Head of the institution: Prof. Gary Hawke, Director

Contact officer: Ms. Sharon Bowling, Executive Officer

Institute of Policy Studies
Victoria University of Wellington
6 Wai-te-ata Road, Kelburn
P.O. Box 600, Wellington
NEW ZEALAND
Tel: (64-4) 471-5307
Fax: (64-4) 473-1261
e-mail • ipos.dir@vuw.ac.nz

Victoria University of Wellington

New Zealand Institute of International Affairs

Background and objectives: The New Zealand Institute of International Affairs, established in 1934, is a nonprofit organization that seeks to create an informed policy-making environment by educating the public about the international issues confronting New Zealand. The Institute has a national office in Wellington and eight branches throughout New Zealand.

Programs: The Institute studies current problems and historical developments in New Zealand's relations with Asia and the Pacific, the Americas, Europe, and the Commonwealth. Recent research projects range from New Zealand trade policy since World War II to culture, ethnicity, and human rights in international relations.

The Institute also organizes meetings and seminars on international issues relevant to New Zealand's political and trade interests, such as New Zealand's relations with the ASEAN countries.

Publications: The Institute publishes the bimonthly journal *New Zealand International Review*. The most recent books published are *New Zealand and Australia: Negotiating Closer Economic Relations* (1995) and *New Zealand's Involvement in Middle East Defense and the Suez Crisis* (1994).

Funding sources: In addition to the provision of accommodation by Victoria University of Wellington, the Institute is funded by a grant from the Ministry of Foreign Affairs and Trade and by corporate, institutional, and individual membership dues.

Staffing: The Institute consists of one director and one secretary. Research activities are staffed on an ad hoc basis.

Notes: Since 1993, with the joint sponsorship of the New Zealand Chambers of Commerce and Industry, the Institute has awarded Media Prizes in print, radio, and television for the best reporting of international events relevant to New Zealand's interests.

Head of the institution: Mr. Giff Davidson, President

Contact officer: Mr. Bruce Brown, Director

The New Zealand Institute of International Affairs
Victoria University of Wellington
6 Waiteata Road, Kelburn
P.O. Box 600, Wellington
NEW ZEALAND
Tel: (64-4) 471-5356
Fax: (64-4) 473-1261

CANADA

Asia Pacific Foundation of Canada

Background and objectives: Headquartered in Vancouver, the Asia Pacific Foundation of Canada (APFC), an independent, nonprofit organization established in 1984 by an Act of Parliament, serves as a conduit for Canadians to meet the opportunities presented by the Asia-Pacific region's increasing economic, cultural, and political influence in the world.

Programs: APFC is the site of the Asia Pacific Economic Cooperation (APEC) Study Centre in Canada. It provides a wide range of information on the Asia-Pacific region and is a focal point for strategic research on Canada-APEC relations. In partnership with the government of Canada, the Foundation is developing a network of Canadian Education Centres in major Asian cities to assist recognized Canadian educational and training institutions market their services to international students and strengthen their ties with the Asia-Pacific. There are seven centers operating in Seoul, Taipei, Kuala Lumpur, Hong Kong, Singapore, Dahka, and Jakarta.

The Foundation also offers various programs aimed at the business community. It manages in-house cross-cultural training programs, Asia-Pacific breakfast updates and business opportunities seminars, as well as a network for Canadian and Asian businesswomen. The Foundation sponsors the GLOBE Series of biennial Expositions on Business and the Environment through its subsidiary, the GLOBE Foundation.

With an eye to building trans-Pacific networks, the Foundation provides the secretariats for two Asia Pacific-based economic groupings: the Canadian Committee of the Pacific Economic Cooperation Council (CANPECC) and the Canadian Committee of the Pacific Basin Economic Council (PBEC). The Foundation maintains computerized databases that include detailed information on corporations, specialists, and organizations that focus on the Asia-Pacific region. APFNET is a communications network that is available on a commercial basis to Canadians who are interested in the Asia-Pacific region. It electronically connects individuals and organizations in twenty countries, allowing a timely, cost-effective means to exchange ideas and information.

Publications: APFC publishes a wide range of research and background material that includes *Canada Asia Review (1997)*, APFC's first annual report on Canada's business and social rela-

tions with the Asia-Pacific; *Issues for APEC,* a series containing the work of the Study Teams of the APEC Study Centre in Canada; *Asia Pacific Papers*, a new series focusing on the policy aspects of contemporary political, economic, and social issues in the Asia-Pacific region; the *Country Backgrounder* series that focuses on Canada's economic relationship with sixteen countries of the Asia-Pacific; and *Succeeding: Profiles of Chinese-Canadian Entrepreneurs*, a report that studies Chinese-Canadian business in the Vancouver area and discusses issues of integration, networks, and bridge building.

In addition, APFC publishes the *Dialogue* newsletter, *Research Network News, Annual Report,* and *APEC Study Centre Reports.*

Funding sources: APFC receives much of its financial support from federal and provincial governments as well as a number of private sector companies. The balance of its revenues are made up of fees paid for Foundation programs.

Staffing: The Foundation employs about fifty people with the head office located in Vancouver, B.C., and regional offices in Saskatchewan, Manitoba, Ontario, and Quebec. The Research and Analysis Division and the APEC Study Centre have a staff of seven, including the vice-president, a director, a manager, and up to three graduate research interns.

Heads of the institution:
Dr. William Saywell, President

Michael E. J. Phelps, Chairman of the Board

Contact officer: Yuen Pau Woo, Director, Research and Analysis

Asia Pacific Foundation of Canada
666-999 Canada Place
Vancouver, BC
V6C 3E1
CANADA
Tel: (604) 684-5986
Fax: (604) 681-1370
e-mail • infoserv@apfc.apfnet.org
URL • http://www.apfnet.org

British Columbia Chamber of Commerce

Background and objectives: The British Columbia Chamber of Commerce is a volunteer, not-for-profit association, and serves its members as the provincial federation of autonomous community chambers of commerce, boards of trade, and corporate members. The Chamber now represents more than 20,000 businesses and ninety local chambers throughout the province. Known to be in operation since 1867, the Chamber was re-established in 1951 with the mandate to develop a true cross-section of opinions of the British Columbia business community and to present these to the provincial and federal governments; to promote trade and commerce; and to improve the economic and human well-being of the people of British Columbia.

Programs: The BC Chamber of Commerce mostly operates in the field of policy advising. It does this through numerous programs in which members participate in developing policy recommendations. The resulting *Policy and Positions Manual* comprehensively addresses the province-wide concerns of business.

Members also provide valuable input through fax polls, receive researched information on issues, and participate in joint initiatives to address policy concerns. The Chamber represents business on numerous provincial task forces, councils, and advisory committees.

Publications: The Chamber publishes the *Policy and Positions Manual;* the *Chamber Express,* a biweekly, single-sheet publication with short articles on multiple topics to keep membership up-to-date on the important issues facing business; the *Chamber Facts,* a single-sheet summary with facts and information on issues of particular importance; *The Voice of BC Business,* a semiannual publication providing coverage of long-term issues and information about major Chamber events; and the *Chamber Press Release,* a concise news "capsule" stating the official view of the Chamber on a public issue.

Funding sources: The Chamber is financed through membership dues.

Staffing: While policy forums and research are conducted on a volunteer basis, several staff assist with organizational functions.

Heads of the institution:
Naomi Yamamoto, Chair

E.A. (Ted) George, Executive Director

Contact officer:
E.A. (Ted) George, Executive Director

British Columbia Chamber of Commerce
1607-700 W. Pender
V6C 1G8
CANADA
Tel: (604) 683-0700
Fax: (604) 683-0416
URL • www.bcchamber.org

Business Council on National Issues

Background and objectives: The Business Council on National Issues is a nonpartisan and not-for-profit organization established in 1976 to enhance the role of Canadian chief executives in international economic, trade, environmental, and foreign affairs. With a membership composed of chief executives of 150 leading Canadian corporations, the Business Council serves as the senior voice of Canadian business on public policy issues in Canada and internationally. Its national focus is to help build a strong economy, progressive social policies, and healthy political institutions.

Programs: The Council engages in an active program of research, consultation, and advocacy. Priority issues are dealt with at the strategic level by the President and Chief Executive, the Executive Committee, and the Policy Committee. In addition to two standing initiatives on competitiveness and global strategy, task forces and committees focus on other priorities. Each task force comprises a small group of members with a specific mandate and a limited time-frame for achieving results.

Over the years, task forces have examined international trade and investment, international competitiveness, foreign policy and international security, sustainable development, educational reform, and monetary policy, among others.

Publications: The BCNI publishes *National and Global Perspectives: Canadian Business Leaders Speak,* a quarterly publication, and issues press releases.

Funding sources: The Business Council is supported through membership fees.

Staffing: An Ottawa-based Secretariat, which reports to the Council's President and Chief Executive, provides policy research and supports the Council's committees, task forces, and initiatives. The Council's Board of Directors, known as the Policy Committee, comprises thirty-six members who meet at least four times annually. BCNI members meet twice yearly to discuss the Council's program. They also can participate directly on committees, task forces, and in periodic forums and roundtables.

Heads of the institution:
Mr. Thomas d'Aquino, President and Chief Executive

Mr. Guy Saint-Pierre, Chairman

Contact officer: Mr. Sam Boutziouvis, Senior Associate, Policy and Economist

Business Council on National Issues
90 Sparks Street, Suite 806
Ottawa, Ontario
K1P 5B4
CANADA
Tel: (613) 238-3727
Fax: (613) 236-8679
e-mail • bcni@flexnet.com

C.D. Howe Institute

Background and objectives: The C.D. Howe Institute was founded in 1973 as an independent, nonprofit, research and educational institution to identify current and emerging economic and social policy issues facing Canadians; to analyze options for public- and private-sector responses; to recommend particular policy options that best serve the national interest; and to communicate the conclusions of its research to a domestic and international audience in a clear, nonpartisan way.

Programs: The Institute provides a wide range of forums for research and analysis of important public policy issues. Its regular policy roundtables are attended by prominent policy makers in Canada. There were twenty-six roundtables in 1995 featuring notable names such as John Crow, former Governor of the Bank of Canada, who reflected upon Canada's zero inflation policy, and Douglas Hurd, former UK Secretary of State, who talked about Britain and the future of Europe.

The Institute regularly holds policy conferences to discuss research work in progress with the Institute's members, senior civil servants, academics, and specialists to help shape the Institute's public policy work. The Institute currently has three committees. The Western Regional Committee (WRC) involves the Institute's members in Western Canada more closely in its ongoing research and advisory activities. The WRC also has an active program of policy roundtable meetings in major cities in Western Canada. The Comité-Québec allows the Institute's members in Quebec to become more actively involved in the Canadian public policy debate. The Institute is also a co-sponsor of the British-North American Committee (BNAC) with the National Planning Association in the United States and the British-North American Research Association in London, England. The BNAC studies and comments on the developing relationships between Britain, the United States, and Canada. It seeks to promote clearer understanding of the economic opportunities and problems facing the three countries, explore areas of cooperation and possible friction, and develop constructive responses. In 1995, working groups examined research on issues such as income disparities, transatlantic relations, and public pensions.

Publications: The Institute publishes the *C.D. Howe Institute Commentary* (occasional); an *Annual Report;* the *Policy Study Series* (occasional); and the *Observation Series* (occasional). The Institute has also published *The Social Policy Challenge* (a fifteen-volume series). Among the Institute's books are *Tomorrow the Pacific* (1991), *Canadian-Japanese Economic Relations in a Triangular Perspective* (1988); and *Nikka Kankei: Japanese-Canadian Relations, the Opportunities Ahead* (1988).

Funding sources: The Institute's main funding sources are members' donations and fees.

Staffing: The Institute's research staff includes two senior and one junior policy analysts. Some outside academics appear in C.D. Howe's publications as Senior Fellows of the institute.

Head of the institution: Mr. Thomas E. Kierans, President and Chief Executive Officer

Contact officer: Ms. Angela Ferrante, Executive Vice President and Chief Operating Officer

C.D. Howe Institute
125 Adelaide Street East
Toronto, Ontario
M5C 1L7
CANADA
Tel: (416) 865-1904
Fax: (416) 865-1866
e-mail • cdhowe@cdhowe.org
URL • http://www.cdhowe.org

Canada-ASEAN Centre

Background and objectives: The Canada-ASEAN Centre (CAC), a project of the Canadian International Development Agency, was established in 1989 to raise awareness and act as a catalyst for new forms of cooperation between Canada and the countries comprising the Association of Southeast Asian Nations (ASEAN), specifically in the areas of science and technology, environment, and infrastructure development. Through building formal and informal networks in these areas, the Centre stimulates the flow of information and collaboration necessary for long-term, mutually beneficial relationships. This is in direct support of Canada's foreign policy objectives and official development assistance efforts.

Programs: The Centre's work focuses in three key industrial areas: science and technology, the environment, and infrastructure. CAC initiatives include the building of formal and informal contact networks, and the dissemination of relevant information to interested parties in the public and private sectors in Canada and ASEAN.

The Centre operates a Media Exchange Support Program, a Speakers Exchange Fund, and Materials Procurement Fund. The Centre also cooperates with the Canadian Embassies and High Commissions in ASEAN to promote Canada through various targeted public relations activities.

The Centre also produces and distributes publicity materials, supporting media initiatives, and facilitating the exchange of selected speakers and experts in fields that parallel the CAC's program areas.

Publications: The Centre publishes *Rapport*, a quarterly newsletter; program newsletters and specific briefing papers; and relevant news articles.

Funding sources: The Centre is funded by the Canadian International Development Agency.

Staffing: CAC's overall operations are overseen by a Joint Committee comprised of representatives from the Canadian International Development Agency and the Department of External Affairs and International Trade. Day-to-day operations are overseen by an executive director and deputy executive director. They are supported by four staff members in Singapore.

Head of the institution: Mr. Ian B. Robertson, Executive Director, Singapore

Contact officer: Mr. Wilfred Hass, Director of Communications

Canada-ASEAN Centre
40 Bukit Pasoh Road
SINGAPORE, 089854
Tel: (65) 325-2300
Fax: (65) 221-7885
e-mail • wilfhass@pacific.net.sg

The Canadian Consortium on Asia Pacific Security

Background and objectives: The Canadian Consortium on Asia Pacific Security (CANCAPS), is a nonprofit association established in 1993 to promote research, publication, and public awareness activities on Asia-Pacific security issues, with a particular emphasis on Canadian involvement.

Programs: CANCAPS's major activities include an annual conference featuring a mix of plenary and workshop sessions dealing with substantive security issues, a business meeting, and various working groups. Currently, there are three working groups dealing with sustainable development and human security in Asia, environmental and oceans issues, shared human security in South Asia, and the regional security outlook.

CANCAPS members are also engaged in informal networking activities with each other and with officials and scholars across Asia-Pacific.

Publications: The Consortium publication program includes *CANCAPS Bulletin*, a newsletter which is published three or four times a year, featuring articles about Asia-Pacific security developments, reports of Canadian government policy, updates on the Council for Security Cooperation in Asia Pacific (CSCAP), and information about new resources and upcoming events; and *CANCAPS Papers,* a series of working papers on Asia-Pacific security issues. Recent titles included "Conditional Multilateralism: Chinese Views on Order and Regional Security," "Unconventional Security and the Republic of Korea: A Preliminary Assessment," "Making Mischief in the South China Sea," "Sustainable Development and Security in Southeast Asia," "Reviewing Regionalism: Organizational Lessons for Asia Pacific Leaders," and "Choosing Multilateralism: Canada's Experience after World War II and Canada in the New International Environment."

The Consortium also publishes *CANCAPS Directory,* a guide to Canadian specialists in Asia-Pacific security issues, as well as to Canadian government officials dealing with Asia.

Funding sources: CANCAPS's main funding source has been the Canadian Department of Foreign Affairs and International Trade. It has also received funding for specific activities from the Canadian Department of National Defense and from the Vancouver Port Corporation. The Consortium is also supported by the University of British Columbia's Institute of International Relations and York University's Centre for International and Strategic Studies, where the two CANCAPS administrative offices are located.

Staffing: CANCAPS is governed by an eleven-member Board of Directors. It has two part-time administrators, one at UBC, one at York.

Notes: CANCAPS membership is open to any Canadian individual interested in Asia-Pacific security.

Heads of the institution:
Dr. David Dewitt, President

Dr. Brian Job, Vice-President

Contact officer: Ms. Shannon Selin, Publications and Communications Coordinator

The Canadian Consortium on Asia Pacific Security
Institute of International Relations
University of British Columbia
C456-1866 Main Mall
Vancouver, BC
V6T 1Z1 CANADA
Tel: (604) 822-5480
Fax: (604) 822-5540
e-mail • cancaps@unixg.ubc.ca

Canadian Council for International Co-operation

Background and objectives: The Canadian Council for International Co-operation (CCIC) is a coalition of Canadian voluntary organizations committed to achieving global development in a peaceful and healthy environment with social justice, human dignity, and participation for all. CCIC serves its member organizations primarily through governmental lobbying and advocacy. Since 1968, this non-governmental organization has supported the work of its members through networking, leadership, information, training, and coordination and represents members' interests to government and others.

Programs: CCIC is composed of several units including Programs, Policy Team, Organizational Development Team, Communications Team, Organizational Services, and the Canada-Haiti Humanitarian Alliance Fund.

During 1995-96, CCIC sought to support and lead a process of transformation in the NGO community by pressing for the establishment of a Transition and Innovation Fund at the Canadian International Development Agency (CIDA) to help NGOs reorganize themselves and diversify sources of financing, and by creating a Task Force on Building Public Support for Sustainable Human Development to help the community identify new roles for NGOs and new ways of working with Canadians to advance international cooperation.

CCIC also launched a dialogue on national unity, debating the implications of various scenarios for international cooperation. As part of its leadership and coordination mandate, CCIC also administers the Canada-Haiti Humanitarian Alliance Fund (CHHAF) under contract with CIDA's Americas Branch. Formerly a component of the Reconstruction and Rehabilitation Fund, the CHHAF was established in 1993 to promote democratization in Haiti during a period of intense civil conflict.

Publications: CCIC publishes *Au Courant,* the Council's newsletter; an *Annual Report;* and *Who's Who in International Development,* containing detailed portraits of 120 Canadian NGOs.

Funding sources: The Council's main support comes from CIDA and membership fees.

Staffing: CCIC has twelve program officers and eleven administrative staff.

Head of the institution: Ms. Betty Plewes, President and Chief Executive Officer

Contact officer: Ms. Maria Desjardins, Executive Assistant

Canadian Council for International Co-operation
1 Nicholas Street
Suite 300
Ottawa, Ontario
K1N 7B7
CANADA
Tel: (613) 241-7007
Fax: (613) 241-5302
e-mail • ccic@web.net
URL • http://www.web.apc.org/ccic-ccci

Canadian Council for International Peace and Security

Background and objectives: The Canadian Council for International Peace and Security, formally known as the Centre for Global Security, helps develop and advance innovative Canadian policies on issues of international peace and security in keeping with Canada's internationalist tradition. The Council comprises Canadians from different walks of life who have a common interest in seeing an independent, informed, reliable voice in Canada on issues of peace and security. The Council promotes public debate and dialogue by providing independent views and sources of information to the Canadian government and public on matters on such issues.

Programs: Based on its continuing research projects, the Council conducts workshops bringing together practitioners, researchers, and other interested individuals including media and NGO representatives. The Council also holds public seminars on issues of international peace and security, cooperating with other organizations as appropriate in sponsoring presentations by distinguished Canadian and international speakers.

Recent topics for workshops, conferences, roundtables, and informal consultations include the following: "Canadian Arms Export Control Regulations," "Developing a UN Mechanism to Monitor the Efficacy and Impact of Sanctions," "Progress in International Efforts to Constrain Light Weapons Transfers," "NATO Enlargement," "Conflict Prevention, Management and Resolution in Southern Africa," "The Comprehensive Test-ban Treaty and Related Issues: An Assessment of the Negotiations and Future Canadian Policy," "Raising the Profile of Peacekeeping in the US Congress," and "The United Nations Operation in Haiti: Lessons Learned."

The Council's activities during 1996 and 1997 also included studies in "Unconventional Means for UN Financing," "The Application of Lessons Learned from Recent Peace Operations," and "NATO and European Union Enlargement: Security Problems of the Central European States."

Publications: The Council publishes *CCIPS Reports,* including timely information and analysis on current issues, and the *Aurora Papers,* presenting the results of research projects and workshops.

Funding sources: The Council raises its core funding from individuals, foundations, and corporations.

Staffing: The Council is composed of a small group of officers, including the vice-chair, the secretary/treasurer, and the executive director.

Heads of the institution:
Mr. Maurice Archdeacon, Chair

Mr. Douglas Fraser, Executive Director

Contact officer: Ms. Hélène Haddad, Administrative Officer

Canadian Council for International Peace and Security
300-1 Nicholas Street
Ottawa, Ontario
K1N 7B7
CANADA
Tel: (613) 562-2736
Fax: (613) 562-2741
e-mail • ccips@web.apc.org
URL • www.web.net/~ccips

Canadian Foundation for the Americas/Fondation Canadienne pour les Amériques

Background and objectives: The Canadian Foundation for the Americas (FOCAL), established in 1990, is an independent, non-profit organization that aims to deepen the knowledge of Canadians and Canadian institutions about Latin America and the Caribbean and contribute to a better understanding of Canada's role in the Americas. It seeks to help develop informed and effective policies enabling Canada to compete successfully in hemispheric markets and to promote lasting linkages between Canadian organizations and their counterparts in the Americas. FOCAL encourages a dialogue on hemispheric affairs between policy makers and other sectors of Canadian society and fosters mutual understanding between the peoples of Canada, Latin America, and the Caribbean.

Programs: FOCAL carries out public education and scholarship programs, as well as research activities. Its Public Education Programs include conferences, seminars, lectures, and workshops in Canada to analyze and assess important policy-relevant issues. These events engage high-profile Latin American, Caribbean, and Canadian speakers in discussions with senior policy makers, academics, and representatives of the private sector and NGOs. Its "Governance in Haiti: Strengthening the State and Democratic Development" conference, held in Ottawa in November 1996, for example, debated the issue of democratic governance by analyzing the Haitian case and examining Canada's involvement in strengthening the state in Haiti.

FOCAL's policy roundtables and meetings provide a forum for the review and analysis of proposed initiatives, current policy, and long-term Canadian strategy in the Americas.

FOCAL's scholarship programs aim to build a cadre of Canadians with special interest and expertise in the region. By enabling Canadian journalists to carry out research in the region on a topic of their choice, its Media Fellowships increase knowledge about the region while building a network of journalists with special interest in hemispheric affairs. Its national MBA Internship Program in the commercial section of Canadian missions educates Canadian MBA students about Canada-Latin America/Caribbean business relations and the business environments of the region.

In addition, FOCAL conducts policy-oriented research on issue or country/region-specific themes that are priorities of Canada's foreign, trade, and development policies. These include hemispheric integration and trade policy; governance and security; democratization and human rights; environment; specific aspects of Canadian policy toward Latin America and the Caribbean; and Canada's bilateral relations and its relations with the region through multilateral organizations.

Publications: *FOCAL Update / Le point FOCAL*, a newsletter, is published three times a year. FOCAL's *Occasional Papers: The FOCAL Papers / Les cahiers de FOCAL*, are published five times annually. Recent books include *Which Future for the Americas? Four Scenarios* (also available in French and in Spanish), *Beyond Mexico* (co-published with Carleton University Press, 1995), and *Natural Allies? Canadian and Mexican Perspectives on International Security* (co-published with Carleton University Press, 1996).

Funding sources: FOCAL receives funding from public and private sources, including the Department of Foreign Affairs and International Trade (Canada) and the Canadian International Development Agency (CIDA).

Staffing: FOCAL employs nine full-time staff at its head office in Ottawa, including five program officers. In addition, it maintains small offices on campuses in Western Canada, Atlantic Canada, and Quebec.

Heads of the institution:
Mr. Dean J. Browne, Executive Director

Ms. Juanita Montalvo, Director of Program

Contact officer: Mr. Brian Cameron, Director of Communications

Canadian Foundation for the Americas (FOCAL)
55 Murray Street, Suite 230
Ottawa, Ontario K1N 5M3
CANADA
Tel: (613) 562-0005
Fax: (613) 562-2525
e-mail • focal@focal.ca
URL • http://www.focal.ca

Canadian Institute of International Affairs

Background and objectives: The Canadian Institute of International Affairs (CIIA) was founded in 1928 as an independent, nonprofit organization to promote an understanding of international affairs by providing interested Canadians with a nonpartisan nation-wide forum for informed discussion, analysis and debate. CIIA's focus is on contemporary world events and trends with particular reference to the concerns of Canadians and the policy options for Canada. CIIA consists of a national office and eighteen branches in cities across Canada: Calgary, Halifax, Kingston, London, Ottawa, St. John, South Saskatchewan, Toronto, Victoria, Hamilton, Kitchener-Waterloo, Montreal, Regina, Saskatoon, Thunder Bay, Vancouver, and Winnipeg.

Programs: CIIA's activities include speakers programs, seminars, conferences, briefing missions designed for CEOs/Chairpersons/Senior Executives, study trips, publications, working groups, and research. A number of CIIA's activities have an Asia-Pacific focus. The Institute has conducted a number of briefing missions for CEOs and equivalents in the Asia-Pacific region including a briefing tour to Tokyo, China, Hong Kong, Southeast Asia (Manila, Brunei, Indonesia, Malaysia, and Singapore), Taiwan, South Korea, and Vietnam. The CIIA held its 60th Anniversary Foreign Policy Conference on the topic of "New Realities in the Pacific."

Publications: Since 1946, CIIA has published *International Journal,* a quarterly journal that provides scholarly analysis of different aspects of international affairs primarily by devoting each issue to a different theme; *Behind the Lines,* a thematically distinctive quarterly pitched to an audience of informed generalists whose concerns span the full spectrum of global issues, this publication has covered topics ranging from the political economy of trade policy and transnational relations, to ethnic politics, migration, and underdevelopment; and *Contemporary Affairs,* a recently revived series of pamphlets on Canadian foreign policy focuses on subjects that examine Canada's national interest.

Funding sources: CIIA is financed by individual and corporate donations.

Staffing: The CIIA has fifteen staff and fellows at its head office in Toronto.

Heads of the institution:
Mr. Peter G. White, Chairman of the Board

Mr. Alan W. Sullivan, President & Chief Executive Officer

Contact officers:
Mr. Mark Adler, Director, Corporate Programs

Ms. Nancy Snelgrove, Office Manager

Canadian Institute of International Affairs
5 Devonshire Place
Toronto, Ontario
M5S 2C8
CANADA
Tel: (416) 979-1851
Fax: (416) 979-8575
URL • http://www.trinity.utoronto.ca/ciia

Canadian Institute of Strategic Studies

Background and objectives: The Canadian Institute of Strategic Studies (CISS) is a nonprofit, nonpartisan organization founded in 1976 to stimulate public awareness and informed opinion on issues of strategic and national security importance to Canada. It considers foreign and defense policy matters; approaches to security and conflict resolution; security arrangements; peacekeeping and conflict resolution; and economic, environmental, and defense industrial strategies. In addition, the Institute is interested in the increase of Canadian participation in regional defense agreements.

Programs: CISS conducts research into national security matters relating especially to Canada's role and interests in national and international affairs and participates in public education through the publication of research and position papers. The Institute's research focuses on military and foreign policy studies, economic and defense industry issues, and alternative security studies.

The Institute hosts two annual seminars. Each spring the CISS conducts a seminar dealing with contemporary issues concerning Canadian foreign and defense policy. The Spring 1996 seminar was on "Canada's Strategic Interests in the New Europe." This seminar served to provide an assessment of Canada's future endeavors in Europe as presented by Ambassadors from Poland, Ukraine, and the European Union along with experts of the Canadian Department of Foreign Affairs & International Trade and the Department of National Defence.

Each autumn the CISS conducts a seminar entitled "The Canadian Strategic Forecast." The topic for 1996 was "CSF97: Canada and the World: Non-Traditional Security Threats."

Recently the Institute had mutual exchange visits with the Beijing International Institute for Strategic Studies and the Shanghai Institute of International Affairs.

Publications: The Institute publishes proceedings of both Spring and Autumn annual seminars. Recent titles have included *Canada's Strategic Interests in the New Europe; The Military in Modern Democratic Society; The Republic of South Africa: Prospects and Problems; The Canadian Defence Policy Review; NATO and Europe: How Relevant to Canadian Security?; Peacekeeping;* and *Peacemaking or War: International Security Enforcement.* Other publications include McNaughton Papers; *Strategic Datalinks,* on topics such as Canada's shrinking defense industrial base; Nigeria's military governance; Canada and Guatemala's struggle for democracy; submarines, Canada and the United States; Bosnia, Eastern Europe and the future of NATO; *Strategic Profile: Canada;* and various books. CIIS has an editorial role in the *Canadian Defence Quarterly.*

Funding sources: CISS's funding is obtained through memberships, grants, and contracts.

Staffing: CISS has a staff of six, including the director of finance and administration and the director of publications.

Heads of the institution:

Dr. Alex Morrison, Executive Director

Mr. James Hanson, Associate Executive Director

Contact officer: Dr. Alex Morrison, Executive Director

Canadian Institute of Strategic Studies
2300 Yonge Street, Suite 402
Box 2321
Toronto, Ontario
M4P 1E4
CANADA
Tel: (416) 322-8128
Fax: (416) 322-8129
e-mail • ciss@inforamp.net
URL • http://www.ciss.ca

Carleton University

Centre for Trade Policy and Law

Background and objectives: The Centre for Trade Policy and Law (CTPL) was established in 1989 to promote greater public understanding of trade and investment policy issues, to foster independent analysis and research on trade policy and legal issues, and to encourage the development of trade policy professionals and practitioners. CTPL is jointly sponsored by the Norman Paterson School of International Affairs at Carleton University and the Faculty of Law at the University of Ottawa.

Programs: Through its conferences and seminar programs, CTPL has successfully brought together experts from within Canada and overseas to discuss key policy issues facing Canada as a trading nation in the 1990s and beyond. CTPL's expanding professional development and executive training programs provide public and private sector specialists with expert advice and specialized training on a number of international economic and trade policy and law issues.

CTPL collaborates jointly with the Centre for Negotiation and Dispute Resolution of the Norman Paterson School of International Affairs (NPSIA). CTPL also acts as the Canadian Secretariat for the Pacific Trade and Development Conference (PAFTAD). The Centre also assists in the development of the Pacific Economic Research Consortium (PERC) whose mandate is to foster greater involvement by economists from a number of universities across Canada in research on trade and investment issues in the Asia-Pacific region.

Senior CTPL staff teach graduate courses on trade policy at NPSIA, Carleton University and on trade law at the Faculty of Law, University of Ottawa.

Publications: CTPL offers a variety of its own publications and those of PAFTAD. Recent books include *China and the World Trade Organization: Requirements, Realities, and Resolution* (1996) and *Managing US-Japanese Trade Disputes: Are There Better Ways?* (1996). The Occasional Papers Series in 1996 included such titles as "Can't See the Forest for the Trees: A Critical Assessment of the Trade and Environment Debate and an Analysis of Proposed Reforms," "Dealing with a 'Single' Market: European Integration and Canada's Market Access Challenge," "Doing the Right Thing: Regional Integration and the Multilateral Trade Regime," "A Multilateral Agreement on Foreign Direct Investment: Why Now?" and "What's Next: Negotiating Rules for a Global Economy." Decision Quebec Series recent titles include "The Implications for US Trade Policy of an Independent Quebec" and "Washington and 'An Act Respecting the Sovereignty of Quebec.'" Donner Canadian Policy Papers recent publications include "International Agreements and the Cultural Industries" and "Constables, Content, Competition, and the 'Information Superhighway.'"

Seminar/Colloquia Series include Proceedings from various roundtables, workshops, and seminars on topics such as Canada-United States-Mexico trade negotiations, economic developments in the Southern Cone of Latin America, the transition of Soviet and East European economies and its implications for China and the Pacific region, the GATT agricultural trade negotiations, ASEAN economic cooperation, APEC, and economic cooperation between Japan, the West Pacific, and the Americas.

In addition, the Centre publishes policy debates and joint policy papers. Examples of PAFTAD publications include "Environment and Development in the Pacific" and "Corporate Links and Foreign Direct Investment in Asia and the Pacific."

Funding sources: CTPL has received funding from the Canadian Department of Foreign Affairs and International Trade through its Centre for International Business Studies (CIBS) program and "in kind" support from the two sponsoring universities. Externally supported research projects, training activities, and publications sales are other important sources of funds.

Staffing: CTPL staff is comprised of one director, five research associates, and three administrative staff members.

Head of the institution: Mr. Dennis Browne, Director

Contact officer: Ms. Maria Isolda P. Guevara, Research Associate

---

Centre for Trade Policy and Law
Social Sciences Research Building, Room 106
Carleton University
1125 Colonel By Drive
Ottawa, Ontario K1S 5B6
CANADA
Tel: (613) 520-6696
Fax: (613) 520-3981
e-mail • ctpl@carleton.ca
URL • http://www.carleton.ca/ctpl

Centre for Asia-Pacific Initiatives

Background and objectives: The Centre for Asia-Pacific Initiatives (CAPI), established in 1988, conducts and supports Asia-Pacific public policy research and related initiatives. CAPI encourages the development of the University of Victoria's Asia-Pacific programs and resources. Linkages are established with other centers on campus for purposes of collaborative research, as well as with individuals and institutions across Canada and in the Asia-Pacific.

Programs: CAPI's research work focuses on development of economic law in Southeast Asia, Sino-Canadian trade and investment in the global context, Chinese property concepts and institutions, and Japanese management paradigms.

CAPI also supports the work of colleagues at the University of Victoria through its Faculty Research Development Grants and its annual Faculty Fellowship Programs. Associates who share research interests are attached to the Centre.

Publications: CAPI publishes the *Asia-Pacific News*, a newsletter published three times a year; the *Occasional Papers Series* that has included such titles as "A Survey of Food Consumption in Thailand," "An Analysis of Import Protection as Export Promotion," "Customized Software: Strategies for Acquiring and Sustaining Competitive Advantage: A Japanese Perspective," "Feminist Perspectives on Development: Why Leprosy Is a Feminist Issue," and "Competition for Power and the Challenges of Reform in Post-Deng China."

Recent CAPI *Conference Proceedings* include "The Asia-Pacific Region and the Expanding Borders of the WTO: Implications, Challenges and Opportunities" and "Institution Building, Capacity Development and the Promotion of Human Rights in Southeast Asia."

Funding sources: Programs are generally funded by third-party sources, such as foundations and ODA agencies, in addition to the University of Victoria.

Staffing: CAPI has eight people on its executive committee, nine faculty/staff, and eight CAPI Associateships.

Head of the institution: Prof. William A. W. Neilson, Director

Contact officer: Ms. Barbara Duffield, Assistant Director

Centre for Asia-Pacific Initiatives
Begbie Building
University of Victoria
P.O. Box 1700
Victoria, BC
V8W 2Y2
CANADA
Tel: (250) 721-7020
Fax: (250) 721-3107
e-mail • CAPISEC@UVVM.UVic.CA
URL • http://www.kafka.uvic.ca/~capiexec

The Conference Board of Canada

Background and objectives: The Conference Board of Canada, established in 1954 as a not-for-profit applied research institution, provides public policy information to help its members anticipate and respond to the changing global economy through the development and exchange of knowledge about organizational strategies and practices, emerging economic and social trends, and key public policy issues. Members are primarily Canadian business, government, and public sector organizations. The Board's partners include organizations with an interest in the Canadian economy, public policies, and organizational practices. The Conference Board also has over a decade of experience dealing with private and public officials in India, China, Japan, Southeast Asia, Europe, Latin America, and other parts of the world.

Programs: The Conference Board offers an extensive international program that aims to be a leading source of insight and intelligence on strategic issues affecting Canadian businesses as they compete globally. The research division provides timely research on trade, investment, and financing issues, and insights on opportunities in new markets to its membership.

The Board also produces concise briefings, *Building Global Business*, which focus on the experiences of Canadian organizations in emerging markets.

Other programs include global business seminars and workshops on specific markets; business briefings based on international business practices in key countries; custom information services to answer questions on specific issues; and counseling, training, and orientation to members (for a fee).

Extensive network systems are offered to bring together executives with similar responsibilities in their organization or with interest in a particular subject in regular closed-door meetings to learn from the experiences of peers. These networks include the Asia Pacific Business Research Council, the Integrated Risk Management Council, the Global Integrated Risk Management Council, the Canadian Council of Logistics, the North American Council of Logistics, the International Human Resources Management, the International Organization and Management, the China Human Resources Council, and the Global Leadership Learning Network.

Publications: The Conference Board publishes *Business Outlook*, a study of Canada's key markets; *World Outlook*, a quarterly global economic forecast covering prospects for the North American, Western European, and Asia-Pacific economies in the next two years; and *North American Outlook*, a detailed annual assessment of the three NAFTA economies. It also publishes technical papers series, in conjunction with a series of monographs, and executive summaries. Some recent examples include *Marketing Case Studies and a Training Curriculum for SME Managers in the APEC Region* (1996); *Prospering in Change—Lessons from the International Executive Study Tour in the Asia Pacific Region* (1995); *Canadian Trade Policy Options in the Asia Pacific Region: A Business View* (1994); and *Industrial Environmental Management in Asia-Pacific—Comparative Report* (1994).

Funding sources: The Conference Board of Canada is funded entirely by contributions of its 600-plus members, consisting primarily of Canadian businesses and government and public sector agencies.

Staffing: The Conference Board has a total staff of 190, of whom six are executive, ninety are research, forty-seven are management, and forty-seven are administrative.

Head of the institution: Dr. James R. Nininger, President and Chief Executive Officer

Contact officer: Dr. Charles Barrett, President, The Niagara Institute and Vice-President, Business Research

The Conference Board of Canada
255 Smyth Road
Ottawa, Ontario
K1H 8M7
CANADA
Tel: (613) 526-3280
Fax: (613) 526-5385
e-mail • barrett@conferenceboard.ca
URL • http://www.conferenceboard.ca

The Fraser Institute

Background and objectives: The Fraser Institute is a nonpartisan, nonprofit organization founded in 1974 to redirect public attention to the role markets can play in providing for the economic and social well-being of Canadians.

Programs: The Institute's research focuses on areas such as welfare reform, privatization, taxation, free trade, government debt, education, poverty, deregulation, health care, labor markets, economic restructuring, and the role of government.

The Institute's work is carried out by different divisions such as the International Centre for the Study of Public Debt, which publishes comprehensive measurements of the extent of government indebtedness; the Fiscal Policy Studies Group, which produces information concerning the taxation and spending behavior of governments at all levels in Canada and makes international comparisons of Canada's fiscal position; and the Events Division, which conducts national and international seminars, conferences, and luncheons.

The Institute also conducts a nationwide series of Student Seminars on Public Policy Issues, which are attended by students from nearly 200 universities and colleges, and the National Media Archive, which maintains the only live data base of the current and historic news and public affairs programming of the two main Canadian television networks.

Publications: The Institute publishes *Fraser Forum*, a monthly publication; *On Balance*, a monthly publication of the National Media Archive; *Critical Issues Bulletins*, which is published six to ten times a year; *Fraser Folio*, a weekly newssheet to radio talk shows; and *Canadian Student Review*. Recent books include *Economic Freedom of the World 1975-1995* (1996), *NAFTA and the Environment* (1993), and *Innovation Policy and Canada's Competitiveness* (1991).

Funding sources: The Fraser Institute has an annual budget of nearly three million dollars. The Institute is financed by the contributions of individual and corporate members, grants, and the sale of its publications.

Staffing: The Institute maintains a core professional staff of nine from a total full-time staff of twenty-five.

Head of the institution: Dr. Michael Walker, Executive Director

Contact officer: David Hanley, Director of Communications

The Fraser Institute
626 Bute Street, 2nd Floor
Vancouver, BC
V6E 3M1
CANADA
Tel: (604) 688-0221
Fax: (604) 688-8539
e-mail • info@fraserinstitute.ca
URL • http://www.fraserinstitute.ca

Joint Centre for Asia Pacific Studies

Background and objectives: The University of Toronto-York University Joint Centre for Asia Pacific Studies recognizes the importance of Canada's economic, political, and cultural ties with the Asia-Pacific. Founded in 1974, the Joint Centre promotes inter-university collaborative research and teaching on East and Southeast Asia.

Programs: Many of the Centre's research projects focus on contemporary policy-related issues, with a broad regional focus. These include a study on regionalization in Eastern Asia and a cluster of activities centering on regional security issues.

The Centre also has a number of country-oriented initiatives, focusing on Hong Kong, Vietnam, and Korea. A new Korea initiative is the Canada-Korea Forum, a high-level group to exchange views on Canada-Korea bilateral relations and larger regional and global developments. The Centre's Asian Business Studies Program offers courses on the business behavior and the cultural, institutional, and political environment of business in Asia-Pacific countries. In addition, the Joint Centre houses the Canada and Hong Kong Resource Centre, which has a collection of over 10,000 books and other materials focusing on developments in Hong Kong, Canada-Hong Kong relations, and Hong Kong immigrant communities in Canada.

Publications: The Joint Centre publishes Eastern Asia Policy Papers, Toronto Studies in Central and Inner Asia, Canada and Hong Kong Papers, Canada and Hong Kong Research Papers, Asia Papers, Working Papers, Discussion Papers, Monographs, and a newsletter.

Funding sources: The Joint Centre obtains support from universities and private and public organizations. Recent support has come from the Canadian International Development Agency (CIDA), the Department of Foreign Affairs and International Trade (Canada), the Donner Canadian Foundation, the Ford Foundation, the Hong Kong Bank of Canada, the International Development Research Centre (IDRC), and Rockefeller Brothers Fund.

Staffing: The Centre has four full-time staff members, and approximately forty scholars, primarily at the University of Toronto and York University, are involved in ongoing research programs.

Head of the institution: Prof. B. Michael Frolic, Director

Contact officer: Ms. Carol Irving, Administrator

Joint Centre for Asia Pacific Studies
York University
4700 Keele Street
North York, Ontario
M3J 1P3
CANADA
Tel: (416) 736-5784
Fax: (416) 736-5688
e-mail • cirving@yorku.ca
URL • http://www.canasiaweb.com

Laval University

Groupe d'études et de recherche sur l'Asie contemporaine

Background and objectives: Groupe d'études et de recherche sur l'Asie contemporaine (GERAC), founded in 1990, is a research institution and academic program primarily concerned with Southeast Asia. It seeks to extend its scope beyond that of research to the application of acquired knowledge to teaching and to prepare students for later work in their respective academic fields. GERAC is interested in the exchange of knowledge between Asia and Canada. Issues surrounding human migration (refugee and immigration movements) also form a significant part of GERAC's mission.

Programs: GERAC's activities focus on teaching, research, and publishing on aspects of culture, health, and inter-ethnic relations. Future studies will investigate human migration within Southeast Asia and between this region and Canada. Current research projects include an analysis of American foreign policy in changing Asia; Sino-Vietnamese dialogue and reconciliation in a multilateral security environment; studies of deforestation in Vietnam and Southeast Asia; networking for global business competitiveness; and agricultural expansion in Southeast Asia.

Publications: GERAC's most recent publications include *Santé et intervention auprès des réfugiés d'Asie du Sud-Est: Recension des publications* (1995); *LAOS: Bibliographie en sciences sociales / A Bibliography in Social Sciences* (1995); *Autour des transferts Orient-Occident: Perspectives anthropologiques* (1994); and *Le défi forestier en Asie du Sud-Est / The Challenge of the Forest in Southeast Asia* (1994).

Funding sources: GERAC receives its funding from the Social Sciences and Humanities Research Council of Canada, the Max Bell Foundation, the Gérard-Dion Foundation, Octroi, Laval University, Department of Foreign Affairs and International Trade (Canada), and the Ministère des relations internationales (Québec).

Staffing: There are ten faculty associated with GERAC and up to eight graduate students as researchers.

Head of the institution: Prof. Albert Lejauld

Contact officer: Prof. L.J. Dorais

Groupe d' études et de recherche sur l'Asie contemporaine
Pavillon Charles-De Koninck
Université Laval
Ville de Québec, Québec
G1K 7P4
CANADA
Tel: (418) 656-2133
Fax: (418) 656-2114
e-mail • Gerac@fss.ulaval.ca
URL • http://www.ulaval.ca

Niagara Institute of International Affairs (A Division of The Conference Board of Canada)

Background and objectives: The Niagara Institute is a private, not-for-profit foundation established in 1971 and became a wholly owned subsidiary of the Conference Board of Canada in 1994. The Institute is dedicated to enhancing the quality of Canadian leadership in business, government, and private organizations. It links leaders of business, labor, and government and provides a forum for sharing experience, assessing issues from a national and international perspective, and considering effective responses. The Institute's programs aim to encourage approaches to decision-making founded upon an understanding of human values; enhance the ability of leaders to anticipate, understand, and respond to critical problems; bridge gaps in perception and communication that separate important parts of the community; and strengthen the capacity of our institutions to adapt to change.

Programs: The Asia-Pacific is a principal area of the Institute's international activities. The Niagara Institute has collaborated with the Asian Institute of Management and has been involved in the development of public sector leadership in Southeast Asia through the Institute on Governance. The Institute has also hosted visiting executives from South Korea.

The Institute offers development programs focusing on specific Asian countries, combining its own expertise in adult education with the Conference Board's extensive research on Asian business.

The Institute, in collaboration with the Centre for Creative Leadership, also offers a Global Leadership Program to help executives appreciate the impact of cultural differences in international business and focus on building individual and organizational capacity to operate effectively internationally.

Publications: A program calendar provides a detailed description of the programs and services offered by the Institute.

Funding sources: The Niagara Institute secures its funding from the contributions of the Conference Board of Canada's Associates.

Staffing: The Niagara Institute has a core staff of eight, who are part of a total of 190 Conference Board staff.

Heads of the institution:
Dr. James Nininger, Chairman

Dr. Charles Barrett, President

Contact officer: Ms. Donna Cook, Program Director

Niagara Institute of International Affairs
255 Smyth Road
Ottawa, Ontario
K1H 8M7
CANADA
Tel: (613) 526-3280
Fax: (613) 526-5385
e-mail • barrett@conference.ca
URL • http://www.conferenceboard.ca

North-South Institute

Background and objectives: The North-South Institute (NSI) is a nonprofit and nonpartisan organization established in 1976 to help Canadians to understand the problems and opportunities facing countries in the developing world. The Institute conducts research on Canada's relations with developing countries and on a wide range of foreign policy issues.

Programs: The Institute recently led a research project, entitled "Gender Equity in Education and Training: Meeting the Needs of APEC Economies in Transition," which focused on the impact of economic restructuring on labor markets and the corresponding education and training needs of women. This study culminated in a two-day conference in Malaysia and the publishing of two overview papers.

The Institute, in conjunction with Lester Pearson International Institute, also coordinated a project and subsequent publication that examined APEC members' experiences with education policy as an instrument for poverty reduction. In addition, the Institute has also recently completed a three-year research project on the impact of global economic reform on women's employment in China.

NSI's APEC program conducts occasional seminars in Canada on APEC Human Resources Development and related issues. The Institute collaborates with many Canadian and international research organizations.

The Institute hosts seminars and conferences on a variety of foreign policy topics and often offers advice to parliamentarians and government policy makers. The North-South Institute is the National Lead Institute for Canada for the Asia Pacific Economic Cooperation (APEC) Human Resources Development Working Group Network on Economic Development Management (APEC HRD NEDM).

Publications: NSI publishes an annual report, briefings, the *Review* (three times annually), and research papers. Recent books include *Gender and Jobs in China's New Economy* (1996); *Partnerships for a New Agenda: Human Resource Development and Poverty Alleviation in the APEC Region* (with Dalhousie University, 1995); *What's in a Job?: Equity in Human Resource Development in Asia-Pacific Economies* (1995); and *From Blackboards to Keyboards: The Fragile Link between Women's Education and Employment* (1994).

Funding sources: The NSI receives funding from a variety of sources including a grant from the Canadian International Development Agency (CIDA). The remainder of the Institute's funding comes from individuals, corporations and institutions, specific research projects, and from the sale of publications.

Staffing: NSI has a small staff of professional researchers and communicators with expertise in international development, foreign policy, and global economic relations.

Heads of the institution:
Dr. Roy Culpepper, President

Mme. Gabrielle Lachance, Chair of the Board

Contact officer: Ms. Melanie Gruer, Communications

The North-South Institute
200-55 Murray Street
Ottawa, Ontario
K1N 5M3
CANADA
Tel: (613) 241-3535
Fax: (613) 241-7435
e-mail • nsi@web.net
URL • http://www.web.net/~nsi

Queen's University

The Centre for Canada-Asia Business Relations

Background and objectives: Founded in 1992, the Centre for Canada-Asia Business Relations (CANAsia) in the School of Business at Queen's University has a range of interdisciplinary programs and activities to foster understanding of the countries of the Asia-Pacific region, promote cooperation, and assist Canadian business in trading relations with Asian countries. The Centre develops and disseminates knowledge of Asia, improves cross-cultural communication, and prepares Canadian business people to enter new markets successfully and provides similar services to interested Asian organizations.

Programs: CANAsia undertakes collaborative and multidisciplinary research, stressing academic rigor and practical relevance. Current research projects include Canadian Success Stories in Japan, Thai-Canadian Negotiations, International Business Training in Companies within Canada, Public Policy Impact on Business Systems in Thailand and Indonesia, Southeast Asian Alliances, and Language Programs (Japanese and Mandarin). CANAsia's products and services include an outreach program of short courses and workshops tailored to specific business needs on a fee-for-service basis; an annual conference at Queen's University on topics related to the Asia-Pacific region; student exchange programs in Asia; internship programs for Queen's students with companies in Asia; and courses related to the Asia-Pacific region at Queen's University.

Publications: CANAsia publishes *Approaching Asia*, a semi-annual newsletter featuring topical issues that affect Canada-Asia business relations as well as the activities and research of the Centre; the *Working Papers* series; and a *Monograph Series* with such titles as *Discovering the New Silk Road: Canadian Venturing into Asia, Proceedings of Far Horizons Fourth Competition and Conference* (1996) and *Benchmarking the Canadian Business Presence in East Asia* (1995).

Funding sources: The Centre has been supported by grants from the Max Bell Foundation, Asia Pacific Foundation of Canada, Hong Kong Bank of Canada, Tanaka Fund, Japan Foundation, and the Canadian Imperial Bank of Commerce.

Staffing: The Centre has a director (half-time position), five research associates working on a project-by-project basis, two program coordinators (one full-time, one part-time), and two part-time research assistants.

Head of the institution: Dr. Lorna Wright, Director

Contact officer: Mr. Thé Tieu, Coordinator

Centre for Canada-Asia Business Relations (CANAsia)
School of Business, Queen's University
Kingston, Ontario
K7L 3N6
CANADA
Tel.: (613) 545-6438
Fax: (613) 545-2321
e-mail • ccabr@qsilver.queensu.ca
URL • http://www.qsilver.queensu.ca/
           business/ccabr/ccabr.htm

Simon Fraser University

Centre for Policy Research on Science & Technology

Background and objectives: The Centre for Policy Research on Science and Technology (CPROST) at Simon Fraser University was established in 1988 to study the interaction of advances in science and technology (S&T), their implementation in the marketplace, and the consequent impact on community and individual interests. CPROST seeks to improve public policy and private decision-making processes by increasing public participation and promoting sound methodologies for the implementation of technological change; promotes understanding of the relationship between private and public sectors as they stimulate, monitor, and control the process of technological innovation; develops and retains researchers skilled in case study techniques, advanced qualitative methods, and the strategic use of information technologies; and enhances the effectiveness and global competitiveness of client organizations by creating and refining tools for managing innovation.

Programs: CPROST is a unique resource of people, information, and networks, working with S&T stakeholders to assist them in analyzing and implementing their policies and programs. CPROST prepares custom briefings and reports for leaders and managers in government, business, and not-for-profit organizations.

CPROST also designs and conducts workshops, seminars, and conferences to address issues raised by changing technologies and to reach collective decisions. Faculty members associated with the Centre have been commissioned to make recommendations to the Canadian government on the future of the Canadian Broadcasting Corporation, the National Film Board, and Telefilm Canada, and to give seminars on the information highway and its public policy implications at a number of locations in the Far East. They also conduct courses at Simon Fraser University on the uses of information technology, retrieval, dissemination, and communications, and on the management of technology.

CPROST's projects and activities include (1) Analysis of Indicators of S&T Performance, which have produced reports on the results of international surveys comparing the awareness of Canadians on S&T issues with citizens of other countries, international and Pacific Rim trade in high-technology products and services, and federal government spending in S&T budget (In April 1996, CPROST organized an international workshop on the management of S&T activities in regional economies.); (2) International Institute on Innovation, Competitiveness, and Sustainability, a 1994 project, which included the first of a series of trinational summer institutes involving scholars, government officials, and business representatives from Mexico, Canada, and the United States; (3) The Scientific Research and Experimental Development Tax Credit Program, which prepared briefing materials on the application of the SR&ED tax credit program for the Tax Foundation of Canada (In October 1994, CPROST hosted a conference on the subject "Government Recipes for Industrial Innovation."); (4) S&T Policy and the Management of Technology in Developing Countries, which includes projects underway in Colombia and Albania to help S&T managers in those countries develop their policy capabilities and improve their technology management programs.

Publications: CPROST prepares public reports on technology management issues, and papers in refereed journals on specific research projects. Selected publications include "A New Picture of the Industrial Landscape in British Columbia," "A Review of the Australian Industry Commission Report on R&D in Australia," "Canadians' Knowledge of S&T and S&T Issues," "Cybernetics and (Real) National Systems of Innovation," and "R&D and Innovation at the Firm Level: Improving the S&T Policy Information Base."

Funding sources: CPROST is a self-supporting institute funded through research contracts and grants from the private sector and all levels of government.

Staffing: CPROST consists of six faculty members, two research associates, and eight research staff.

Head of the institution: Dr. Peter Anderson, Director

Contact officer: Adam Holbrook, Adjunct Professor

Centre for Policy Research on Science and Technology
Simon Fraser University
515 West Hastings Street
Vancouver, BC
V6B 5K3
CANADA
Tel: (604) 291-5114
Fax: (604) 291-5165
e-mail • anderson@sfu.ca
**   jholbroo@sfu.ca**
URL • http://edie.cprost.sfu.ca/cprost

Simon Fraser University

David Lam Centre for International Communication

Background and objectives: David Lam Centre for International Communication was established in 1989 as an interdisciplinary center integrating university, government, professional, and business resources. The Centre's education, training, and research and development activities concentrate on communication for effective international, intercultural, and interlingual cooperation in the Pacific region.

Programs: The Centre's four major programs include (1) Seminars and courses in international communication for professionals, with an emphasis on identifying, articulating, and overcoming obstacles to effective East-West cooperation through a context-sensitive understanding of communication theory and practice; (2) East Asian Culture and Communication Programs, whose activities include public lectures, exhibitions, performances, non-credit courses, seminars, and workshops on East Asian culture and communication for Canadians, and on Canadian culture and communication for people from East Asia. The Centre also offers immersion, intensive, and non-intensive courses in Japanese, Mandarin Chinese, Cantonese, Bahasa Indonesian, and Korean languages and cross-cultural competence; (3) Pacific Region Forum on Business and Management Communication, which provides an ongoing arena for the periodic reporting, analyzing, discussing, and debating of new and old strategies for articulating relationships within and between businesses and their environments around the Pacific Region; (4) International Communication Research and Development Projects, which includes the Canadian Liaison Office of the China Council for International Cooperation on the Environment and Development (CCICED); the Asia Pacific Curriculum Resources Database, presented in cooperation with the Asia Pacific Foundation of Canada, offering on-line access to reviews of hundreds of books, videotapes, and other teaching materials focusing on the Asia-Pacific region; and developing computerized methods for easier and more efficient learning of Chinese and Japanese languages and communication.

Publications: The Centre publishes an *Annual Report* and *Forum Reports*, which is an ongoing print and on-line electronic publication that provides summaries of presentations made at the Pacific Region Forum on Business and Management Communication. Recent reports include "Communicating Across the Pacific: A European's View," "Environment Creating Corporations," "Will Shanghai Re-emerge as an International Financial Market? Sino-Foreign Strains on the Bund," "Mandarins and Markets: Government Intervention in East Asian Markets and What It Means for Canadian Investors," "Issues of Multiculturalism in Canadian Workplaces," and "Socialization of Asian Managers into North American Firms: Fit or Misfit?"

Funding sources: The Centre's main funding sources are the David Lam Endowment interest; government and non-governmental grants; and tuition income.

Staffing: The Centre has a total staff of twenty people, of whom twelve are research/program-oriented while eight are administrative.

Head of the institution: Dr. Jan W. Walls, Director

Contact officer: Edith Lo, Assistant to the Director

David Lam Centre for International Communication
SFU at Harbour Centre
515 West Hastings Street
Vancouver, BC
V6B 5K3
CANADA
Tel: (604) 291-5111
Fax: (604) 291-5112
e-mail • dlam-info@hoshi.cic.sfu.ca
URL • http://hoshi.cic.sfu.ca

Université de Montréal

Centre d'études de l'Asie de l'Est

Background and objectives: The Centre d'études de l'Asie de l'Est (CETASE), a multidisciplinary program of the Faculty of Arts and Sciences at the Université de Montréal, was established in 1976 to provide general training on East Asia for students who aim to work in various fields of exchange and cooperation between Canada and East Asia, and to prepare undergraduate students to continue their studies at the M.A. and Ph.D. levels.

Programs: CETASE's main activities concentrate in teaching and research. The core of its multidisciplinary program is the teaching of East Asian languages. CETASE offers joint B.A. degrees on East Asia with twelve departments in the Faculty of Arts and Sciences; M.A. and Ph.D. joint direction with five departments of the Faculty of Arts and Sciences and one department of the Faculty of Education.

In addition, it also offers M.A. Joint Seminars with Polytechnique de Montréal, a Post B.A. Cooperative Program in Business Administration and Communication with the Centre for East Asian Studies at McGill University, and an Intensive Summer Course in Chinese Language in cooperation with Nankai University in China.

CETASE's research programs focus on Japan, China, and Korea. Its past and ongoing research projects include "Social Structure and Economic Development," "Esthetics and National Identity," and "Literature and Gender Studies" (Japan); "Transport and Land Utilization in the Shanghai Area," in collaboration with Shanghai Institute of Mechanical Engineering and Shanghai Academy of Social Sciences, "The Paradigm of the Westerner in Contemporary Chinese Culture," "Philosophy and Political Culture in the Han Dynasty," in collaboration with Centre National de la Recherche Scientifique, Paris; and "Popular Culture and Religion in Northern Henan," and "Exile Poetry in the Chinese Tradition" (China). The China, Japan,

Korea institutional research project examines "Models of Modernization in East Asia: Culture, Society, and Economy."

CETASE's Specialized Library on East Asia holds 23,250 monographs, 172 current periodicals in Chinese, Japanese, and Korean languages, and 11,174 monographs in French and English.

Publications: CETASE publishes the periodical *Cahiers du Centre d'études de l'Asie de l'Est*.

Funding sources: CETASE is entirely funded by the Faculty of Arts and Sciences of the Université de Montréal. There have also been several institutional grants from the governments of Québec and Canada and from foundations such as the Asia Pacific Foundation, Japan Foundation, and Korea Foundation.

Staffing: CETASE has eight professors and eight lecturers. In addition, it has three professors from other departments and five staff members in its library.

Head of the institution: Dr. Charles Le Blanc, Director

Contact officer: Dr. Charles Le Blanc

Centre d'études de l'Asie de l'Est
Université de Montréal
Case postal 6128, Succursale Centre-Ville
Montréal, Québec
H3C 3J7
CANADA
Tel: (514) 343-5800
Fax: (514) 343-7716
e-mail • leblanch@ere.umontreal.ca

Université du Québec á Montréal and Concordia University

Joint Centre for Asia Pacific Communication Research / Centre conjoint de Recherche en Communication sur l'Asie Pacifique

Background and objectives: The Joint Centre for Asia Pacific Communication Research was established in 1992 to promote awareness and understanding through the study of communication, media, and information issues related to Canada and the Asia-Pacific region and Asian communities in Eastern Canada, most specifically in Québec. The Joint Centre provides institutional support for academics from a number of countries to come together with graduate students and community, business, and government interests to create a critical mass of expertise that facilitates the development of programs and initiatives with an Asian-Pacific focus and from an intercultural perspective. It is located in the Communications Department at Université du Québec á Montréal (UQAM) and in the Journalism Department at Concordia University.

Programs: The Joint Centre promotes collaborative research, offers research training opportunities to graduate students, develops and provides information services, and co-sponsors community group projects of a cultural nature or on issues of social importance to Asia-Pacific communities in Canada.

The Joint Centre's research projects currently focus on communication policies and technologies; communication and development with emphasis on Official Development Assistance (ODA) and human resources development; intercultural communication and immigration; and international communications and institution building. Some ongoing research projects include "The Information Superhighways in Asia: Key Issues and Policy Orientations for the Creation of an Appropriate Regulatory Framework in the Context of the Convergence of Technologies"; "Impact of New Information Technologies and of Internet within APEC Countries"; "Comparative Analysis of Japanese and Canadian ODA Policies and Programs within the Asia Pacific"; "Comparative Analysis of Intercultural Communication and Integration Problems of Asian Immigrants to Canada"; and "Negotiating Trilateral Relationships between Canada, Japan and China."

The Joint Centre offers M.A. and Ph.D. seminars in international communication and cooperation with the Asia-Pacific on an annual basis. It also sponsors major conferences linking community needs with academic expertise, such as the 1994 National Conference of the National Association of Japanese Canadians.

In addition, the Joint Centre has been involved in the development of pedagogical material for the Asia Pacific Foundation of Canada, and with Simon Fraser University and the Chinese Embassy, it has been conducting the Hanyu Shuiping Kaoshi (Chinese-Language Proficiency Test) for Eastern Canada since 1992.

Publications: The Joint Centre publishes Series of Monographs. Recent titles include *Cultural Identity and Development:* *Communication Practices and the Creation of a New Discourse on Local Development. A Case Study of Nishikawa-ChO, Yamagata Prefecture, Japan, 1975-1995* (1996); *Japanese and Canadian ODA within the Asia Pacific* (1996); *SOGO SHOSHA: Une culture organisationnelle centrée sur la circulation de l'information. Analyse de cas de Mitsubishi* (1996); and *A Communication Approach to Development: Recipient Perspectives towards Japan Bilateral ODA to Ethiopia* (1996). The Joint Centre also publishes working papers. Recent issues include "A Growing Uncertainty: Japan Security Issues within the Asia Pacific Region" (1996) and "The China Emerging Security Threat: The Japanese Perspective" (1996).

Funding sources: The Joint Centre receives funding from a wide range of domestic and international, public and private sources, which include the Canadian Department of Foreign Affairs and International Trade, the Canadian International Development Agency (CIDA), International Development Research Centre (IDRC), The Max Bell Foundation, Canada-ASEAN Centre, the Japan Foundation, The Chinese State Education Commission, the Korea Foundation, and UNESCO.

Staffing: The Joint Centre has five full-time, nine part-time faculty members, four post-doctoral fellows, and ten Ph.D. candidates. It has three administrative staff.

Notes: The Joint Centre has an Advisory Board. Its President is Professor Kong Fah Lee, a leader of the Montreal Chinese community; its honorary President is Professor Chian Wei Chang, President of Shanghai University in China.

Heads of the institution:
Prof. Claude-Yves Charron, Co-director, Université du Québec á Montréal and Scientific Director, International Network of UNESCO Chairs in Communication ORBICOM

Prof. Lindsay Crysler, Co-director, Chair, Journalism Department, Concordia University

Contact officer: Dr. Claude-Yves Charron

Joint Centre for Asia Pacific Communication Research
Université du Québec á Montréal
P.O. Box 8888, Station "Centre Ville"
Montreal, H3C 3P8
CANADA
Tel: (514) 987-3000 Ext. 4046
Fax: (514) 987-0249
e-mail • charron.claude-yves@uqam.ca
crysler@vax2.concordia.ca

University of British Columbia

Centre for Asian Legal Studies

Background and objectives: The Faculty of Law at the University of British Columbia (UBC) established the Centre for Asian Legal Studies to provide a focal point for the exchange of ideas and information through education and research regarding Asian legal systems and law. The Centre also encourages creative approaches to Canada-Asia legal issues with the aim of promoting Pacific Rim cooperation.

Programs: The Centre has three major programs of teaching and research: Chinese Legal Studies, Japanese Legal Studies, and Southeast Asian Legal Studies. It hopes to expand to cover other Asian legal systems in the near future.

The Chinese Legal Studies program, established in 1987, offers general and specialized training in the field of Chinese law and promotes scholarly exchanges with outside institutions, in particular the Faculty of Law at Peking University and the National Taiwan University with which the Law Faculty has agreements for the exchange of scholars and graduate students. The program also has close ties with the Law Institutes of both the Chinese Academy of Social Sciences in Beijing and the Shanghai Academy of Social Sciences as well as the University of Hong Kong Law Faculty. Research projects include a Chinese Legal Culture Project, a Chinese Securities Market Project, a Chinese Justice Project, and a Chinese Foreign Investment Law Project. Publications have appeared in the *China Quarterly*, the *East Asian Executive Reports*, *The China Law Reporter*, and the *UCLA Pacific Rim Law Journal*.

The Japanese Legal Studies program, inaugurated in 1980, has established formal cooperation and exchange relationships with the Law Faculties of Japanese national universities in Osaka, Hokkaido, and Niigata and with Chukyo in Nagoya. Each year students are selected to study under a University Education Abroad Agreement at Sophia University in Tokyo. Japanese Legal Studies also sponsors a number of visiting scholars and guest lecturers from Japan, Australia, the United States, and other countries who contribute to the academic and professional activities of the Faculty. The main research project is a six-year investigation into the cultural, social, legal, economic, administrative, and medical context of mental health care in Japan and the situation of psychiatric patients and their families.

The Southeast Asian Legal Studies program, launched in 1993, provides an opportunity for legal scholars from the region to come to UBC to participate in teaching, research, and publication. The program covers legal systems and government, law making, court systems and dispute settlement, foreign investment and trading laws, and natural resources and environmental laws. The research and publication program evolved through consultations with law schools in the region, federal and provincial governments, the Canadian private sector, and non-governmental organizations. Research projects include the development of cooperative ocean policies in the South China Sea, and the Vietnam-Canada Ocean and Coastal Cooperation Project aimed at assisting the Vietnamese government in the development of its marine policy and policy and law.

Publications: A series of workshop reports, meeting reports, and working papers have been produced in conjunction with each of the programs.

Funding sources: The Centre receives support from the Max Bell Foundation, the Law Foundation of British Columbia, the Social Sciences and Humanities Research Council of Canada, the Canadian International Development Agency, and the Chiang Ching-kuo Foundation.

Staffing: There are seven researchers and one administrator working with the Centre.

Head of institution: Dr. Pitman Potter, Director

Contact officer: Dr. Pitman Potter

Centre for Asian Legal Studies
Faculty of Law
1822 East Mall
University of British Columbia
V6T 1Z1
CANADA
Tel: (604) 822-4780
Fax: (604) 822-8108
e-mail • potter@law.ubc.ca

University of British Columbia

Institute for Asian Research

Background and objectives: The Institute for Asian Research (IAR) was founded in 1978 to promote contemporary, issue-oriented research on Asia and the Pacific and to facilitate interaction among people of different disciplines and backgrounds, from the academic community and other areas, who share a common interest in the region.

Programs: The Institute is now focusing on human values and expression; cultural learning and behavior; political economy and organizational innovation; globalism, regionalism, and localism; science, technology, and the environment; and policy, futures, and the Asia-Pacific region. IAR carries out and sponsors research related to the Asia-Pacific region; studies and recommends policy options to academic, government, industry, and public service organizations; organizes seminars and programs on Asia for faculty, students, and interested members of the community; promotes worldwide networking and sharing of information through publications, conferences, data, and knowledge base development; and hosts visiting researchers and scholars and dignitaries from the Asia-Pacific region.

In 1992, the Institute opened five new research centers dealing with China, Korea, Japan, Southeast Asia, and South Asia research. The Institute has carried out projects on agricultural development in Asia, Canadian-Asian communities, and British Columbia's economic relations with East Asian countries.

The Institute also provides a forum for seminar presentations, art exhibitions and cultural performances, as well as lectures by Asian specialists. The Institute organizes workshops, conferences, and seminars.

Publications: IAR publishes *Asia Pacific Report*, a quarterly newsletter; *Canada and the Changing Economy of the Pacific Basin*, a series of working papers; occasional papers series; and special series on political economy and organizations, science, technology, and the environment in the Asia-Pacific region, culture, learning, and behavior, and policy options.

Funding sources: IAR receives some funding from the University of British Columbia, as well as endowments for chairs and programs. Research grants form an important source of funding.

Staffing: The Institute's professional staff includes the director, a senior researcher (Konwakai Research Chair), the directors of the constituent research centers, and a manager for administration and programs.

Notes: IAR and its constituent centers moved to a new research center, C.K. Choi Building, in 1996.

Head of the institution: Dr. Terry D. McGee, Director

Contact officer: Dr. Terry D. McGee, Director

Institute for Asian Research
University of British Columbia
1855 West Mall
Vancouver, BC
V6T 1Z2
CANADA
Tel: (604) 822- 4688
Fax: (604) 822- 5207
e-mail • capri@unixg.ubcca
          tmcgee@unixg.ubc.ca
URL • http://www.iar.ubc.ca

University of British Columbia

Institute for International Relations

Background and objectives: The Institute for International Relations was established in 1970 as a nonprofit, research organization to promote and organize internationally oriented, multidisciplinary research projects and curricula among the faculty and students of the University of British Columbia (UBC) and other institutions. The Institute conducts research on international politics and organization, diplomatic history, strategic studies, international legal problems, and trade and development. Research with a policy-relevant perspective has focused on Canada's place in international ocean regimes, trading regimes, and security relationships such as NATO. Asia-Pacific security affairs have become a major focus of the Institute's work.

Programs: The Institute does not offer courses or degree programs. Rather, it supports individual or group research projects at the graduate, post-doctorate, and faculty levels through grants, graduate and post-doctoral fellowships, professional conferences, publication subsidies, and other services. IIR's areas of primary interest include Canada and the transformation of the international system; Canada and the evolving order of the Asia-Pacific region; regional conflict and conflict management in the "new world order," and the international community and the prospects for collective security, human rights, and human security in the evolving world order. The Institute supports and organizes conferences, symposia, and seminars on areas of specialization. Among the recent conferences organized or co-sponsored by the Institute were "Canada in a Networked Environment: The Internet, International Relations and Foreign Policy" (co-sponsored with the Department of Foreign Affairs), and "Hong Kong: The Countdown."

The Institute also organizes many lectures and seminars for visiting scholars and officials, addressing topics such as "Canada and the Politics of the G-7 Meetings," "ASEAN towards the 21st Century," "US Perspectives on Current Issues of Asian Economic Integration," "UN Peacekeeping after 50 Years: Dilemmas and Opportunities," and "Development and Security in Southeast Asia."

The Institute also serves as an administrative center for the Canadian Consortium on Asia Pacific Security (CANCAPS).

Publications: IIR publishes an *Annual Report;* the *CANCAPS Bulletin;* and a *Working Paper Series.* Recent titles include *New Powers, Old Patterns: Dangers of the Naval Buildup in the Asia Pacific Region* (1995); *The Logic of Japanese Multilateralism for Asia Pacific Security* (1994); *Asia Pacific Arms Buildups. Part One: Scope, Causes and Problems* and *Part Two: Prospects for Control* (1994); *Multilateralism: The Relevance of the Concept to Regional Conflict Management* (1994); and *The Geostrategic Foundations of Peace and Prosperity in the Western Pacific Region* (1994).

Funding sources: IIR receives support from numerous sources such as the Asia Pacific Foundation of Canada, Department of Foreign Affairs and International Trade (Canada), Department of National Defence, Hong Kong Economic and Trade Office, Maritime Forces Pacific Headquarters, University of British Columbia, and Vancouver Port Corporation.

Staffing: IIR research and academic staff include the director, assistant director, eight professors, one assistant professor, two associate professors, two research associates, two post-doctoral fellows, and one secretary.

Head of the institution: Dr. Brian Job, Director

Contact officer: Allan Castle, Assistant Director

Institute for International Relations
University of British Columbia
C456-1866 Main Mall
Vancouver, BC
V6T 1Z1
CANADA
Tel: (604) 822-5480
Fax: (604) 822-5540
e-mail • instir@interchange.ubc.ca
URL • http://www.iir.ubc.ca

York University

Centre for Research on Latin America & the Caribbean

Background and objectives: The Centre for Research on Latin America & the Caribbean (CERLAC) at York University, established in 1978, is Canada's only university-based research center specializing in Latin American and Caribbean studies. It aims to contribute to knowledge about political, economic, social, and cultural aspects of Latin America and the Caribbean.

Programs: CERLAC's research program emphasizes interdisciplinary work and collaborative research with scholars and research institutions in Latin America and the Caribbean. CERLAC's past and ongoing research projects include the study of the Caribbean as a whole, Canadian-Latin American relations, and group research in the Andean region (Ecuador, Colombia, Peru, and Bolivia) and in Chile, Mexico, Argentina, Brazil, Costa Rica, and other countries in the region.

CERLAC receives visiting scholars and public figures from Latin America and the Caribbean and periodically holds conferences and cultural events. It plays an important role in York University's Graduate Diploma in Latin American and Caribbean Studies.

Publications: The Centre publishes a newsletter, occasional papers, edited volumes, and working papers. Recent Project and Conference Books and Monographs include *A Report on Reforming the Organization of Latin American States to Support Democratization in the Hemisphere: A Canadian Perspective* (1995), and *Popular Participation and Development: A Bibliography on Africa and Latin America* (1992), jointly published with the Centre for Urban and Community Studies at the University of Toronto. Recent *CERLAC Working Papers* include "Trade, Employment and the Rural Economy," "Indigenous Ecology and the Politics of Linkage in Mexican Social Movements," "Mexican Meltdown: NAFTA, Democracy and Peso," "Cooperation and Polarization beyond Borders: The Transnationalization of Mexican Environmental Issues during NAFTA Negotiations," "Neoliberalism and the Transformation of Mexican Authoritarianism," "Development Paths at Crossroads: Peru in Light of the East Asian Experience," and "Economic Reforms and Political Democratization in Mexico: Reevaluating Basic Tenets of Canadian Foreign Policy." *CER-*

LAC Colloquia Papers recent titles include two Rapporteur's Reports, "Mexico after NAFTA: A Public Forum for Social and Labour Activists on the Current Mexican Crisis" and "Critical Perspectives on North American Integration." *CERLAC Occasional Papers* include "The United Nations in El Salvador: The Promise and Dilemmas of an Integrated Approach to Peace" and "The Role of Ideas in a Changing World Order: The Case of the International Indigenous Movement, 1975-1990."

Funding sources: CERLAC's research projects have been supported by various agencies and institutions, including the Social Sciences and Humanities Research Council of Canada, the International Development Research Centre (IDRC), the Canadian International Development Agency (CIDA), the Canadian Donner Foundation, and others.

Staffing: CERLAC's research fellows are drawn from faculty members at York University and various universities across Canada. It currently has ninety-three fellows (including visiting fellows), and eleven research associates and twenty-one graduate associates, representing a wide range of fields in the social sciences, humanities, law, and education. CERLAC has a Director, one Deputy Director who is also the Graduate Diploma Program Coordinator, a Cultural Coordinator, and several faculty members who volunteer to maintain the Documentation Centre and contribute as Communications Coordinator.

Head of the institution: Dr. Ricardo Grinspun, Director

Contact officer: Ms. Liddy Gomes, Administrative Assistant

Centre for Research on Latin America & the Caribbean
240 York Lanes
York University
4700 Keele Street, North York
Ontario, M3J 1P3
CANADA
Tel: (416) 736-5237
Fax: (416) 736-5737
e-mail • CERLAC@yorku.ca

York University

York Centre for International and Security Studies

Background and objectives: The York Centre for International and Security Studies (YCISS), founded in 1982, supports and encourages innovative theoretical and empirical research in international relations and security studies. The Centre fosters scholarly research of interest to academic and policy communities in Canada and abroad. The Centre also coordinates and facilitates a variety of scholarly activities including conferences, workshops, lectures, seminars, and research publications.

Programs: The Centre organizes its principal programs under four thematic areas: Strategic Studies, focusing on theoretical and policy-oriented aspects of strategic studies, the determinants and formulation of foreign and defense policies, civil-military relations, arms control and disarmament, weapons proliferation, confidence-building measures, and approaches to peacekeeping; Political Economy of Security, concentrating on the politicization of global economic relations and the emergence of new forms of international cooperation and competition, and economic factors that affect Canadian security; Regional Conflict, examining theoretical and empirical aspects of regional conflicts including those in Asia-Pacific, the Middle East, the Horn of Africa, southern Africa, and Latin America, with research that includes an examination of the origins of regional conflicts, their contemporary characteristics and dynamics, and the prospects for successful management/resolution; and Non-Traditional Analyses of Conflict and Security, focusing on alternative approaches to the study of conflict and security, including those informed by contemporary methodological and theoretical debates in the social sciences.

Many of the classical issues in international relations, such as security, power, and war, are addressed in terms of various critical analytical postures, including feminist scholarship, postmodern analyses, and linguistic studies.

In addition, faculty have been instrumental in establishing two Canadian non-governmental associations on Asia-Pacific security (North Pacific Cooperative Security Dialogue and Canadian Consortium on Asia Pacific Security) as well as one international non-governmental agency with representation from all major Asia-Pacific countries (Council for Security Cooperation in the Asia Pacific).

Publications: The Centre has three publication series: occasional papers, working papers, and a monograph series. The Centre also publishes specialized papers in support of specific research projects. For example, the Centre publishes the *Canadian Consortium on Asia Pacific Security* (CANCAPS) Paper series, as well as the *Multilateral Institutions and Global Security Working Papers*.

Funding sources: The Centre's substantial financial support has come from the Faculty of Arts, the Faculty of Graduate Studies, and the Office of the Associate Vice-President (Research) at York University. Nevertheless, YCISS supports its activities primarily through external sources to the University such as the Social Sciences and Humanities Research Council of Canada (SSHRC), the Canadian International Development Agency, the CRB Foundation, the Donner Canadian Foundation, the Department of Foreign Affairs and International Trade (Canada), the United Nations University (Tokyo), the North Atlantic Treaty Organization, and Energy Mines and Resources Canada. A special role is played by funding provided through the competitive Security and Defence Forum (formerly the Military and Strategic Studies Program) of the Department of National Defence.

Staffing: The Centre is built around three core groups: resident York University and visiting faculty; graduate students, postdoctoral fellows, and other resident research associates; and research and administrative staff. In addition, the Centre has developed a network of external associates who are engaged in scholarly or professional activities relating to the Centre's research streams.

Head of the institution: Prof. David B. Dewitt, Director

Contact officers:
Prof. David B. Dewitt, Director

Andrew Latham, Assistant Director (1996-1997)

York Centre for International and Security Studies
3rd Floor, York Lanes
York University
4700 Keels Street
North York, Ontario
M3J 1 P3
CANADA
Tel: (416) 736-5156
Fax: (416) 736-5752
e-mail • yciss@yorku.ca
URL • http://www.yorku.ca/research/ciss

LATIN AMERICA

Centro de Investigaciones Europeo-Latinoamericanas

Background and objectives: The Center for European-Latin American Research was established in 1983 to study contemporary international relations between Europe and Latin America and other aspects related to Latin American countries and regions from an economic, political, strategic, and international point of view and from a Latin American perspective. EURAL is building a distinctive academic profile based on an ethical and scientific preference for the critical paradigm in social sciences in general, and political science in particular.

Programs: EURAL's research activities are undertaken within three defined areas. The Area of Economic Studies is currently working on the restructuring of the automobile industry in Brazil and Argentina in the context of economic integration, social actors and economic integration in Europe and MERCOSUR, a comparative analysis of transportation in Europe and MERCO-SUR, a comparative study of privatization of public enterprises, and the effects of the change of agrarian policies in Europe on Latin American exports. The Area of Political Studies and Government has traditionally focused on democratic transitions in Europe and Latin America. It has recently incorporated issues such as the problem of structural adjustment and poverty, the quality of representative institutions, and state reform in Latin America and Argentina. The Area of International Studies and Defense started its activities with a project on European strategic interests in Latin America in 1985. Since then, it has focused on Argentina's foreign policy, the militaries, and the Malvinas/Falkland conflict. EURAL has a core group of military affairs experts. One research team specializes in military industry and nuclear development in Argentina, with emphasis on the Argentinean missile Condor II and nuclear safeguards between Argentina and Brazil. A second team is currently studying the military industry reconversion in Argentina, Chile, Peru, Bolivia, and Paraguay and its impact on the formulation of public policy.

Publications: EURAL's researchers publish articles in academic journals and chapters in books.

Funding sources: EURAL's research activities are supported by diverse national and international contributors. A major national funding source is the National Council of Scientific and Technological Research (CONICET). EURAL has also received support from the Ford Foundation, the Pew Foundation, the Tinker Foundation, the Friedrich Ebert Foundation, the Berghof Foundation, the Commission of the European Communities, and the United Nations Development Program.

Staffing: EURAL has four full-time researchers and three part-time researchers and an administrative staff of three.

Head of the institution: Dr. Atilio Boron, Director

Contact officer: Mrs. Merchy Puga Marin, Executive Secretary

Centro de Investigaciones Europeo-Latinoamericanas (EURAL)
Rivadavia 2358, Piso 5
(1034) Buenos Aires
ARGENTINA
Tel: (54-1) 954-3673
Fax: (54-1) 951-3416
e-mail • eural@clacso.edu.ar

Consejo Argentino para las Relaciones Internacionales

Background and objectives: The Argentine Council for International Relations is a private academic institution created in 1978 to advance the analysis of relevant international issues from a national perspective. CARI is also a forum where outstanding personalities meet to discuss economic, political, social, and cultural aspects of contemporary international relations to promote peace, development, and better understanding among countries.

Programs: CARI's Permanent Studies Committees include Latin American affairs; Malvinas, Georgias, and South Sandwich Islands; Argentina-U.S., Argentina-Canada, and Argentina-Mexico relations; European affairs; Asian affairs; African, Arabian, and Middle East affairs; communications and media; study, prevention, and resolution of conflicts; international organizations; Antarctic studies; nuclear policy; environment affairs, etc. CARI also has Study Committees for specific subject matters such as the role of Argentina in restructuring the Latin American Free Trade Association, the foreign debt, and GATT and the Uruguay Round; armed forces and the integration process in the Southern Cone; and the role of journalism in the integration between Argentina and Chile. CARI's Committee for Services to Enterprises provide services to the business sector to bridge the gap between businessmen and foreign policy decision makers and to make them aware of relevant issues in contemporary international relations. Other academic activities include conferences, courses, seminars, symposiums, roundtables, and scholarships. The Institute of International Law and the Institute of International Security and Strategic Affairs, also part of CARI, have carried out activities since 1993 and 1994, respectively.

Publications: CARI publishes *International Developments,* a monthly newsletter featuring a synthesis of Argentina's international activities, and *CARI Noticias*, a biannual publication with information on CARI activities and events. Recent books include *Argentine Foreign Policy* (1996), *European Union and MERCO-SUR: Rounds of Reflection* (1996), *Argentina and Brazil Facing the XXI Century* (1995), and *Argentina-Chile Relations: Economic, Foreign and Defense Policy* (1995).

Funding sources: CARI is funded by a corporate affiliate program that allows companies, individuals, and public agencies to establish continuing relationships with CARI.

Staffing: CARI has six full-time researchers and twenty-seven part-time researchers. The administrative work is carried out by fourteen employees.

Notes: CARI's individual membership categories comprise honorary members, which include Chiefs of State and Government; correspondent members such as foreign cabinet members, ministers, heads of international organizations, and distinguished individuals; counselors, who are high-ranking civil servants and Argentine business figures; and consultants, who are mainly scholars that design and develop CARI's programs.

Head of the institution: Dr. Carlos Manuel Muñiz, President

Contact officer: Dr. Jose Maria Llados, Academic Secretary

Consejo Argentino para las Relaciones Internacionales
Uruguay 1037, Piso 1
1016 Buenos Aires
ARGENTINA
Tel: (54-1) 811-0071 to 0074
Fax: (54-1) 811-0072
e-mail • info@cari.org.ar
URL • www.intr.net/mercosur/cari.htm

Facultad Latinoamericana de Ciencias Sociales (FLACSO)

Área de Relaciones Internacionales

Background and objectives: The Latin American School of Social Science is an intergovernmental organization created in 1957 by recommendation of the United Nations Organization for Education, Science and Culture to promote research, teaching, and technical assistance in Latin America. The Secretariat-General is located in San Jose, Costa Rica. FLACSO-Argentina was established in 1974, and the Area of International Relations began its activities in 1984.

Programs: The Area of International Relations conducts research on international politics and international political economy. The main research topics are Argentina's economy, foreign policy, and international relations; trade policy and the international trade system; markets and financial institutions; U.S.-Latin American economic and political relations; regional integration, with emphasis on MERCOSUR; international environmental negotiations; and multilateral peace and security issues. FLACSO-Argentina offers an M.A. degree in international relations through a two-year interdisciplinary program focusing on international political economy and integration. The Area of IR organizes seminars, conferences, and workshops as well as short specialized courses for professionals and graduates. This Area also provides technical assistance to national and foreign institutions like the Ministry of Foreign Relations of Argentina, the Ministry of Foreign Relations of Brazil, the Inter-American Development Bank, the United Nations Development Program, the Organization of American States, and the Latin-American Economic System.

Publications: The Area of IR publishes working papers that result from research findings. Recent issues include *La dimension politica del MERCOSUR: Actores, politizacion e ideologia* (1995), *La agenda economica del MERCOSUR: Desafios de politica a corto y mediano plazo* (1995), and *Coercive Strategy, Democracy and Free Markets in Latin America* (1995). This Area has published more than twenty books through publishers located in Latin America, the United States, and Great Britain, which have included *America Latina en la Posguerra Fria: Ensayos Criticos* (1996), *Economic Integration in the Western Hemisphere* (1994), and *The Inter-American Development Bank* (1993).

Funding sources: The academic activities of the Area of IR are supported by the National Council of Scientific and Technical Research (CONICET, Argentina). The Area also received support from international contributors such as the Ford Foundation, the Rockefeller Foundation, the Tinker Foundation, the MacArthur Foundation, the Mellon Foundation, the International Development Research Center, and the United Nations Development Program.

Staffing: The Area of International Relations has four senior researchers and seven research assistants, and an administrative staff of two.

Notes: FLACSO member states are Argentina, Brazil, Chile, Costa Rica, Cuba, Ecuador, El Salvador, Guatemala, Mexico, and the Dominican Republic.

Head of the institution: Dr. Diana Tussie, Coordinator

Contact officer: Ms. Celsa Dominguez, Administrative Coordinator

Área de Relaciones Internacionales FLACSO-Argentina
Ayacucho 551
Buenos Aires
ARGENTINA
Tel: (54-1) 375-2435
Fax: (54-1) 375-1373
e-mail • rrii@flacso.cci.org.ar

Fundación de Investigaciones Económicas Latinoamericanas

Background and objectives: The Foundation for Latin American Economic Research is a private, nonpartisan institution dedicated to theoretical and applied research on Latin American and Argentinean economic issues. It was founded in 1964 by the Bolsa de Comercio de Buenos Aires, the Camara Argentina de Comercio, the Sociedad Rural Argentina, and the Union Industrial Argentina. FIEL is directed by a Council made up of members of these founding institutions and CEOs of leading Argentine private companies.

Programs: FIEL focuses on the international economy, labor markets, economic growth, industrial organization, agriculture, the economy of the public sector, and financial markets. New research areas include the environment, transportation, and fiscal decentralization. FIEL collects and compiles basic economic information for its research activities. DATAFIEL, the Foundation's database, has more than 3,000 original series on economic and related variables that are used by FIEL specialists for short-run studies. FIEL takes polls on short-run economic indicators such as demand, production, sales, stocks, wages, and investments, among others. Since 1992, FIEL has been preparing "Informe Sectorial," economic sectoral reports. In 1995, FIEL also began to offer macroeconomic forecasts for main economic indicators in Argentina.

Publications: The Foundation publishes *Indicadores de Coyuntura,* a monthly journal that provides a general perspective on economic, fiscal, monetary, and financial issues, as well as on the conditions of the labor market and the industrial, rural, and external sectors. FIEL also publishes *Reseña Anual de la Actividad Economica,* an annual report on Argentinean industries and other sectors of the economy, and *Informe sobre el Mercado de Trabajo,* a monthly report on the labor market. FIEL also pub-

lishes *Documentos de Trabajo* and other books based on its research work.

Funding sources: FIEL revenues come from the regular contributions of approximately 200 sponsors, the sale of publications and services such as the economic sectoral reports, and occasional contributions from national and foreign sources. The latter contributors include the Centro International para el Desarrollo Economico (CINDE, San Francisco/Panama), the Center for International Private Enterprise (CIPE, Washington, D.C.), the World Bank, the British Council, the Inter-American Development Bank, the Ford Foundation, the Volkswagen Foundation, the Konrad Adenauer Foundation, the United Nations Development Program, the Tinker Foundation, and the International Development Agency.

Staffing: FIEL's research is carried out by a technical team of more than twenty specialists in the fields of economics, statistics, law, engineering, systems, and social sciences. FIEL's core staff is made up of two academics and four chief economists.

Head of the institution: Ing. Victor L. Savanti, President

Contact officer: Ing. Eduardo Losso, Public Relations Manager

**Fundación de Investigaciones
    Económicas Latinoamericanas**
Cordoba 637 - 4to. Piso
(1054) Buenos Aires
ARGENTINA
Tel: (54-1) 314-1990
Fax: (54-1) 314-8648
e-mail • postmaster@fiel.org.ar
        fiel@datanar.com.ar

Instituto de Relaciones Internacionales de Asia-Pacífico

Background and objectives: The Institute of Asian-Pacific International Relations was founded in 1994 by a group of experts and professionals interested in economic, political, and cultural affairs in the Asian-Pacific countries; the international involvement of that region; and the evolution of its economic relations with Argentina-MERCOSUR, Chile, and Latin America in general. IRIAP aims to strengthen public and private economic links between the countries of the Asia-Pacific and the Southern Cone.

Programs: IRIAP's activities include teaching, research, advising, and publishing. Its research programs focus on Argentina and MERCOSUR relations with the Asia-Pacific region, Japan, China, and Southeast Asia.

Publications: IRIAP's first book, *Vietnam: Doi Moi (Renovacion) ¿Del Socialismo al Mercado?,* was published in 1995 by Grupo Editor Latinoamericano, Buenos Aires. The Institute will also publish works on domestic and foreign affairs in China, the evolution of small and medium-sized enterprises in the Asia-Pacific, and the process of economic integration in Asia.

Funding sources: IRIAP's economic support comes from individuals, foundations, enterprises, and international organizations.

Head of the institution: Dr. Carlos Juan Moneta, Founder-Director

Contact officers:
Lic. Ricardo Parera, Deputy Director

Lic. Sergio Cesarin, Coordinator

Instituto de Relaciones Internacionales de Asia-Pacífico (IRIAP)
Maipu 26, Dpto. 13G
1084 Buenos Aires
ARGENTINA
Tel. and Fax: (54-1) 343-5265
e-mail • iriap@wamani.org.ar

Instituto para la Integración de América Latina y el Caribe

Background and objectives: The Institute for Integration of Latin America and the Caribbean is an international organization created by an agreement between the Inter-American Development Bank (IDB) and the government of Argentina in 1964. As part of the Integration and Regional Programs Department at the IDB, INTAL has been actively involved in promoting regional integration through studies, training of public officials, information dissemination and by providing technical assistance to countries and the various sub-regional integration schemes. INTAL also assists the region's governments to bring the private sector, including representatives of the business community, labor, and non-governmental organizations (NGOs), into their integration policy deliberations.

Programs: INTAL's main activities during the 1996-2000 period include: (1) regional and national projects that provide technical support to sub-regional and hemispheric integration processes, particularly programs that support infrastructure links among countries, regional development of border areas, and legal aspects of integration as well as accession to new agreements. The Institute also provides technical support to the hemisphere-wide process of integration agreed upon during the Summit of the Americas in 1994 as well as fulfillment of the WTO disciplines; (2) policy-oriented forums for government officials, entrepreneurs, trade unionists, experts, NGO representatives, and sub-regional integration organizations to analyze issues in sub-regional and regional integration and generate practical proposals to governments participating in such integration schemes; (3) integration studies commissioned through specialized institutions on issues relating to the process of trade liberalization and integration within Latin America and the Caribbean and intra-regional links between the Western Hemisphere and the rest of the world; and (4) publications and information services provided by INTAL's Documentation Center, which specializes in information related to trade and integration in Latin America and the Caribbean and in non-regional blocs. INTAL also offers electronic access to its DATAINTAL, a database that contains timely foreign trade statistics on exports and imports of Latin America and the Caribbean countries.

Publications: INTAL produces *Integration & Trade* (published in English and Spanish), a journal on integration processes and trade relations within Latin American countries that is published every four months, and *Carta Mensual INTAL* (also published in both languages), a monthly newsletter providing information on regional events, meetings, agreements, and publications relating to integration. This newsletter also contains a bibliography section and institutional information about INTAL.

Funding sources: INTAL is primarily financed by a four-year technical cooperation grant of the Inter-American Development Bank and the government of Argentina. Other Latin American and Caribbean countries contribute on a voluntary basis.

Staffing: INTAL's core staff is made up of twelve.

Head of the institution: Mr. Juan Jose Taccone, Director

Contact officer: Mr. Uziel Nogueira, Deputy Director a.i.

Instituto para la Integración de América Latina y el Caribe
Esmeralda 130, piso 17
Casilla de Correo 39 - Sucursal I
(1401) Buenos Aires
ARGENTINA
Tel: (54-1) 320-1850
Fax: (54-1) 320-1865
e-mail • juantac@iadb.org
uzieln@iadb.org
int/inl@iadb.org

Universidad de Buenos Aires

Facultad de Ciencias Sociales

Background and objectives: The School of Social Sciences at the University of Buenos Aires (UBA), one of the most prestigious universities in Latin America, was created in 1988 as a teaching and research institution in the social sciences.

Programs: The School offers undergraduate and graduate programs through the Political Science, Sociology, Social Communications, Labor Relations, and Social Work departments. In the field of international relations, there is a Specialization Program within the Political Science Department that offers such courses as international relations theory, contemporary international relations, international economics, foreign policy, international law, and regional integration. The School has M.A. degree programs in social science research, political science, and communication and culture and a Ph.D. degree in the social sciences. Course instructors conduct research either in the multidisciplinary Research Institute of the School of Social Sciences, or in other public or private research centers. The Research Institute is an academic unit with more than 100 researchers, professors, and fellows. The Institute's research focuses on such topics as population, health and society, conflict and social change, labor studies, rural studies, gender, and public sector and state reform.

Publications: Since 1992, the School has published *Sociedad*, a biannual academic journal including relevant contributions and discussions among the social science academic community. The School's Research Institute publishes *Serie Libros Coleccion Sociedad*, featuring its research findings; *Serie Jovenes Investigadores*, which is co-edited with the Gino Germani research institute at UBA; and *Serie Documentos de Trabajo*.

Funding sources: The School is funded by the University of Buenos Aires, a public institution.

Staffing: The School has more than 100 full-time and 800 part-time researchers and professors, and an administrative staff of 270.

Head of the institution: Lic. Juan Carlos Portantiero, Dean

Contact officer: Lic. Olga Pisani, Executive Secretary

Facultad de Ciencias Sociales
Universidad de Buenos Aires
Marcelo T. de Alvear 2230
Buenos Aires
ARGENTINA
Tel: (54-1) 961-5964
Fax: (54-1) 962-2531
e-mail • opisani@gstion.fsoc.uba.ar

Centro de Estudos Estratégicos

Background and objectives: The Center for Strategic Studies (CEE) was established in 1992 by the Secretariat of Strategic Affairs (SAE), a department of ministerial status within the Presidency of the Republic of Brazil, to develop research projects and foster debate of relevant issues in the field of international security. The Center's mission is to promote studies and meetings that analyze global changes relevant to Brazil; to evaluate their consequences and point out options to cope with these changes; and to foster strategic thinking in all aspects of government.

Programs: The Center's programs are directed by the SAE and focus on four areas of analysis. In their *Strategies for Development* program, CEE promotes activities and meetings organized jointly with other SAE agencies to analyze proposals for reforming the Brazilian state and modernizing the public sector. In their *Global Strategic Insertion* program, CEE develops studies to evaluate Brazil's opportunities and risks present in new regional and global initiatives as well as in the development of strategic partnerships. In their *Strategic Management* program, the Center takes part in studies and activities that relate to national and organizational strategic management, including defense policy, crisis management, and strategic scenarios. In their *International Security and National Defense* program, CEE evaluates changes and transformations in a variety of international regimes and regional security, and their impact on Brazil's interests and policies.

Since its inception, the Center has promoted more than 400 events, including lectures, conferences, seminars, workshops, and courses, on such topics as state reforms, information highways, international capital flows, and Brazil's strategic perceptions. The Center coordinated and implemented the First National Meeting of Strategic Studies in 1994.

The Center houses a Documentation and Reference Center open to the public.

Publications: The Center issues the series "Documentos de Trabalho" (Working Papers) and in 1996 began publishing the journal *Parcerias Estratégicas* (Strategic Partnerships).

Funding sources: The Center is fully financed by the government of Brazil.

Staff: No information provided.

Head of the institution: Edmundo Sussumu Fujita, Undersecretary for Analysis and Evaluation, Secretariat for Strategic Affairs of the Presidency, Director Pro-Tempore, Center for Strategic Studies

Contact officer: Ms. Marcia Maro Da Silva, Coordinator of Events

Centro de Estudos Estratégicos
Seção de Divulgação-CEE
Setor Policial, Área 5, Quadra 3, Bloco A
CEP.70.610-200 - Brasilia - DF
BRAZIL
Tel: 55-061-245-5711 / 216-3112
Fax: (55-61) 245-4911 / 216-3947
e-mail • fujita@cepesc.gov.br
          ceecdr@cepesc.gov.br
URL • http://www.cepesc.gov.br

Instituto de Estudos Econômicos, Sociais e Políticos de São Paulo

Background and objectives: The São Paulo Institute of Economic, Social, and Political Studies (IDESP), founded in 1981, is an autonomous nonpartisan and not-for-profit private research institution that promotes public debate on economic, social, and political issues related to the consolidation of representative democracy, the modernization of the economy, and the achievement of social equity in Brazil.

Programs: IDESP conducts research, gives advice to governmental and non-governmental organizations, and organizes seminars and conferences in Brazil and abroad. IDESP's research areas include Political and Economic Reform (which addresses such issues as transitions from military to civilian rule in Brazil and Latin America); Judicial Studies (projects include measuring the economic costs of judicial inefficiency in Brazil); Political Parties and Elections (focusing on electoral and partisan history in Brazil, public opinion and electoral behavior, voting preferences in the National Congress elections, the functioning of the Electoral Branch, and electoral and party system reforms); Cultural and Scientific Development (which examines the science and art in Brazil, scientific interchange between Brazil and the United States and Europe, public policies on science, art, and culture, and the social and cultural history of immigration in Brazil); and Analysis and Evaluation of Public Policies (which studies human resources training, women's role, public transportation policies, and agricultural policies among other topics). In January 1996, together with the Center for Policy Studies of South Africa, IDESP organized a comparative Brazil-South Africa seminar in Johannesburg.

Publications: IDESP has published many books, which include *Brasil and Africa do Sul / Uma Comparação* (vol. 1, 1996), *História das Ciências Sociais no Brasil* (vol. 1, 1989 and vol. 2, 1995), *Imigração Política em São Paulo* (vol. 6, 1995), *O Judiciário em Debate* (1995), and *Uma Introdução ao Estudo da Justiça* (1995).

Funding sources: IDESP activities are funded primarily by grants and research and advisory contracts. International contributors include the Ford Foundation, the Tinker Foundation, the Andrew W. Mellon Foundation, and the Inter-American Development Bank. The most important national supporters are Brazilian government organizations such as FINEP (Financiadora de Estudos e Projetos), IPEA (Instituto de Pesquisa Econômica e Aplicada), CNPq (Conselho Nacional de Desenvolvimiento Científico e Tecnológico), and FAPESP (Fundação de Amparo à Pesquisa do Estado de São Paulo).

Staffing: IDESP has a part-time professional staff that includes a director, a research director, seven senior researchers, and seven researchers. It also has an administrative staff of eight.

Head of the institution: Dr. Sergio Miceli Pessoa de Barros, Director-President

Contact officer: Ms. Sandra Regina das Neves

Instituto de Estudos Econômicos,
    Sociais e Políticos de São Paulo
Rua Desembargador Guimarães No. 21
CEP 05002-050 (Agua Branca)
São Paulo
BRAZIL
Tel: (55-11) 864-7500
Fax: (55-11) 263-1605
e-mail • idesp@eu.ansp.br

Instituto de Estudos Políticos e Sociais

Background and objectives: The Institute of Political and Social Studies (IEPES), a nonprofit independent research center founded in 1979, is one of the leading social science research center in Latin America. The Institute's research projects seek to improve understanding of the major problems of Brazil, clarify the issues at stake in international relations, and examine the conditions of contemporary man in mass society.

Programs: IEPES's research is carried out by independent scholars who are appointed among a large group of professors and specialists connected with the Institute. The directors of the firms that form the Council of Institutional Members participate in discussions that critically evaluate the work of the Institute. These discussions allow the academic scholars to exchange views with those involved in the practical aspects of development, international relations, and the problems of contemporary society. IEPES's major studies include "Brazil, Democratic Society" (1983-84), which acknowledged that the democratic consolidation of Brazil will not be possible as long as 60% of the population remains marginalized; "Towards a New Social Pact" (1985-88), which critically surveyed the social problems of Brazil and examined the prerequisites for solving these problems; and the "Alvorada Project" (1988-91), which evaluated the issues of economic integration among Brazil, Argentina, and Uruguay and discussed the plausibility of integrating Mexico and Venezuela into the Latin American economic sphere. In 1995 the Institute concluded the second phase of this research project, focusing on specific issues related to MERCOSUR. Another proposed project, "Society, State, and Political Parties in Contemporary Brazil," envisions a large comparative study of the Brazilian public system in relation to three Latin American countries (Argentina, Mexico, and Venezuela) and three European nations (Germany, Italy, and Portugal). IEPES is also conducting a five-year research project, "A Critical Study of History" (1994-98), sponsored and financed by UNESCO. Its main goal is to survey the major civilizations in history according to a threefold analysis of the main factors that influenced the emergence, development, and eventual decline of each civilization. This project is directed by Professor Helio Jaguaribe, and the central research group includes Italian ambassador Ludovico Incisa Di Camerana and Professors Torcuato S. Di Tella (University of Buenos Aires), Manfred Mols (University of Mainz), Ulpiano T. Bezerra de Meneses (University of São Paulo), and Vicente de Paulo Barretto (Institute of Political and Social Studies). Eighteen scholars from European and American universities participate as thematic consultants within their academic specialties. Professors Albert O. Hirschman and Gabriel Almond are general consultants to the project.

Publications: IEPES publishes books based on its studies. Among the most important are *Transcendence and the World at the Turn of the Century* (1993); *Society, State, and Political Parties in Contemporary Brazil* (1992); *Brazil 2000* (1989); *Brazil: Reform or Chaos* (1988); and *Brazil, Democratic Society* (1985).

Funding sources: IEPES receives support from its institutional members to cover the Institute's daily maintenance; funds from public institutions such as FINEP, the Federal Agency for Financing Projects, CNPq, and the National Council for Research; and grants from international contributors such as UNESCO and the Ford Foundation.

Staffing: IEPES has a senior professional staff of seven, and one executive assistant.

Heads of the institution:
Dr. Israel Klabin, President

Prof. Helio Jaguaribe, Dean and Director of Academic Activities

Contact officer: Ms. Maria Augusta Leal Soares, Chief Secretary

Instituto de Estudos Politicos e Sociais-IEPES
Rua Barao de Oliveira Castro, 22
Rio de Janeiro, 22460-280 - RJ
BRAZIL
Tel: (55-21) 294-5243
Fax: (55-21) 259-4943

Instituto Universitario de Pesquisas do Rio de Janeiro

Background and objectives: The Rio de Janeiro University Research Institute (IUPERJ) was established in 1963 as a private nonprofit research and graduate education center in the social sciences. IUPERJ is part of Conjunto Universitario Candido Mendes, Sociedade Brasileira de Instrucao (SBI). It is directed by a Board of Directors and a Management Group.

Programs: IUPERJ's researchers study social and political theory (projects include "Democracy or Demosclerosis: Facts, Versions, and Outlooks" and "Social Crisis and Theoretical Deadlock: Convergence and Divergence"); social history and political studies (projects include "Politics and Culture in Brazil, 1950-68" and "The Evolution of Citizenship in Brazil"); state, formation of the state, and public policies (projects include "Stabilization, Reform, and Democratic Institutionality in Brazil," "Political Opportunities and Hurdles against Economic Modernization in Brazil," "Governability, Governance, and State Reform," "Bureaucracy and Politics in Contemporary Brazil," and "Strategic Elite, Political Culture, and Development Dilemmas"); social policy and social structure (projects include "Social Stratification and Mobility," "Racial and Gender Inequalities," and "Gender and Development"); urban studies (projects include "Social Organization and Daily Life in Rio de Janeiro," "Social Policy and Poverty in Brazil," and "Governability and Poverty in Urban Brazil"); sociology of intellectuals and professional occupations (projects include "Social Scientists and Public Life" and "The Magistrate and Judiciary Power"); and political parties, elections, and political participation (projects include "Presidential Elections in Brazil," "Comparative Study of Electoral Systems," "Multiple Political Parties, Parliamentary Majority, and Democracy," and "Institutional Reform in Contemporary Brazil").

IUPERJ maintains a Data Bank to support its research. *Urbandata* gathers information on literature, institutions, and persons in Brazil dedicated to urban research. IUPERJ also has a political indicator database that compiles information on election results and the operation of the Legislative, Executive, and Judiciary Branches.

IUPERJ offers master's degree and doctoral programs in political science and sociology.

Publications: Since 1966, IUPERJ has published *Dados-Revista de Ciencias Sociais*, an academic journal open to social scientists in Brazil and abroad and *Cadernos de Cojuntura*, a publication that focuses on political issues such as elections and the decision-making process. Monograph papers, as well as lectures and conferences delivered at IUPERJ, are published in the *Serie Estudos*. The Institute also publishes *Seminarios Friedrich Naumann / IUPERJ*, a journal of intellectual debate on public issues. As part of its academic activities, IUPERJ organizes seminars and conferences.

Funding sources: IUPERJ receives institutional support from Sociadade Brasileira de Instrucao (SBI), the Ford Foundation, and MEC/CAPES. Support for IUPERJ's research program and seminars during 1995 came from specific contributors such as the Ford Foundation, Financiadora de Estudos e Projetos (FINEP), Instituto Friedrich Naumann, the Andrew W. Mellon Foundation, and the University of Toronto.

Staffing: IUPERJ maintains a permanent faculty of twenty professor-researchers, and visiting professors join the faculty each semester.

Head of the institution: Dr. Renato Lessa, Executive Director

Instituto Universitario de Pesquisas do Rio de Janeiro
Rua da Matriz, 82 - Botafogo
22260-100, Rio de Janeiro - RJ
BRAZIL
Tel: (55-21) 537-8020
Fax: (55-21) 286-7146
e-mail • iuperj@omega.lncc.br
          rlessa@omega.lncc.br

Federation of Industries of the State of São Paulo / Center of Industries of the State of São Paulo

Background and objectives: The Federation of Industries of the State of São Paulo (FIESP) and the Center of Industries of the State of São Paulo (CIESP) have been working together for the last sixty years. FIESP, as the leader of the employers' organizations, deals with major policy decisions; CIESP offers services to the industrial companies in the state. FIESP/CIESP seeks to inform, support, and assist its members in matters related to economics, politics, law, technology, and environment. It also operates as a center of information gathering, research, development, and dissemination of ideas and facts on industry and service issues at the state level.

Programs: Most of FIESP/CIESP work is carried out by its departments. The Economics Department studies the economic performance of industry in São Paulo and Brazil as a whole; the Department of International Trade focuses on commercial relations with other countries and the supply of services to companies associated with CIESP; the Department of Industrial Infrastructure concentrates on areas such as energy, telecommunications, sanitation, transport, and mail; the Department of Documentation, Research, and Evaluation contributes to strategic planning of the Brazilian industrial sector; the Department of Technology promotes the technological capability and competitiveness of industry; the Department of Micro, Small, and Medium-sized Companies strives to improve the quality and the productivity of this sector through information on modern management systems, technological processes, and administrative and operational efficiency; the Department of Labor Relations helps affiliated unions with labor negotiations and pay settlements, and advises companies associated to CIESP on issues connected with industrial unrest and strikes; the Department of the Environment and Land Use ensures that the development of industry in the State of São Paulo takes environment issues into account; and the Department of International Affairs fosters international links between businessmen, foreign institutions, and international organizations by encouraging commercial ties and improving contacts abroad. CIESP also has forty-one regional offices throughout the state of São Paulo to decentralize the services to the companies.

Publications: FIESP/CIESP publishes *Revista da Industria*, the institution's weekly magazine, and proceedings of its most important meetings. It also issues daily fax reports on industry-related news.

Funding sources: Main support comes from FIESP's institutional members, the CIESP's associated companies, and the sales of services.

Staffing: FIESP/CIESP has approximately 600 employees.

Notes: Three other institutions are linked to FIESP/CIESP. The National Service for Industrial Training-SENAI provides technical professional training for the industry; Social Service for the Industry-SESI offers basic education, leisure, and social assistance to the industry workers; and the Roberto Simonsen Institute offers a forum for debate and exchange of ideas among business leaders and the society.

Head of the institution: Mr. Carlos Eduardo Moreira Ferreira, President

Contact officer: Mr. Luiz Antonio Martinez Vidal, Head of the President's Cabinet

FIESP/CIESP
Avenida Paulista, 1313
01311-923 - Cerqueira Cezar
São Paulo
BRAZIL
Tel: (55-11) 252-4200
Fax: (55-11) 284-3611

Fundação Getúlio Vargas

Background and objectives: The Fundação Getúlio Vargas is a private, nonprofit institution dedicated to the development and teaching of the social sciences. Created in 1944, it has played a strategic role in spreading ideas of economic efficiency in both public and private administration in Brazil. Headquartered in Rio de Janeiro, it also has centers in São Paulo, Brasilía, Manaus, and Curitiba.

Programs: Research and teaching in public and business administration, economics, history, and environmental protection are structured within the following main units: (1) The Instituto Brasileiro de Economia (IBRE), created in 1951, was Brazil's pioneer in the preparation of economic statistics. Now it has expanded its statistical research into applied economic analysis and is committed to publishing its findings for both decision makers and the general public. The Institute's regular projects focus primarily on agriculture, corporations, economics and government, and prices and trend analysis. IBRE publishes the monthly review *Conjuntura Econômica,* which includes brief analyses of current economic issues as well as database information for both research and commercial purposes. (2) Escola Brasileira de Administração Pública (EBAP), founded in 1952, was the first school of administration in Brazil. It has played an important role in training senior university and government staff in Latin America. EBAP's research agenda includes projects in the fields of government and administration, public sector management, public policies, public administration education, and short-term analysis of the public sector.

EBAP offers a master's program in Public Administration, and a doctoral program on management was scheduled to start in 1997. EBAP publishes the quarterly *Revista de Administração Pública* (RAP).

(3) Escola de Administração de Empresas de São Paulo (EAESP), which pursues teaching, research, and consulting with an emphasis on the area of business administration. Teaching programs include four-year undergraduate courses in business and public administration, and Master's of Science, MBA, and Ph.D. programs in business administration, public administration, and business economics. (4) Escola de Pós-Graduação em Economia (EPGE), a graduate program in economics that began its activities in 1966. Its main publications are the *Revista Brasileira de Economia* (RBE), currently featuring articles in both Portuguese and English; a collection of its theses in book form; and a collection of research papers. (5) Centro de Pesquisa e Documentação de História Contemporânea do Brazil (CPDOC), founded in 1973, which assembles and maintains an open collection of private documents and recorded oral testimonies by noteworthy public figures in post-1930 Brazilian political history such as Getulio Vargas, Oswaldo Aranha, Gustavo Capanema, Ulysses Guimaraes, and Tancredo Neves. It also conducts research work on contemporary Brazilian history such as citizenship and civil rights, elementary education, Rio de Janeiro's elites and Brazilian thought, foreign policy and international affairs, and the military. The Center publishes *Estudos Históricos,* a biannual journal open to social scientists from Brazil and abroad, as well as occasional papers. The Center has produced over 750 titles, including reference works, books, articles, theses, dissertations, and working papers.

Funding sources: The Fundação Getulio Vargas has three main sources of income: services, contributions, and endowment. Most funds come in the form of income from paid courses, consulting and other services, especially those related to the use of the Center's database; donations from private foundations, international organizations, the Brazilian government, state governments, and corporations; and income from real estate investment.

Staffing: No information provided

Head of the institution: Dr. José Alfonso Barbosa, General Director

Fundação Getúlio Vargas
Praia de Botafogo, 190 - 22253-900
Caixa Postal 62.591 - CEP 22.257-70
Rio de Janeiro
BRAZIL
Tel: (55-21) 536-9305
Fax: (55-21) 553-6372
e-mail • celina@fgvrj.br
URL • http://www.fgv.br

Instituto Brasileiro de Economia (IBRE)
Antonio Salazar Pessoa Brandao, Director
Tel: (55-21) 536-9219
e-mail • abrandao@fgvrj.br

Escola Brasileira de Administração Pública (EBAP)
Armando Santos Moreira da Cunha, Director
Tel: (55-21) 536-9150
e-mail • acunha@fgvrj.br

Escola de Administração de Empresas de São Paulo (EAESP)
Alain Florent Stempfer, Director
Tel: (55-11) 283-5444
e-mail • stempfer@eaesp.fgvsp.br

Escola de Pós-Graduação em Economia (EPGE)
Carlos Ivan Simonsen Leal, Director
Tel: (55-21) 536-9246
e-mail • civan@fgvrj.br

Centro de Pesquisa e Documentação de História
    Contemporânea do Brazil (CPDOC)
Lucia Lippi Oliveira, Director
Tel: (55-21) 536-9412
e-mail • llippi@fgvrj.br

Pontifícia Universidade Católica do Rio de Janeiro

Instituto de Relações Internacionais

Background and objectives: The Institute of International Relations (IRI) was established in 1979 by the Pontifical Catholic University in Rio de Janeiro as a research and graduate teaching institution dedicated to the study of international affairs.

Programs: IRI concentrates on several research areas within the field of international relations. In its Regionalization and Integration Processes program, IRI focuses on the formation of MERCOSUL from a comparative perspective with other similar initiatives such as the European Community. It seeks to provide a historical, institutional, and functional analysis with emphasis on its political, institutional, and social aspects.

The International Institutions program investigates the ways the international system is stabilized as well as analyzes existing international authority structures. It has as its main areas of research international and transnational organizations, international regimes, and the principles and mechanisms of hegemonic order in the international system.

The Brazilian Foreign Policy and International Relations program focuses on foreign policy analysis from different theoretical perspectives to explain Brazilian contemporary foreign policy. In addition, the program addresses the political, economic, and military variables that explain Brazilian international relations.

The International Political Economy program investigates the relationship between transnational economic processes and the political power structure of the international system.

The Security Issues in the Contemporary World program examines such topics as security issues in a post-Cold War world.

The Environment and International Relations program examines the impact of environmental questions on international relations.

IRI also offers a master's degree program in international relations.

Publications: IRI publishes *Contexto International*, a biannual academic journal featuring articles by Brazilian and foreign experts on international relations and comparative politics. IRI also publishes *IRI-Textos*, which presents research by IRI's academic staff.

Funding sources: IRI's main contributors include CAPES, CNPq, FAPERJ, and the Ford Foundation.

Staffing: The permanent research staff consists of four full-time and one part-time researchers and five visiting scholars or professors from other academic departments.

Head of the institution: Ms. Sonia de Camargo, Director

Contact officer: Ms. Maria Helena Marques, Assistant

Instituto de Relações Internacionais
Pontifícia Universidade Católica do Rio de Janeiro
Rua Marques de São Vicente 225
Casa 19- Gavea - 22453-900
Rio de Janeiro - RJ
BRAZIL
Tel: (55-21) 529-9494
Fax: (55-21) 274-1296
e-mail • iripuc@rdc.puc-rio.br
URL • http://www.puc-rio.br

Universidade de São Paulo

Núcleo de Pesquisa em Relações Internacionais

Background and objectives: The Research Center for International Relations at the University of São Paulo, founded in 1989, is a multidisciplinary research institution that studies international relations, international political economy, and security and defense; teaches courses and seminars at the undergraduate, graduate, and post-graduate levels; publishes research and teaching materials; and provides consultancy and advisory services in its areas of study and expertise.

Programs: The Center's research projects have examined such topics as the history of Brazilian foreign policy; the obstacles to hemispheric integration; the implications of regional economic integration in the Americas and the Pacific Rim; Brazilian-Japanese relations and the international context that may affect them; China's economic reforms and their international effects; and the role of multilateralism in security matters in the Asia-Pacific region. The Center's ongoing projects include "Sixty Years of Brazilian Foreign Policy," a history of Brazilian foreign policy since 1930; and "Forum MERCOSUR/NAFTA," through which non-governmental leaders and academics from the MERCOSUR and NAFTA countries study obstacles to hemispheric integration and recommend a policy agenda.

Publications: The Center publishes *Politica Externa*, a quarterly journal co-edited by the Editora Paz e Terra Publishing House; *Carta International*, a monthly newsletter featuring analysis and comments on international news from a Brazilian point of view; *Serie Politica Internacional* and *Serie Carta Internacional*, occasional papers featuring the Center's research and activities.

Other publications include *O Futuro do Brasil: A America Latina e o fim da Guerra Fria* (1992) and *Anais do Coloquio Internacional "Integraçao Economica Regional: Objetivos e perspectivas"* (1992).

Funding sources: The Center's main support comes from FAPESP, the Ford Foundation, and FUNAG at the Ministry on Foreign Relations of Brazil.

Staffing: The Center's permanent staff is made up of two directors, six researchers, and one administrative officer.

Heads of the institution:
Dr. Jose Augusto Guilhon Albuquerque, Co-Director

Dr. Henrique Altemani de Oliveira, Co-Director

Contact officer: Ms. Janina Onuki, Researcher

Núcleo de Relacoes Internacionais da Universidade de São Paulo
Rua do Anfiteatro, 181, Colmeia, Favo 7
Cidade Universitaria
05508-900, São Paulo - SP
BRAZIL
Tel: (55-11) 818-3061
Fax: (55-11) 210-4154
e-mail • guilhon@usp.br

University of Brasília
Instituto de Ciência Política e Relações Internacionais

Departmento do Relações Internacionais

Background and objectives: The Department of International Relations, which is part of the Institute of Political Science and International Relations (IPR) of the University of Brasilia, seeks to train professionals to work in the international area, conduct research on international issues and Brazilian foreign policy, and interact with Brazilian and foreign institutions to promote joint academic activities and provide services that require expertise in the field of international affairs. Since its formation in the mid-1970s, the Department has worked in close cooperation with the Brazilian Ministry of Foreign Affairs through joint seminars, regular participation of diplomats in the Department courses, and in that of University professors in the preparation of young diplomats. Recently the Department has also developed partnerships with other public agencies, like the Secretariat for Strategic Affairs of the Presidency of the Republic.

Programs: The Department has undergraduate and M.A. degree programs in international relations. The B.A. in international relations enrolls forty students per semester and at present has 292 students. The master's program selects ten candidates per semester and currently has fifty-one graduate students. The Department also has a tutorial program financed by the Brazilian Ministry of Education to prepare undergraduate students to pursue an academic career.

The Department's main research areas include political economy and international political economy; environment and natural resources; science, technology, and culture; strategic studies, security, and national defense; regional integration and human rights; telecommunications and media studies; and drug trafficking and international relations.

The Department also organizes seminars as well as specialization courses such as the management of international technical cooperation, which was recently targeted to Brazilian civil servants.

Publications: The Department works in partnership with the Department of History of the University of Brasilia to support the oldest Brazilian publication on international affairs, the *Brazilian Review of International Politics*, to which our faculty contributes regularly. The Department also publishes a series of occasional papers. In the last two years, most books published by faculty members focused on international protection of human rights, environment, drug trafficking, and globalization.

Funding sources: The Department is mainly funded by the University of Brasilia, a federal university. It also receives funds from governmental agencies such as the Ministry of Education and the Ministry of Science and Technology to support specific research projects and programs.

Staffing: The Department of International Relations has nineteen permanent professors, most of whom are Ph.D.s. The Department usually hosts three to four associate researchers, who conduct research, teach courses, and supervise student work. The Department has a secretary responsible for administrative tasks, but faculty also rely on IPR's administrative staff.

Notes: At present, the Department is consolidating and institutionalizing its research programs in order to reach greater autonomy in financial and administrative terms.

Head of the institution: Prof. Antonio Jorge Ramalho da Rocha

Contact officers:
Prof. Antonio Jorge R. da Rocha

Prof. Marcus Faro de Castro, Coordinator for Graduate Studies

Department of International Relations
University of Brasília
Caixa Postal 04561, 70910-900, Brasilia, D.F.
BRAZIL
Tel: (55-61) 348-2426 / 348-2865
Fax: (55-61) 273-3930
e-mail • ajrrocha@nutecnet.com.br
           mfcastro@guarany.cpd.unb.br

Centro de Estudios del Desarrollo

Background and objectives: The Development Studies Center (CED) is an independent nonprofit private institution established in 1980 to discuss public policy strategies and policies on issues that affect civil society and the political system. It seeks technically and politically feasible ways to promote sustained development, equity, and democratic stability.

Programs: CED's thematic research areas are territorial development and decentralization, with emphasis on local and regional governments, urban and regional development, and other issues; security and domestic peace; environment, with a focus on Chilean environmental law, environmental impact assessment, and environmental management at both public and private levels; gender and development; civil-military relations; international relations and foreign policy, with an emphasis on international trade and investment; and entrepreneurial cooperation, legal and commercial information systems, the effects of global, regional and national economic policies, and financial and negotiation strategies. Some recent studies include "NAFTA and the Environmental Impact of the Agreement on the Chilean Regions," "Environmental Future Scenarios and Free Trade Agreements," and "Economic Relations of Chile and the Impact of Trade Agreements on Different Sectors." During 1995-96, CED also organized three workshops on "Free Trade Agreements and the Agricultural Sector in Chile," "Chile and the Asia-Pacific Countries," and "Economic International Relations between Chile and the United States."

Publications: CED publishes *Materiales para la Discusion* and *Cuadernos del CED* series.

Funding sources: To support its activities, CED has developed institutional, technical, and financial cooperation agreements with such institutions as the Ministry of Defense, the Ministry of Foreign Affairs, the European Union, USAID, the Ford Foundation, and many other private companies.

Staffing: CED has twelve full-time researchers and eighteen part-time researchers, and an administrative staff of nine.

Heads of the institution:
Mr. Gabriel Valdes, Honorary President

Mr. Patricio Silva, Chairman

Contact officer: Mr. Eduardo Dockendorff, Executive Director

Centro de Estudios del Desarrollo
Nueva de Lyon 0128
Providencia, Santiago
CHILE
Tel: (56-2) 231-2723
Fax: (56-2) 232-6860

Centro de Estudios Públicos

Background and objectives: The Center for Public Studies (CEP), founded in 1980, is an academic nonprofit private foundation dedicated to the study of principles and institutions that sustain a democratic free society. CEP seeks to influence public opinion and policy in favor of individual liberties, private property rights, and democratic government.

Programs: CEP's research focuses on issues such as environment, macroeconomics, finance, social policy, law, public health, education, public opinion polls, and political philosophy. In addition to its research, CEP organizes seminars, conferences, and roundtables. During 1996, CEP's relevant seminars included "Economic Effects of Urban Regulation," "The Industrial Revolution: Past and Future," and "South and North in the New World Culture: Tradition and Innovation in American Populations." Over the last years, CEP has sponsored seminars and conferences by Mario Vargas Llosa, Peter Berger, Giovanni Sartori, Juan Litz, Salman Rushdie, Arnold Harberger, Claudio Veliz, and Francis Fukuyama, among others. CEP also conducts public opinion polls.

Publications: CEP publishes *Estudios Publicos,* a quarterly journal, and Documentos de Trabajo, Puntos de Referencia, Serie de Antecedentes, and Al Dia. CED has published *Competitividad. El Gran Desafio de las Empresas Chilenas* (1996), *Analisis Empirico del Tipo de Cambio en Chile* (1996), *Chile hacia el 2000: Ideas para el Desarrollo* (1995), and *La Salud en el Siglo XXI: Cambios Necesarios* (1995), among others.

Funding sources: CEP's economic support comes mainly from individual and local business groups, as well as foreign donors. CEP has received support from international foundations such as the Institute for the Study of Economic Culture (Boston University), Hanns-Seidel-Stiftung of Munich, the Ford Foundation, the Tinker Foundation, the Educational Innovation Center of the Manhattan Institute, and the Atlas Economic Research Foundation. It also has received support from the United States International Development Agency (USAID).

Staffing: CEP has eleven permanent researchers and ten associated researchers. Much of CEP's work is carried out through contract research.

Head of the institution: Mr. Arturo Fontaine Talavera, Executive Director

Contact officer: Ms. Ximena Hinzpeter

Centro de Estudios Públicos
Monsenor Sotero Sanz No. 175
Providencia, Santiago
CHILE
Tel: (56-2) 231-5324
Fax: (56-2) 233-5253
e-mail • cep@iactiva.cl
URL • http://www.iactiva.cl/ep

Comisión Económica para América Latina y el Caribe

Background and objectives: The Economic Commission for Latin America and the Caribbean (ECLAC) was set up in 1948 to coordinate policies for the promotion of economic development in the Latin American and Caribbean regions. ECLAC's main objectives are to improve the level of economic activity in the region; to study economic and technical problems of development in the region; to collect, evaluate, and disseminate economic data; to help formulate practical policies for regional development; and to collaborate in technical assistance programs of the United Nations. ECLAC has sub-regional headquarters in Mexico City, serving Mexico, Central America, and the Spanish-speaking Caribbean, and in Port of Spain, for the non-Spanish-speaking Caribbean. It also has offices in Bogota, Brasilia, Buenos Aires, Montevideo, and Washington. The Executive Secretariat functions in Santiago, Chile.

Programs: ECLAC conducts research, disseminates information, provides technical assistance, participates in seminars and conferences, and gives training courses. In recent years, ECLAC has focused on such issues as social policy, environmental and demographic trends, educational reform and development, and the need to improve regional integration and the region's position in the world economy. ECLAC conducts programs in Economic Development; Social Development; International Trade, Development Financing, and Transport; Industrial, Agricultural, and Technological Modernization; Environment, Natural Resources, and Human Settlements; Statistics and Economic Projections; Integration of Women in Development; and Regional Integration and Cooperation. In 1957, ECLAC established the Latin American Demographic Center (CELADE) to collaborate with governments in formulating population policies and to provide demographic estimates and projections, documentation, data processing, and training facilities. In 1962, it established the Latin American and Caribbean Institute for Economic and Social Planning (ILPES) to undertake research and to provide training and advisory services in the region on such issues as public policy planning, decentralization and development, regional development, and public investment management.

Publications: ECLAC publishes the following documents and periodicals: *Economic Survey of Latin America and the Caribbean* (Spanish and English versions, annual), *Economic Panorama of Latin America* (Spanish and English versions, annual), *Social Panorama of Latin America* (Spanish and English versions, annual), *CEPAL Review* (Spanish and English versions, three issues per year), *Preliminary Overview of the Economy of Latin America and the Caribbean* (Spanish and English versions, annual), *Statistical Yearbook for Latin America and the Caribbean* (bilingual, Spanish and English, annual), *CEPALINDEX* (annual), *PLANINDEX* (twice yearly), *Cuadernos Estadisticos de la CEPAL, Demographic Bulletin* (bilingual, Spanish and English, twice yearly), *Notas de Poblacion* (two issues per year), *DOCPAL-Resumenes sobre Poblacion en America Latina* (twice yearly), *ECLAC's Chronicles* (Spanish, English, and Portuguese, monthly), *Notas sobre la Economia y el Desarrollo* (monthly), *Boletin de Facilitacion del Comercio y Transporte-FAL* (bimonthly), *Cooperation and Development* (Spanish and English, quarterly), *Micronoticias* (weekly), *Estudios e Informes de la CEPAL,* and *Cuadernos de la CEPAL.* ECLAC also publishes books, studies, reports, and bibliographical bulletins.

Funding sources: ECLAC's share of the United Nations budget for the biennium 1995-1997 was approximately US$90.65 million. It has been estimated that for this same period, ECLAC will receive voluntary contributions of approximately US$17.65 million from the Official Development Assistance activities of different countries both within and outside Latin America and the Caribbean. These funds are used to finance specific research, training, and technical assistance projects.

Staffing: ECLAC's Executive Secretariat has 639 staff members, 224 of which are international (56 women), and 415 local (227 women).

Notes: ECLAC member states are Antigua and Barbuda, Argentina, Bahamas, Barbados, Belize, Bolivia, Brazil, Canada, Chile, Colombia, Costa Rica, Cuba, Dominica, Dominican Republic, Ecuador, El Salvador, France, Grenada, Guatemala, Guyana, Haiti, Honduras, Italy, Jamaica, Mexico, the Netherlands, Nicaragua, Panama, Paraguay, Peru, Portugal, Saint Kitts and Nevis, Saint Lucia, Saint Vincent and the Grenadines, Spain, Suriname, Trinidad and Tobago, the United Kingdom of Great Britain and Northern Ireland, the United States of America, Uruguay, and Venezuela. Its associate members are Aruba, the British Virgin Islands, Montserrat, the Netherlands Antilles, Puerto Rico, and the United States Virgin Islands.

Head of the institution: Dr. José Antonio Ocampo, Executive Secretary

Contact officer: Mr. Ernesto Ottone, Secretary of the Commission

Economic Commission for Latin America and the Caribbean
Edificio Naciones Unidas
Avenida Dag Hammarskjold
Casilla 179-D
Santiago de Chile
CHILE
Tel: (56-2) 210-2000
Fax: (56-2) 208-0252 / 208-1946
Cable: UNATIONS
Telex: 340295 UNSTGO CK
e-mail • postmaster@eclac.cl
URL • http://www.eclac.cl

Comisión Sudamericana de Paz

Background and objectives: The South American Commission for Peace was established in 1987 as a nonprofit private advisory and research institution to strengthen democracy in the region and to promote democratic concepts of regional security and peace. As a non-governmental organization, it serves as a consultative member of the United Nations Economic and Social Committee (ECOSOC).

Programs: CSP's activities include research and advising and dissemination of information on Latin American peace and security issues. The Commission's main interests are regional integration, democratization, security, drug trafficking, the environment, mutual confidence measures, social development, and citizen security and violence. CSP also organizes seminars and conferences on related topics, which recently included the seminar "Styles of Making Politics and the Necessary Reforms for Governability in South America" (October 1996).

Publications: The Commission publishes *Dialogos*, a quarterly journal. Recent books include *Reforma Politica, Gobernabilidad, Desarrollo Social: Retos del Siglo XXI* (1996), *Desarrollo Social* (1995), and *America Latina: Una realidad expectante* (1994).

Funding sources: CSP funding comes mainly from Latin American governments (Brazil, Bolivia, Uruguay, and Chile). It also receives support for specific activities and projects from international organizations such as the Inter-American Development Bank, the European Union, and from governmental organizations such as the States' Secretariat for International Cooperation and for Iberoamerica (SECIPI), Spain; and Corporacion Andina de Fomento (CAF), Venezuela.

Staffing: The Commission has three part-time consultants and is supported by an administrative staff of seven.

Heads of the institution:
Mr. Juan Somavia V., General Secretary

Mr. Carlos Contreras, Executive Secretary

Contact officer: Mr. Carlos Contreras, Executive Secretary

Comisión Sudamericana de Paz
Juan Williams Noon 643
Providencia
Casilla 16085, Correo 9
Santiago
CHILE
Tel: (56-2) 235-3073 / 235-7117
Fax: (56-2) 235-0279
e-mail • Comdepaz@Reuna.cl
              Compaseg@Reuna.cl

Corporación de Investigaciones Económicas para Latinoamerica

Background and objectives: The Economic Research Corporation for Latin America (CIEPLAN), founded in 1976, is a private, nonprofit institution that carries out economic and social research to improve economic policies and development strategies in Chile and Latin America.

Programs: CIEPLAN's activities include research studies, conferences, seminars, workshops, publications, and extension activities. CIEPLAN's research field is divided into four areas. The first area deals with macroeconomic policies, focusing on short-term economic problems such as inflation or balance-of-payment disequilibria. The analysis is based on econometric models, with an emphasis on how economic policies affect employment, inflation, growth, etc. The second area is devoted to international economy and trade policies. Originally, CIEPLAN focused on the Latin American integration process, trade policies, and foreign investment policies. Ongoing research in this area deals with bilateral and multilateral free trade and the competitiveness of Chilean exports. The third area, social policies and income distribution, addresses the problems of poverty and inequality in Chilean society, the impact of specific social policies on these problems, and the possible policy alternatives. The fourth area focuses on the long-term formulation of economic and social development strategies, with emphasis on institutional aspects. A more recent line of research analyzes the transformations undergone by the state in the context of development, with special reference to relationships with the private sector and the formulation of industrial policies. Recently, CIEPLAN conducted research on Chilean commercial policies and strategies, export development, and Chilean economic relations with NAFTA, MERCOSUR, APEC, and the European Union. CIEPLAN is also studying economic relations between Chile and the Asia-Pacific countries. During 1990-95, CIEPLAN organized a Seminar on Economic Policies for Latin America (SPEAL) in collaboration with other research centers in South America, to promote discussion of political economy issues, improve the analytical skills and methodological tools of Latin American economists, and strengthen relations among research institutions in the region. This program comprised thirty-three conferences and seminars that took place in nine South American capitals. In 1995, this project was extended for five more years but focusing only in Bolivia, Ecuador, Paraguay, and Peru.

Publications: CIEPLAN disseminates its research results through such publications as *Coleccion Estudios CIEPLAN*, a biannual academic journal containing the final versions of the most significant studies, and two working papers: *Notas Tecnicas,* focusing on methodological and technical aspects of the Corporation's research, and *Apuntes,* which presents general conclusions of CIEPLAN's works to the public.

Funding sources: CIEPLAN's activities are economically supported by grants from international foundations such as CIDA and IDRC from Canada, the Ford Foundation, and SAREC and through projects prepared for Chilean ministries and other public sector institutions.

Staffing: The Corporation has eight senior researchers, two of them on a part-time basis. They all hold Ph.D. degrees either in economics or sociology. There are also three junior researchers and three research assistants.

Head of the institution: Mr. Joaquin Vial R-T, Executive Director

Corporación de Investigaciones Económicas para Latinoamerica
Mac Iver 125, Piso 17
Casilla 16496, Correo 9
Santiago
CHILE
Tel: (56-2) 633-3836 / 638-3246
Fax: (56-2) 632-6677
e-mail • cieplan@cieplan.cl

Fundación Chilena del Pacifico

Background and objectives: The Chile-Pacific Foundation is a nonprofit institution established in 1994 as a joint initiative of the Chilean government, the private sector, and academic institutions interested in the development of trade and investment across the Pacific Basin. The Foundation aims to improve the information available in Chile on the Pacific Basin economies, as well as to increase the levels of economic, social, and political information on Chile throughout the Pacific area.

Programs: The Foundation's program of activities seeks to integrate and coordinate public, private, and academic initiatives on Chile's links to the Pacific Basin. The Foundation participates in all major programs of the Pacific Economic Cooperation Council (PECC), in its capacity as the Chilean Committee of Pacific Economic Cooperation: PECC Trade Policy Forum, Food and Agriculture Forum, Financial Markets Development Program, Minerals Forum, and others. The Foundation supports Chilean participation in ABAC (APEC Business Advisory Council), and serves as consultant to the government on APEC policies.

Publications: The Foundation together with the Institute of International Relations at the University of Chile has published *La Participacion de Chile en los Organismos Multilaterales de la Cuenca del Pacifico* (1996), and *Las Economias de Asia Pacifico: Desarrollo Economico, Comercio Internacional e Inversion Extranjera* (1997).

Funding sources: The Foundation receives support from a public budget appropriation (50%) and private donations and contracts (50%).

Staffing: The Foundation has a core staff that includes the executive secretary, a consultant, and three administrative staff.

Notes: In January 1995, the Foundation took over the tasks of Pacific Economic Cooperation Council (PECC) coordination from the Economic Division of the Ministry of Foreign Relations. It serves as a consultant to the Chilean government on APEC policy. The Foundation has also been named by the Chilean government as Chile's APEC Study Center. The Foundation cooperates closely with the Chilean Chapter of the Pacific Basin Economic Council (PBEC), by scheduling joint events and exchanging information on matters of common interest.

Head of the institution: Mr. Edgardo Boeninger, Chairman

Contact officer: Manfred Wilhelmy, Executive Secretary

Chile-Pacific Foundation
Av. Los Leones 382, Oficina 701
Providencia, Santiago de Chile
CHILE
Tel: (56-2) 334-3200
Fax: (56-2) 334-3201
e-mail • chilpec@reuna.cl
URL • http//:www.funpacifico.cl

Libertad y Desarrollo

Background and objectives: Freedom and Development, founded in 1990, is a private research institution that promotes economic development within a free social order.

Programs: Freedom and Development has six research programs. The Economic Program emphasizes the promotion of economic development based on individual freedom and private property; the Social Program focuses on the analysis and eradication of extreme poverty; the Political Program analyzes national issues such as crime, family, municipal and congressional elections, and the penitentiary and judicial systems; the Legislative Program analyzes legislative initiatives and projects; the Center for International Economy studies global economic and financial events, especially within the Latin American countries; and the Communications Program is responsible for the dissemination of Freedom and Development's studies and proposals. The institution also gives advice to governmental organizations, especially the Chilean Congress, through juridical, economic, and technical analyses.

Publications: Freedom and Development publishes the following periodicals: *Serie Programa Economico, Social, Politico-Institucional y Legislativo,* with in-depth studies on key national issues; *Temas Publicos,* a weekly newsletter featuring brief analyses of public issues; *Reseña Legislativa,* a weekly publication that covers legislative proposals under discussion in the Congress; *Informe de Coyuntura Economica,* a monthly report on relevant national economic issues; *Revista Libertad y Desarrollo,* which presents opinions on current political, economic, and social issues; and *Coyuntura Internacional,* featuring economic and financial information on the developed world and the most important Latin American economies. Each issue of this journal focuses on a specific country but includes regional and global economic analysis as well. Freedom and Development has also published *Ecologia de Mercado* (1995), *Las Tareas de Hoy: Politicas Sociales y Economicas para una Sociedad Libre* (1994), *La Pobreza. Desafios de Ayer y Hoy* (1994), *La Transformacion Economica de Chile: Del Estatismo a la Libertad Economica* (1993), and *Private Solutions to Public Problems* (1993).

Funding sources: Libertad y Desarrollo finances its activities through studies and researches that are prepared for various private institutions, enterprises, and individuals. It also receives support from institutions such as the Tinker Foundation, the Center for International Private Enterprise, and the Atlas Foundation.

Staffing: Libertad y Desarrollo has fifteen full-time and seven part-time professionals, and eleven administrative staff.

Heads of the institution:
Mr. Carlos F. Caceres C., President of the Board

Mr. Cristian Larroulet V., Executive Director

Libertad y Desarrollo
San Crescente 551
Las Condes, Santiago
CHILE
Tel: (56-2) 234-1894
Fax: (56-2) 234-1893
e-mail • ild@mailnet.rdc.cl
URL • http://www.his.com/~ild

Universidad de Chile

Centro de Económia Internacional y Desarrollo

Background and objectives: The International Economy and Development Center (CENDES) was established as a research institution within the Economic Science Department at the University of Chile in 1992 to organize research programs and disseminate publications on growth and international economic issues regarding Chile and its trading partners.

Programs: CENDES's studies and teaching activities concentrate on the international economy and its impact on development. One major activity is the monitoring of commercial and financial agreements in which Chile participates, such as those related to APEC. CENDES has a research program on Asia-Pacific that has encouraged the preparation of papers in connection with the Chilean participation in APEC, and collaborates with the government on trade policy. Currently, CENDES is conducting a joint study with the University of Tsukuba (Japan) and the University of Buenos Aires (Argentina) on science and technology policies in Japan and the possibility of applying them in Latin America.

Publications: CENDES research is published through the Department of Economics at the University of Chile, which publishes *Estudios de Economia*, an academic journal.

Funding sources: The Center is funded by the University of Chile.

Staffing: CENDES has four full-time and two part-time professors, and an administrative staff of two.

Head of the institution: Dr. Manuel R. Agosin, Director

Centro de Económia Internacional y Desarrollo
Universidad de Chile
Diagonal Paraguay No. 257
Oficina 1801
Santiago
CHILE
Tel: (56-2) 678-3464
Fax: (56-2) 222-0775
e-mail • magosin@decon.facea.uchile.cl
URL • http://www.decon.facea.uchile.cl

Universidad de Chile

Instituto de Estudios Internacionales

Background and objectives: The Institute of International Studies of the University of Chile is an educational and research center offering post-graduate and professional training in political, legal, economic, and historical fields. Since its creation in 1966, the Institute has taken an interest in Chilean and Latin American foreign relations in the framework of the Pacific Basin. The Institute is a leading member of the Chilean APEC Study Centers Consortium.

Programs: The Institute has organized several national and international conferences to promote Chilean and Latin American participation in the Pacific Basin cooperation schemes and to enhance understanding of the region's political, economic, and cultural diversity. Conferences devoted to Asia-Pacific issues include "Asia-Pacific: Economic and Political Dimensions and the Role of Chile" (1996); "Regionalization and Mineral Resources," supported by the Mineral Resources and Energy Task Force of the PECC (1993); and "The Business Community and the Pacific" (1989 and 1991). Institute faculty members participate in working groups sponsored by the Pacific Basin entities and cooperation organizations, such as PBEC and PECC. The Institute has also supported the Chilean Committee for the PECC since its creation in 1991.

Publications: Since 1967, the Institute has published *Estudios Internacionales*, a quarterly journal. The Institute has also edited books and studies on the Pacific region, such as *Elaboration of a Strategy for International Relations of Chile with Multilateral Organizations of the Pacific Basin* (1994), *Comparative Perspectives of Cooperation and Regional Integration in Southeast Asia and Latin America* (German version 1993, Spanish version 1995), *The Exclusive Economic Zone and the Regime of the Fisheries* (1982), and *The Pacific Community in Perspective* (1980).

Funding sources: The Institute's main funding comes from the University of Chile and from services provided by the Institute such as courses, seminars, and publications. Specific institutional projects are financed by different sources, which include local companies, the Ministry of Foreign Affairs, the Organization of American States, the Canadian Embassy, the Tinker Foundation, and the Volkswagen Stiftung.

Staffing: The Institute has a professional staff of four.

Heads of the institution:
Dr. Alberto van Klaveren (on leave), Director

Prof. Joaquin Fermandois, Acting Director

Contact officer: Prof. Hernan Gutierrez, Coordinator for Pacific Affairs

Instituto de Estudios Internacionales
Universidad de Chile
Av. Condell 249
Santiago
CHILE
Tel: (56-2) 274-5377
Fax: (56-2) 274-0155
e-mail • inesint@abello.dic.uchile.cl
URL • http://www.uchile.cl/facultades/estinter

Universidad Gabriela Mistral

Instituto de Estudios del Pacífico

Background and objectives: The Institute for Pacific Studies at the Gabriela Mistral University, created in 1985, is a research and advisory institution dedicated to the study of Pacific Rim issues. It hopes to become a national center on information, contacts, interchanges, and projects related to the Pacific area, and to establish links with academic and business institutions and leaders in the Pacific Rim countries.

Programs: The Institute organizes seminars and conferences on Pacific Rim issues and countries. These events focus on topics such as cooperation and integration, economic development, and international and political relations.

Publications: Since 1986, the Institute has published *Boletin del Instituto del Pacifico*, a bimonthly publication issued in English and Spanish; *Profile of Chile*, an annual publication with brief summaries of the Chilean economic, political, and social situation; and the *Asian Pacific Economic Council and Its Members,* with information on the main geographic, political, social, cultural, and economic aspects of the APEC countries. The Institute has a radio program, *Una Ventana al Pacifico*, which has been broadcasting daily since 1994. Leading academics, politicians, businessmen, and senior diplomats interested in the Pacific Rim are invited to appear on this program. The Institute also publishes *Seleccion de Programas: Una Ventana al Pacifico*, a monthly publication featuring the most interesting programs broadcast by radio.

Funding sources: The Institute is totally supported by the University.

Staffing: The Institute has three full-time and three part-time researchers, and one secretary.

Notes: The Institute was an active member of the organizing committee for PEEC's General Annual Meeting, which was held in Santiago, Chile, in 1997.

Heads of the institution:

Mrs. Alicia Romo, President, Universidad Gabriela Mistral

Mr. Erik Haindl R., Director

Mr. Jesus Gines Ortega, Executive Secretary

Contact officer: Mr. Jesus Gines Ortega

Instituto de Estudios del Pacífico
Universidad Gabriela Mistral
Ladislao Errazuriz 2073
Providencia
Santiago
CHILE
Tel: (56-2) 204-9073
Fax: (56-2) 204-9074
e-mail • jgines@ugm.cl

Fundación para la Educación Superior y el Desarrollo

Background and objectives: The Higher Education and Development Foundation (Fedesarrollo) was established in 1970 as a private, nonprofit, independent research center. Its goals are to promote cultural awareness, scientific knowledge, and higher education to further social and economic development.

Programs: Fedesarrollo's research concentrates on macroeconomics, development economics, international economics, economic forecasts, sectoral studies, income distribution and labor markets, health economics, and environmental economics. It organizes seminars on a variety of topics to provide timely and accurate analysis on economic and social issues. Fedesarrollo conducts quarterly economic debates in which experts from academia, government, and business sectors discuss the most controversial economic and social issues. Every six months, Fedesarrollo provides economic forecasts. This exercise is of great relevance for the design of policies in Colombia. Fedesarrollo also conducts public opinion polls to sense the business climate and to assess the situation of the industrial, commercial, and construction sectors. Fedesarrollo provides intense training to young economists through research and active participation in seminars and conferences within and outside the institution. Recently, Fedesarrollo has organized the Inter-American Seminar on Economics (jointly with the NBER), and the Latin-American Network of Macroeconomics (jointly with the IDRC from Canada). In 1997 it hosted the second meeting of the Latin American and Caribbean Economic Association (LACEA). Fedesarrollo also has a visiting fellows program.

Publications: Fedesarrollo publishes *Coyuntura Economica*, a quarterly journal with current economic analysis; and *Coyuntura Social*, a biannual journal devoted to the analysis of social issues. Recent books include *Informe de la Misión de Estudios del Mercado de Capitales, Inflación, Estabilización y Política Cambiaria en América Latina: Lecciones de los años noventa* and *El Crecimiento Económico en América Latina: Teoría y práctica.*

Funding sources: Fedesarrollo's revenues come from research projects carried out for domestic and international agencies. The World Bank, the United Nations Development Program, the Inter-American Development Bank, the Economic Commission for Latin America and the Caribbean, and other multilateral organizations have sponsored Fedesarrollo's research activities. Grants from the Ford Foundation and the International Research Center of Canada have also been important. The sale of publications, along with seminar and conference fees, account for one third of the institution's income.

Staffing: Fedesarrollo's professional staff is made up of twenty-five economists and social scientists. Its activities are supported by an administrative staff of fifteen.

Head of the institution: Dr. Mauricio Cardenas S., Executive Director

Contact officer: Claudia Duarte, Secretary General

Fundacion para la Educación Superior y el Desarrollo
Calle 78 No. 9-91
Apartado Aéreo 75074
Santafe de Bogota
COLOMBIA
Tel: (57-1) 312-5300
Fax: (57-1) 212-6073
e-mail • fedesarr@openway.com.co
URL • http://www.openway.com.co/fedesarrollo

Universidad de los Andes

Centro de Estudios Asiáticos

Background and objectives: The Asian Studies Center (CEA) was created in 1989 to promote the study of Asian languages and to provide a multidisciplinary academic environment in which different schools at the University of Los Andes can work to improve mutual understanding and cooperation between Colombia and the Pacific Basin countries.

Programs: CEA has four main areas of activity. The Language program offers instruction in Chinese, Japanese, and Korean; the Cultural program fosters academic and social links between Colombia and Asia; the Research program studies economic, social, scientific, technological, and cultural progress among Asian countries, especially in relation to Colombian and Latin American development; and the Exchange program coordinates interaction between academic institutions in Korea, China, and Japan and the schools, departments, and research centers at the University of Los Andes to develop joint projects on science, technology, and culture. Since 1993, CEA has been organizing workshops with the participation of leading scholars from the Asia-Pacific region. Recent events included a three-week Summer Seminar on Relations between Asia and Latin America (1996), and a workshop on how to do business with Asian countries, which was sponsored by PBEC and the Bogota Chamber of Commerce (1995). In October 1997, CEA organized the IX Conference of the Latin American Association of Afro-Asian Studies (ALADAA).

Publications: The Center annually publishes a special issue of *Texto y Contexto*, the University multidisciplinary publication. In 1995, this special publication was entitled "Encounters with Japanese Culture." CEA also publishes occasional papers.

Funding sources: CEAS's economic support comes mainly from the Japanese government, the Japan Foundation, the Korea Foundation, and the Organization of American States. The Center's national sponsors include ICETEX, the Colombian Institute of Educational Credit Loans and Studying Abroad, and COLCIENCIAS, the Colombian Institute for Science and Technology.

Staffing: CEA has one full-time and one part-time researcher, and four associate professors. It is supported by one librarian and one administrative employee.

Notes: The Center serves as the secretariat for COLPECC, the Colombian National Committee of the Pacific Economic Cooperation Council, and chairman of the Colombian chapter of ALADAA.

Head of the institution: Mr. Jaime Barrera Parra, Director

Centro de Estudios Asiáticos
Universidad de los Andes
Carrera 1 Este No. 18A-10, Casita Rosada piso 2
A.A. 4976 Santafe de Bogota
COLOMBIA
Tel: (57-1) 284-9911 ext. 2136
Fax: (57-1) 284-1890
e-mail • jbarrera@uniandes.edu.co
URL • http://www.prof.uniandes.edu.co/~bicenesa

Universidad de los Andes

Centro de Estudios Internacionales

Background and objectives: The Center for International Studies (CEI) of the Universidad de los Andes, founded in 1982, encourages research in the field of international relations to promote Colombia's integration into an increasingly complex and interdependent world order.

Programs: In geographic terms, the CEI focuses on Venezuela, the United States, Central America, the Caribbean, the Andean Region, the Southern Cone, the European Community, and the Pacific Basin. Its thematic emphases include theory of international relations, theory and practice of negotiations, international humanitarian law and peaceful resolution of conflict, the environment, drug trafficking, regional integration, comparative politics, democratization and governability, commerce and international economic relations, and international political economy. The CEI also sponsors conferences, seminars, and roundtable discussions especially on issues related to drug trafficking, the environment, political economy of arms, politics of integration, and international relations theory.

Publications: CEI's research findings are usually published as books or in the Center's journals, *Colombia Internacional* and *Documentos Ocasionales*. CEI's researchers also write in national and regional newspapers and news magazines on topics such as Colombia-U.S. relations, regional integration agreements, and interstate conflicts.

Funding sources: CEI relies upon grants from international organizations such as the Organization of American States (OAS), the United Nations Program for Development (UNPD), the Ford Foundation, and the Tinker Foundation.

Staffing: CEI's staff consists of a director, an administrative coordinator, six full-time researchers, associate researchers, and research assistants.

Head of the institution: Dr. Rafael Rivas Posada, Director

Centro de Estudios Internacionales
Universidad de los Andes
Santafe de Bogota
COLOMBIA
Tel: (57-1) 286-7504 / 286-7505
Fax: (57-1) 286-8091
e-mail • carodrig@uniandes.edu.co

Universidad Externado de Colombia

Facultad de Finanzas, Gobierno y Relaciones Internacionales

Background and objectives: The School of Finance, Government, and International Relations was established as an academic program by the Universidad Externado de Colombia in 1986. The School's mission is to provide multidisciplinary training with an emphasis on politics, economics, law, finance, and business administration.

Programs: The School has two undergraduate programs, one in finance and international relations and the other in government and international relations. It also offers four graduate programs in government, management and public affairs, transnational business, and finance and international cooperation. The School's graduate program on government, management, and public affairs is offered jointly with the School of International and Public Affairs of Colombia University in New York. During 1995-96, the School completed two research projects, "An Evaluation of Ecofondo's work," and "The History of the Chamber of Commerce of Bogota."

In 1994, the School established the Center for Research and Special Projects (CIPE) to carry out research, provide consulting services, and disseminate studies in national and international areas relevant to Colombia. CIPE is also a forum for debates and discussions. The Center's research areas include sustainable development, international relations, municipal development, and history.

Publications: The School publishes *Pretextos*, which has recently included titles such as "Colombia's Multilateral Relations and the Developing World" (1995), "The OAS and the Inter-American Relations: An Agenda for the XXI Century" (1995), and "Leadership and Autonomy: Colombia and the United Nations Security Council" (1993).

Funding sources: The School only receives University funds.

Staffing: Approximately 110 professors teach at the School, supported by an administrative staff of nineteen. CIPE has two full-time researchers, five part-time researchers, and two secretaries.

Head of the institution: Mr. Roberto Hinestrosa, Dean

Contact officer: Ms. Milena Gomez de Gaviria, Assistant Dean

Facultad de Finanzas, Gobierno y Relaciones
    Internacionales, Universidad Externado de Colombia
Calle 12 No. 1-17 Este
Santafe de Bogota
COLOMBIA
Tel: (57-1) 283-9282 / 341-8038
Fax: (57-1) 341-7066
e-mail • Uexterrn3@trauco.colomsat.co

Universidad Nacional de Colombia

Instituto de Estudios Políticos y Relaciones Internacionales

Background and objectives: The Institute of Political Studies and International Relations (IEPRI), established by the National University of Colombia in 1986, uses a multidisciplinary approach effort to enhance intellectual debate, encourage critical thinking on political problems, expand public awareness of peace issues, and identify and forecast political trends in the medium term. IEPRI's main commitment is to human rights, democracy, and social equity.

Programs: IEPRI's four main working areas include international relations; illegality and violence; governability, democracy and human rights; and political culture. IEPRI's international section is conducting research on integration policies of the Cesar Gaviria administration, Colombia and the Non-Alignment Movement's presidency, Latin America and the European Union, and United States policy towards Colombia in relation to Cuba, among other topics. The Institute also organizes seminars, conferences, and other academic events. During 1995-96, IEPRI organized together with FESCOL four workshops on the Colombian political system focusing on such topics as the role of the opposition, political participation, justice and democracy, and political representation. In 1996, the Institute jointly with the North-South Center of Miami organized an international workshop seminar on the challenges and problems of democratic transitions. IEPRI's staff also teaches post-graduate courses in the University's Law and Human Sciences Programs, as well as other courses on political issues and human rights. Since 1994, the Institute has coordinated the master's program in political studies, which was approved by the National University of Colombia.

Publications: IEPRI publishes *Analisis Politico*, an academic journal published three times a year, and *Sintesis*, an economic, social, and political annual report that assesses Colombian life in the realms of society, state and politics, economics, and international relations. The Institute has also co-published books including *Citizenship in Latin America* (1996), *The Armed Forces in Colombia's Recent History* (1996), *Political Actors in the 1990s* (1996), *Democracy and Economic Reforms in Latin America* (1996), *Violence in Colombia: Present and Past* (1995), and *Colombia-Cuba: Historical Relations* (1995). IEPRI also disseminates its ideas in the Colombian media. The Institute has an institutional weekly newspaper column in *El Espectador;* broadcasts *Analisis Politico*, a thirty-minute program on National University Radio; and conducts *Huso de Razon*, a thirty-minute weekly TV program broadcast on the Colombian cultural channel.

Funding sources: Most of IEPRI's funding comes from the Institute of Political Studies and International Relations' Friends Foundation, which supports, promotes, sponsors, and collaborates with IEPRI's activities. The Institute has also received support from local private and public institutions such as COLCIENCIAS, ICFES, and the Justice Ministry, as well as from international foundations including the Ford Foundation, the Friedrich Ebert Foundation, and the Nauman Foundation.

Staffing: IEPRI's teaching staff is made up of sixteen permanent professors, eleven special and adjunct professors, and six associate researchers. The Institute has nine administrative personnel.

Head of the institution: Dr. Alvaro Camacho Guizado, Director

Contact officer: Ms. Gloria Muñoz Martinez, Executive Secretary

**Instituto de Estudios Políticos y Relaciones Internacionales
Universidad Nacional de Colombia
Edificio Manuel Ancizar, 3er Piso, Oficina 3026
Santafe de Bogota
COLOMBIA
Tel: (57-1) 368-1579
Fax: (57-1) 368-7471**

Corporación de Estudios para el Desarrollo

Background and objectives: The Development Studies Corporation (CORDES) was founded in 1984 as a private non-profit research institution for development studies, with emphasis on economic, social, and political problems that affect Ecuador and Latin American development.

Programs: CORDES's research focuses on education, governability, social policies and poverty, and the macroeconomic and economic situation. CORDES organizes national and international seminars, conferences, and roundtables to discuss economic, social, and political issues.

Publications: CORDES publishes *Economic and Financial Trends,* twice a year, and *Economic Letter,* a bimonthly publication. Recent books include *Education, Growth and Equity* (1995), *Ecuador and Peru: Economy and Development* (1995), and *Social Policies and Poverty* (1994).

Funding sources: CORDES is funded mainly by the Konrad Adenauer Foundation. It also receives economic support from domestic and international institutions such as FISE (Fondo de Inversion Social de Emergencia), the Inter-American Development bank (IDB), and the United Nations Development Program (UNDP).

Staffing: CORDES has ten full-time researchers, four part-time researchers, and four administrative personnel.

Head of the institution: Dr. Osvaldo Hurtado L., President

Contact officer: Mr. Esteban Vega U., General Director

Corporación de Estudios para el Desarrollo
Suecia 277 y Avenida Los Shyris
Edificio Suecia, piso 2
Quito
ECUADOR
Tel: (59-32) 455701 / 454406 / 432799 / 452094
Fax: (59-32) 446414
e-mail • general@cordes.ecx.ec
        general@cordes.org.ec

Centro de Estudios Monetarios Latinoamericanos

Background and objectives: The Center for Latin America and Monetary Studies (CEMLA), formally established in 1952 at the Third Meeting of Central Bank Technicians of Latin America, is a teaching and research institute for the exchange of information among monetary authorities in the region. CEMLA aims to promote a better understanding of monetary and banking matters in Latin America as well as other aspects of fiscal and exchange policies; assist in improving the qualifications of central bank and other financial agencies' personnel through the organization of seminars and special training courses and the publication of surveys and research studies; conduct research and systematize the results of past experience in the above fields; and provide information to member banks on developments of international and regional interest on monetary, fiscal, and banking policies. CEMLA headquarters is located in Mexico City.

Programs: The Center's work is carried out in three main areas. The Research Department prepares technical studies, monographs, and working papers; the Training Department performs technical and administrative tasks related to CEMLA's programs and organizes seminars for students and professionals; and the Information and International Relations Department publishes the Center's books and reviews on central banking, financial and monetary policies and issues, and collaborates with CEMLA's associated and collaborating [affiliated] central banks in organizing technical meetings for the various levels of the central bank's staff.

CEMLA acts as executive secretariat of the Association of Banking Supervisory Authorities of Latin America and the Caribbean, which was established in 1991 to promote and maintain close communications among authorities of supervision and financial direction and control in the region; provide a high-level forum for the discussion and exchange of ideas, techniques, technologies, and experience of its members; and encourage research, training programs, the furnishing of technical services and, in general, all activities related to the functions of its members.

Publications: No information provided.

Funding sources: CEMLA's activities are supported by annual contributions from the associate and collaborating members. Specific projects have been made possible through partial financial assistance from the International Monetary Fund (IMF), the Inter-American Development Bank (IDB), the Ford Foundation, the U.S. Agency for International Development (USAID), and the Rockefeller Foundation.

Staffing: No information provided.

Notes: CEMLA has a total of sixty-five members, including thirty associates and thirty-five collaborating members. The former, which have the right to speak and vote at the Assembly, include the Central Banks of Argentina, Aruba, Bahamas, Barbados, Belize, Bolivia, Brazil, Colombia, Costa Rica, Cuba, Chile, Ecuador, El Salvador, Guatemala, Guyana, Haiti, Honduras, Jamaica, Mexico, Netherlands Antilles, Nicaragua, Panama, Paraguay, Peru, Dominican Republic, Surinam, Trinidad and Tobago, Uruguay, Venezuela, and the Eastern Caribbean Central Bank.

Heads of the institution:
Mr. Sergio Ghigliazza, Director

Mr. Luis A. Giorgio, Deputy Director

Contact officer: Mr. Juan Manuel Rodriguez S., Head, Information and International Relations Department

Centro de Estudios Monetarios Latinoamericanos (CEMLA)
Durango No. 54
Col. Roma
Mexico DF, 06700
MEXICO
Tel: (52-5) 533-0300 to 09
Fax: (52-5) 207-7024

Centro de Investigación para el Desarrollo

Background and objectives: The Center for Development Research, founded in 1980, is an independent, not-for-profit research institution devoted to exploring policy options for the country's medium- and long-term development. Its projects are designed to help shape public opinion and to provide analysis on which policy decisions can be based. The Center seeks to help Mexico become more competitive in the international economy while building a strong democratic and pluralistic political system.

Programs: CIDAC systematically monitors economic and political decision making and its professionals work on specific projects. Currently, research is being conducted on environmental policy; the informal and underground economies; political decision making in Mexico; domestic savings and economic development; municipal governments and foreign investments; democracy, markets, and the rule of law; and labor markets in Mexico. Among its activities, CIDAC has held over forty conferences since 1990. CIDAC's professionals also address academic, policy, and business forums regularly.

Publications: The Center has published thirty-eight books on economic, political, and international policy issues; released forty-five monographs; and published more than 2,000 op-ed pieces in Mexican, American, and European newspapers and news magazines in the last six years. Its more important publications are *Economic Development and Regional Inequality* (1995), *Industrial Integration Mexico-United States* (1992), *How Will NAFTA Impact Mexico?* (1992), *The U.S.-Mexico Free Trade Agreement* (1991), *Mexico and the U.S.-Canada Free Trade Agreement* (1989), *Mexico and the Pacific Basin* (1988), and *Cooperation or Rivalry? Regional Integration in the Americas and the Pacific Basin* (1996).

Funding sources: About 80% of CIDAC's expenditures come from an endowment received upon its creation in 1980. The remainder is covered by grants from foundations, sales of publications, and material contributions such as direct sponsoring of conferences and other events.

Staffing: CIDAC has eleven researchers and six administrative personnel.

Head of the institution: Dr. Luis F. Rubio, Director

Contact officer: Ms. Velia Luz Hernandez, Coordinator

Centro de Investigación para el Desarrollo A.C. (CIDAC)
Jaime Balmes No. 11, Edificio D, 2 Piso
Los Morales, Polanco
Mexico, D.F. 11510
MEXICO
Tel: (52-5) 395-5402
Fax: (52-5) 395-9174
e-mail • 74174.56@compuserve.com

Centro de Investigación y Docencia Económicas, A.C.

Background and objectives: The Center for Economic Research and Teaching (CIDE), founded by the Mexican Ministry of Education in 1974, is a public institution of higher education and research in social sciences devoted to the study of some of the country's major national and international problems.

Programs: CIDE offers three M.A. degree programs in economics, health economics, and public administration and three B.A. degree programs in economics, political science/international relations, and administration.

CIDE's research work is structured in four disciplinary divisions. The Economics Division covers a broad spectrum of specialization in the field, although its priority is the empirical study of the Mexican economy. Its projects include macroeconomic models, international finance, and microeconomic analysis of institutions and actors in specific sectors. Other projects analyze trade policy and its effects on the industrial and agricultural trade balance, fiscal and exchange rate policies, and privatization in Mexico. Recent research includes "Non-linear dynamics in the stock exchange," "Demographic and genetic models in conservation biology: Applications and perspectives for tropical rain forest trees," "Technological capability in developing countries: A case study of industrial biotechnology in Mexico," "Re-exploring financial diversification: The Mexican case," and "Domestic savings in Mexico and pension system reform."

Research projects in the International Studies Division deal mostly with policy, theoretical, and empirical problems derived from changes taking place in North America. Some specific projects include "Actors, interests and coalitions in North American international negotiations," "Mexican foreign policy in the post-cold war era: From nationalism to imperfect interdependence," and "Multinational corporations in the automobile industry in North America."

The projects in the Political Studies Division are concentrated in two main areas: political institutions and processes and state policies. Ongoing projects include "Regime transitions: The Mexican case in comparative perspective," "Camarillas: Political groups in the PRI and the Mexican bureaucracy," "Entrepreneurs and politics in Mexico," "Politics and policy decisions in education," and "Constitutionalism and the judiciary in Mexico and Latin America."

The Public Administration Division conducts two major projects: "Policies and strategies of modernization and change in public administration," which studies the processes of change in the public administration in Mexico and other countries, and "Modernization policies in local and municipal administrations," which elaborates proposals for the improvement of municipal governments.

These academic divisions organize seminars and international workshops with the participation of national and foreign scholars from other research centers.

Publications: CIDE's publications program includes books, working papers, and three journals: *Economía Mexicana: Nueva Epoca*, *Política y Gobierno*, and *Gestión y Política Pública*. Recent books include *Tres ensayos sobre desarrollo y frustración: Asia Oriental y América Latina* (1997), *La compra de Louisiana y las ideas sobre la expansión territorial en Estados Unidos* (1996), *Regionalismo y poder en América: Los límites del neorrealismo* (1996), and *Una búsqueda incierta: Ciencia, tecnología y desarrollo* (1996).

Funding sources: CIDE is mainly funded by the Mexican government. Some specific activities are supported by grants from national and international institutions such as the Ford Foundation, the Korea Foundation, and the Mexican Science and Technology Council.

Staffing: CIDE's permanent faculty is composed of sixty-one research professors (forty-four of them have Ph.D. degrees or are Ph.D. candidates, and seventeen have an M.A. degree in different social sciences). Their work is supported by thirty assistants with B.A. degrees. The services and administrative staff is composed of 150 employees.

Heads of the institution:
Dr. Carlos Elizondo Mayer-Serra, General Director

Dra. Blanca Heredia, Academic Director

Dra. Ma. Emilia Janetti, General Secretary

Contact officer: Prof. Denise Maerker, Director of the Communication Office

Centro de Investigación y Docencia Económicas, A.C.
Carretera México-Toluca 3655 (km. 16.5)
Col. Lomas de Santa Fe
Delegación Alvaro Obregón
01210 México, D.F.
MEXICO
Tel: (52-5) 727-9800
Fax: (52-5) 292-1772
e-mail • denise@dis1.cide.mx

Centro de Investigaciones sobre América del Norte

Background and objectives: The Center for Research on North America (CISAN) was founded in 1989 to promote multidisciplinary research on the region, focusing on the United States and Canada and their relation with Mexico, and to encourage better relations among these three countries through a broad range of academic and networking activities.

Programs: CISAN's academic activities fall into three main areas: United States Studies, United States-Mexico Studies, and Canadian Studies. At present, CISAN has twenty-seven research projects in progress on foreign policy, public policy, economics, law, and strategic, literary, cultural, and social issues. CISAN periodically organizes national and international seminars, colloquia, lectures, roundtables, and other academic gatherings on subjects related to its core interests. Since its inception, the Center has hosted 210 foreign lecturers, as well as eighteen visiting scholars.

Publications: The Center publishes *Voices of Mexico*, a quarterly review with in-depth and up-to-date coverage of Mexico's cultural, social, political, and economic life. CISAN has also edited twenty-seven books, three of them co-edited with foreign and national universities. Recent books include *Dilemas estadounidenses en los noventa: Impactos sobre Mexico* (1996), *Canada en Transicion* (1996), and *California: Problemas economicos, politicos y sociales* (1995).

Funding sources: CISAN's activities have been sponsored by UNAM along with institutions such as the Flora and William Hewlett Foundation, the John D. and Catherine MacArthur Foundation, and the United States Embassy in Mexico.

Staffing: CISAN's faculty comprises nineteen researchers, eighteen technical assistants, and thirty-six administrative personnel.

Notes: CISAN is linked to more than fifty-five foreign institutions and universities through collaborative agreements, as well as twenty-four Mexican educational institutions. It is also an active member of fourteen international professional associations.

Head of the institution: Dr. Pazconsuelo Márquez Padilla, Director

Contact officer: Ms. Silvia Nuñez G., Academic Secretary

Centro de Investigaciones sobre América del Norte
Torre II de Humanidades, 110 Piso., Ciudad Universitaria
México D.F.., C.P. 04510
MÉXICO
Tel: (52-5) 623-0300 to 0309
Fax : (52-5) 550-0379
e-mail • nugar@servidor.unam.mex
silvel@servidor.unam.mex

El Colegio de la Frontera Norte

Background and objectives: El Colegio de México and the Secretaria de Educacion Publica established the Centro de Estudios Fronterizos del Norte de México in 1982 to study the northern border area and the United States. In 1986, this autonomous research and teaching institution officially adopted the name of El Colegio de la Frontera Norte-COLEF (The North Border Research Institute). Among its institutional aims, COLEF promotes the scientific understanding of social, economic, cultural, demographic, political, urban, and environmental issues in the Mexican regions close to the United States. It uses this knowledge to formulate regional plans in accordance with national plans such as "Programa Paisano." COLEF also identifies and defines obstacles to the development of the border region and to productive relations between Mexico and the United States.

Programs: COLEF's various academic departments use a multidisciplinary approach to analyze border issues. The Department of Social Studies focuses on modernization and social change on Mexico's northern frontier; the Department of Gender and Family Studies explores gender relations in the economic, social, demographic, and cultural spheres; the Department of Demographic Studies carries out quantitative and qualitative research on the relations between growth, reproduction, and population mobility in the Mexico-United States border area; the Department of Cultural Studies analyzes anthropological, sociological, cultural, and historical issues in the frontier region, with an emphasis on identity and history; the Department of Economic Studies examines the economic situation of the northern frontier within the context of the national and international economy; and the Department of Public Administration Studies evaluates local government activities focusing on the advancement of decentralization, assesses the regional presence of the federal government, and analyzes binational relations that affect the economy, politics, culture, and public services in the northern frontier area. COLEF's Program of Japanese Studies aims to establish strong cultural links between Mexico and Japan, while the Program of North American Studies focuses on domestic, intra-regional, and inter-regional politics in the United States, Canada, and Mexico. As a teaching institution, COLEF offers a doctoral program in social science and master's programs in regional development, integral administration of the environment, population studies, and applied economics.

Publications: COLEF publishes *Frontera Norte*, a semiannual multidisciplinary review, and *El Correo Fronterizo*, a bimonthly publication with information on research projects, academic events, and recent publications that deal with frontier issues and Mexico-United States relations. COLEF also publishes the following series: *Coleccion Cuadernos*, with news on research projects and COLEF researchers; *Coleccion COLEF*, which includes work submitted at the biannual academic evaluation event; and *Coleccion Memorias,* with the results of academic events organized by the institution.

Funding sources: COLEF has received support from several institutions in the United States such as the MacArthur Foundation, the Tinker Foundation, the Ford Foundation, the Hayes Foundation, the Hewlett Packard Foundation, the Border Progress Foundation, the National Science Foundation, and the Rockefeller Foundation, as well as the Carnegie Corporation, the Arizona-Mexico Border Health Foundation, the Research Fund for Studies at Michigan State University, UC-Mexus, AT&T, and the University of California-Davis. COLEF has also received support from federal agencies and public institutions in Mexico such as the Consejo Nacional de Ciencia y Tecnologia and the Consejo Nacional de Poblacion, and from state and municipal governments.

Staffing: COLEF's research staff, including its regional offices, is made up of approximately 100 people.

Notes: COLEF has regional departments in Mexicali, Baja California; Nogales, Sonora; Ciudad Juarez, Chihuahua; Piedras Negras, Coahuila; Nuevo Laredo and Matamoros, Tamaulipas; Monterey, Nuevo Leon; and one representative office in Mexico City.

Head of the institution: Dr. Jorge A. Bustamante, President

Contact officer: Ms. Erendira Paz, Associate Director for International Affairs

El Colegio de la Frontera Norte
Blvd. Abelardo L. Rodriguez 2925
Zona del Rio, CP 22320
Tijuana, Baja California
MÉXICO
Tel: (52-66) 13-3540 / 13-3535, / 84-2226 / 84-2068
Fax: (52-66) 13-3555 / 13-3065
International P.O. Box: "L"
Chula Vista, CA 91912, USA
e-mail • jorgeb@dns.cincos.net

El Colegio de México

Background and objectives: El Colegio de México is a graduate-level research and teaching institution in the humanities and social sciences. It was founded in 1940 with the support of the federal government, Banco de México, the National Autonomous University of Mexico, and the Fondo de Cultura Economica.

Programs: El Colegio de México is divided into seven research centers: the Center for Linguistic and Literary Studies (CELL), the Center for Historical Studies (CEH), the Center for International Studies (CEI), the Center for Asian and African Studies (CEAA), the Center for Economic Studies (CES), the Center for Demographic and Urban Development Studies (CEDDU), and the Center for Sociological Studies (CES). It also supports the Mexican APEC Study Program.

The Center for International Studies (CIS), founded in 1960, focuses on education and research in the fields of international relations, political science, federal and local public administration, the Mexican political system, and Mexico's foreign policy, as well as area studies concerning the United States, Canada, Europe, and Latin America. In 1979, El Colegio de México created a program within the CIS on Mexican-U.S. relations, now called the U.S.-Canadian Studies Program. Emphasizing the dynamics that affect Mexico's place and future in the post-NAFTA political, economic, and social setting, the program focuses on trade and investment, environmental issues and comparative U.S.-Mexican environmental law, national security, drug trafficking, immigration and culture, nationalism, and education. The CIS also offers undergraduate programs in international relations and public administration. CIS publishes *México-Estados Unidos-Canada,* an annual publication that includes papers prepared by U.S. and Canadian participants in the U.S.-Canadian Studies Program's activities. This program also offers a Summer Program on Contemporary Mexico for Mexican, U.S., and Canadian undergraduates and graduate students, featuring courses on Mexican history, society, politics, arts, literature, and economy and Mexican-U.S. bilateral relations. CIS has twenty-two full-time researchers, five visiting professors, eight research fellows and an administrative staff of nine.

In 1964, the Center for Asian and African Studies (CEAA) was established, with UNESCO support, as the Oriental Studies Department of CIS at the El Colegio de México. In 1982, the CEAA became independent and adopted its current name with the inclusion of Sub-Saharan Africa as an area study. The CEAA has six research areas: China, India, Japan, West Asia (the Middle East) and North Africa, Sub-Saharan Africa, and the Asia-Pacific region. CEAA offers a three-year master's degree program in Asian and African studies. The Center publishes *Estudios de Asia y Africa*, a quarterly journal, and the *Asia Pacifico Yearbook*, an annual report featuring CEAA's research work on political, economic, and social issues concerning the Asia-Pacific countries. The Yearbook also includes articles written by invited national and international specialists.

El Colegio de México also conducts special research programs such as the Interdisciplinary Program on Women's Studies; the Program for Science, Technology and Development, the Program for Translators, Dictionary of Mexican Spanish Program, and the Institute for Studies of European Integration.

The APEC Study Program at El Colegio de México was established in 1996 to promote research and cooperation on Asia-Pacific affairs. As the Mexican APEC Study Center, it aims to act as a communication channel between universities, research centers, and persons from the private and public sectors in Mexico interested in the Asia-Pacific region, and to establish links with similar institutions in this area. The PE-APEC organized a series of conferences on China called "1997: The Year of the 'Great' China?" It is also preparing, together with the Centre for Asian and African Studies (CEAA), a series of conferences on ASEAN, with specialists from the region, and a bilateral meeting with Canadian specialists on Canada's and Mexico's work in APEC. The PE-APEC is helping CEAA in the preparation of a master's degree program on South East Asia at El Colegio de México. The PE-APEC has already published five working papers, and starting in 1998 it will be responsible for the publication of the yearly report on Asia at El Colegio de México.

Funding sources: El Colegio de México's annual budget is financed mainly from the Ministry of Education. Minor contributions come from some national and international organizations for specific programs and research projects.

Staffing: An average of 150 full-time researchers and 110 national and foreign visiting scholars work at El Colegio de México.

Head of the institution: Dr. Andres Lira, President

Contact officer: Mr. Alberto Palma, Joint Academic Secretary

El Colegio de México
Camino al Ajusco 20
Col. Pedregal de Santa Rosa
México D.F. 10740
MÉXICO
Tel: (52-5) 645-5955
Fax: (52-5) 645-0464
e-mail • webmaster@colmex.mx
URL • http://www.colmex.mx

Centro de Estudios Internacionales
Dr. Ilan Bizberg, Director
Tel: (52-5) 645-2458
Fax: (52-5) 645-0464
e-mail • ilan@colmex.mx

Centro de Estudios de Asia y Africa
Dr. Flora Botton, Director
Tel: (525) 645-4954
Fax: (525) 645-0464
e-mail • botton@colmex.mx

Programa de Estudios APEC
Prof. Eugenio Anguiano, Coordinator
Tel: (52-5) 645-5955 ext. 5008/5102
Fax: (52-5) 645-0464 / 554-3263
e-mail • eroch@colmex.mx
**   mromero@colmex.mx**
**   postmaster@colmex.mx**

Universidad de Colima

Centro Universitario de Estudios e Investigaciones sobre la Cuenca del Pacífico

Background and objectives: In 1989, the University of Colima initially established the Pacific Basin Program within the Center for Social Research. The Program became the Pacific Basin Studies and Research Center (CUEICP) in 1995. The Center promotes scientific cooperation between researchers of social, economic, cultural, and political aspects related to the Pacific Basin through the Mexican National Network of Researchers on the Pacific Basin (RNICP). This Network participates in the Mexican National Committee for Pacific Basin Cooperation (MXCPEC) and in the Pacific Economic Cooperation Council (PECC) meetings. The Network's Technical Secretariat is located at the Center.

Programs: CUEICP's research work focuses on the study of Pacific Basin countries in the areas of transportation, telecommunications, and tourism; education; financial flows; minerals and energy; intellectual property; international organizations; and agricultural and international trade.

Publications: CUEICP publishes two series, *Mexican Outlook on the Pacific Basin* (1992) (in English), and "Aportes de la Universidad de Colima" (1989) (in Spanish). CUEICP has also jointly edited "Restructure of the Mexican Economy. Integration to World Economy and the Pacific Basin" and "Japan Inc. in Mexico: Japanese Firms and Labor Models," with the Universidad Autonoma Metropolitana-Azcapotzalco; and "Models of Economic Growth in the Globalization Era" with the Universidad Autonoma de Puebla, among others.

Funding sources: CUEICP has received support from the Secretaria de Educacion Publica and Consejo Nacional de Ciencia y Tecnologia.

Staffing: The Center has seven research staff.

Head of the institution: Dr. Fernando A. Rivas Mira, Director and Technical Secretary of the National Network of Researchers on the Pacific Basin

Centro Universitario de Estudios e Investigaciones sobre la Cuenca del Pacífico
Universidad de Colima
Av. Gonzalo de Sandoval 444
Col. Oriental
26040 Colima
MÉXICO
Tel: (52-3) 314-1841
Fax: (52-3) 313-5009
e-mail • arivas@cgic.ucol.mx

Universidad de Guadalajara

Departmento de Estudios del Pacífico

Background and objectives: The Department of Pacific Studies (DEP) at the University of Guadalajara, originally established in 1990, is devoted to the academic study of the Pacific Basin. DEP promotes and conducts both applied and theoretical research in the fields of Pacific studies and international relations, offers courses at both the graduate and undergraduate levels, and organizes seminars, conferences, and cultural activities on Asia-Pacific to disseminate research findings and to promote cultural exchange.

Programs: The Department's teaching and research activities concentrate on (1) international political economy with an emphasis on the international division of labor in the Pacific Rim, multinational corporations and transpacific capital flows, trading-bloc formation, foreign direct investment and regional integration, and food security and transpacific trade; (2) geopolitical and strategic studies with special reference to Mexico's foreign policy in the Pacific and regional security issues in Asia-Pacific; (3) macroeconomic and development studies, which include macroeconomic analyses by country, industrial and sectoral studies, and comparative development strategies; technology transfer and development, particularly on comparative technological development, and transnational corporations and technological innovation; and (4) history, culture, and society in the Pacific with an emphasis on Mexico-Asia cultural links, comparative historical and literary studies, social and political studies focusing on government structure and public institutions, and the nature and role of the state.

The Area Study Programs focus on Asia's cultures (China, Japan, and Korea) and on major regions, mainly Southeast Asia and Oceania. These programs carry out research, teaching, and extension activities, including international exchange of scholars, seminar and lecture series, the integration of country-specific bibliographic collections, and the organization of cultural events. Current research projects include "Foreign direct investment and regional integration in Asia Pacific: The case of Greater South East China," "The electronics and computer industry in Jalisco: Localized industrial district or export-oriented industrial enclave," "Food security and agricultural policies in the Pacific Rim: The cases of China, Japan," "Fiscal policy and income distribution in post-war Japan," "Origin and evolution of Zen Buddhism in modern Japanese thought," and "The interaction of domestic and foreign factors in the international political economy: NAFTA's two-level game."

Recent academic and cultural events include symposiums on "Korea, Image and Reality" and "Japan, Culture and Society," both within DEP's Pacific Encounters Series; the 3rd International Congress of the Mexican Association for Canadian Studies; and lectures such as "Politics, culture and development in South East Asia: The cases of Malaysia and Indonesia," "Towards a new Mexican diplomacy," "The Arab-Israeli process: Present reality and perspectives," "Culture and society in contemporary China," and "Development strategies in East Asia and Latin America."

Publications: DEP's recent books include *Japan, Culture and Society* (1996) (proceedings of symposium); *Historia Minima de Japon, Fondo de la Cultura Economica* (forthcoming), and *Industrializacion y Desarrollo Regional en Jalisco: Por una Politica Estatal de Planeacion* (1997)

Staffing: DEP's academic staff consists of eleven full-time researchers and five part-time associates. It has an administrative and technical support staff of five.

Funding sources: DEP's major funding sources are the University of Guadalajara, the Federal Ministry of Public Education, the National Council of Science and Technology, the Japan Foundation, and the government of the state of Jalisco.

Notes: DEP has been a member of the Interministerial Mexican Commission for the Pacific Basin since 1990, and of Mexico's National Committee for PECC since 1991.

Head of the institution: Dr. Juan Jose Palacios, Director

Contact officer: Mr. Dagoberto Amparo, Administrative Coordinator

Departmento de Estudios del Pacífico
Universidad de Guadalajara
P.O. Box 6-341 C.P. 44602
Guadalajara
MÉXICO
Tel: (52-3) 853-3318
Fax: (53-3) 853-3053
e-mail • jpalacio@ udgserv.cencar.udg.mx

Universidad Nacional Autónoma de México

Centro de Relaciones Internacionales

Background and objectives: The Center for International Relations (CRI) at the Universidad Nacional Autonoma de Mexico was founded in 1971 with the aim to strengthen teaching and interdisciplinary research to help students respond more effectively to national and international problems.

Programs: The Center offers a B.A. degree in international relations. CRI's research and teaching addresses theory and methodology; politics, economics, and law; and regional and Mexico studies. Current research projects investigate pragmatism, globalism, and postmodernism; economic integration processes from a geopolitical perspective; changing social actors in the Mexican productive sector; the formulation of Mexico's foreign policy and the integration of Mexico in North America; and economic integration processes in Latin America.

The Center also organizes conferences, roundtable discussions, seminars, and symposiums. Recent academic events include "Mexico in a changing world: Priorities, challenges and opportunities" and "50th anniversary of the United Nations and the challenges of Mexico."

CRI also conducts "Foro Nacional de Politica Exterior," an annual conference to discuss most important recent Mexican foreign policy decisions and issues. The topic of the 1995 conference dealt with the role of foreign policy and the Mexico economic crisis.

Publications: Since 1973, CRI has published *Relaciones Internacionales*, a quarterly journal. The Center also publishes *Cuadernos de Relaciones Internacionales* to support its teaching activities. CRI's faculty has published various books such as *Pragmatismo y Globalismo: Una aproximacion a la politica contemporanea* (1997), *Mexico ante los procesos de regionalizacion economica en el mundo* (1996), and *La nueva relacion de Mexico con America del Norte* (1994).

Funding sources: The Center's main economic support comes from the University. It also receives funds from the UNAM Foundation and the European Community.

Staffing: The Center has thirty-four full-time and forty-eight part-time professors. It also has an administrative staff of five.

Head of the institution: Mtra. Consuelo Davila, Coordinator

Contact officer: Mtro. Roberto Dominguez Rivera, Academic Secretary

Centro de Relaciones Internacionales
Universidad Nacional de México
Circuito Mario de la Cueva s/n
Edificio E, Planta Baja
México D.F., C.P. 04510
MÉXICO
Tel: (52-5) 622-9412 / 622-9413
Fax: (52-5) 666-8384
e-mail • mcdp@servidor.unam.mx
**   CRI@sociolan.politicas.unam.mx**

Centro de Estudios y Promoción del Desarrollo

Background and objectives: The Center for Development Studies and Promotion (DESCO), a nonprofit private institution founded in 1965, is dedicated to building democracy and development by assisting Peru's marginal populations in the areas of economic production, culture and learning, and democratic participation in civil society. DESCO's promotional outreach programs target peasants, formal and informal workers, and shantytown populations. DESCO's concerns focus on production and management of natural resources, market access and relations, poverty and social policies, education and employment, and the redefinition and strengthening of the political system and institutional framework.

Programs: DESCO's thematic working areas include the Development Cooperation Area, which has recently completed a study on NGOs and local governments; the Development Alternatives Area, which includes various geographical and topical programs, the Research Group, and the Institutional Strengthening and Training of NGOs Program (FICONG), a cooperative institutional effort with FUPROVI (Costa Rica) and IIED-AL (Argentina) to reduce urban poverty in Latin America; and the Communication and Information Area, which includes DESCO's Data Bank, Documentation Center, and Publications Unit. Current research projects include "Bossism: Everyday life, mercantile circuits and power structure in the Andes: XIX and XX centuries"; "Urban poverty and politic violence"; "Comparative analysis of teachers' role in educational reforms in three South American countries"; "Post-stabilization, institutionality and entrepreneurial interest groups in Peru"; and "Labor market in metropolitan Lima: Segmentation and wage structure 1985-95."

Publications: DESCO publishes *QUEHACER*, a bimonthly journal of political, social, economic, and cultural analysis; *Resumen Semanal*, a weekly synthesis of the most important events reported in Peruvian newspapers and magazines; *Pretextos*, an academic journal published twice a year; *Coyuntura Laboral*, a monthly newsletter covering political and labor legislation; *Reporte Especial*, a monthly newsletter on political violence and crime; and *Cooperacion*, a monthly bulletin on social and development policies aimed at cooperation agencies and NGOs. Recent books include *Social Policy and NGOs* (1996), *The Challenges of Cooperation* (1996), *The Worlds of Development* (1996), *Structural Reform and Entrepreneurial Reconversion: Conflicts and Challenges* (1996), and *Education: Challenges and Hopes: Agenda and Proposals for an Educational Policy* (1995).

Funding sources: DESCO's main economic support comes from international agencies and institutions devoted to development and research, such as BILANCE-Catholic Organization for Development Co-operation, the Netherlands; EZE, Germany; MISEREOR, Germany; SAREC-Swedish Agency for Research Cooperation with Developing Countries; the Canadian Agency for International Development; the Spanish Agency for International Cooperation; Caritas, Switzerland; the Ford Foundation; the Overseas Development Institute, England; among others.

Staffing: DESCO has six professionals working in the Research Group, nineteen other professionals with research skills in charge of development projects, and six administrative personnel.

Head of the institution: Mr. Luis Peirano, President

Centro de Estudios y Promoción del Desarrollo
Leon de la Fuente 110, Lima 17
PERÚ
Tel: (51-1) 264-1316
Fax: (51-1) 264-0128
e-mail • postmaster@desco.org.pe
URL • http://www.desco.org.pe

Centro de Investigación de la Universidad del Pacífico

Background and objectives: The Universidad del Pacífico Research Center (CIUP) was established in 1972 to conduct interdisciplinary research on Peru's political, economic, and social problems, and to propose strategies for building a more democratic, just, and developed society.

Programs: CIUP's research focuses on six areas: natural resources and environment protection, with emphasis on regulation policies; social policies, with emphasis on health and education; international trade and integration; growth and saving; regulation of natural monopolies and antitrust policies; and business administration, a program that prepares teaching materials for students at the Administration and Accounting Department and the Graduate School at the Universidad del Pacifico.

In 1996, CIUP concluded a "Study of the ongoing situation of Peru," a "Study to determine the need to apply compensatory duties to the imports of Chinese textiles and shoes," and "Costs and demand analysis of health services in Peru."

An important ongoing project is the "Administrative autonomy of government institutions in Latin America." CIUP's Coyuntura Economica is a special project created in 1981 to support CIUP's research activities with updated statistical information. This project has built a database that takes into account more than 200 economic variables over the last forty years. Recently, CIUP created the Asia Pacific Economy and Management Program (PEGAP) to teach undergraduate and graduate courses on the Asia-Pacific region, to carry out joint research activities with Asian academics, and to provide advisory and information services to public and private institutions interested in the Asia-Pacific region. CIUP also serves as a pluralistic forum for debate on Peru's problems. CIUP's seminars and conferences include INTERQUORUM, a thirty-day training program designed to help young political leaders from Lima and Peru's provinces develop analytical skills and capacity for dialogue on issues such as the functioning of markets, public administration, economic growth, and Peru's democratization; INTERFORUM, a specialized seminar on micro and small businesses; and INTERCAMPUS, a gathering of political, intellectual, and business leaders who assemble to discuss urgent national problems. Recent INTERCAMPUS topics were "The Social Market Economy," "Population and Poverty: Challenges and opportunities," "Growth, Employment and Social Development," and "Dialogue for Democracy."

Publications: CIUP's research results are published in two series, *Cuadernos de Investigacion* and *Documentos de Trabajo*. CIUP also publishes *Apuntes*, a specialized biannual academic social science journal; and *Punto de Equilibrio*, a monthly economic journal. The Center also publishes *Apuntes de Estudio* and *INTERCAMPUS*. Recent books include *Crossroads: The Reality of Urban Employment in Peru* (1996), *The Big Small Businesses in Peru* (1996), *The Japanese Economy without Mysteries* (1996), and *Export Promotion and Macroeconomic Policy* (1996).

Funding sources: CIUP's activities are funded mainly through its own resources and support from international organizations such as the International Development Research Center of Canada, the U.S. Agency for International Development, the United Nations Development Program, the Inter-American Development Bank, the Ford Foundation, and the Japanese International Cooperation Agency. CIUP has also received local contributions from Comision de Promocion de la Inversion Privada (COPRI), Honda del Peru, Toyota del Peru and the Ministry of Industry.

Staffing: CIUP has twenty-two full-time researchers, ten part-time researchers, and an administrative staff of seven.

Head of the institution: Dr. Jorge Fernandez-Baca, Director

Contact officer: Ms. Maria Isabel Quevedo, Assistant to the Director

Centro de Investigacion de la Universidad del Pacífico
Av. Salaverry 2020
Lima 11
PERÚ
Tel: (51-1) 471-2277 / 472-9635
Fax: (51-1) 470-9747
e-mail • jfernanb@up.edu.pe
URL • http://www.up.edu.pe

Centro Peruano de Estudios Internacionales

Background and objectives: The Peruvian Center for International Studies (CEPEI) was established in 1983 to provide a scientific and academic perspective on international issues that concern Peru. Its activities include research, analysis, consulting, promoting public debate of international issues, and publishing.

Programs: CEPEI's working areas include regional and hemispheric affairs; international economic negotiations and economic affairs; security, democracy, and governability; environment, development, and maritime issues; and specific issues in Peruvian foreign policy.

CEPEI's research has included governability and democracy, promotion of democracy in the inter-American system, the role of the military in a democratic Peruvian society, and the challenges of the Southern Pacific Permanent Commission in the Pacific Basin, among others.

CEPEI also organizes conferences and seminars to analyze global and national issues that influence Peruvian international relations and foreign policy. Most important events include "Peruvian-European Union Relations in Perspective," "Peru and Foreign Capital: Debt and Investment," "Towards a National Security and Defense Agenda," "Democracy and Collective Security in the Inter-American System," "Perspectives of the Pacific Basin in the Global Economy," and "Relations between Peru and Ecuador."

Publications: CEPEI publishes *Analisis Internacional*, an academic journal published three times a year, featuring essays by political, economic, social, and international experts and policy specialists. Recent publications include *Towards a Foreign Policy National Agenda* (1995), *Debt and Foreign Investment* (1995), and *Promotion of Democracy in the Inter-American System* (1995).

Funding sources: CEPEI is funded mainly through private foundations and contributions from international organizations. CEPEI has received support from the Ford Foundation, the MacArthur Foundation, the National Endowment for Democracy, and the United States Agency for International Development, among others. The Center also received support from local companies such as Cotecna-Peru, the Occidental Petroleum Corporation of Peru, and Southern Peru.

Staffing: CEPEI has a small professional and administrative staff.

Head of the institution: Dr. Drago Kisic, Executive President

Contact officer: Mr. Ramón Bahamonde, Adjoint Director

Centro Peruano de Estudios Internacionales
Las Camelias 141
Lima 27
PERÚ
Tel: (51-1) 442-9591
Fax: (51-1) 221-2696

Comisión Andina de Juristas

Background and objectives: The Andean Commission of Jurists (ACJ), founded in 1982, is an international non-governmental organization that works at a regional level to promote democratic institutions, the rule of law, and human rights in the Andean countries of Bolivia, Chile, Colombia, Ecuador, Peru, and Venezuela. ACJ, which is comprised of jurists from the Andean region, is headquartered in Lima, Peru. It also has a branch in Bogota, Colombia. ACJ is affiliated to the International Commission of Jurists based in Geneva. It also has consultative status with the United Nations Economic and Social Council.

Programs: ACJ activities target three specific areas: democratic reform, administration of justice, and human rights. In the area of democratic reform, ACJ has focused on constitutional and legal reforms designed to protect citizens' fundamental rights, procedures for protecting constitutional rights, and institutions and mechanisms for direct public participation. To shape an independent, modern, and democratic administration of justice, ACJ supports public participation in the election of magistrates and public control over the manner in which judges perform their duties. ACJ also supports the ratification and incorporation of international human rights instruments in national legislation, offers training courses and outreach activities to help judicial and political authorities uphold international human rights standards, promotes discussion and cooperation between human rights-oriented specialists and NGO representatives, and evaluates the situation of human rights and the administration of justice in the Andean region. ACJ also proposes alternative control policies to confront drug trafficking problems, promotes their adoption, and encourages the recognition and respect of the rights of indigenous peoples. To achieve these objectives, ACJ prepares studies and proposals, organizes regional seminars, workshops, and courses aimed at training and specialization, and maintains an information center with bibliographic material, news, and information related to the ACJ's activities.

Publications: ACJ publishes *Regional Report*, an annual publication with information and comparative analysis of diverse problems confronting the Andean countries; *Andean Newsletter*, a monthly publication on issues concerning the rule of law, human rights, and drug trafficking; and *Constitutional Readings*, a periodical publication featuring issues on democratic institutions and constitutional law. ACJ also publishes and edits publications and reports with the results of its studies, as well as proceedings of ACJ's seminars and conferences.

Funding sources: ACJ's main funding sources include the Ministry of Technical Cooperation (Holland), ICCO (Holland), the Ibis Foundation (Denmark), the Ford Foundation, and the Catholic Relief Services.

Staffing: ACJ has an executive director, an academic director, and a general secretary. It also has seven full-time and four part-time researchers and an administrative support staff of twelve.

Heads of the institution:
Dr. Diego Garcia Sayan, Executive Director

Dr. Enrique Bernales, Academic Director

Contact officer: Mr. Javier Ciurlizza, General Secretary

Comisión Andina de Juristas
Los Sauces 285
Lima 27
PERÚ
Tel: (51-1) 440-7907 / 442-8094
Fax: (51-1) 442-6468
e-mail • DGS@cajpe.org.pe

Grupo APOYO

Background and objectives: Grupo APOYO is a consulting firm founded in 1977 to serve companies, government institutions, and non-governmental organizations. APOYO hopes that its input will help clients improve the quality of their decisions and increase their competitiveness, and promote the well-being of society.

Programs: Grupo APOYO S.A., as the holding company, directs the development of five affiliate companies. APOYO Consultoria S.A. offers consulting services on economic and financial issues, carries out sector and market studies and investment valuations, and provides advice on business developments and equity restructuring; APOYO Asociados Internacionales S.A. assesses the risk classification for companies and financial instruments in Peru; APOYO Opinion y Mercado S.A. carries out field work and research in marketing, public opinion, and other areas where polling, focus groups, and other similar techniques may be useful to its clients; APOYO Comunicaciones S.A. publishes specialized publications and develops other communications projects, edits books, and provides advice on mass media and the press; and APOYO Administrativo S.A. offers administrative and management services.

Publications: APOYO's periodicals include *Peru Economico*, a monthly publication which offers in-depth analysis on most relevant issues of Peru's economy such as capital markets, privatizations, private investments outlook, and infrastructure; *Semana Economica*, a weekly publication that synthesizes the most useful and relevant information regarding Peru's current economic, political, entrepreneurial, and financial situation; and *Debate*, a bimonthly publication featuring political, economic, and cultural issues.

Funding sources: No information provided.

Staffing: In all APOYO companies, there are 150 employees, of which ninety are full-time professionals.

Head of the institution: Dr. Felipe Ortiz de Zevallos M., President

Grupo APOYO S.A.
Parque Ruben Dario 162
Lima 18
PERÚ
Tel: (51-1) 444-6262
Fax: (51-1) 445-8811
e-mail • foz@apoyo.org.pe

Grupo de Análisis para el Desarrollo

Background and objectives: The Development Analysis Group (GRADE), a private nonprofit institution founded in 1980, pursues theoretical and empirical research on national and international development issues, formulates and evaluates related policies, and promotes quality in education.

Programs: GRADE's four working areas are macroeconomics and sectoral policy; higher education, science, and technology; governance and development; and natural resources and the environment. The Macroeconomics and Sectoral Policy area develops research projects, monitors the economy, builds economic models, updates statistical databases, and provides advisory support to the public sector. Research projects during 1993 included "Macroeconomic adjustment and food security," "Agricultural commercialization in Peru," "Rural credit markets in Peru," "Peruvian rural labor markets," "The impact of trade reform on manufactured production, trade and employment," and "Recent trends in the Peruvian urban labor market: The impact of changes in the foreign trade regime." GRADE's Education, Science, and Technology area has expanded from its original focus on higher education to the primary, secondary, and vocational levels, through such projects as "Income effects of public and private education in Peru," "Education, income and structural adjustment," "Academic culture and democratic values in teacher training institutions," "Teacher training in Peru: Current situation and prospects," "The Cajamarca University sociology graduates," "The Lima labor market for technicians," and "The graduates of the Catholic University's school of Social Sciences." The area of Governance and Development studies how power and authority are exercised within and among countries, with a special focus on the social aspects of the development process in Peru and other Latin American nations. Its projects have included "Crisis and perspectives of Peruvian political parties," "Democratic governance, public spaces and gender," and "Reinterpreting international development from a science and technology perspective." The Natural Resources and the Environment area focuses on exploiting mineral resources efficiently and in an environmentally sound manner. Its main projects in 1995 were "The environmental impact of small-scale gold mining in the Peruvian jungle" and "Tax incentives for environmental regulation." GRADE also organizes seminars and conferences such as "A proposal for methodological guidelines for public sector reform," "Social theory, education and gender," and "Simulation models for foreign debt negotiation and the Brady Plan."

Publications: GRADE publishes *Notas para el Debate*, an occasional collection of papers with research results and policy recommendations. GRADE also publishes working papers.

Funding sources: GRADE's main economic and technical support has come from international organizations such as the Canadian International Development Agency (CIDA), the International Development Research Center (IDRC), the Ford Foundation, the Swedish Agency for Research Cooperation with Developing Countries (SAREC/SIDA), the Carnegie Corporation, Deutsche Gesellschaft für Technische Zusammenarbeit (GTZ), the Intermediate Technology Development Group (ITDG), the Mellon Foundation, Junta del Acuerdo de Cartagena, USAID, UNDP, and the World Bank.

Staffing: GRADE has approximately thirty full-time and fifteen part-time people working as researchers, assistants, and interns, and seventeen people carrying out administrative, coordination, and support duties.

Head of the institution: Dr. Patricia McLauchlan de Arregui, Executive Director

Grupo de Análisis para el Desarrollo
Av. del Ejercito 1870, Lima 27
PERÚ
Tel: (51-1) 264-1887 / 264-1889 / 264-3325
Fax: (51-1) 264-1882
e-mail • arregui@grade.org.pe
          postmaster@grade.org.pe
URL • http://www.rcp.net.pe (under "organismos")

Instituto de Estudios Peruanos

Background and objectives: The Peruvian Studies Institute, the oldest social science research center in Peru, was founded in 1964 as an independent, pluralistic forum for analysis of the country's main social, political, and economic problems. It is a private nonprofit organization, with no religious or partisan affiliations. The Institute aims to contribute to Peru's economic development with social equity, to strengthen its democratic institutions, and to foster greater awareness of the country's rich cultural diversity.

Programs: The Institute's researchers work in the fields of anthropology, sociology, political science, economics, and history. The Institute's main research areas include rural development, social policies, and unemployment; democratic governance, decentralization, regionalization, and local government; macroeconomic analysis as it relates to development; ethnic and cultural pluralism; gender; Andean ethnohistory; the changes and continuities in state reforms; social and economic history; the history of public health and technology; and the process of democratization and citizenship.

In 1990, the Institute began sponsoring Civic Awareness and Leadership Workshops to complement the educational training of young political, union, and media leaders, and mayors and city councilors, through seminars on democracy, government, political economy, institutional reforms, and national and cultural identity.

Publications: The Institute has published almost 300 titles in seventeen thematic series. Since 1994, it has also publicized its research through a radio program and the publication of *Argumentos*, a monthly bulletin focusing on the relationships between political, economic, and cultural change.

Funding sources: Most of the Institute's funding comes from external sources such as the United Nations Economic Commission for Latin America and the Caribbean (ECLAC), the United Nations Development Program (UNDP), the Regional Employment Program for Latin America and the Caribbean (PREALC), the International Labor Office (ILO), Pan American Health Organization (PAHO), the United Nations Children's Fund (UNICEF), the Inter-American Development Bank (IDB), and Consejo Latinoamericano de Ciencias Sociales (CLACSO). It has also received support from the Ford Foundation, the Inter-American Foundation, the Tinker Foundation, and the Batelle Foundation in the United States; the Instituto de Cooperacion Iberoamericana in Spain; the Naumann Foundation, the Ebert Foundation, and the Volkswagen Foundation in Germany; the SAREC Foundation in Sweden; and the Canadian International Development Agency and the International Development Centre in Canada.

Staffing: IEP has twenty-five full-time researchers and an administrative staff of fourteen.

Head of the institution: Dr. Cecilia Blondet Montero, Director

Instituto de Estudios Peruanos
Horacio Urteaga 694
Lima 11
PERÚ
Tel: (51-1) 432-3070 / 424-4856 / 431-6603
Fax: (51-1) 432-4981
e-mail • postmaster@iep.org.pe

Instituto Libertad y Democracia

Background and objectives: The Institute for Freedom and Democracy (ILD), founded in 1980, is devoted to the study of the informal sector. Its mission is to develop strategies necessary for the peaceful and purposeful transition to a market economy and a stable democratic society. These strategies draw upon spontaneously indigenous institutions and are informed by successful models from developed countries.

Programs: ILD has conducted research to advance understanding of the nature and extent of property in the informal sector of the economy, and of the role and importance of property formalization in economic and social development. ILD has also been working on strategies and procedures for the efficient formalization of informal property in the Third World. ILD's work concentrates on economic and political issues, development, property rights, and land tenure. ILD also organizes national and international conferences, symposiums, and seminars; press conferences; briefings and presentations for the government as well as the opposition and political and industry organizations; public lectures; and training programs.

Publications: The Institute occasionally publishes the *ILD Newsletter* in English.

Funding sources: Almost 75% of ILD's funds come from USAID.

Staffing: ILD has fifteen full-time researchers, five part-time researchers, and twenty-three administrative personnel.

Head of the institution: Mr. Hernando de Soto, President

Contact officer: Mr. Manuel Mayorga, General Manager

Instituto Libertad y Democracia
Av. Benavides 881, Lima 18
PERÚ
Tel: (51-1) 447-0916 / 444-3500
Fax: (51-1) 447-8604
e-mail • postmaster@ild.org.pe

Instituto Venezolano de Estudios Sociales y Políticos

Background and objectives: The Venezuelan Institute of Social and Political Studies (INVESP), founded in 1986, is an independent nonprofit private institution dedicated to promoting and developing scientific research on the social, economic, and political areas at both domestic and international levels. INVESP mainly designs, prepares, and coordinates research studies in international relations and social-political problems in Latin America and the Caribbean.

Programs: INVESP's research program focuses on regional and international relations and sociopolitical studies. INVESP's permanent research areas include international relations and integration in Latin America and the Caribbean; Venezuelan foreign policy and global changes; peace, security, and disarmament in Latin America and the Caribbean; international relations, economics, and the environment; global reforms and regional studies; and the political-economic and social research areas.

The Institute, together with the Woodrow Wilson Center and Centro de Estudios de America (CEA), is conducting a research project on "Cuba and the Caribbean after the Cold War." INVESP is also organizing, together with ILDIS, a seminar on "Integration and Foreign Policy." Past research projects include "The Caribbean towards the Year 2000," "Venezuelan Foreign Policy toward the Year 2000," "Environmental Security and Regional Cooperation in the Caribbean," "The Group of Three (Colombia, Mexico and Venezuela): Evaluation and Perspectives," "Perceptions and Relations between Latin America and the non-Hispanic Caribbean," and "Colombia and Venezuela Political Systems and the Impact of Political and Economic Reforms: A Comparative Study."

INVESP also organizes seminars and workshops to discuss national and international issues. Recent academic events include the 1st Regional Workshop on "Political Actors and Regional Integration in the Caribbean," which was co-organized with SELA, CLAIP, IPRA, and IRIPAZ, in Guatemala, and an international symposium, "The Socio-Political Agenda of the Caribbean Integration Process."

Publications: INVESP publishes working papers with research advances and *Cuadernos del INVESP*, an occasional publication featuring some of the issues discussed within the Institute. Recent books include *Distant Cousins, Caribbean and Latin American Connections* (1996), *Retos de la Cooperacion Ambiental: Caso del Caribe* (1996), and *El ocaso de las islas: El Gran Caribe frente a los desafios globales y regionales* (1996).

Funding sources: INVESP has received support from Comision para la Reforma del Estado de Venezuela (COPRE), Consejo Britanico, the Friedrich Ebert Foundation, the Ford Foundation, the John D. and Catherine T. MacArthur Foundation, the Mellon Foundation, Fundacion Gran Mariscal de Ayacucho, North-South Center at Miami University, and the Organization of American States.

Staffing: INVESP's academic staff comprises seven permanent researchers and ten associated researchers, and a small administrative staff of four.

Head of the institution: Dr. Francine Jacome, Director

Contact officer: Lic. Adriana Marin, Assistant

Instituto Venezolano de Estudios Sociales y Políticos
Quinta Marielvi, Avenida Gil Fortoul
Santa Monica, Caracas
VENEZUELA
Tel/Fax: (58-2) 662-1655
(58-2) 661-2933
(58-2) 661-5196
e-mail • INVESP@dino.conicit.ve

Sistema Económico Latinoamericano

Background and objectives: The Latin American Economic System (SELA) is an intergovernmental regional organization that encompasses twenty-seven Latin American and Caribbean countries. Founded in 1975, SELA fosters a system of consultation and coordination for the adoption of joint regional strategies and common positions on economic and social issues. It also promotes cooperation and integration among its Latin American and Caribbean countries.

Programs: SELA is working in the areas of trade (including intra-regional trade, hemispheric negotiations, WTO rules, trade in services, rules of origin, and implementation of the Uruguay Round agreements); the economic relations of Latin American and Caribbean countries with the United States and NAFTA, the European Union, the Asia-Pacific region, Japan, China, Korea, and the ASEAN countries, and Central and Eastern Europe; financing and investment (including external debt, domestic savings, foreign investment, financing for integration, liberalization of the financial system, and privatization); regional cooperation and integration in MERCOSUR, the Andean Community, the Central American Common Market, CARICOM, the Group of Three, and the Association of Caribbean States; social policies issues (including the linkage between economic and social policies, criteria for efficiency and evaluation in social spending, etc.); intellectual property (including the effects of the TRIPS Agreement, and the legislative and institutional evolution of intellectual property and copyright law); and industrialization (including industrial policies, new paradigms for productive management, linkage of the research and development sector with the productive sector, and human resource training for competitiveness). SELA holds an annual Council Meeting at the ministerial level and convenes consultation and coordination meetings with its member states on a regular basis. It also organizes meetings for experts on specific issues; organizes regional forums on trade, development financing, intellectual property, industrial policy, development and social equity, and productive sectors and technological innovation, with the participation of governmental and private sector representatives; prepares annual analyses and studies on these issues; and maintains a close relationship with public and private organizations at the regional and international levels.

Publications: SELA publishes in Spanish and English *Capitulos*, a quarterly magazine of economic studies, and three monthly bulletins: *Strategic Notes, SELA-Antenna in the United States*, and *Latin American and Caribbean Integration*. Among its forthcoming publications is the *Yearbook on Economic Relations between Latin America and the Caribbean and Asia-Pacific.*

Funding sources: SELA's main support comes from the government and contributions from external sources.

Staffing: SELA's Permanent Secretariat has twenty international civil servants and specialists and fifty-six administrative staff.

Notes: SELA member states are Argentina, Barbados, Belize, Bolivia, Brazil, Chile, Colombia, Costa Rica, Cuba, the Dominican Republic, Ecuador, El Salvador, Grenada, Guatemala, Guyana, Haiti, Honduras, Jamaica, Mexico, Nicaragua, Panama, Paraguay, Peru, Suriname, Trinidad and Tobago, Uruguay, and Venezuela.

Heads of the institution:
Amb. Carlos Juan Moneta, Permanent Secretary

Dr. Luis Alberto Rodriguez, Deputy Permanent Secretary

Contact officer: Mr. Gerardo O. Noto, Head of Projects

Secretaria Permanente del SELA
Avda. Francisco de Miranda, Torre Europa, 4to Piso
Chacaíto, Caracas
Apartado de Correos 17035, Caracas 1010-A
VENEZUELA
Tel: (58-2) 905-5111
Fax: (58-2) 951-6953 / 951-7246 / 951-7263
e-mail • gnoto@sela.org
URL • http://www.sela.org
http://lanic.utexas/~sela

WESTERN UNITED STATES

American Graduate School of International Management/Thunderbird, Center for International Business Education and Research

Background and objectives: Thunderbird, formally known as the American Graduate School of International Management, has been recognized by the U.S. Department of Education as a Center for International Business Education and Research (CIBER). The Thunderbird CIBER fosters links with the business community through programs designed to be beachheads for study, research, and conferences that will help small, medium-sized, and large businesses move into the global marketplace.

Programs: Thunderbird/CIBER has developed several programs, which include six centers and institutes, faculty development programs, overseas programs, undergraduate linkages, and cooperative degree programs. The International Management of Technology Institute is designed to help business integrate technology into firms' strategic objectives, assess and evaluate technology more effectively, and improve new product development processes; the International Risk Management Institute is the first U.S. clearinghouse for information on international risk management; the Institute for International Business Ethics focuses its efforts on the generation and stimulation of research into the international aspects of business ethics, reporting its findings to the academic and business community, and exchanging ideas with researchers in the field; the International Health Management Institute is designed to create programs that will enhance the basic health degree program, focusing on such topics as privatization and legal and ethical questions affecting medical decisions; the International Environmental Management Institute broadens the Master of International Management program (MIM) by integrating courses in international environment policy and management and conducting research in environmental management; and the North American Free Trade (NAFTA) Center is a resource for companies adapting to the new rules of business between the U.S., Canada, and Mexico. Thunderbird CIBER offers the Faculty Development in International Business (FDIB) program, which teaches faculty in other schools how to add an international dimension to courses they are already teaching. This two-week program has seminars in international studies and world business topics, and is primarily for business professors who teach at the undergraduate level. Thunderbird also operates an International Campus Consortium with thirteen member MBA programs whose students and faculty members are able to study or teach at one of Thunderbird's foreign campuses. Thunderbird operates year-round campuses in Archamps, France, and in Tokyo, Japan, as well as a summer campus in Guadalajara, Mexico.

Publications: Thunderbird publishes *Discussion Papers in International Business*, approximately twelve issues per year. Thunderbird also houses four academic journals in international business, international studies, and languages.

Funding sources: Thunderbird CIBER is mainly funded by the School itself, by a grant from the U.S. Department of Education, by corporate contributors, and by tuition and fees paid by participants in the various programs that are operated by CIBER.

Staffing: CIBER at Thunderbird has two professors responsible for day-to-day activities as well as management of the overall program, a full-time secretary, and four student assistants. In addition, about two dozen of the School's faculty members participate actively in CIBER programs, with seven professors having administrative roles in the CIBER-related institutes and centers.

Head of the institution: Dr. Robert Grosse, Director

Contact officer: Dr. Bert Valencia, Executive Director

Thunderbird Center for International Business Education and Research (CIBER)
15249 North 59th Avenue
Glendale, AZ 85306-6000
USA
Tel: (1-602) 978-7150
Fax: (1-602) 843-6143
e-mail • grosser@t-bird.edu
　　　　valenciab@t-bird.edu

The Asia Foundation

Background and objectives: The Asia Foundation was established in 1954 to promote U.S.-Asian understanding and cooperation. It is a private grantmaking organization based in San Francisco, with fourteen field offices and programs in thirty-seven countries in the Asia-Pacific region. It also has a liaison office in Washington, D.C. The Foundation makes over 1,500 grants each year to government agencies and non-governmental organizations in the region. Grants are used to support training, technical assistance, start-up costs for new organizations, and exchange of ideas; non-governmental organizations and citizen groups have invested the funds in projects involving everything from legal aid and conflict resolution to environmental protection and women's rights. The Foundation also promotes democratic governance and the rule of law, the development of open markets, and improved U.S.-Asian relations by working to strengthen institutions, improve policies, and develop leadership in these areas.

Programs: In addition to its field-based programs, the Foundation has several U.S.-administered programs. The Foundation's Center for Asian Pacific Affairs (CAPA), created in 1985, seeks to improve policy dialogue between Americans and Asians on issues of mutual interest (including political, economic, and security issues) through seminars, conferences, and working groups. CAPA's work also helps to inform the Foundation's field-based grantmaking. CAPA has assisted the United States National Committee for Pacific Economic Cooperation in producing the *Pacific Economic Outlook*, a compilation of short-term economic forecasts for the member states of the Pacific Economic Cooperation Council. The Center also organizes an annual conference of young professionals from around the Asia-Pacific region. Other Foundation programs are the Partnership for International Education and Training, an Asia-America Exchange Program, the Luce Scholars Program, and a Women in Politics Program.

Publications The Foundation publishes the *CAPA Report Series* and *Occasional Paper Series,* which analyze the challenges fac-
ing the Asia-Pacific region. On behalf of the Pacific Economic Cooperation Council, the Foundation also produces the annual *Pacific Economic Outlook,* a compilation of short-term economic forecasts for the member states of the Pacific Economic Cooperation Council.

Funding sources: The Foundation receives an annual appropriation from the U.S. Congress. Its public and private sector contributors include corporations, foundations, trusts, and individuals in the United States and Asia. The Foundation also receives gifts in kind, including more than one million American books and journals each year.

Staffing: The Foundation's total staff includes 220 people, of whom 100 are based in the United States.

Notes: In fiscal year 1993, the Asia Foundation distributed more than $34 million in cash and in-kind benefits to its country programs and U.S.-administered programs. The Books for Asia program, the Foundation's oldest project, distributes nearly one million donated books and journals each year to institutions in the Asia-Pacific region.

Head of the institution: Dr. William P. Fuller, Director

Contact officer: Ms. Carolyn Iyoya Irving, Communications and Outreach Manager

The Asia Foundation
465 California Street, 14th Floor
P.O. Box 193223
San Francisco, CA 94119-3223
USA
Tel: (1-415) 982-4640
Fax: (1-415) 392-8863
e-mail • tafpa@igc.org
URL • http://www.asiafoundation.org

The Asia Society / California Center

Background and objectives: The Asia Society, founded in 1956 by John D. Rockefeller III, is dedicated to increasing American understanding of Asia and improving communication between the peoples of the United States and Asia. A nonprofit and non-political educational organization, it is headquartered in New York and has regional offices in Hong Kong, Houston, Los Angeles, and Washington, D.C.

The Asia Society California Center was started as an advisory council in 1980.

Programs: The Asia Society California Center, in support of the Asia Society nationwide, organizes a full range of activities from corporate and contemporary affairs to art, culture, and education, and presents these in a variety of forums, dialogues, seminars, conferences, and study missions. Recent program initiatives include a conference on media and entertainment in Asia; a policy briefing with the New Zealand Minister of Finance; the Annual Ambassador dinner, featuring the U.S. and Korean Ambassadors; seminars on business, politics and entrepreneurship in China, and Japan's role in post–Cold War Asia; dance performances by Taiwan's Cloud Gate and the Ballet Philippines and discussions of modern art in China; an update on Cambodian socioeconomic reconstruction and progress toward building a democratic society; and educational initiatives with two local middle schools under the Asian Educational Resource Center's TeachAsia. The Asia Society's Corporate Affairs Department based in New York presents approximately thirty meetings, briefings, and conferences in the U.S. and Asia each year. In these gatherings, Asian and American policy makers, specialists, and business leaders assess key developments in the U.S.-Asia business environment and in the global economy that affect the Asia-Pacific region. The Asia Society annual corporate conference in Asia is the highlight of the year's events. Since 1989, this conference has featured distinguished Asian and American guests. The recent 1996 Conference in Seoul was attended by the President of Korea, the Prime Minister of New Zealand, the Minister of Trade and Industry from Vietnam, the Vice Minister of Foreign Trade and Economic Cooperation from China, and both the Korean Foreign Minister and American Ambassador to Korea.

Publications: Asia Society publications include annual briefings on China, Korea, and India; *Asian Americans in Transition*, a survey of the current state of Asian American affairs; and the "Asian Update" series, which provides background and analysis of newsworthy issues and events in Asia and U.S.-Asia relations. The Society also publishes *Asia*, a newsletter.

Funding sources: The Society's regional centers are funded entirely through local corporate and individual membership as well as program-generated revenues. However, the California Center draws on both the New York office and other regional centers for content and speaker support.

Staffing: Asia Society / California Center is made up of four full-time staff.

Head of the institution: Mr. Gary Larsen, Executive Director

Contact officer: Ms. Wendy Hsieh, Program Associate

Asia Society / California Center
Arco Plaza, Level C
505 South Flower Street
Los Angeles, CA 90071
USA
Tel: (1-213) 624-0945
Fax: (1-213) 624-0158
e-mail • garyl@asia.soc.org
URL • http://www.emasia.com

The Asia Society
Ambassador Nicholas Platt
President
725 Park Avenue
New York, NY 10021
USA
Tel: (1-212) 288-6400
Fax: (1-212) 517-8315

The Asia Society / Texas Center
4605 Post Oak Place
Suite 205
Houston, TX 77027
USA
Tel: (1-713) 439-0051
Fax: (1-713) 439-1107

The Asia Society / Hong Kong Center
The Chinese Bank Building
14th Floor
61-65 Des Voeux Road
Central District
HONG KONG
Tel: (011-852) 523-9922
Fax: (011-852) 524-9926

The Asia Society / Washington, D.C.
1800 K Street, N.W., Suite 1102
Washington, DC 20006
USA
Tel: (202) 833-2742
Fax: (202) 833-0189

Brigham Young University / University of Utah

Center for International Business Education and Research

Background and objectives: The BYU/Utah CIBER is one of the twenty-six centers designated by the Department of Education as a national resource for international business education and research. The BYU/Utah CIBER is the only joint CIBER in the country, with professors and students from both schools working together on many of the CIBER programs. The BYU/Utah CIBER aims to add superior business skills to the foreign language skills and international experience of the students and faculty; be a resource to the business community of the Inter-Mountain West, focusing on the key economic sectors of the region; and provide leadership and support to International Business professors throughout the Inter-Mountain West.

Programs: The BYU/Utah CIBER organizes and sponsors MBA student consulting teams capable of doing company research and consulting in the language where the company or branch office is located; sponsors a global network of business schools to provide a comprehensive exchange program for students and faculty; funds and promotes academic research on international business, and sponsors conferences for the business community such as "How to Successfully Do Business in Asia," "Going Global: How Utah's Information Technology Industry Can Do Business Internationally," and "The Bio-Medical Device Industry and International Business."

The Center also organizes and sponsors the Rocky Mountain International Business association, for professors of international business in the region.

Publications: The BYU/Utah CIBER has funded over fifty published journal articles and working papers.

Funding sources: CIBER is mainly funded by the U.S. Department of Education (75% of its budget). It also receives support from corporations and foundations, including Emma Eccles Jones Foundation and the KITO Corporation.

Staffing: The Center has two half-time co-directors, one full-time program manager, one full-time secretary, and numerous part-time researchers.

Heads of the institution:

Prof. C. Brooklyn Derr, University of Utah, Co-Director

Prof. Lee H. Radebaugh, Brigham Young University, Co-Director

Contact officer: Mr. Steve Hurlbut, Program Officer

Center for International Business Education and Research (CIBER)

At Utah
David Eccles School of Business
University of Utah
Salt Lake City, UT 84112
USA
Tel: (1-801) 585-3360
Fax: (1-801) 581-3666
e-mail • ciber@business.utah.edu
URL • http://www.business.utah.edu/CIBER

At BYU
Marriott School of Management
660 TNRB
Brigham Young University
Provo, UT 84602
USA
Tel: (1-801) 378-6495
Fax: (1-801) 378-5984
e-mail • Terri_Hagler@byu.edu
URL • http://msm.byu.edu/c&i/cim

Center for Continuing Study of the California Economy

Background and objectives: The Center for Continuing Study of the California Economy was founded in 1969 as an independent, private economic research organization focusing on long-term economic and demographic trends in California and its major economic regions. Working with public and private institutions, this for-profit organization analyzes the economic growth process and creates detailed quantitative projections to help decision makers develop long-term strategic plans regarding business and public policy.

Programs: The Center performs customized California economic research and prepares customized presentations to public and private sector decision makers. Twice a year, using its own economic model, CCSCE prepares long-term projections on jobs by sector, population/household characteristics, and income spending to the year 2010 for the entire state and four of its major economic regions: the Los Angeles Basin, the San Francisco Bay Area, the San Diego Region, and the Sacramento Region. Recent projects include analysis of the impact of air quality regulations on the California economy and investigation of defense conversion issues in Silicon Valley. CCSCE has also supported public agencies such as the California Economic Strategy Panel, the Metropolitan Water District of Southern California, and the South Coast Air Quality Management District by providing an independent assessment of the California economy to policy makers.

Publications: CCSCE publishes three annual report series: *California Economic Growth*, an analysis of trends in jobs, housing, income, and spending throughout California; *California Population Characteristics*, which describes consumer market segments; and *California County Projections*, which presents selected projections for all fifty California counties.

Funding sources: CCSCE conducts contract research for clients and sells annual reports and database service to subscribers.

Staffing: No information provided.

Head of the institution: Dr. Stephen Levy, Director and Senior Economist

Contact officer: Dr. Stephen Levy

Center for Continuing Study of the California Economy
610 University Avenue
Palo Alto, CA 94301
USA
Tel: (1-650) 321-8550
Fax: (1-650) 321-5451
e-mail • calecon@aol.com

Center for the New West

Background and objectives: The Center for the New West, established in 1989, is a nonpartisan, Denver-based institution for policy research on education and economic development. The Center focuses on changes that increasingly characterize U.S. society and the U.S. economy. These changes include increased global competition, rapid technological advances, demographic shifts, and the growing impact of small business and entrepreneurship.

Programs: The Center's current programs include four areas. The High Performance Communities Program offers seminars and studies on the roles of trade, technology and entrepreneurship, the Small Office/Home Office (SOHO) movement, and enterprise-friendly policies in economic development. The Information Policy and Culture Program addresses the impact of telecommuting technologies on how our communities live, work, play, learn, move about, and govern. The Center's Policy Studies focuses on public lands management, water resources, migration, urbanization, economic diversification, globalization, gentrification, and other issues shaping the American West. The Center's roundtables convene periodically to assemble Center members and regional, national, and international leaders to address topical issues.

Publications: The Center publishes *Profile of Western North America: Indicators of an Emerging Continental Market,* a reference source offering statistical information on the twenty-three western states of the U.S. and provinces and states of Canada and Mexico. Along with some 350 comparative indicators, this publication includes essays on income, population, health, housing, and energy. Other recent publications include *Strong Growth Drives a Dramatic Economic Transition in the West, Voices from the Heartland: New Tools for Decentralizing Management of the West's Public Lands,* and *California: A 21st Century Prospectus,* a report on the dramatic changes in the California economy. *Points West Chronicle* is the Center's quarterly newsletter on current Center programs.

Funding sources: The Center is supported by membership fees from more than 250 corporations, foundations, community organizations, and individuals including US West Communications Group, GTE Telephone Operations, Arizona Public Services Co., and Goldman Sachs & Co. The Center also draws on grants, fees for briefings, a speakers bureau, and other services. The Center's annual budget is $3 million.

Staffing: The Center has a network of forty senior fellows and associates, most of them part-time. It is also supported by a permanent staff of twenty professionals.

Head of the institution: Dr. Philip M. Burgess, President

Contact officer: Mr. Bob Wurmstedt, Director of Communications

Center for the New West
600 World Trade Center
1625 Broadway
Denver, CO 80202
USA
Tel: (1-303) 572-5400
Fax: (1-303) 572-5499
e-mail • cnwinfo@newwest.org
URL • http://www.newwest.org

Claremont Graduate School

Program in Politics and Policy

Background and objectives: The Claremont Graduate School, established in 1925, offers the Program in Politics and Policy to analyze the political dynamics of present and future society. The Program, founded in 1987, aims to integrate broad theoretical concerns about politics and political values with focused questions of applied policy analysis.

Programs: The Program offers four M.A. programs in international studies, politics, and public policy, as well as a doctoral degree in political science. The School's policy clinics propose creative solutions to public problems and address the political and institutional obstacles facing these innovative ideas. Examples of recent clinic topics include air pollution in Southern California, ethnic diversity in Los Angeles, and the uses and limitations of market-based approaches to environmental improvement. Current research projects related to the Pacific Rim include "Economic and Political Transitions in China" and U.S.-Mexico relations under NAFTA. A new project in collaboration with the Tomás Rivera Center for Hispanic and Public Policy Studies, funded by a grant from the Irvine Foundation, aims to advance Latino policy research in California and the Southwest, focusing on international political economy in Latin America and other areas of interest to American Latinos.

Funding sources: The Claremont Graduate School receives funds from foundations and corporations such as the Irvine Foundation, City Bank, the Lincoln Foundation, General Electric, and the Southern California Auto Club.

Staffing: The Program has thirteen full-time faculty and three full-time staff.

Head of the institution: Dr. John Maguire, President

Contact officer: Ms. Sandra Seymour, Office Administrator, Center for Politics and Economics

The Claremont Graduate School
Program in Politics and Policy
170 E. Tenth Street
McManus Hall 225
Claremont, CA 91711-6163
USA
Tel: (1-909) 621-8171
Fax: (1-909) 621-8545
e-mail • cgscpp@cgs.edu
URL • http://cgs.edu

Claremont McKenna College

Keck Center for International and Strategic Studies

Background and objectives: Founded in 1983, the Keck Center supports the study of critical issues in world affairs at Claremont McKenna College (CMC), one of the six Claremont Colleges which together have an enrollment of approximately 6,000 students.

Programs: The Keck Center sponsors lecture series on topics such as American Foreign Relations in the 21st Century, Fascism in Asia, and the Future of Communism; fellowships; visiting scholars; research associates; conferences; research publications; and student internships. The Center's research focuses on diplomatic, economic, and strategic issues in Northeast Asia, especially Japan, China, and Korea. Normally, the Keck Center sponsors approximately two annual conferences, at least one of which spotlights the Asia-Pacific region on issues such as State and Society in China, the United States and Japan, North Korea after Kim Il Sung, and the U.N. in a New World Order. In addition, the Center hosts workshops and seminars, primarily on East Asia and Europe. Recent speakers include Ambassador James Lilley, Professor Robert Scalapino of the University of California, Berkeley, Dr. Michel Oksenberg of the East-West Center, and Dr. Jonathan Pollack of RAND. The Center has a small library with an emphasis on international strategic studies and Asian and European developments.

Publications: The Center publishes a monograph series, a collection of essays and articles on timely international topics, including Pacific Rim affairs. Approximately two monographs are published each year. The Center has published monographs on topics such as the United States and Japan, U.S.-Japan Partnership in Conflict Management, the Korean War, and the Prospects for Korean Reunification.

Funding sources: The Keck Center is funded primarily by private foundations, including the Japan, Keck, Korea, and Luce Foundations and the Yenching Educational Fund.

Staffing: No information provided.

Head of the institution: Dr. Chae-Jin Lee, Director and Bank America Professor of Pacific Basin Studies

Contact officer: Ms. Mary Anderson, Administrative Assistant

Keck Center for International and Strategic Studies
Claremont McKenna College
850 Columbia Avenue (P-6)
Claremont, CA 91711-6420
USA
Tel: (1-909) 621-8213
Fax: (1-909) 621-8756
e-mail • marykeck@cyberg8y.com

The Commonwealth Club of California

Background and objectives: The Commonwealth Club of California, founded in 1903, is a public affairs forum and a nonprofit educational organization with a national membership of more than 15,000, most from Northern California. It is engaged in the nonpartisan study of current issues.

Programs: The Commonwealth Club's activities include over 500 meetings a year including luncheons, receptions, and dinners; and Sections, or regional programs. Speakers who addressed the Commonwealth Club in recent years included Jiang Zemin of the People's Republic of China, Fidel Ramos of the Philippines, Vaclav Havel of the Czech Republic, and Jean-Bertrand Aristide of Haiti.

The Friday noon luncheon programs, the hallmark of the Commonwealth Club, are held every Friday at major hotels in downtown San Francisco. The Commonwealth Club also holds early evening receptions at which influential speakers discuss issues of the day. Discussion Sections have had a history of providing for the in-depth examination of a variety of key issues through the format of a small, intimate forum. Current Sections cover such subject areas as the Arts, Asia Pacific Affairs, Business and Economics, Environment & Natural Resources, Food and Farming, Health and Medicine, Human Resources, International Relations, National Security, Nonprofit Sector, and Science and Technology. In recent years, the Commonwealth Club of California has expanded its programming to include meetings held in six Bay Area sites outside of San Francisco (Alameda County, Contra Costa County, Marin County, Peninsula, Silicon Valley, and Sonoma County).

The Club hosts a radio show, which started in 1924, and is now carried on more than 225 stations across the country. The program is transmitted live via the National Public Radio satellite, and sent on tape to commercial stations, as well. In 1995, the Club began regular broadcast of selected programs on public television's KQED in Northern California and via C-SPAN programming on cable systems nationally. The Commonwealth Club Book Awards, which began in 1931, are the oldest awards exclusively for California writers.

Publications: *The Commonwealth* is published weekly by the Commonwealth Club.

Staffing: The Commonwealth Club has twenty-three staff members.

Funding sources: Funds are derived from membership dues, foundation grants, corporate memberships, individual contributions, and program revenues.

Head of the institution: Dr. Gloria Duffy, Chief Executive Director and Officer

Contact officer: Mr. Daniel Miller, Office Manager

The Commonwealth Club of California
595 Market Street, 2nd Floor
San Francisco, CA 94105
USA
Tel: (1-415) 597-6700
Fax: (1-415) 597-6729
e-mail • cwc@sirius.com
URL • http://www.sfgate.com/~common

Silicon Valley Forum of the Commonwealth Club
306 S. Third Street
San Jose, CA 951121
USA
Tel: (1-408) 298-8342
Fax: (1-408) 298-0832

Head of the Institution: Mr. Tom Gewecke, Executive Director

Discovery Institute

Background and objectives: The Discovery Institute, founded in 1991, is a center for analysis of national and international affairs. Its philosophy is that good public policy requires exploration, civilized debate, and common sense about the possibilities and limits of political action.

Programs: The Institute conducts research on a variety of policy issues. The High Technology and Public Policy program examines how technologies of the computer age are transforming business, education, and government. Specific topics include government telecommunications policy, the impact of new technologies on law firms and the legal process, and the importance of using technology to revitalize U.S. national defense; the Cascadia project seeks to promote cooperation between the Northwestern U.S. and Western Canada on trade, transportation, and tourism. This project has generated two new regional institutions: the Cascadia Task Force, a bi-national working group of government leaders chaired by Seattle mayor Norm Rice; and the Cascadia Economic Roundtable, a bi-national group devoted to improving the business climate in the region; the Environment and People program explores new methods of environmental protection through economic and social incentives; the Religion, Liberty and Civic Life program aims to re-articulate for the 21st century the proper role that faith should play in public life and politics; the Revisioning Defense program emphasizes new technologies and new challenges faced by the United States as it maintains an effective, flexible, and affordable defense; the Representative Government and the Future of Public Life aims to restate the purposes of robust and effective representative democracy, advocating a reform of the reforms, strengthened political parties, and revived commitment to public service; and the Center for the Renewal of Science and Culture brings together leading scholars from the natural sciences and those from the humanities and social sciences, to explore how new developments in biology, physics, and cognitive science raise serious doubts about scientific materialism and have re-opened the case for the supernatural.

Discovery Institute also sponsors conferences, luncheons, workshops, seminars, and lectures throughout the year in various locations across the United States and Western Canada.

Publications: The Institute's publications include the newsletter *Discovery Institute Journal, Discovery Institute Inquiry,* featuring essays by Discovery Fellows, and *Discovery Institute Views,* a compilation of articles by and about the Institute and its Fellows.

Funding sources: The Institute is supported by contributions by foundations such as the MJ Murdock Charitable Trust, the Stewardship Foundation, and the Agnes Klingensmith Charitable Foundation. Income also comes from membership dues.

Staffing: Discovery Institute has over thirty Fellows and Adjunct Fellows including George Gilder, Edwin Meese III, Mark Plummer, Dr. Philip Gold, and Dr. John West. The Institute headquarters in Seattle, Washington, has a full-time administrative support staff of fourteen, and often employs numerous part-time staff and interns.

Head of the institution: Hon. Bruce Chapman, President

Contact officer: Mr. Robert L. Crowther II, Director of Public and Media Relations

Discovery Institute
1201 Third Avenue, 40th Floor
Seattle, WA 98101
USA
Tel: (1-206) 287-3144
Fax: (1-206) 583-8500
e-mail • discovery@discovery.org
URL • http://www.discovery.org

East-West Center

Background and objectives: The U.S. Congress established the EWC in 1960 to foster mutual understanding and better relations between the United States and the nations of the Asia-Pacific region through programs of cooperative study, training, and research. The EWC, officially named the Center for Cultural and Technical Interchange Between East and West, is a public, non-profit national educational institution with an international board of governors. Each year over 2,000 scholars, government and business leaders, educators, journalists, and other professionals from throughout the region collaborate with the Center's staff to address a wide variety of issues relevant to the Asia-Pacific region.

Programs: The EWC's mission is to share ideas and promote greater understanding of the various cultures, institutions, and values both of the peoples of the U.S. and of the Asia-Pacific region. To accomplish this mission, the EWC convenes international conferences on various topics such as population, environment, resources (energy and minerals), economic development, international relations, communications, and culture. The Center offers training for corporate executives and the business community as well as elementary and high school teachers. In cooperation with the University of Hawaii, the EWC supports 100 degree students from throughout the region at the undergraduate and graduate level. The EWC frequently welcomes distinguished visitors. In recent years, these have included the Emperor of Japan, the Dalai Lama of Tibet, and the President of the United States.

Publications: The results of research, training, and conference activities are disseminated to a wide audience of government policy makers, industry, media, and academe through EWC's publications, newsletters, and refereed journal articles. The EWC publications series, *Asia Pacific Issues* and *East-West Center Special Reports*, provide timely analysis from Center experts and visiting fellows. The EWC book series is produced in collaboration with Stanford University Press. Recently published books include *Political Legitimacy in Southeast Asia: The Quest for Moral Authority*, and *Making Majorities: Comprising the Nation in Japan, China, Korea, Malaysia, Fiji, Turkey, and the United States*.

Funding sources: The Center receives half of its funds from the U.S. Congress and the rest from governments in Asia and the Pacific, public and private institutions, and from private contributions.

Staffing: A core staff of about twenty-five fellows and a steady stream of visiting fellows publish their research and engage in educational, training, and networking activities, including working with post-doctoral and pre-doctoral fellows and degree students.

Head of the institution: Mr. Kenji Sumida, President

Contact officer: Ms. Karen Knudsen, Director, Office of Public Affairs

**East-West Center
1777 East-West Road
Honolulu, HI 96848
USA
Tel: (1-808) 944-7111
Fax: (1-808) 944-7970
URL • http://www.ewc.hawaii.edu**

Economic Development Corporation of Los Angeles County

Background and objectives: The Economic Development Corporation of Los Angeles County (LAEDC) is a private, non-profit organization established in 1981 to provide proactive leadership and substantive programs that retain, enhance, and expand businesses, jobs, enterprises, and economic resources in Los Angeles County. Supporters of the LAEDC are a diverse group of small, medium, and large businesses, cities, and public agencies that have a vested interest in the health of the local economy.

Programs: The LAEDC seeks to address the needs of the business community through three major programs: the Business Assistance Program (BAP), Research and Information Services, and the Los Angeles Regional Technology Alliance (LARTA).

The LAEDC's Business Assistance Program, funded by the New Los Angeles Marketing Partnership, provides personalized, professional support to businesses and economic development organizations throughout Los Angeles County to secure a robust economic environment providing growth in both gross county product and jobs. The LAEDC's ongoing development and management of a regional economic business assistance network ensures the coordination and leveraging of all business assistance programs throughout Los Angeles County.

The LAEDC's Business Assistance Managers are versed on the latest initiatives designed to help the company best leverage the many assets, talents, and programs available throughout Los Angeles County to support the growth of industry. They are strategically placed in regions throughout the County, with each manager assisting economic development professionals from those sub-regions to deliver program objectives.

The LAEDC researches and publishes key current and forecasted data on Southern California's economy to assist companies in the area.

The LAEDC also offers an economic consulting practice on such areas as the financial services industry, international economics including country analysis, and regional economic trends and regional industry analysis. The practice can be accessed by both members and non-members of the LAEDC.

The Los Angeles Regional Technology Alliance (LARTA) is dedicated to retaining and expanding the overall technology base in Southern California's five-county region (Los Angeles, Ventura, Orange, San Bernardino, and Riverside). LARTA helps local technology-based businesses find partners, access resources, and expand their markets in emerging and mature industries.

Publications: The LAEDC publishes *The Essential LA* guide, which highlights the most significant attributes of the Los Angeles area as a place to do business; *The Business Resource Guide*, a comprehensive resource directory for businesses of all sizes; and *The Economic and Industry Forecast of the Los Angeles Five-County Area*, which provides the most comprehensive regional forecast for Southern California's economy. Various other demographic studies and statistical databases are also available.

Funding sources: Funding is through membership dues and grants from both the private and public sectors.

Staffing: The LAEDC has a staff of approximately twenty-five professionals and administrative staff performing a wide array of activities including program management, research, consulting, membership development, marketing, and publication development and sales.

Head of the institution: Mr. Lee K. Harrington, President and CEO

Contact officer: Ms. Gabriele Greene, Director of Marketing and External Relations

**The Economic Development
   Corporation of Los Angeles County**
515 South Flower Street, 32nd Floor
Los Angeles, CA 90071
USA
Tel: (1-213) 622-4300
Fax: (1-213) 622-7100
e-mail • ghuang@laedc.org

Federal Reserve Bank of San Francisco

Center for Pacific Basin Monetary and Economic Studies

Background and objectives: Established in 1990 by the Federal Reserve Bank of San Francisco, the Center for Pacific Basin Monetary and Economic Studies seeks to further international understanding of major Pacific Basin monetary and economic policy issues. Since 1974, the Federal Reserve Bank of San Francisco has promoted cooperation among central banks in the Pacific Basin and enhanced public understanding of economic policy issues. Since establishing the Center within its Economic Research Department, the Bank has sought greater participation by researchers from other central banks, universities, research institutes, and international organizations who share its interest in the Pacific Basin.

Programs: Up to three visiting scholars are received by the Center for a period of six months. The Center organizes and hosts major Pacific Basin economic policy conferences at two- or three-year intervals, and also sponsors occasional conferences jointly with other institutions. The Center's most recent major conferences on Asia-Pacific issues include "Managing Capital Flows and Exchange Rates: Lessons from the Pacific Basin" (1996) and "Exchange Rate Policy in Pacific Basin Countries" (1992).

Publications: The Center publishes *Pacific Basin Research Abstracts,* which contain summaries of Center Associates' research papers, and distributes working papers by staff members and visiting scholars. Recent examples include "The New Regionalism and Asia: Impact and Options" (1995), "Monetary Policy in Japan: A Structural VAR Analysis" (1995), and "Comparative and Absolute Advantage in the Asia-Pacific Region" (1995). Conference papers are published in commercial book form. The Center also distributes relevant articles from the Bank's *Economic Letter* and *Economic Review* series.

Funding sources: The Center is internally financed by the Federal Reserve Bank of San Francisco.

Staffing: The Center has four full-time research economists, three research associates, one administrative staff assistant, and up to three visiting scholars.

Head of the institution: Dr. Reuven Glick, Vice President and Director

---

Center for Pacific Basin Monetary and Economic Studies
Federal Reserve Bank of San Francisco
101 Market Street
San Francisco, CA 94105
USA
Tel: (1-415) 974-3184
Fax: (1-415) 974-2168
e-mail • Reuven.glick@sf.frb.org
URL • http://www.frbsf.org

The Hoover Institution

Background and objectives: The Hoover Institution on War, Revolution, and Peace at Stanford University is a research center devoted to advanced study of domestic public policy and international affairs. Founded by Herbert Hoover in 1919, the institution is home to approximately seventy resident fellows—specialists in economics, education, history, international relations, law, political science, and sociology—who focus their research on economic, political, and social issues of current relevance to public policy makers.

Programs: Hoover fellows conduct research on many and varied issues of public policy, most of which are identified with one of three major research programs. The Program on American Institutions and Economic Performance studies policies that enable the U.S. economy to perform better, thereby providing an ever-higher quality of life, increased economic opportunity, and greater economic proficiency, while at the same time solving or providing relief from persistent social problems.

The Program on Democracy and Free Markets analyzes the factors, particularly in nations evolving from socialism to democracy and market economies, that help build and sustain democratic practices and institutions and that, in the economic sphere, promote free markets and liberty.

The Program on International Rivalries and Global Cooperation focuses on the changing context of international relations with a view to identifying and understanding relationships of conflict and cooperation.

Many Hoover fellows also conduct research relating to specific geographic regions of the world, including East Asia, Russia and the other republics of the former Soviet Union, Europe, Africa, the Middle East, and the Americas.

Studies relating to the Pacific Rim focus on modern economic and political developments in China, Taiwan, Hong Kong, Korea, and Japan, as well as strategic security problems throughout the region. With respect to China, specific areas of inquiry include economic modernization, evolution of the socialist economy, foreign investment, the Communist party and other political institutions, trends toward decentralization of power, prospects for political reform, Chinese intellectual history, U.S.-China relations, Chinese influence in the Pacific Basin, and the transition of Hong Kong from British to Chinese sovereignty. Studies on Taiwan relate to postwar democratization, economic development, and the new business class. Research on Korea has examined questions relating to unification, strategic security, and democratization. With respect to Japan, studies have focused on Japanese imperial expansion, postwar economic and political development, and U.S.-Japanese postwar relations.

Fellowships for visiting scholars are offered in various fields. These include National Fellowships for junior scholars at U.S. colleges and universities to pursue public policy studies, the Susan Louise Dyer Peace Fellowship, National Security Affairs and Diplomatic Affairs Fellowships for U.S. foreign service and military officers, the Robert Wesson Fellowship in Scientific Philosophy and Public Policy, Media Fellowships for journalists and other professionals in the communications field, and the Stuart Distinguished Visiting Scholar Fellowship in Education Policy.

Many scholars, diplomats, government officials, and others also spend varied periods of time in residence as visiting scholars.

Publications: The Institution's research output is disseminated through books, essays, articles, a television program, conferences, seminars, videotapes, media interviews, a quarterly newsletter, and congressional testimony. The Hoover Institution Press publishes books on both domestic and international affairs, with a number of titles on East Asia. *The Hoover Digest*, which is published quarterly, presents short articles and opinion pieces by Hoover fellows.

Staffing: The Hoover Institution has almost 100 fellows in residence, and approximately 200 administrative staff members.

Funding sources: The Institution's operating budget of $18 million is funded by income from endowment (39%); expandable gifts from individuals, foundations, and corporations (33%); allocation from Stanford University's operating funds for the Hoover Library and Archives (22%); government grants (4%); and miscellaneous income (2%).

Notes: Hoover fellows include three Nobel laureates, nineteen members of the American Academy of Arts and Sciences, six members of the American Philosophical Society, eleven members of the Econometric Society, and nine members of the National Academy of Sciences. The Hoover Library and Archives house one of the largest and most complete private collections in the world on economic, political, and social change in the 20th century, which includes 1.6 million books and periodicals and forty million documents.

Head of the institution: Dr. John Raisian, Director

Contact officer: Ms. Michele Horaney, Acting Public Affairs Manager

The Hoover Institution
Stanford, CA 94305-6010
USA
Tel: (1-650) 723-1454
Fax: (1-650) 725-8611
e-mail • info@hoover.stanford.edu
URL • http://www.hoover.stanford.edu

Human Rights Watch / California

Background and objectives: Human Rights Watch (HRW), an independent, non-governmental organization, began in 1978 as Helsinki Watch, which is now its European division. This non-profit organization is headquartered in New York and includes five divisions covering Africa, the Americas, Asia, the Middle East, and the countries that are signatories of the Helsinki accords. The organization has nearly 100 staff members who monitor and promote human rights by conducting regular, systematic investigations of human rights abuses in approximately seventy countries. The Los Angeles office of HRW, opened in 1989, primarily organizes public discussions by HRW staff recently returned from the field. The California Committee of HRW is composed of prominent members of the LA community who have worked hard to stimulate media attention to human rights issues and involve California citizens in the human rights movement.

Programs: In addition to its five geographical divisions, HRW has convened thematic projects on arms transfers, children's rights, and women's rights. In the Asia-Pacific region, HRW has published their findings on human rights in Burma, Cambodia, China, East Timor, India, Indonesia, Nepal, Pakistan, the Philippines, South Korea, Sri Lanka, and Vietnam. In addition, HR Americas Watch has reported extensively on all of Latin America since 1981. In addition, HRW has written two dozen reports on the United States. HRW seeks to maximize the impact of its reports through the press, testimony before the U.S. Congress, and contacts with the European Union, the World Bank, the United Nations, and other international organizations.

Publications: Each year, HRW publishes approximately 100 reports of varying lengths, which are available for purchase through regional or topical subscriptions. Release of reports to the press, citizens' organizations, policy makers, the academic community, and libraries is the main vehicle by which HRW distributes its findings.

Funding sources: HRW is supported by contributions from private individuals and foundations worldwide. The organization does not accept any funds from governments.

Staffing: HRW has three full-time professionals engaging in education, communications, program development, advocacy, and administrative duties.

Head of the institution: Mr. Kenneth Roth, Executive Director

Contact officer: Mrs. Pam Bruns, California Director

**Human Rights Watch
333 S. Grand Avenue, Suite 430
Los Angeles, CA 90071-1504
USA
Tel: (1-213) 680-9906
Fax: (1-213) 680-9924
e-mail • hrwla@hrw.org
URL • http://www.hrw.org**

Institute for Contemporary Studies

Background and objectives: The Institute for Contemporary Studies (ICS) was founded in 1972 to promote the self-governing and entrepreneurial way of life. The general philosophy of the Institute is that self-governing political, social, and economic institutions offer the greatest hope for individuals and families to live productive and fulfilling lives.

Programs: The ICS focuses on entrepreneurship, the environment, education, governance and leadership, and social policy. A central aim of the ICS Entrepreneurship Program is to analyze the effects of policy on entrepreneurial activity. The ICS has also created the Center for Social Security Reform with the purpose of beginning and sustaining a broad national discussion, through in-depth forums and aggressive use of the media, to help frame avenues of action that can foster real change to the Social Security system. In addition, ICS has sponsored a long-term education program to promote sound environmental positions. Initial research indicates that when environmental policies are based on science, self-governance, and entrepreneurship, people are more likely to work to produce a clean environment than when such policies are imposed by bureaucratic mandates. ICS's program for school reform seeks to help citizens create schools that bring the values of self-governance to students. The Institute's model for neighborhood self-governance and empowerment employs local action foundations (LAFs) composed of community leaders, entrepreneurs, and interested citizens united by common social and community concerns. One LAF at work in the San Francisco Bay Area is CACE (the Citizens' Alliance for Community Empowerment), an association of public housing tenants, business people, and community activists working on resident management of public housing and choice in education. LAFs reward initiative and responsibility in the areas of housing, education, and child care. The International Center for Self-Governance (ICSG) carries out the Institute's international activities. ICSG's objective is to promote self-governance—the process of men and women actively participating in the design and operation of the institutions that affect their lives—as a strategy for economic, social, and political development. ICSG works with policy institutes and organizations throughout Asia that are members of its international network. ICSG has also conducted seminars and workshops in the Philippines and Nepal and has published books and videos on self-governing projects in several Asian countries.

Publications: The Institute's leading vehicle for disseminating its findings is ICS Press, which has published over 100 books, including the writings of six Nobel laureates. The early work of the Institute on energy policy helped influence the deregulation of oil prices in 1981, and President Bush's plan for educational reform, America 2000, includes many ideas set forth in the ICS book *Winning the Brain Race*.

Funding sources: The ICS relies on individual and corporate support to fund its activities.

Staffing: ICS has thirteen full-time researchers and three part-time researchers.

Head of the institution: Mr. Robert B. Hawkins, Jr., President and CEO

Contact officer: Ms. Perenna P. Fleming, Chief Operating Officer

Institute for Contemporary Studies
720 Market St., 4th floor
San Francisco, CA 94102
USA
Tel: (1-415) 981-5353
Fax: (1-415) 986-4878
e-mail • 3711,477@compuserve.com
URL • http://www.self-govern.com

Institute of the Americas

Background and objectives: The Institute of the Americas is an independent, inter-American institution studying some of the major challenges facing the countries of the Western Hemisphere. Located on the campus of the University of California, San Diego, the Institute aims to encourage and analyze economic and social reform in Latin America and the Caribbean; identify opportunities to enhance the private sector's contributions to progress; and promote public-private cooperation in the region.

Programs: The Institute carries out its work primarily through membership networks, private sector-oriented conferences, research and publications, joint programs with collaborating institutions at the University of California at San Diego, linkages with other organizations in Latin America and Canada, and joint programs with government and multilateral agencies.

Some of the issues on which the Institute has concentrated include sustainable development, energy, and the environment; democratization and governance; market-oriented economic reforms, including privatization; and free trade and economic integration.

The Institute is collaborating with the U.S. Department of Commerce and the Environmental Export Council on a $1.2 million project, the Market Development Cooperator Program, aimed at building exports of U.S. goods and services to Latin America in the environmental and energy sectors.

The Institute's project on Regionalization of the World Economy explores ways to ensure the compatibility of regional trade agreements with an open global system.

In a joint effort with the Inter-American Development Bank, the Institute has sponsored conferences and seminars analyzing social security pension reforms in the U.S. and Latin America. In the realm of privatization and investment, the Institute holds conferences on health care reform, telecommunications, and infrastructure finance and development.

Publications: The Institute's publications include monographs on the political and economic outlook for major Western Hemisphere countries; the "Inside the Americas" series; and *Hemisfile,* the Institute's flagship periodical of economic and political trends published bimonthly and distributed to some 66,000 readers. This publication features concise articles written by distinguished scholars and specialists. It is free to members of the Institute of the Americas and available through subscription to others.

Funding sources: The Institute is funded through membership dues (both individual and corporate) and grants from foundations, corporations, and U.S. and multilateral development agencies. The Institute has some one hundred corporate members, including major U.S. corporations such as Bank of America, Bechtel, and Enron, as well as corporations from Canada and Latin America. Major foundations supporting the Institute have included the Mellon Foundation, the Ford Foundation, the Hewlett Foundation, and the Pew Charitable Trusts.

Staffing: The Institute has a professional and administrative staff of approximately fifteen individuals, including four program directors, a director of development, an editor, finance director, and office manager. The Institute also has several program and development assistants, student interns, and volunteers.

Head of the institution: Hon. Paul H. Boeker, President

Contact officer: Ms. Colleen S. Morton, Vice President & Director of Research

Institute of the Americas
10111 North Torrey Pines Road
La Jolla, CA 92037
USA
Tel: (1-619) 453-5560
Fax: (1-619) 453-2165
e-mail • cmorton@weber.ucsd.edu
URL • http://www.ioal92-92.ucsd.edu
       http://www.132.239.192.92

Japan Policy Research Institute

Background and objectives: The Japan Policy Research Institute (JPRI) was founded in 1994 by Chalmers Johnson and Steven Clemons. It is a nonprofit membership organization devoted to public education about Japan and trans-Pacific international relations. One of its goals is to bring home to educated people around the Pacific the need for in-depth area studies on Japan and other countries in East Asia, as distinct from the social science theory approaches prevalent in many university departments.

Programs: Through the use of an international electronic network, JPRI promotes communications among scholars, journalists, government officials, business leaders, and students. JPRI collaborates with the New Mexico U.S.-Japan Center in organizing and sponsoring a series of workshops and conferences. On September 27-28, 1996, JPRI, together with the Center for the Pacific Rim at the University of San Francisco, organized the conference "Legacies of the Cold War: Constraints on Post-Cold War Security Policy in East Asia." There were panels on the Kwangju Massacre in South Korea, current U.S. China Policy, and the Japanese-American Security Treaty and the Okinawan issue.

Publications: JPRI publishes monthly *Working Papers, Occasional Papers,* and the *JPRI Critique* for its members.

Recent examples include the working paper by Gavan McCormack, entitled "Afterbubble: Fizz and Concrete in Japan's Political Economy," and the working paper by Chalmers Johnson, entitled "Nationalism and the Market: China as a Superpower."

Funding sources: JPRI is funded primarily through individual membership dues.

Staffing: The Institute has three part-time researchers in California (all with Ph.D. degrees), one half-time editor and accountant in California, and one full-time administrative assistant in New Mexico.

Head of the institution: Dr. Chalmers Johnson, President

Japan Policy Research Institute
2138 Via Tiempo
Cardiff, CA 92007
USA
Tel: (1-619) 944-3950
Fax: (1-619) 944-9022
e-mail • jpri@nmjc.org
          cjohnson@ucsd.edu
URL • http://www.nmjc.org/jpri

Japanese American Citizens League

Background and objectives: Founded in 1929, the JACL is the oldest and largest Asian American volunteer organization in the United States. A membership-driven organization, its mission is to secure and protect the rights of Americans of Japanese ancestry and others, and to preserve the cultural heritage and values of Japanese Americans. The organization has 22,300 members nationwide, 111 chapters across the U.S., and one chapter in Japan. The National JACL is headquartered in San Francisco, California. Regional offices are located in Los Angeles, Fresno, Seattle, and Chicago. An office is also maintained in Washington, D.C.

Program: The League's National Youth Council Program (NYC), seeks to introduce the JACL to new members, particularly youth and students, and recruit them into local JACL chapters. NYC sponsors programs to improve the leadership skills of young Japanese Americans and to establish ties and coalitions with other Asian Pacific Islander American (APIA) groups. Through workshops and resource guides on topics such as anti-Asian violence, the glass ceiling, affirmative action, inter-Asian racism, and inter-racial dating, the Council hopes to promote awareness of these issues within the APIA community. The NYC also supports the creation of ethnic studies programs on college campuses and the creation of a network among universities to monitor hate crimes, admissions policies, tenure proceedings, and other issues affecting APIAs in higher education. Since 1946, the JACL has operated a National Scholarship Program through which members or their children may apply for scholarship funds that total over $65,000 annually. JACL distributes grants to JACL chapters for a variety of programs to develop oral histories and anti-Asian violence programs. It also convenes a biennial convention that is the largest gathering of Japanese American leaders in the nation.

Publications: The *Pacific Citizen* is the newspaper of the National JACL and serves as an independent informational forum for the members of the organization. The JACL also publishes an educational Curriculum and Resource Guide about the experiences of Japanese Americans during World War II.

Funding sources: The JACL is funded through its membership dues, donations, grants, and fees.

Staffing: JACL has ten full-time and four part-time program staff members and five full-time administrative staff.

Notes: JACL's advocacy was crucial in passing legislation that obtained naturalization rights for, and provided redress to, those Japanese Americans placed in internment camps during World War II.

Head of the institution: Mr. Herbert Yamanishi, National Director

Japanese American Citizens League
National Headquarters
1765 Sutter Street
San Francisco, CA 94115
USA
Tel: (1-415) 921-5225
Fax: (1-415) 931-4671

Leadership Education for Asian Pacifics, Inc.

Background and objectives: Leadership Education for Asian Pacifics, Inc. (LEAP) is a national, nonprofit, nonpartisan community-based organization founded in 1982. LEAP's mission is to achieve full participation and equality for Asian Pacific Americans through leadership, empowerment, and policy.

Programs: LEAP is the umbrella organization for the Leadership Management Institute and the Asian Pacific American Public Policy Institute. The Leadership Management Institute (LMI), LEAP's flagship program, builds leadership and managerial skills among Asian Pacific Americans in public, private, student, and community sectors through workshops and a five-day Leadership Development Program that is offered twice a year on the West and East coasts. The LMI educates both Asian Pacific Americans and non-Asians in issues of cultural diversity, awareness, and identity, and seeks to increase Asian Pacific American representation in leadership ranks. The Institute has conducted over 535 workshops to a national audience of more than 27,000 people since 1983. LMI's recent workshops include "Bridging the Gap: Key Issues in Understanding Asian Pacific Americans," "Risk Taking: Making Changes Happen," and "Understanding Your Cultural Values."

The Asian Pacific American Public Policy Institute (PPI) aims to raise public awareness of policy issues as they impact the Asian Pacific American community. The PPI sponsors original research and publishes policy reports on Asian Pacific American affairs. The PPI also regularly convenes policy roundtables in several major U.S. cities to discuss its research findings and to collectively discuss policy recommendations that promote Asian Pacific American interests on national and local levels.

Publications: LEAP publishes *LEAP Connections*, a quarterly newsletter (cir. 18,000) summarizing current events and programs of interest to the Asian Pacific American community. The PPI has six publications to date, including three 300-page volumes under the annual title series *The State of Asian Pacific America*. Other recent publications include *Reframing the Immigration Debate* (1996), and *Common Ground Perspectives on Affirmative Action and Its Impact on Asian Pacific Americans* (1995).

Funding sources: LEAP is funded through private foundations such as the Ford Foundation and the Carnegie Corporation of New York and corporation grants. The Leadership Management Institute is partially financed through workshop and program fees.

Staffing: LEAP has four full-time staff, which includes the executive director, the administrative director, a program manager, and a development manager.

Head of the institution: Mr. J.D. Hokoyama, President and Executive Director

Contact officer: Ms. Linda Akutagawa, Administrative Director

Leadership Education for Asian Pacifics, Inc. (LEAP)
327 East Second Street, Suite 226
Los Angeles, CA 90012-4210
USA
Tel: (1-213) 485-1422
Fax: (1-213) 485-0050
e-mail • leap90012@aol.com
URL • http://www.leap.org/leap

Los Angeles Urban League

Background and objectives: The National Urban League is an African-American civil rights organization and social service agency with 114 affiliates across the country. The Los Angeles Urban League (LAUL) is one of the organization's largest affiliates and has served the Los Angeles community for seventy-six years with programs in South-Central Los Angeles, Pomona, Pasadena, and Inglewood, California.

Programs: The LAUL sponsors or co-sponsors a variety of programs that are geared toward building business and employment skills for its constituents. The Ron Brown Information Technology and Business Center was established as a partnership between the LAUL, the ARCO Foundation, and private industry.

The Center provides technical and business development assistance to existing small and medium businesses and assists aspiring entrepreneurs in creating, developing, and successfully managing new businesses.

The LAUL offers on-line access to public agency procurement departments and major corporations, conference facilities, seminars on business issues, a business resource library, and computer training. The Information Technology program portion of the center trains individuals for careers in information technology and office administrative support.

Another program, the LAUL-Toyota Automotive Training Center in Los Angeles's Crenshaw District, is a nonprofit vocational center that provides inner-city residents with skills training and job placement in the automotive repair field at no cost.

In addition to these employment-related programs, the LAUL sponsors several other social services that include Head Start/preschool education, employment counseling services, volunteer opportunities, health examinations, meals for Head Start children, college scholarships, and training programs.

Publications: LAUL publishes an annual report and a quarterly newsletter.

Funding sources: LAUL's operations are funded by United Way, and by corporate donations, program partnerships, and membership dues.

Staffing: LAUL has a small professional and administrative staff.

Head of the institution: Mr. John W. Mack, President

Contact officer: Ms. Sandra S. Carter, Vice-President, Programs

Los Angeles Urban League
3450 Mt. Vernon Drive
Los Angeles, CA 90008
USA
Tel: (1-213) 299-9660
Fax: (1-213) 299-0618
URL • http://www.careermosaic.com:80/cm/ul

The Mansfield Center for Pacific Affairs

Background and objectives: The Mansfield Center is the public policy and international outreach arm of the Maureen and Mike Mansfield Foundation, which was established in 1983 to advance Ambassador Mansfield's lifelong goal of improved understanding between the U.S. and Asia. The Mansfield Center addresses the political, economic, cultural, and social factors that affect policy decisions in both the United States and Asia. The Center maintains offices in Washington, D.C., and Missoula, Montana.

Programs: Focusing on policy makers and opinion leaders (especially young emerging leaders) the Mansfield Center promotes and nurtures enduring relationships for the exchange of ideas and information. Its lectures, forums, seminars, conferences, and publications provide avenues for in-depth exploration of issues that influence relationships among Pacific Rim nations and between these countries and the United States. Programs focus on such topics as Hong Kong's "Next Century"; deregulation in Japan; the trilateral relationship of China, Japan, and the U.S.; and the impact of national news media on international relations and policy debates. The Center also administers the Mansfield Fellowship program, which sends U.S. government officials to Japan for one year of work in Japanese government ministries, following a year of full-time Japanese-language training. Finally, the Center sponsors special programs to enhance the long-standing ties between Montana and nations on the far side of the Pacific Rim.

Publications: No information provided.

Funding sources: Many of the Center's activities are co-sponsored by other organizations and agencies, including the Pacific Basin Institute, the World Environment Center, the U.S. Library of Congress, the NHK Broadcasting Culture Research Institute, and the Keizai Koho Center. Center activities are also funded by the Maureen and Mike Mansfield Foundation, other foundations and private sector companies, and the United States Information Agency.

Staffing: No information provided.

Head of the institution: Ms. Tovah LaDier, Executive Director

Contact officer: Ms. Joyce Piquette, Administrative Assistant

The Mansfield Center for Pacific Affairs
Mansfield Library
University of Montana
Missoula, MT 59812
USA
Tel: (1-406) 243-2214
Fax: (1-406) 243-2181

601 Thirteenth Street, N.W.
Suite 400 South
Washington D.C. 20005
USA
Tel: (1-202) 347-1994
Fax: (1-202) 347-3941

Mexican American Legal Defense and Educational Fund

Background and objectives: The Mexican American Legal Defense and Educational Fund (MALDEF), founded in San Antonio, Texas, in 1968, is a national nonprofit organization whose mission is to protect and promote the civil rights of the over twenty-six million Latinos living in the United States. It is particularly dedicated to securing such rights in employment, education, immigration, political access, and language and leadership development. Headquartered in Los Angeles in the MALDEF Anheuser-Busch Nonprofit Center, MALDEF has regional offices in Los Angeles, San Francisco, Chicago, and Washington D.C., with a satellite office in Sacramento, California, and program offices in Fresno, California, and El Paso, Texas.

Programs: The organization achieves its objectives through litigation, advocacy, community education, collaboration with other groups and individuals, and by offering scholarship awards in law and communications. MALDEF has been at the forefront of civil rights litigation, setting precedent in many cases and establishing new systems to elect officials, hire and promote employees, and educate children.

On the non-litigation side, MALDEF has worked extensively on the issues of redistricting and census adjustment. Through its leadership programs MALDEF has empowered and trained Latinos to join boards of directors and commissions in their communities and parents to become advocates for their children's education. For example, the School and Parent Partnership for Educational Achievement Right program (SPEAR initiative) provides a national infrastructure through which teachers, school administrators, policy makers and elected officials, and parents can work together to bring down the barriers that prevent Latino children from full educational attainment.

Publications: MALDEF publishes *MALDEF*, the institution newsletter, the Leadership newsletter, and the Annual Report.

Funding sources: MALDEF's activities are supported by corporate and private foundations, corporations, and individuals.

Staffing: MALDEF's Board of Directors is comprised of thirty-two leaders from the public and private sectors, government, and law firms. Its staff of over seventy-five employees includes twenty-two attorneys.

Head of the institution: Ms. Antonia Hernandez, President and General Counsel

Contact officer: Mr. Thomas B. Reston, Board Chair

Mexican American Legal Defense and Educational Fund (MALDEF)
National Office
634 South Spring Street, 11th Floor
Los Angeles, CA 90014
USA
Tel: (1-213) 629-2512
Fax: (1-213) 629-8016
e-mail • maldefone@aol.com

Monterey Institute of International Studies

Background and objectives: The Monterey Institute of International Studies (MIIS) is an independent professional graduate school that seeks to prepare students for international careers in the private, public, nonprofit, and education sectors. An emphasis on second language acquisition and cross-cultural understanding is woven throughout the school's curricula.

Programs: The Institute offers master's degree programs in International Management, International Policy Studies, International Public Administration, International Environmental Policy, Language Teaching, and Translation and Interpretation. The Institute's 750 students come from over fifty countries, and more than 90% of them have lived, worked, or studied outside their native countries. In addition to the academic degree programs, the Monterey Institute offers several special programs, including the Summer Intensive Language Program (SILP), with classes in ten languages at the elementary and intermediate levels; and Custom Language Services (CLS), which facilitates communication across languages and cultures, through such services as specialized language and cultural training, document translation, and language skills assessment.

The Center for East Asian Studies (CEAS), established in 1991, sponsors research, lectures, and workshops on subjects related to East Asia. Currently, the Center is conducting three research-conferences projects: First, the project on "Economic Relations and Regional Security," involving researchers from Japan, Korea, Mongolia, Russia, and the United States, examines the changing economic relations among these countries and their security implications. A seminar on this topic was held in September 1996. Second, the "Intercultural Communication and Management in Japanese Business in the United States" project has conducted research into human resources development and personnel management in California-based Japanese firms and developed a series of recommendations for improving human relations. Finally, "INFORM" (Information Network for Ocean Resources/Environment, Monterey) is part of a larger MIIS-based project, Project OCEANS, which is developing electronic databases on the state of global ocean environment, ocean-related technologies, and ocean-related laws, policies, and treaties. Contact Information: Dr. Tsuneo Akaha, Director.

The Center for Trade and Commercial Diplomacy (CTCD) offers training for business executives and international trade specialists, conducts research, provides public information, and supplies a forum for leaders from the public and private sectors to learn about and discuss international trade and competition issues. Contact Information: Mr. Geza Feketekuty, Director.

The Center for Nonproliferation Studies (CNS) maintains a wide-ranging program of non-proliferation study, analysis, and training. The CNS analyzes key proliferation issues affecting U.S. national security and the stability of the international community; maintains databases that track commerce in weapons technologies; provides education and training in non-proliferation and arms control; and conducts outreach to inform the U.S. and international body politic about the dangers inherent in continued proliferation and the best ways to mitigate those threats. Within the Pacific region, the CNS follows nuclear, missile, and advanced conventional arms trade for all countries. It also has more focused research projects covering nuclear problems in the Russian Far East, North Korea, and China. Contact Information: Dr. William Potter, Director.

Publications: The Institute publishes the *International Experts Guide*, a directory of faculty and research scholars from MIIS who have indicated a willingness to offer their insights and expertise on more than 200 subject areas.

Funding sources: MIIS depends on private support as well as tuition revenues to fund its academic and research programs and to provide scholarship assistance to students. The Institute received contract support from the federal government to establish the Center for Trade and Commercial Diplomacy. Additional federal funding and foundation grants support the Center for Proliferation Studies. The Monterey Institute has received support from the S. H. Cowell Foundation, the Ford Foundation, the John D. and Catherine T. MacArthur Foundation, the Joyce Mertz-Gilmore Foundation, the Rockefeller Foundation, the Volkswagen Foundation, and the W. Alton Jones Foundation.

Head of the institution: Dr. Robert G. Gard, Jr., Professor and President

Contact officer: Mr. Mark Hucklebridge, Director of Public Affairs

Monterey Institute of International Studies
425 Van Buren Street
Monterey, CA 93940
USA
Tel: (1-408) 647-3581
Fax: (1-408) 647-4199

National Association of Japan-America Societies

Japan-America Society of Southern California

Background and objectives: The Japan-America Society of Southern California was founded in 1909 and is a nonprofit, non-political organization. The Society's membership includes individuals and organizations with an interest in Japan and in U.S.-Japan relations. The Society seeks to foster understanding and strengthen the links between the U.S. and Japan in the spheres of business, culture, trade, politics, and the arts.

Programs: The Society offers an active and diverse schedule of events, including frequent breakfast and luncheon programs and special seminars and workshops on contemporary U.S.-Japan affairs. Roundtable groups provide opportunities to discuss industry-specific topics. These meetings feature distinguished Japanese and American officials, community and industry leaders, artists, and scholars.

In addition, the Society hosts art, music, fashion, film, and performing arts programs as well as other special activities such as golf tournaments and gala dinners. The Society's "5:01 Clubs"—established in downtown, Westside, and South Bay—meet monthly at changing locations and provide an opportunity to socialize in an informal setting.

Publications: The Japan-America Society publishes a newsletter that highlights the Society's activities and provides advance notice of all programs and events.

Funding sources: Funds are drawn primarily from membership dues, contributions, and program fees.

Staffing: The Society's staff consists of a president, vice president, program director, and office manager.

Head of the institution: Mr. E. B. Kehn, President

Japan-America Society of Southern California
505 South Flower Street
Level C
Los Angeles, CA 90071
USA
Tel: (1-213) 627-6217
Fax: (1-213) 627-1353

Other Japan-America Societies
in the Western part of the United States:

Japan-America Society of Colorado
Mr. Brian Pendleton, President
1200 Seventeenth Street
Suite 3000
Denver, CO 80202
Tel: (1-303) 298-9633
Fax: (1-303) 293-9222

Japan-America Society of Dallas/Fort Worth
Mr. Dean Vanderbilt, President
P.O. Box 58095
Dallas, TX 75258
Tel: (1-214) 761-1791
Fax: (1-214) 761-1793

Japan-America Society of Hawaii
Mr. Yoshiharu Satoh, President
P.O. Box 1412
Honolulu, HI 96806
Tel: (1-808) 524-4450
Fax: (1-808) 524-4451

Japan-America Society of Houston
Mr. Wesley J. Grove, President
Suite 1760
1360 Post Oak Boulevard
Houston, TX 77056
Tel: (1-713) 963-0121
Fax: (1-713) 963-8270

Japan-America Society of Nevada
Mr. Kenneth R. Ivory, President
P.O. Box 26267
Las Vegas, NV 89126-0267
Tel: (1-702) 252-0277
Fax: (1-702) 253-0075

Japan-America Society of Northern California
Ms. Kathleen Kimura, President
312 Sutter Street 4F
San Francisco, CA 94108
Tel: (1-415) 986-4383
Fax: (1-415) 986-5772

Japan-America Society of Oregon
Mr. Adolf Hertrich, President
221 N.W. Second Avenue
Portland, OR 97209
Tel: (1-503) 228-9411 ext. 235
Fax: (1-508) 228-5126

Japan-America Society of the State of Washington
Mr. Gary Severson, President
1800 Ninth Avenue, Suite 1550
Seattle, WA 98101-1322
Tel: (1-206) 623-7900
Fax: (1-206) 343-7930

The National Bureau of Asian Research

Background and objectives: The National Bureau of Asian Research (NBR) is a nonprofit, nonpartisan institution that conducts research and serves as an international clearinghouse on policy issues in the Asia-Pacific region. Envisioned as a bridge between the policy, academic, and business communities, NBR was founded in 1989 with a major grant from the Henry M. Jackson Foundation. The organization concentrates exclusively on the Asia-Pacific region, including Russia and Central Asia.

Programs: NBR research is conducted by leading experts in the Asia-Pacific field, wherever they may be based, rather than exclusively by in-house research staff. The organization's research is interdisciplinary, drawing upon specialists in Asian politics, economics, business, defense, the environment, and other fields. Research is made public through written reports, conferences, meetings with policy makers and staff, testimony before congressional committees, and outreach to the media. Recent projects have focused on the Asia-Pacific Economic Cooperation (APEC) forum, Russia's changing role in Asia, Japanese and American leadership in the Asia-Pacific region, China's most-favored-nation status, Korean reunification, and the evolving security environment in Southeast Asia. NBR maintains a major database for the project *AccessAsia*, the only international resource that tracks specialists and their current research on policy-related issues in the Asia-Pacific region. With the recent establishment of an NBR-led global consortium of institutions in Europe, Asia, and North America, *AccessAsia* has become the global clearinghouse of Asia specialists and their research.

Publications: The organization publishes *NBR Analysis*, a journal featuring essays and reports by policy specialists, and *NBR Executive Insight*, a publication exploring business-related topics in Asia through timely reports utilizing NBR's network of contacts. NBR also publishes a book series with M.E. Sharpe and an annual directory *AccessAsia,* a guide to specialists and current research with information on the current research interests of Asia experts and decision makers in government, private, and academic institutions in the United States and abroad. Approximately 2,000 specialists are included in the 1996 edition.

Funding sources: NBR's research is funded by private foundations, the government, and the private sector.

Staffing: NBR has a staff of seventeen.

Notes: NBR's operations are governed by a Board of Directors made up of corporate and academic leaders with strong interests in the Asia-Pacific region. NBR's research agenda is guided by the Board of Advisors, which includes experts from research centers, universities, corporations, and government organizations, as well as thirty-four members of Congress.

Head of the institution: Dr. Richard Ellings, Executive Director

Contact officer: Ms. Jennifer Linder, Executive Assistant

The National Bureau of Asian Research
715 SAFECO Plaza
Seattle, WA 98185
USA
Tel: (1-206) 632-7370
Fax: (1-206) 632-7487
e-mail • nbr@nbr.org

National Center for APEC

Background and objectives: The National Center for APEC's mission is to support and promote the Asia Pacific Economic Cooperation process in the United States. As a private, nonprofit organization established following the 1993 meetings of the APEC Leaders and Ministers in Seattle, the Center conducts a wide variety of related activities and programs that follow up on those auspicious meetings.

Programs: The Center's activities fall into the five areas of providing direct support for the U.S. representatives to the APEC Business Advisory Council (ABAC), hosting APEC ministerial and other official events, facilitating private sector involvement in the APEC policy process, conducting public outreach programs to increase the awareness of APEC and its benefits to the United States, and issuing publications related to the Center's work. Recent programs sponsored by the Center included the 1995 APEC Next Generations Program, an event designed to build relationships among rising new Pacific leaders that serve the development of regional foreign policy and cooperation for the coming decades; the 1996 Executive Roundtable in Del Mar, California, which gathered key representatives of industry and Asia-related business associations together to outline how the U.S. private sector could provide input to the ABAC; and the Forum on U.S. Agriculture and Food Trade Policy in APEC, which developed a policy recommendation to create a "Pacific Rim Food System." Other events include an APEC-wide round-table on "best practices" for infrastructure development and a series of roundtables focusing on key topics including capital markets formation and human resource development.

Publications: The Center has published *U.S. Business Views of APEC: A Survey, APEC at the Crossroads,* a summary of key issues on the APEC agenda, and other papers and documents resulting from National Center conferences.

Funding sources: The Center's initial funding came from the surplus raised by the 1993 APEC Host Committee and the Washington Council on International Trade. Currently, the National Center's Board of Governors (all from private sector companies) provide financial support on an annual basis.

Staffing: The National Center has five senior staff members and four full-time graduate interns.

Head of the institution: Mr. Michael C. Mullen, Director

Contact officer: Ms. Monica H. Whaley, Deputy Director

National Center for APEC
2601 Fourth Avenue, Suite 340
Seattle, WA 98121-1253
USA
Tel: (1-206) 441-9022
Fax: (1-206) 443-3828
e-mail • ncapec@ncapec.org
URL • http://www.laurasian.org/ncapec_home.html

Nautilus Institute for Security and Sustainable Development

Background and objectives: Founded in 1981, the Nautilus Institute for Security and Sustainable Development is a policy-oriented research and consulting organization that promotes international cooperation for security and ecologically sustainable development. The Institute's programs focus on emerging regional environmental and energy and security issues, with a focus on the Asia-Pacific region.

Programs: Nautilus produces reports, organizes seminars, and provides educational and training services for policy makers, media, researchers, and community groups. The Institute's research draws from many disciplines including environmental economics and science, energy and resource planning, and international relations.

The Institute has several programs related to the Asia-Pacific. The Sustainable Development Program works to promote integration of environmental objectives into national economic policies and international economic institutions, especially within Asia. Current research concentrates on linkages between trade, environment, and development; ecologically sound macroeconomic policies; and regional environmental cooperation.

The Institute's Asia Pacific Regional Environmental Network (APRENET) is an international electronic network of people interested in Asia-Pacific environmental issues. Its participants include analysts and activists from research institutions, environment and development citizen groups, government, and business. The Network encourages dialogue and promotes regional environmental advocacy. A primary focus is to stimulate debate about institutional evolution and policy alternatives on trade, environment, and development issues at APEC.

The Peace and Security Program seeks to identify ways to avoid and resolve conflicts without resort to force, with particular emphasis on Northeast Asia. Current research in this program includes nuclear weapons and nuclear proliferation, confidence building between states, military postures and doctrines, and environmental security.

The Northeast Asia Peace and Security Network (NAPSNET) is a transnational network that includes non-proliferation specialists, regional security experts, and non-governmental organizations from Northeast Asia and North America. The Network commissions expert papers from scholars around the world and distributes them on electronic networks.

The Institute's Energy, Security, and Environment in Northeast Asia (ESENA) program brings these issues together via a policy development process that includes conferences, policy papers, and a school curriculum.

Publications: The Institute publishes a Daily Report, available via electronic mail and the World Wide Web, which covers recent developments in the region. There is also a periodic APRENET report, and Nautilus has authored many studies and books.

Funding sources: Nautilus is a nonprofit organization funded primarily by grants and contributions. Supporting foundations include the Rockefeller Foundation, the Ploughshares Fund, the John Merck Fund, the Ford Foundation, the W. Alton Jones Foundation, and the Winston Foundation for World Peace.

Staffing: Nautilus's core staff is based in Berkeley, with associates in Tokyo, Seoul, Shanghai, and other locations. There are five program staff members and two administrative personnel at the Berkeley office.

Heads of the institution:
Mr. Peter Hayes, Co-Executive Director

Ms. Lyuba Zarsky, Co-Executive Director

Contact officer: Mr. Steve Freedkin, Managing Director

Nautilus Institute for Security and Sustainable Development
1831 Second Street
Berkeley, CA 94710-1902
USA
Tel: (1-510) 204-9296
Fax: (1-510) 204-9298
e-mail • nautilus@nautilus.org
URL • http://www.nautilus.org

The North America Institute

Background and objectives: The mission of the North America Institute is to advance discussion and understanding on the common issues confronting the societies of Canada, the United States, and Mexico. Its goal is a prosperous North American region that functions equitably, democratically, and sustainably. Established in 1989, NAMI has branches in Vancouver, Mexico City, and Santa Fe, which also houses the secretariat.

Programs: NAMI programs revolve around three main issues: trade and the environment, the emerging North American Community, and trinational institution-building. Recent forum titles include "Managing the Relationship: Perspective from the States and Report on the New NAFTA Institutions" (June 1996), "Renewing Federalism in North America: Diversity of Peoples, Community of Purpose" (March 1996), and "NAFTA's Relationship to the Caribbean and Central America: Informal and Formal Integration and the Question of Cuba" (November 1995). Participants are invited from an informal and growing trinational network of leading thinkers from academia and education, business and nonprofit institutions, government, labor, and the media. Many of NAMI's forums and colloquia result in publications available from the organization.

Publications: The Institute publishes *NAMINEWS*, a quarterly newsletter that monitors and disseminates information about events, publications, and research with potential policy implications for Canada, the United States, and Mexico.

Funding sources: NAMI is financed through private donations and foundation support from the Hewlett Foundation and the Ford Foundation, among others.

Staffing: NAMI's staff include a part-time executive director, a full-time office manager/director of communication, and a part-time intern. The president also works on a part-time schedule and directs research efforts along with the executive director.

Notes: NAMINET, the Institute's on-line information service, offers NAMI's publications and links to other NGOs in this policy area. Information is provided in English and Spanish.

Head of the institution: Dr. John D. Wirth, President

Contact officer: Mr. Kevin Drennan, Director of Communications

The North America Institute
708 Paseo de Peralta
Santa Fe, NM 87501
USA
Tel: (1-505) 982-3657
Fax: (1-505) 983-5840
e-mail • naminet@ santafe.edu
URL• http://www.santafe.edu/~namient

Pacific Basin Economic Council

Background and objectives: Pacific Basin Economic Council (PBEC) is an association of business leaders that promotes the expansion of trade and investment through open markets. Founded in 1967, PBEC serves as a forum in which regional business leaders create new business relationships and address issues in the Pacific and global economies. It includes more than 1,100 corporate members in twenty economies: Australia, Canada, Chile, the People's Republic of China, Colombia, Ecuador, Fiji, Hong Kong, Indonesia, Japan, Korea, Malaysia, Mexico, New Zealand, Peru, the Philippines, Russia, Chinese Taipei, Thailand, and the United States.

Programs: The Member Committees conduct a wide range of programs, including conferences, seminars, training programs, and regular meetings with government officials. Since 1987, for example, PBEC's Japan Member Committee has conducted the "Training Course in Private Sector Middle Management," which provides middle managers from the Pacific region with hands-on training at private companies in Japan. PBEC also provides advice and counsel to governments on issues affecting the development of the Pacific region. It recently adopted a policy paper, entitled "Implementing Free Trade and Investment in the Pacific Region," that identifies key business issues in the region and makes comprehensive recommendations to the Asia-Pacific region's governments regarding trade and investment in the region. PBEC has also produced a *Pacific Basin Charter on International Investments*, a *PBEC Statement to APEC*, and a *PBEC Statement of Environmental Policy*. The Council cooperates with international organizations, such as the Asia-Pacific Economic Cooperation, the World Bank, and the Pacific Economic Cooperation Council, to ensure that business sector viewpoints are considered in public policy making. Through its Business Symposiums, PBEC focuses on improving the business climate in the Asia-Pacific region. Recent speakers include Tomiichi Murayama, Prime Minister of Japan; Fidel V. Ramos, President of the Philippines; Ryutaro Hashimoto, Japanese Minister of International Trade and Industry; and Alvaro Garcia Hurtado, Chilean Minister of the Economy. PBEC's annual International General Meeting (IGM) brings together more than 700 business leaders, government ministers and officials, and heads of state from approximately twenty-five economies around the Pacific to discuss emerging business opportunities and trade issues facing the region. In 1993 and 1994, PBEC has led business opportunity missions to the Russian far East and Vietnam that allowed Pacific Basin business and government officials to showcase their countries.

Publications: PBEC publishes *International News,* a quarterly newsletter on the organization's activities with a calendar of events, as well as an Executive Summary of the IGM. In addition, a biennial report entitled *PBEC Statistics* is published by the PBEC Japan Committee, which gives a comprehensive overview of the Pacific region.

Funding sources: PBEC is funded through membership dues.

Staffing: PBEC's International Secretariat currently has six full-time staff and regularly employs part-time researchers and fellows to assist in PBEC's activities and programs. Each PBEC Member Committee also has its own dedicated staff who work on the individual programs of the Committee.

Heads of the institution:
Mr. Gary L. Tooker, Chairman, Vice Chairman & CEO, Motorola Inc. (USA)

Dr. Helmut Sohmen, Vice Chairman, Chairman, World-Wide Shipping Agency, Ltd. (Hong Kong)

Contact officer: Mr. Robert G. Lees, Secretary General

Pacific Basin Economic Council
900 Fort Street, Suite 1570
Honolulu, HI 96813
USA
Tel: (1-808) 521-9044
Fax: (1-808) 521-8530
e-mail • jon@pbec.org
URL • http://www.pbec.org

The Pacific Basin Institute

Background and objectives: The PBI was founded in 1979 to stimulate American interest in the Pacific Basin through multimedia programming (including films, videotapes, and publications), as well as more conventional research studies and conferences.

Programs: The PBI has worked with scholars, journalists, film producers, business leaders, public policy makers, foundations, research institutes, and public broadcasting stations to sponsor films, publications, and conferences. These efforts include *The Pacific Century,* a telecourse that includes a ten-part, award-winning PBS television series, as well as the book *Pacific Century,* study guides, and a book of readings on the history and economics of the Pacific Basin. PBI's Library of Japan program has translated and published six of a planned thirty-volume series on contemporary and traditional Japanese writing, both fiction and nonfiction, for general readers. PBI initiated a conference on "Asia's Emerging Middle Class," held in Claremont in October, 1995, in conjunction with Pomona College, Claremont-McKenna, and Claremont Graduate School. *Reshaping the Japanese Marketplace,* a study sponsored by the Sasakawa Peace Foundation and conducted in cooperation with the Mansfield Center for Pacific Affairs, features papers by leading Japanese and American economists, journalists, and public officials on the problem of over-regulation and bureaucracy in the Japanese economy. The centerpiece of a Keidanren conference held in Japan in March 1996, the study was published by Brookings Institution in 1997. Previous programs have included documentary films on Japanese industrial productivity; a seminar on media coverage of the Pacific Basin featuring U.S., Chinese, and Japanese journalists; and publication of economic data on the Pacific Basin nations. PBI also serves as principal consultant to the British Open University's new multimedia program on Pacific Studies.

Publications: PBI's recent books include *Taken Captive* (John Wiley, 1996), *The Third Opening of Japan* (Kodansha in Japan, 1995), *Senso* (M.E. Sharpe, 1995), and *Battle for Okinawa* (John Wiley, 1995).

Funding sources: Organizations that have cooperated with and supported PBI include the Asia Foundation, the Japan Foundation, the Ford Foundation, NHK Japan, the Sasakawa Peace Foundation, the Sumitomo Foundation, the Times Mirror Corporation, and the Annenberg/Corporation for Public Broadcasting Project.

Staffing: PBI has a small core staff and uses interns and outside contributors for most of its projects.

Head of the institution: Mr. Frank B. Gibney, President

Contact officer: Ms. Linda Jones, Administrative Director

The Pacific Basin Institute
c/o Pomona College
156 West 7th Street
Claremont, CA 91711
USA
Tel: (1-909) 607-8035
Fax: (1-909) 607-7468
e-mail • 73423.3134@compuserve.com

Pacific Council on International Policy

Background and objectives: The Pacific Council on International Policy, an independent, nonpartisan membership organization, seeks to help leaders from many different sectors and perspectives understand better and respond more effectively to a rapidly changing world. It aims to inform and improve policy making in both the private and public sectors, promote public understanding of global trends and their implications, and facilitate international cooperation on shared concerns, particularly around the Pacific Rim. Established in 1995 in cooperation with the Council on Foreign Relations of New York, the Pacific Council brings together diverse leaders—primarily from the western region of the United States but also from elsewhere in the U.S., Canada and Mexico, Pacific Asia, South America, and Europe—to exchange ideas and develop policy recommendations on economic, social, and political issues with important international dimensions. It is headquartered on the campus of the University of Southern California.

Programs: The Pacific Council's programs include briefings, workshops, Study Groups, and Retreats, and a Visiting Fellows program. The Pacific Council has held some forty membership meetings and briefings (two to three per month), on issues ranging from trends in China, Japan, Korea, Mexico, Russia, and Taiwan to economic regionalism, "big emerging markets," ethnic conflict, immigration policy, narcotics, peacekeeping, and the relation of social values and institutions to economic development. It has also organized membership retreats as well as several different workshops and Study or Discussion Groups. The three Annual Retreats—in Los Angeles (1995), in San Francisco (1996), and in Santa Monica (1997)—attracted about 125 members for intense exchanges on key topics. In close cooperation with the International Forum on Democratic Studies of the National Endowment for Democracy, it co-organized and hosted a two-day workshop on "Constructing Democracy and Markets: Comparing Latin America and East Asia," which involved scholars and practitioners from East Asia and Latin America. The Pacific Council also co-organized and hosted, together with the Foreign Policy Project of the Overseas Development Council and the Henry L. Stimson Center, a half-day western regional forum on "The United States and Asia in the 21st Century." In cooperation with the Council on Foreign Relations, the Pacific Council held five meetings during 1995-96 of a western regional discussion group on "Rethinking U.S. Interests," one of a number of parallel groups meeting around the country. The Pacific Council has also been holding a series of discussions on International Intellectual Property Policy; these meetings led to a brief policy report, to be distributed in 1998. During 1996-97, the Studies Program launched two Study Groups, one on "The Future of China" (being co-organized and co-sponsored by RAND's Center for Asia-Pacific Policy) and one on "The American West and the International Economy." The Pacific Council will organize Task Forces from time to time to engage relatively small numbers of members in focused efforts to reach findings and recommendations on specific policy issues. In its first year, the Visiting Scholars program and an International Visiting Fellows program attracted four academic researchers and one international fellow. The full-scale International Visiting Fellows program will attract six to eight Fellows to Los Angeles each year: one each from Canada, Mexico, China, and Japan and two to four from other countries, mainly from around the Pacific Rim.

Publications: The Pacific Council publishes *Pacific Council Dateline*, a periodic newsletter (three per year), and will inaugurate soon a series of "policy briefs," drawing on Pacific Council meetings, workshops, Task Forces, and Study Groups. The Pacific Council has also published the *Directory of Pacific Rim Institutions on International Policy,* which provides concise profiles of some 290 international policy institutions around the Pacific Rim, and a *Membership Directory*, available only to members of the Pacific Council. The Pacific Council's first publication, *Coping With An Uncertain World* (1996), provides highlights from the Inaugural Retreat.

Staffing: The Pacific Council's staff includes a president, vice president for programs and administration, director of public affairs, events coordinator, director of membership affairs, career officer of the Department of State who joins the Council's staff under the terms of the Department's James Pearson Program, director of studies, two program assistants, and a junior associate. The administrative support staff personnel includes an executive assistant to the president, coordinator of computer and information services, coordinator of membership services, financial assistant, and a receptionist and clerical assistant.

Funding sources: The Pacific Council's main support comes primarily from foundations, corporations, individuals, and international sources. It receives support from the Ahmanson Foundation, the Carnegie Corporation of New York, the Ford Foundation, the General Service Foundation, the William and Flora Hewlett Foundation, the Conrad N. Hilton Foundation, the James Irvine Foundation, the John D. and Catherine T. MacArthur Foundation, and the Andrew W. Mellon Foundation. More than twenty different corporations have become Founding Corporate Sponsors, committing themselves to multi-year support. Support from individuals comes from membership dues and voluntary contributions.

Notes: The Pacific Council has nearly seven hundred members, including decision makers in business and labor, politics and government, religion, the media, law, entertainment, science and technology, education, and other professions—all of whom share the conviction that international developments are increasingly significant and ever more connected with domestic concerns.

Head of the institution: Dr. Abraham F. Lowenthal, President

Contact officer: Ms. Charlotte Kennedy, Vice-President for Programs and Administration

Pacific Council on International Policy
University of Southern California
Los Angeles, CA 90089-0035
USA
Tel: (1-213) 740- 4296
Fax: (1-213) 740-9498
e-mail • pcip@usc.edu
URL • http://www.pcip.org

Pacific Forum CSIS

Background and objectives: Pacific Forum CSIS is a nonprofit, nonpartisan policy-study institute based in Honolulu, Hawaii. Founded in 1975, it operates as the autonomous Asia-Pacific arm of the Center for Strategic and International Studies (CSIS) in Washington, D.C. The Forum organizes policy studies on political, economic, and security issues in the Asia-Pacific region and engages the region's government, academic, and corporate leaders in an effort to develop cooperative policies and solutions. Pacific Forum CSIS collaborates with a network of more than thirty research institutes around the Pacific Rim.

Programs: The Council for Security Cooperation in the Asia-Pacific (CSCAP) is a non-governmental organization of sixteen policy research institutes founded in 1993 to promote multilateral security dialogue. Each institute is mandated to establish broad-based member committees; Pacific Forum organizes the USCSCAP which meets biannually in Washington D.C. The work of CSCAP is conducted through biannual Steering Committee meetings as well as four working groups that focus on confidence and security-building measures, Northeast Asia security, maritime cooperation, and comprehensive security. The consensus that emerges from CSCAP feeds into and helps inform the inter-governmental security dialogue conducted in the ASEAN Regional Forum (ARF). With the International Trade and Business Institute (ITBI) of Seoul, the Pacific Forum co-sponsors the United States-Korea Wisemen Council, founded in 1990 to engage senior, experienced individuals to evaluate emerging concerns in U.S.-Korean bilateral relations. The results of the Council's deliberations are conveyed to the White House and the Blue House and to relevant cabinet officials. The Forum, in cooperation with institutes in Tokyo and Beijing, is also undertaking a project aimed at improving the three-way U.S.-Japan-China relationship. Other initiatives include an annual conference, co-sponsored with the Japan Institute of International Affairs, which involves senior policy officials and scholars from both countries to assess changing aspects of the bilateral security alliance. The Forum also co-sponsors, with the Policy Study Group and the Okazaki Institute in Tokyo, a series on revitalizing the U.S.-Japan alliance which involves younger scholars in both nations. Another new initiative evaluates the prospects for conflict in the South China Sea and the Spratly Islands. The Visiting Fellows Program invites promising young Asia-Pacific scholars to conduct research at the Pacific Forum.

Publications: The Forum's weekly *PacNet Newsletter* analyzes Asian-Pacific trends and issues and is sent to more than 400 recipients throughout the U.S. and the region. The Forum also publishes the *Policy Report Series*, which conveys policy recommendations from the Forum's research programs, and the *Occasional Papers*, which are in-depth studies by participants in the Pacific Forum's research conferences. The Forum publishes monographs and other research work in the CSIS *Significant Issues Series* and in *The Washington Quarterly*.

Funding sources: Pacific Forum is funded by grants from foundations, corporations, individuals, and governments. The Forum's annual budget is $1.2 million.

Staffing: The Forum has one part-time and three full-time professionals and a support staff of four.

Notes: An international Board of Governors guides the Pacific Forum's work. The Board is chaired by Brent Scowcroft, former Assistant to the President for National Security Affairs.

Head of the institution: Mr. James A. Kelly, President

Contact officer: Ms. Jane Khanna, Assistant Director for Programs and Development

Pacific Forum CSIS
1001 Bishop Street
Pauahi Tower, Suite 1150
Honolulu, HI 96813
USA
Tel: (1-808) 521-6745
Fax: (1-808) 599-8690
e-mail • 70672.106@compuserve.com
URL • http://www.csis.org

Pacific Institute for Women's Health

Background and objectives: The Pacific Institute for Women's Health is dedicated to improving the health and well-being of women both locally and globally. Founded in 1993 as part of the Western Consortium for Public Health, the Institute aims to create worldwide partnerships with community groups, policy makers, researchers, service providers, and advocates to facilitate the sharing of information and lessons and to plan for future actions.

Programs: The Institute has developed several domestic and international projects including a research project documenting the impact of Proposition 187 on basic health care for women and families; an analysis of factors that promote or impede access to both primary care and specialty services in managed care plans for all women (in collaboration with UCLA's Center for Health Policy Research); an initiative that draws on international expertise and experience to improve the quality and effectiveness of family planning services in California; and the Americas Program, which examines demographic and health outcomes of economic integration in the NAFTA and MERCO-SUR regions. The program has three principal components: a workshop series, a research program, and international partnerships; it furthers research on cultural influences on reproductive and contraceptive behavior among recent immigrant populations and adaptation of international social marketing, communications, and health education materials to address these populations.

Publications: The Institute has published its annual report, *First Year's Report: 1994-1995.*

Funding sources: The Pacific Institute receives most of its funding from private foundations, as well as government agencies and international organizations.

Staffing: Unlike many organizations that retain a large on-site research staff, the Pacific Institute supports associates interested in implementing women's research and advocacy projects while continuing their various responsibilities with community-based and academic institutions. The Institute has four full-time administrative employees.

Heads of the institution:
Ms. Francine Coeytaux, Co-Director

Ms. Helen Rodriguez-Trias, MD, Co-Director

Contact officer: Ms. Veronique Autphenne, Communications Specialist

Pacific Institute for Women's Health
2999 Overland Avenue, Suite 111
Los Angeles, CA 90064
USA
Tel: (1-310) 842-6828
Fax: (1-310) 280-0600

Public Policy Institute of California

Background and objectives: The Public Policy Institute of California is a nonprofit private operating foundation established in 1994 with an endowment from William R. Hewlett. The mission of the Institute is to provide independent, nonpartisan information and analysis to help formulate public policy in California. While not a grant-making foundation, the Institute collaborates extensively with individuals and institutions to focus the state's intellectual resources on major public policy debates.

Programs: The Institute's research activities currently focus on three program areas: Population, Economy, and Governance and Public Finance. Initial projects include studies of income distribution, public assistance, block grants, immigration, redevelopment agencies, the statewide revenue burden, and the role of special districts in the public sector. The Institute holds policy seminars, publishes reports and background papers, offers visiting fellowships, and hosts a summer intern program. It also funds external research contracts under its new Extramural Research Program.

Publications: Most recent PPIC publications include *Dynamics of Immigration: Return Migration to Western Mexico* (January 1997), *Nursing Staff Trends in California Hospitals: 1977 through 1995* (October 1996), *Undocumented Immigration to California: 1980-1993* (September 1996), and *Distribution of Income in California* (July 1996).

Staffing: The Institute has twenty full-time research staff and is arranging work with an equal number of external research contractors.

Funding sources: With its endowment of $150 million, the Institute currently has an annual operating budget of $5.6 million.

Head of the institution: Dr. David W. Lyon, President and CEO

Contact officer: Dr. Joyce Peterson, Director of External Affairs

Public Policy Institute of California
500 Washington Street, Suite 800
San Francisco, CA 94111
USA
Tel: (1-415) 291-4400
Fax: (1-415) 291-4401
e-mail • info@ppic.org
URL • http://www.ppic.org

RAND

Background and objectives: RAND is a private, nonprofit institution that seeks to improve public policy through research and analysis. RAND has a broad research agenda aimed at strengthening the nation's economy, maintaining its security, and improving its quality of life by informing policy makers' choices in national defense and foreign policy, education, health care, and criminal and civil justice, among other areas. RAND has been known for its research on national security since its inception in the days following World War II. It has maintained a large and influential program for research and analysis of domestic issues since the late 1960s. The RAND graduate school is a fully accredited academic program that awards more doctorate degrees in policy analysis than any other institution in the country.

Programs: Research divisions and programs include Project AIR FORCE, Army Research Division, the National Security Research Division; Criminal Justice, Health Sciences, Education and Training, Labor and Population, and the Institute for Civil Justice. Research centers include the Critical Technologies Institute, the European-American Center for Policy Analysis, the Center for Asia-Pacific Policy, the Drug Policy Research Center, the Center for Research on Immigration Policy, the Center for Information Revolution Analysis, the Greater Middle East Studies Center, the Center for Russia and Eurasia Studies, and the California Initiative Project. The Center for Asia-Pacific Policy (CAPP), founded in 1993, explores, analyzes, and explains the changes in the Asia-Pacific by focusing in three areas: international security; international political economy, including transnational manufacturing, trade, investment, and high-technology relations in the Asia-Pacific region; and social issues, including health care, transportation, and environmental standards in the Asia-Pacific. The California Initiative Project conducts research on education, health, immigration, fiscal constraints, environmental resources, economic resources, and community resources. The project is now studying the relationship between state and local governments in California and the implications of federal block grants for welfare on the quality and financing of public services in California. The Center for Research on Immigration Policy monitors international migration trends, assesses the effects of immigration on sending and receiving countries, and studies the integration of immigrants in receiving societies and how immigration issues affect international relations. Currently, the Center is conducting an empirical cost-benefit assessment of how Asian and Hispanic immigration has affected California's demography, economy, demand for public services, and community relations and is studying how immigration is affecting U.S.-Mexico relations. The Center for Russian and Eurasian Studies (CRES) provides scholars, policy makers, and citizens with an in-depth understanding of developmental processes in Russia, East Europe, and Eurasia. The CRES program of scholarly research, policy support, professional training, and public education currently includes a study of migration within and from the former Soviet Union; collaboration with several Russian research centers to upgrade independent policy-analytic capabilities in Russia; and research on the foreign and security policies of Soviet successor states.

Publications: The methods and findings of research at RAND are reported mainly through the organization's publications and briefings. RAND publishes books, monographs, issue papers, research briefs, congressional testimony, conference proceedings, and RAND graduate school dissertations.

Funding sources: RAND's research is supported by a broad range of sources, the largest of which are U.S. government agencies.

Staffing: RAND employs some 600 research professionals in its offices in Santa Monica, California, and Washington, D.C. It also employs more than 500 professional consultants.

Head of the institution: Dr. James A. Thomson, President and Chief Executive Officer

Contact officer: Mr. Jess Cook, Director, Public Information Office

RAND
1700 Main Street
P.O. Box 2138
Santa Monica, CA 90407-2138
USA
Tel: (1-310) 451-6913
Fax: (1-310) 393-4818
e-mail •
General questions:
correspondence@rand.org
Individuals:
firstname_ lastname@rand.org
URL • http://www.rand.org

Center for Asia-Pacific Policy (CAPP)
Dr. Michael D. Swaine, Director
Tel: (1-310) 393-0411 ext. 7488
Fax: (1-310) 393-4818

California Initiative Project
Dr. Kevin F. McCarthy, Director
Tel: (1-310) 451-6919
Fax: (1-310) 393-4818

Center for Research on Immigration Policy
Dr. Georges Vernez, Director
Tel: (1-310) 393-0411 ext. 6211
Fax: (1-310) 393-4818

Center for Russian and Eurasian Studies (CRES)
Dr. Jeremy Azrael, Director
Tel: (1-310) 393-0411 ext. 6351
Fax: (1-310) 393-4818

Rice University

The James A. Baker III Institute for Public Policy

Background and objectives: The James A. Baker III Institute for Public Policy seeks to provide a nonpartisan forum for scholars and policy makers to exchange ideas about selected issues in foreign and domestic policy. Founded in 1993, the Institute is named in honor of the 61st U.S. Secretary of State, who takes an active role in its development.

Programs: The Institute is defining its research agenda. So far it has initiated research on energy supply, security, and pricing, with a special focus on the Middle East-Central Asia region; the Middle East peace process; and issues in Mexico, Latin America, and China. Preliminary work is also underway on tax reform and urban problems, and the Institute plans to work with the Texas Medical Center on health policy issues. The Institute does not confer academic degrees, but Institute Scholars and Fellows offer courses through Rice University's academic departments, serve as mentors, and interact informally with students. The Institute's first Annual Conference, "Foreign Policy Challenges at the End of the Century," took place in November 1995. Three panels explored "Economic Reform in Russia and China," "Political-Military Factors and the Future of Warfare," and "The Impact of Cultural, Ethnic, and Religious Factors on Foreign Policy." The Enron Prize for Distinguished Public Service was awarded to General Colin Powell at this conference. The Shell Lecture Series, numbering two to four per year, has included presentations by UN Secretary General Boutros-Ghali on UN peacekeeping, and Tunisian Foreign Minister Ben Yahya on Islam. In February 1996, the Baker Institute co-sponsored the annual conference of the Asia Society, "China, the United States, and Asian Challenges for U.S. Policy and Business." The Institute has also participated in a number of Council on Foreign Relations events and study groups, and has created a study group to examine the prospects for the Middle East peace process. Events are open to the public whenever possible.

Publications: The Institute publishes the *Baker Institute Report,* which serves as the newsletter of the Institute, and the *Baker Institute Studies*, which summarize policy problems and offer recommendations. The first two studies concentrated on U.S. policy toward Islam and the status of the peace process in the Middle East in the aftermath of the Israeli elections. The Baker Institute also plans on having a reprint series and a working paper series. Many of these publications will be accessible through the Institute's World Wide Web site.

Funding sources: University resources have been committed to the Institute, and the first phase of a fund-raising campaign has been completed. Funding comes from a variety of sources: individuals, groups, foundations, and corporations. Currently, Institute research is being supported by the Center for International Political Economy and the National Tax Research Committee.

Staffing: Currently, seven people do administrative work at the Institute. Most research is conducted by Rice faculty on a part-time basis. At present, sixteen people are engaged in full- or part-time research for the Institute.

Notes: Completed in spring of 1997, the Institute's building includes an international conference facility that will permit simultaneous translation, video-conferencing, and satellite link-up to other locations in the United States and abroad.

Head of the institution: Amb. Edward P. Djerejian, Director

Contact officer: Dr. Richard J. Stoll, Associate Director for Academic Programs

The James A. Baker III Institute for Public Policy
Rice University-MS-40
6100 Main Street
Houston, TX 77005-1892
USA
Tel: (1-713) 527-4683
Fax: (1-713) 285-5993
e-mail • bipp@ruf.rice.edu
URL • http://www.riceinfo.rice.edu/projects/baker

San Diego State University

Center for International Business Education and Research

Background and objectives: The Center for International Business Education and Research (CIBER) at San Diego State University (SDSU) was established in October 1989 by a grant from the U.S. Department of Education to enlarge and enhance international business education, to promote research into international business issues, and to increase U.S. competitiveness in the global economy.

Programs: As part of its mandate, SDSU CIBER created the Bachelor of Arts in International Business degree program, the largest of its kind in the nation. The International Business degree requires students to develop fluency in a foreign language as well as a regional specialization. CIBER has developed significant linkages with the business community by sponsoring seminars, lectures, and business development programs and providing courses in Business Japanese, Business French, and Business Spanish.

CIBER has also established close ties with the California State University system, the California Community College Centers for International Trade and Development network, the language programs of local high schools, and the International Baccalaureate programs offered at several of these schools.

CIBER is the testing site for the Madrid and Paris Chamber of Commerce Language Certification examinations, which are used as assessment tools by a number of institutions in Europe and are required for admission to many European business schools.

The CIBER Global Issues Forum brings together faculty from the Schools of Business Administration and Arts and Letters, in addition to invited members from the business community, for a semester-long series of discussions on central themes of consequence in international business and politics.

CIBER directors also serve on the International Business Establishment Team, members of which are available on demand to make site visits to institutes of higher education to propose a detailed and realistic plan for the establishment of interdisciplinary international business programs and to provide strategies for the integration of the business and liberal arts curricula at the host campus.

Publications: SDSU CIBER publishes working paper series to provide an active medium for the initial publication of SDSU and CSU faculty research work funded wholly or in part by CIBER. Many of the working papers or abstracts are available for viewing via the Internet.

Funding sources: SDSU CIBER is funded primarily by the San Diego State University, and the U.S. Department of Education.

Staffing: SDSU CIBER has from ten to twenty professional staff and an administrative staff of three.

Notes: The CIBER Grant Program provides funds for SDSU and CSU faculty to engage in research related to international business and gain international exposure through faculty development overseas. Since 1989, CIBER has awarded over $300,000 in such grants to faculty throughout the CSU system.

Heads of the institution:
Dr. Alvord G. Branan, Co-Director

Dr. Michael L. Hergert, Co-Director

Contact officer: Mr. David P. Earwicker, Associate Director

Center for International Business Education and Research (CIBER)
San Diego State University
San Diego, CA 92182-7732
USA
Tel: (1-619) 594-6023
Fax: (1-619) 594-7738
e-mail • ciber@mail.sdsu.edu
URL • http://www.sdsu.edu/ciber

Southern California Association of Governments

Background and objectives: The Southern California Association of Governments is a voluntary organization of cities and counties that have come together for regional planning and coordination. The organization comprises 184 cities located in Ventura, Los Angeles, Orange, Riverside, San Bernardino, and Imperial counties. The Association's decisions are made by the Regional Council, a seventy-member group of locally elected officials from across Southern California who are elected by their peers to serve on the Council. The Association's policies, plans, data, and coordination activities can help local governments comply more efficiently with federal and state mandates to assess the development activities of neighboring communities.

Programs: The Association prepares regional policies and action plans for issues that transcend city and county boundary lines, such as transportation, air quality, housing, growth, hazardous waste, water quality, and the economy. The Association also solicits public opinion and the views of businesses and nonprofit organizations on these issues. The Association is also responsible for Southern California's rideshare services.

Publications: The Association publishes the *Regional Comprehensive Plan and Guide*, a resource tool that provides a comprehensive overview of Southern California and its interrelated metropolitan service systems. The document identifies key issues facing the region and provides strategies to deal with those issues. A major portion of this document is the Regional Transportation Plan.

Funding sources: The Association's planning work is supported by grants from federal and state agencies, and by the dues paid by its members, cities, and counties.

Staffing: The Association has approximately 170 employees, with approximately ninety-five employees dedicated to research and analysis, forty employees conducting rideshare to member jurisdiction services, and thirty-five employees performing administrative support activities.

Notes: The Association also acts as a clearinghouse for some federal grants to local governments. This ensures that major projects seeking federal funds conform to state and federal requirements, as well as to the Association's overall plans for the region.

Head of the institution: Mr. Mark Pisano, Executive Director

Contact officer: Mr. Fernando del Rio, Manager of Communications

Southern California Association of Governments
818 West Seventh Street, 12th Floor
Los Angeles, CA 90017
USA
Tel: (1-213) 236-1800
Fax: (1-213) 236-1825
e-mail • pisano@scag.ca.gov
URL • http://www.scag.ca.gov

Southwest Voter Research Institute

Background and objectives: The Southwest Voter Research Institute (SVRI) is a tax-exempt, nonprofit, nonpartisan organization chartered in 1984 to conduct research aimed at improving the level of political and economic participation in Latino communities. SVRI provides information to Latino leaders relevant to the needs of their constituents and to empower them to shape public and international agendas accordingly, and informs the Latino leadership and public about the impact of public and international policies on Latinos and political opinions and behavior of Latinos.

Programs: SVRI's international program aims to develop, through training sessions, delegations, seminars, polls, and publications, a large group of Latino leaders articulate in the key issues of U.S.-Latin America relations.

The Program coordinates the Institute's initiatives in Mexico, Central America, and the Caribbean, supporting grassroots democracy and sustainable economic development through training and other technical assistance to non-governmental organizations.

Since 1990, the Institute has helped found the Centro Pro Desarrollo Socio Economico (CEDESEC) in Nicaragua and the Instituto de Educacion Civica Salvadoreña (INDEC) and Camino a la Paz (CAPAZ) in El Salvador. In addition, the Institute conducts fact-finding and election observation delegations in the same areas, as well as voter education consulting in South Africa.

The Economic Empowerment Program is designed to analyze public policy issues that directly affect the Latino community. Through policy research, it attempts to determine how Latinos are specifically impacted by policy decisions and how well their views are being represented when elected officials make decisions on public policy.

Since the early 1990s, the Institute has been tracking the effects of the U.S.-Mexico economic integration, first launching studies that determined the effects of NAFTA on both sides of the border and continuing with ensuring NAFTA-created institutions, such as the North American Development Bank (NADBank) and the Border Environment Cooperation Commission (BECC).

The Institute also conducts research and community outreach to analyze the implementation of guidelines and project criteria from the NADBank's Community Adjustment and Investment Program (CAIP) as well as the implementation of the Department of Labor's NAFTA-specific Trade Adjustment Assistance Program.

The Survey Research Project is designed to provide quantitative data on public opinion and political behavior for Latino leaders and other Institute constituents. The Institute conducts all aspects of survey research, including survey design, sampling, and data collection and reduction analysis. The Center tracks the level of political activity by Latinos and analyzes those factors that affect their turnout at the polls. The Institute analyzes official registration rolls, election returns and information collected from various Institute polls, and other demographic data to generate an accurate picture of Latino participation levels.

Publications: The Institute's publications include research reports on various policy issues and two newsletters published quarterly: the *Southwest Research Notes,* which reports on polling data, and *De las Americas,* which reports on the Institute's binational and international activities.

Funding sources: The Institute's main support comes from private foundations and government grants.

Staffing: In addition to specific project consultants, the Institute staffs full-time personnel at its headquarters office in San Antonio, Texas, and offices in Montebello, California.

Head of the institution: Mr. Antonio Gonzales, President

Contact officers:
Mr. Ricardo Castañon, M.A., Public Policy and International Programs Coordinator., Montebello Office

Ms. Angela Acosta, M.A., Economic Policy and Research Coordinator, San Antonio Office

Southwest Voter Research Institute
403 E. Commerce, Suite 260
San Antonio, Texas 78205
USA
Tel: (1-210) 222-8014
Fax: (1-210) 222-8474
California Office:
1712 W. Beverly Blvd., Suite 201
Montebello, California 90640
USA
Tel: (1-213) 728-5613
Fax: (1-213) 728-1020
e-mail •
svrica@aol.com (Los Angeles: Public Policy and International projects)
svriborder@aol.com (San Antonio: Public Policy and Binational projects)
svrinfo@aol.com (San Antonio: Research and Polling projects)
URL • http://naid.sppsr.ucla.edu/southwest/index.html

Stanford University

Asia/Pacific Research Center

Background and objectives: The Asia/Pacific Research Center (A/PARC), established in 1976, is dedicated to the study of key economic, political, and security issues in the Asia-Pacific region. The Center, operating under the auspices of the Stanford Institute for International Studies, comprises eighty-five Stanford faculty and graduate students working in collaboration with visiting scholars, senior fellows, and leaders from the Asia-Pacific.

Programs: The A/PARC's work is concentrated in three areas: research, education and training, and public outreach. One major research project at the Center is "Asian Regionalism," a study of the underlying forces behind economic growth and regional interdependence throughout the Asia-Pacific. This research analyzes the role of information and technology flows, foreign direct investments, and labor migration in economic and security interdependence in the region. A second project uses econometric techniques to isolate the effects of various factors on China's economic growth and to assess the impact of economic reform on Chinese development. A third research project, on Japanese technology, includes comparative studies of Japanese and American software industries, advanced information networks, and the role of government in large-scale national research projects. A final project examines comparative health care among the Asia-Pacific nations. The Center has assembled a team of experts from Stanford and Japan to study the medical, technological, and economic aspects of health care. In its teaching and training roles, the A/PARC and its multidisciplinary faculty offer courses in economics, political science, anthropology, history, engineering, chemistry, law, medicine, and business. A course on the rise of industrial Asia, for example, is taught by an interdisciplinary team of ten scholars who seek to explain why Asia has grown faster than other regions and how that growth has affected the rest of the world. The A/PARC also provides financial support and research training for a number of undergraduate and graduate students. The newly initiated Asia-Pacific Scholars program, modeled after the Rhodes Scholarship, will bring to Stanford approximately twenty-five future leaders from the Asia-Pacific for two years of graduate study in the field of their choice at the University. In its public outreach activities, the Center sponsors conferences such as the U.S.-Japan Forum and the Asia-Pacific Leaders' Roundtable. The annual U.S.-Japan Forum

seeks to open new channels of communication between the U.S. Congress and the Japanese Parliament by bringing together a limited group of leaders for candid, off-the-record discussions on policy issues. The annual Asia-Pacific Leaders' Roundtable, established in 1994, seeks to promote dialogue and conflict resolution among leaders of the region. The last two meetings were co-hosted by Senator Bill Bradley and former Secretary of State George P. Shultz and discussed trade imbalances, illegal immigration, and rising military expenditures. The Center's seminar series features informal discussions led by Stanford faculty, business executives, and guest speakers from Asia.

Publications: The A/PARC publishes occasional papers and has a working paper series. Recent publications include *A United States Policy for the Changing Realities of East Asia: Toward a New Consensus* (1996), *Managing U.S. Relations with China* (1996), *The China-United States Bilateral Trade Balance: How Big Is It Really?* (1996), and *A "Mediterranean" Model for Asian Regionalism: Cosmopolitan Cities and Nation States in Asia* (1995).

Funding sources: The Center is funded through its Corporate Affiliates program and through grants from private foundations, including Smith Richardson, Japan-United States Friendship Commission, JR Foundation, the Rockefeller Foundation, and the Tamaki Foundation.

Staffing: A/PARC has three Senior Fellows, a Director of Research, an Administrative Manager, and about ten full- and part-time researchers.

Head of the institution: Dr. Daniel I. Okimoto, Director

Asia/Pacific Research Center
200 Encina Hall
Stanford University
Stanford, CA 94305-6055
USA
Tel: (1-650) 723-9741
Fax: (1-650) 723-6530
URL • http://www.iis.stanford.edu/aparc/aparc

Stanford University

Center for East Asian Studies

Background and objectives: The Center for East Asian Studies was formed in the early 1960s to increase interdisciplinary communication among linguists, historians, art historians, political scientists, anthropologists, and others whose research, teaching, or study focuses on China or Japan. The Center now encourages and supports instructional, research, and special activities in the University related to China, Korea, and Japan.

Programs: The Center administers Bachelor's and Master's Degree programs in East Asian Studies and is involved in a number of programs, including the China and Japan Projects of the Stanford Program on International and Cross-Cultural Education (SPICE), that link the University's resources on China and Japan with civic groups, secondary schools, and local colleges in the San Francisco Bay Area. The people involved in these projects develop innovative curricular materials, organize teacher workshops, and visit classrooms in the area to foster Asian Studies education at the elementary and secondary school levels. Center-sponsored colloquia feature prominent scholars, diplomats, and other professionals. Faculty-student workshops on East Asian topics have addressed such issues as business in Japan, the history and culture of Taiwan, Buddhism, and women in Asia.

Publications: No information provided.

Funding sources: The Center for East Asian Studies receives University funds, as well as grants to support its activities.

Staffing: The Center has fifty faculty members and an administrative staff of three.

Head of the institution: Mr. Peter Duus, Director

Contact officer: Ms. Connie Chin, Program Administrator

Center for East Asian Studies
Room 14, Littlefield Center
300 Lasuen Street
Stanford University
Stanford, CA 94305-5013
USA
Tel: (1-650) 723-3362
Fax: (1-650) 725-6119
e-mail • connie.chin@forsythe.stanford.edu
URL • http://www.leland.stanford.edu/dept/ceas

Stanford University

Center for International Security and Arms Control

Background and objectives: The Center for International Security and Arms Control (CISAC), which originated in the early 1970s as the Arms Control and Disarmament Program, is a multidisciplinary community dedicated to research and training on issues of international security. The Center brings together scholars, policy makers, area specialists, business people, and other experts to focus on a wide range of contemporary security questions. The Center is part of Stanford's Institute for International Studies.

Programs: CISAC currently focuses on such issues as ethnic and civil conflict and conflict resolution, industrial demilitarization in the former Soviet Union and China, nuclear proliferation and safety, and security relations in the Asia-Pacific region. The Center approaches these topics from perspectives ranging from the technical and scientific to the historical, political, and ethical. The "Project on Peace and Cooperation in the Asia-Pacific Region," directed by Professor John W. Lewis, focuses on easing regional tensions and fostering more cooperative security relations among the region's most powerful states. Recent efforts include initiating a dialogue on cooperation among the major navies of the North Pacific; improving U.S.-China relations through military-to-military contacts and defense conversion cooperation; and denuclearizing the Korean peninsula. The Center has established working relationships with a number of institutions in the Asia-Pacific region. For instance, in China, members of this project have worked for more than twenty years with individuals in the Ministry of Foreign Affairs, the Chinese Academy of Sciences, national and regional foreign policy institutes, and several branches of the military. During the next three years, the Asia-Pacific project plans to focus on U.S.-China security relations, U.S. defense posture in the Asian-Pacific region, and security issues in Northeast Asia. Seminars, conferences, and workshops are also an important part of CISAC's intellectual life. Recent examples include talks on "Ethnicity, the State, and Security" and "Commercializing High Technology: East and West." With support from the Carnegie Corporation of New York, the Center brings together scientists and engineers to examine technical and policy aspects of national security, arms control, and international peace and security. The Center also sponsors several fellowship programs, which select a small number of scholars for training in issues related to international security. Three Science Fellowships, for instance, are available for scientists or engineers who are interested in doing research on technical and policy problems related to arms control and defense conversion. Fellows spend up to a year at CISAC on their independent research projects. The CISAC scholars sponsor an interdisciplinary course on "International Security in a Changing World."

Publications: The Center publishes reports, working papers, and reprints. Examples include *Cooperative Security in Northeast Asia* (report published in English and Russian) and *The Transformation of the Asian-Pacific Region: Prospects for the 1990s* (conference report).

Funding sources: The Center is supported by grants from private foundations, including the MacArthur and W. Alton Jones Foundations, the Carnegie Corporation, the Corporate Affiliates program, and individual Center Associates. The Corporate Affiliates program allows corporate leaders to participate in discussions of U.S. defense policy and issues in international security.

Staffing: The Center has Pre- and Post-Doctoral Fellows, Science Fellows, MacArthur Consortium Scholars, Research Staff, and Resident Faculty.

Notes: Secretary of Defense William J. Perry was co-director of CISAC from 1989 to early 1993.

Heads of the institution:
Dr. David Holloway, Co-Director and Professor

Dr. Michael May, Co-Director and Professor

Contact officer: Ms. Melanie Greenberg, Associate Director

Center for International Security and Arms Control
320 Galvez Street
Stanford University
Stanford, CA 94305-6165
USA
Tel: (1-650) 723-9625
Fax: (1-650) 723-0089
e-mail • hf.jgw@forsythe.stanford.edu
URL • http://www.leland.stanford. edu/group/cisac

Stanford University

Center for Latin American Studies

Background and objectives: Since its creation in the 1960s, the Center for Latin American Studies has fostered interdisciplinary research by faculty and students on a broad range of policy issues. The Center has over seventy affiliated faculty members throughout the university, offers both undergraduate and master's degree programs, and coordinates a variety of academic conferences and lectures. In conjunction with the University of California at Berkeley, the Center constitutes a Title VI National Resource Center for the study of Latin America.

Programs: The Center's research and teaching initiatives address the following topics: Democratization, Peace and Human Rights, which includes work on the resolution of civil conflicts, prospects for consolidation of new democracies, and the defense of human rights, especially those of women and children; Sustainable Development, and Comparative Development Strategies, which examines the interface between economic, political, and ecological systems, and the historical roots and implications of diverse development patterns, such as regional trade agreements, financial markets, and agricultural practices; Culture, History and Identity, which explores areas ranging from imagery and identity in film and literature to customary law, gender relations, and ethnic practices. In cooperation with other Stanford groups, the Center actively sponsors interdisciplinary faculty-graduate student working groups, such as the Working Group on Comparative Democratization. Now in its second year, this group, co-sponsored by the Institute for International Studies, draws over thirty active participants from throughout the university, representing regional interests in Eastern Europe, South Africa, Asia, and Latin America. Other current interdisciplinary research of the Center for Latin American Studies includes a medical anthropology project in Chiapas, Mexico, and research on ecosystem conservation in Costa Rica and Brazil. The Center also collaborates with Stanford's North American Forum, which concentrates on labor markets, debt and growth, and trade relations in the North America Free Trade Area. A weekly lecture series as well as frequent seminars, films, and colloquia presented by Latin American specialists number over 100 annually and have recently featured Brazilian President Fernando Henrique Cardoso, Nobel Prize winners Rigoberta Menchu and Oscar Arias, Uruguayan author Eduardo Galeno, and Mexico's former Minister of Finance, Pedro Aspe. The Center annually hosts one or two senior scholars from Latin America or Iberia as Tinker Visiting Professors, as well as a distinguished scholar from Brazil as the Nabuco Visiting Professor in Brazilian Studies.

Publications: No information provided.

Funding sources: The Center is supported by a combination of University operating monies, a Title VI grant, individual gifts and donations, the Tinker Foundation, the Ayacucho Fund, and an endowment.

Staffing: The Center has a small professional staff.

Head of the institution: Dr. Terry L. Karl, Director

Contact officer: Dr. Kathleen B. Morrison, Associate Director

Center for Latin American Studies
Bolivar House, 582 Alvarado Row
Stanford University
Stanford, CA 94305-8545
USA
Tel: (1-650) 723-4444
Fax: (1-650) 723-9822

Stanford University

North America Forum

Background and objectives: The North America Forum, which originated in 1980 as the U.S.-Mexico project, carries out policy research on issues of regional integration in Canada, Mexico, and the United States. The Forum's activities fall under the umbrella of Stanford's Institute for International Studies.

Programs: The Forum is currently engaged in several major research projects. These include the North American Agricultural Policy Research Consortium, a network organized in 1992 to exchange research findings on the future of agricultural policy in North America. Through reports on the findings of Forum-sponsored workshops and conferences held throughout North America, this project resulted in a published volume, *Toward a North American Agricultural Policy.* A series of regional case studies on regional integration in North America explore regional economic integration among the three North American states. These cases were published in a volume titled *Integrating Cities and Regions: NAFTA and the Caribbean Face Globalization.* A project titled "The U.S. and Mexico: Conflict and Convergence" focuses on the lingering effects of Mexico's recent economic crisis and its implications for policy making and institution building.

Publications: *Toward a North America Agricultural Policy* (1997) and *Integrating Cities and Regions* (1997).

Funding sources: The Forum is funded through institutional support from the Ford Foundation, the Hewlett Foundation, and the government of Canada.

Heads of the institution:
Prof. William F. Miller, Director

Dr. Clint E. Smith, Executive Director

North America Forum
200 Encina Hall
Stanford University
Stanford, CA 94305-6055
USA
Tel: (1-650) 723-3096
Fax: (1-650) 725-2010
URL • http://www.iis.stanford.edu

Texas A&M University

Center for International Business Studies

Background and objectives: The Center for International Business Studies (CIBS) is a division of the College of Business Administration and is responsible primarily for internationalizing business education at Texas A&M University. CIBS consists of the Center for International Business Education and Research (funded by the U.S. Department of Education), the Center for the Study of Western Hemispheric Trade (funded by the U.S. Customs Service), and the North American Business and Public Policy Studies Program (funded by endowments from the Canadian government and America's private sector). The Center and its supporting units design and implement education, research, and outreach programs dedicated to enhancing the international competitiveness of American businesses and accelerating the economic progress of the state of Texas, the Southwest region, and the nation.

Programs: CIBS is responsible for identifying and conducting internationally oriented programs for students, faculty, and the business community. Examples include student exchange programs with Japanese institutions, technical assistance for the University of Indonesia's business faculty, and a conference on business opportunities in ASEAN for American businesses.

CIBS's annual Faculty Development in International Business (FBIB)-East Asia program, conducted jointly with the University of Hawaii, exposes American business faculty to East Asia's business environment. Visits to the region's financial and commercial centers are coupled with field trips and seminars focusing on the region's business practices and culture.

CIBS co-sponsors, with the University of Texas at Austin, the annual Conference on Internationalizing Business Education, designed to assist faculty from regional business colleges with the internationalization of their business curriculum.

Publications: The Center's research findings are published in major refereed journals in the business and economics disciplines. CIBS research that has been published includes *Customer Service as a Strategic Weapon in International Operations* (1995), *Cost Structures in Multinational and Domestic Banking* (1995), and *Understanding Strategic Intent in the Global Marketplace* (1994).

Funding sources: CIBS receives University support for its administrative operations, but relies on government and private sector funds for research, outreach, and educational enrichment programs.

Staffing: CIBS has fifty professors and a full-time administrative staff of six.

Head of the institution: Dr. Kerry Cooper, Executive Director

Contact officer: Dr. Julian Gaspar, Director

Center for International Business Studies
College of Business Administration
Texas A&M University
College Station, TX 77843-4116
USA
Tel: (1-409) 845-5234
Fax: (1-409) 845-1710
e-mail • jgaspar@unix.tamu.edu
URL • http:cibs.tamu.edu

The Tomás Rivera Policy Institute

Background and objectives: The Tomás Rivera Policy Institute (TRPI), an independent and national institute for policy studies on Latino issues, was established in 1985 by a group of college presidents and business executives with the aim of improving public policies affecting education, employment, and human services available to the nation's Latino community. The Institute is affiliated with the Claremont Graduate School in Claremont, California, and the Department of Government at the University of Texas at Austin. The Institute has offices in California and Texas.

Programs: The TRPI currently focuses on three main issues. The first, integrating Latino immigrants into American society, includes research on the economic impact of immigration, California's Proposition 187 (affirmative action), and Black/Latino relations.

The second area, Latinos and Western Hemisphere integration, includes research on the role of Latino-owned firms in U.S.-Mexico trade, as well as the analysis of how U.S. Latinos are impacting foreign policy towards Latin America.

The third area, developing intellectual resources for the Latino community, aims to recruit Latinos into the teaching profession.

The TRPI also sponsors a variety of briefings and roundtable discussions for policy makers to further its research agenda. In May 1996, the Institute convened members of the California Legislative Caucus to apprise them on its research findings on the contributions of immigrants to the state of California. In 1994, the Institute organized a seminar featuring leaders from many segments of the national Latino community to discuss foreign policy as it relates to Latinos.

In collaboration with the Joint Center for Political and Economic Studies, the TRPI is examining the sources of conflict between African Americans and Latinos in the U.S. The project will target the urban areas in Texas and California where these two communities coexist. The TRPI was also commissioned by the U.S. Department of Labor's Glass Ceiling Commission to examine gender and ethnic group wage disparities in different sectors of the California and Texas economies.

In the area of education, TRPI is researching alternative teacher certification as a viable means to augment the teacher labor force.

Publications: The Institute publishes *TRPI Review,* a newsletter that describes TRPI news, recent publications, and research findings. Two publications came out of the TRPI's investigation: the Labor Department's *Good for Business: Making Full Use of the Nation's Human Capital* and the Tomás Rivera Policy Institute's own *Affirmative Action Sourcebooks* (California and Texas). TRPI also publishes two types of reports: *TRPI Policy Briefs,* which summarize and analyze the institute's research findings, and *TRPI Sourcebooks,* which document the circumstances of Latinos in specific geographic areas. Using surveys, questionnaires, personal interviews, and focus groups, TRPI staff have published major surveys and national surveys of Mexican Americans, Cuban Americans, and Puerto Ricans.

Funding sources: Financial support for the Institute is provided by corporations, foundations, and individuals, which include the Carnegie Corporation of New York, the Ford Foundation, the Andrew Mellon Foundation, the Times Mirror Foundation, as well as Nissan North America and Levi Straus & Co.

Staffing: The California Office has ten researchers and an administrative staff of eight. The Houston Office is made up of nine researchers and one administrative assistant.

Head of the institution: Dr. Harry P. Pachon, President

Contact officer: Ms. Karen Escalante, Director of Operations/ Development

The Tomás Rivera Policy Institute
241 E. Eleventh Street
Steele Hall, 3rd Floor
Claremont, CA 91711-6194
USA
Tel: (1-909) 621-8897
Fax: (1-909) 621-8898
e-mail • trc@cgs.edu
URL • http://www.cgs.edu/inst/trc.hmtl

Texas Office
Department of Government
Burdine Hall 536
UT, Austin
Austin, TX 78712
USA
Tel: (1-512) 471-2872
Fax: (1-512) 471-2873

Town Hall Los Angeles

Background and objectives: Town Hall, founded in 1937, is a nonprofit, nonpartisan organization for discussion of public issues. Its diverse speakers have included numerous leaders from government, business, media, and the arts and sciences.

Programs: Town Hall meetings, which are held at breakfast, lunch, and dinner, usually involve twenty minutes of prepared remarks by the speaker(s) and twenty minutes of questions and answers. Town Hall also holds early evening receptions, which are informal and discussion-oriented. Recent speakers include Mikhail Gorbachev, Jimmy Carter, Margaret Thatcher, F.W. de Klerk, Henry Kissinger, Warren Christopher, and Indonesian Trade Minister Hartarto. Programs aimed specifically at young people include the Associates Program, for members aged thirty-five and under, and the American Heritage Program, which enables local high school students to attend Town Hall events.

Publications: Town Hall meetings are publicized through the twice-monthly *Town Hall Journal,* the weekly "Town Hall on the Air" radio broadcast, and other national and local media outlets.

Funding sources: Town Hall is funded primarily through membership dues, both corporate and individual.

Staffing: Town Hall staff includes seven full-time and three part-time professionals and many interns.

Head of the institution: Ms. Adrienne Medawar, President

Town Hall Los Angeles
900 Wilshire Boulevard, Suite 1500
Los Angeles, CA 90017-4716
USA
Tel: (1-213) 628-8141
Fax: (1-213) 489-3327

United States-Mexico Border Progress Foundation

Background and objectives: The United States-Mexico Border Progress Foundation (BPF) was created in 1991 as a binational nonprofit institution, to help find and utilize private resources to solve public problems and meet vital needs on the 2,000-mile international border that is undergoing major demographic, environmental, and economic change.

BPF supports the advance of sustainable development along the border by integrating efforts and resources through public-private partnerships to enhance the region's viability, environment, and quality of life. It also promotes communication, mutual respect, and cooperation to resolve common problems, and educates the public on border issues, including those affecting the long-term health of residents.

Programs: BPF developed a series of educational forums to help ensure that businesses become more responsive to the concerns and priorities of the communities in which they operate.

Using funds from a historic $2.5 million settlement against a U.S. company accused of dumping lead in Tijuana, Mexico, BPF developed a comprehensive lead education project to apprise the residents of Tijuana of potential risks and ways to minimize exposure to lead, particularly for children. Partnering with Arizona, BPF established the U.S.-Mexico Border Volunteer Corps to promote environmental, public health, and safety initiatives through voluntary service.

Publications: BPF publishes *Border Links,* a newsletter aimed at giving the border region with all its challenges and opportunities a greater audience.

Funding sources: BPF has received generous contributions from the James Irvine Foundation, U.S. Environmental Protection Agency, AmeriCorps, Mexico's SEDESOL, AT&T, Los Angeles District Attorney's Office, and Johnson & Johnson, among others.

Staffing: BPF has an executive director, an assistant to the director, and two full-time employees.

Notes: The United States-Mexico Border Progress Foundation is a nonprofit 501(c)(3) organization in the U.S. It is also a recognized charitable foundation in Mexico. The recognition in Mexico makes the Foundation unique, as this designation has been bestowed to only a limited few binational organizations.

Head of the institution: Ms. Elsa R. Saxod, Executive Director

U.S.-Mexico Border Progress Foundation
1615 Murray Canyon Road, Suite 1000
P.O. Box 33419
San Diego, CA 92108
USA
Tel: (1-619) 298-2952
Fax: (1-619) 692-3107
e-mail • Saxod@aol.com
URL • http://www.borderprog.org.mx/fbp.html

University of California, Berkeley

Berkeley APEC Study Center

Background and objectives: The Berkeley APEC Study Center (BASC) was created in October 1996 at the University of California at Berkeley to promote multidisciplinary research activities on the Berkeley campus related to APEC—the Asia-Pacific Economic Cooperation forum created in 1989 by countries in the Asia-Pacific. In particular, BASC will investigate the compatibility between globalism and regionalism and consider the implications of continued regional cooperation for governments, firms, and citizens.

Programs: BASC's current research includes an examination of American, European, and Japanese corporate market and non-market strategies in the Asia-Pacific. This project, funded in part by the UC Center for German and European Studies, draws on the expertise of political scientists, economists, and business school professors to analyze different approaches used by corporations to advance their position in the context of their regional and global strategies, and to study the link between trade policy and the environment and the prospects for reconciling regional and international governance. This work will attempt to provide policy advice on the ways in which the sometimes conflicting objectives of groups in trade and the environment might be reconciled, and an analysis of the management of health care in the Asia-Pacific region. This project focuses on understanding how regional institutions might be helpful in developing national policy coordination on health issues, particularly with respect to the spread of communicable diseases.

Publications: In cooperation with the East-West Center, BASC sponsored an edited volume on the future of institutions in the Asia-Pacific that appeared in 1997. BASC also has a Working Paper series and a Policy Paper series with discussion of issues of current interest. A semiannual newsletter reports on BASC activities.

Funding sources: BASC is a unit of the Institute of International Studies at Berkeley, which in turn is part of International and Area Studies. Specific projects are supported by foundations and corporate sponsors.

Staffing: BASC currently has a staff of two full-time researchers and several research assistants. It has a large number of Faculty Associates, both from Berkeley and elsewhere, working on specific projects.

Head of the institution: Prof. Vinod K. Aggarwal, Director

Contact officers:
Stephen Rudman, Associate Director

Trevor Nakagawa, Project Director

Berkeley APEC Study Center (BASC)
802 Barrows Hall #1970
University of California
Berkeley, CA 94720-1970
USA
Tel: (1-510) 643-1071
Fax: (1-510) 643-1746
e-mail • basc@globetrotter.berkeley.edu
URL • http://globetrotter.berkeley.edu/basc

University of California, Berkeley

Berkeley Roundtable on the International Economy

Background and objectives: The Berkeley Roundtable on the International Economy (BRIE), founded in 1982 by a group of faculty at the University of California, Berkeley, is a multidisciplinary research project that focuses on international economic competition and the development and application of advanced technologies. BRIE's overarching philosophy is that any attempt to analyze the complex international dynamics of politics and markets must be rooted in the study of industrial production and competition. The Roundtable's core research examines the different ways that industrialized countries create competitive advantage and how these differences affect international economic and political relations.

Programs: BRIE's research is organized along three themes. The first, "Competing Capitalisms and Regionalization," examines how asymmetries between regional economic zones affect industrial competition and geopolitics. The second, "Technology Development and Application," looks at the impact of new technology on economic growth and assesses how America can adapt its technological strengths and convert Cold War assets to commercial benefit. Finally, BRIE's research on trade and investment analyzes how multilateral commitments to expand trade and investment can be maintained in an era of sectoral, bilateral, and regional bargains.

Publications: Representative books published by BRIE's researchers include *The Highest Stakes* (1992), *Who's Bashing Whom: Trade Conflicts in High Technology Industries* (1992), *Competing for Control: America's Stake in Microelectronics* (1988), and *Manufacturing Matters: The Myth of the Post-Industrial Economy* (1987).

BRIE authors publish their work in periodicals and newspapers such as *Foreign Affairs*, the *New York Times*, and the *Financial Times*, as well as in the in-house working papers, project reports, and monographs of BRIE.

Funding sources: BRIE is funded principally by private foundations. Other support comes from public funding for specific research projects, corporate support, and unrestricted gifts.

Staffing: BRIE's research and administrative staff varies from roughly ten to thirty-five.

Heads of the institution:
Dr. Michael Borrus, Co-Director

Dr. Stephen S. Cohen, Co-Director

Dr. John Zysman, Co-Director

Contact officer: Ms. Marybeth Schubert, Project Coordinator

Berkeley Roundtable on the International Economy
University of California at Berkeley
2234 Piedmont Avenue
Berkeley, CA 94720-2322
USA
Tel: (1-510) 642-3067
Fax: (1-510) 643-6617
e-mail • brie@garnet.berkeley.edu
URL • http://server.berkeley.edu/BRIE

University of California, Berkeley

Institute of East Asian Studies

Background and objectives: The Institute of East Asian Studies (IEAS) was established in 1978 at the University of California, Berkeley to promote research on the history, cultures, and contemporary affairs of East Asia. The Institute brings together the major East Asian programs on campus, including the Center for Chinese Studies; the Center for Japanese Studies; the Center for Korean Studies; the Group on Asian Studies, an interdisciplinary degree program; and the East Asian National Resource Center.

Programs: The IEAS and its centers sponsor both research and teaching by providing internal funds to and administering extramural grants for Berkeley faculty, and by providing funds to fill gaps in the East Asian course offerings of Berkeley departments. The Institute and its centers organize frequent seminars and colloquia to facilitate both intellectual exchange across academic departments and community access to information about East Asia. The Institute also provides resources and programs for California teachers. A recent program was a summer institute targeted at middle school teachers entitled "Waters of Life: River Civilizations of China, the Middle East, and South Asia," organized in collaboration with other area centers on campus. Recent lectures and seminars include "The Status of 'Tradition' in Japanese Studies," the 1996 Regional Seminar of the Center for Japanese Studies (May 1996); "Economic Policies of the Northeast Asian Countries on the Eve of the 21st Century," a lecture by the Honorable Cho Soon, Mayor of Seoul, Republic of Korea (April 1996); "Landscape, Culture and Power in Chinese Society," and the 1996 Annual Symposium of the Center for Chinese Studies (March 1996).

IEAS now administers the Inter-University Board for Chinese Language Study (IUB), a fourteen-university-sponsored program for advanced Chinese language study in Beijing and Taipei.

Publications: IEAS administers *Asian Survey*, a monthly journal on contemporary Asia published by the University of California Press. The Institute also publishes the China, Japan, Korea, and Indochina Research Monograph series. Recent titles include "Putting Class in Its Place: Worker Identities in East Asia" (1996), "The Korean Business Conglomerate: Chaebol Then and Now" (1996), and "Negotiating Ethnicities in China and Taiwan" (1996). It also publishes the Research Papers and Policy Studies series, which include conference reports, technical studies, and manuscripts addressing East Asian issues such as "Cultural Nationalism in East Asia: Representations and Identity" (1993).

Funding sources: Support for the Institute comes from the state and federal governments, as well as from foundations such as the Ford Foundation, the Mellon Foundation, the Henry Luce Foundation, the MacArthur Foundation, the Chiang Ching-Kuo Foundation, the Korea Research Foundation, the Japan Foundation, and the National Endowment for the Humanities. The Institute also receives private gifts and endowments.

Staffing: In addition to six academic personnel, the IEAS and its centers have twenty-one administrative staff members.

Notes: Since 1973, Berkeley has been designated a National Resource Center for East Asian Studies by the U.S. Department of Education.

The East Asian Library contains one of the most comprehensive collections in East Asian languages in the United States. The Center for Chinese Studies Library is the world's largest repository of materials on contemporary China outside of China itself.

Head of the institution: Dr. Frederic E. Wakeman, Director

Contact officer: Ms. Joan Kask, Assistant Director

Institute of East Asian Studies
University of California, Berkeley
2223 Fulton Street #2318
Berkeley, CA 94720-2318
USA
Tel: (1-510) 642-2809
Fax: (1-510) 643-7062
e-mail • jkask@garnet.berkeley.edu

University of California, Berkeley

Institute of International Studies

Background and objectives: The Institute of International Studies (IIS) was established in 1955 to promote interdisciplinary research in international, comparative, and policy studies.

Programs: The Institute's current programs emphasize the following themes: peace and security after the Cold War; environment, demography, and sustainable development; comparative development; and globalization and the transformation of the global economy.

Institute activities include noon seminars featuring presentations by faculty, students, and policy analysts from various departments and institutions. Recent topics included "Contrasts in Small Business Policy: A Comparative Analysis of Japan and the United States" and "Vietnam's Development Policy in Comparative Perspective."

In the spring of 1995, the Institute began hosting six workshops collectively titled "Global Governance: The United Nations and the Next Fifty Years," to discuss issues such as population, migration, and refugees; environment and sustainable development; and human rights. In late 1995, the IIS hosted an international conference entitled "Reentering the Global Economy: A Comparative Analysis of Nicaragua, South Africa, and Vietnam," which addressed such issues as income equality and isolationism.

The Center's newest program, "The Moral Economy of Islam," focuses on how the interaction of political, social, and economic forces shape the Islamic visions of economic justice. Topics include tensions in Islamic societies between individual and collective utilities, equality and growth, and the institutional arrangements governing the economy. These workshops and conferences are meant to help faculty develop long-term research interests.

Colloquia for faculty and advanced graduate students provide an avenue for open discussion of ongoing research. Among these programs are the Colloquium for Research on International Politics and Economics (CRIPE) and the International Relations Theory Colloquium.

Publications: The IIS publishes *Policy Papers in International Affairs*, *Insights in International Affairs*, and the Institute newsletter, *Currents*, which describe upcoming IIS events and other topics of interest to the International Studies community.

Funding sources: The IIS is funded by grants from private foundations such as the Ford Foundation, the MacArthur Foundation, and the Rockefeller Foundation.

Staffing: The Institute employs an Executive Director, a Director, a Senior Administrative Assistant for Financial Affairs, an Editorial and Program Assistant, an Administrative and Payroll Assistant, and a Program Assistant.

Head of the institution: Prof. Michael J. Watts, Director

Contact officer: Mr. Harry Kreisler, Executive Director

University of California, Berkeley
Institute of International Studies
215 Moses Hall #2308
Berkeley, CA 94720-2308
USA
Tel: (1-510) 642-2472
Fax: (1-510) 642-9493
e-mail • iis@globetrotter.berkeley.edu
URL • http://globetrotter.berkeley.edu

University of California, Irvine

Global Peace and Conflict Studies

Background and objectives: Global Peace and Conflict Studies (GPACS), established in 1983 with an appropriation from the University of California, San Diego-based Institute on Global Conflict and Cooperation (IGCC), is dedicated to teaching, research, and public service in the study of international conflict resolution.

Programs: GPACS's research focuses on the interaction of foreign policy and domestic affairs; ecological and environmental factors; the nature, strategy, and ethics of violence and force in international relations; the role of international organizations; and human attitudes and perceptions relating to peace and conflict. GPACS also hosts visiting scholars and an annual research colloquium series on a central contemporary topic in international studies. The Thursday afternoon Forum series brings a continuous stream of outstanding speakers on international issues.

Other special events feature such distinguished guests as Robin Williams, Immanuel Wallerstein, Peter Wallensteen, and Noam Chomsky. GPACS's annual Julius Margolis Lecture also brings a statesman or scholar to the campus each year for a formal address. Presentations have been given by McGeorge Bundy, Hans Bethe, Les Aspin, Vladimir Lukin, Stephen Solarz, and A. Kim Campbell.

GPACS also sponsors the Irvine Research Unit (IRU), which pursues interdisciplinary research on the international and domestic conditions necessary to avert war and promote a stable peace.

Publications: GPACS publishes a working paper series and edited volumes from its annual colloquia. Recent publications in the series International Society and Institutions include *Negotiating Institutions: Framing State Choice and the Montreal Protocol* (1996) and *The Future of International Environmental Governance* (1996).

Funding sources: GPACS's main funding support comes from the Institute on Global Conflict and Cooperation, a permanent peace endowment, three endowed chairs, and the Office of Academic Affairs and the Research and Graduate Studies, both at UCI.

Staffing: GPACS has three full-time researchers and fifty affiliated research faculty, as well as two full-time and two part-time administrative staff.

Head of the institution: Prof. Patrick M. Morgan, Director

Contact officer: Dr. Paula Garb, Associate Director

Global Peace and Conflict Studies
Social Science Tower 721
University of California, Irvine
Irvine, CA 92697-5100
USA
Tel: (1-714) 824-6410
Fax: (1-714) 824-3589
e-mail • gpacs@uci.edu
URL • http://www.socsci.uci.edu/gpacs

University of California, Los Angeles (UCLA)

Asian American Studies Center

Background and objectives: The Asian American Studies Center, founded in 1969, is dedicated to exploring the history, culture, and status of Asian Americans. Emerging out of the civil rights struggles of the 1960s, the Center has developed active core programs in research, teaching, publication, archival collection, student leadership, joint university-community research, and public education.

Programs: The Center's research focuses on everything from Asian American mental health to politics to the transnational flow of capital and migrants in the Pacific Rim region. Current research topics include interracial conflicts and coalition building in Los Angeles and New York, the persistence of poverty and welfare dependency among Asian Pacific Americans, and unique cultural responses to medical crises. The Center's archival collection program includes the Japanese American Research Project Collection, the country's largest archive on the Japanese American experience. The Center is also supporting the next generation of Asian American filmmakers by offering classes and workshops in Asian American film, theater, and journalism and co-sponsoring the annual Asian Pacific American International Film Festival.

Publications: The Center's publications include monographs, books, works of literature, bibliographies, and the national *Amerasia Journal*, the oldest interdisciplinary journal in Asian American Studies. A notable Center publication is the 1971 book *Roots: An Asian American Reader*, the first textbook for the Asian American Studies field. *Crosscurrents*, published twice per year, provides information on Center events and programs.

Funding sources: The Center's activities are funded by private donations, University funds, and grants from foundations and government agencies such as the Rockefeller Foundation, the Ford Foundation, the Ahmanson Foundation, and the federal government.

Staffing: Thirty-nine professors make up the Center's faculty and affiliated faculty. The Center has a staff of thirteen.

Head of the institution: Dr. Don T. Nakanishi, Director and Professor

UCLA Asian American Studies Center
3230 Campbell Hall
405 Hilgard Avenue
University of California, Los Angeles
Los Angeles, CA 90095-1546
USA
Tel: (1-310) 825-2974
Fax: (1-310) 206-9844
e-mail • dtn@ucla.edu
URL • http://www.sscnet.ucla.edu/aasc

University of California, Los Angeles

Center for International Business Education and Research

Background and objectives: Founded in 1989, CIBER UCLA seeks to enrich the international content of the Anderson School curriculum through sponsorship of retreats for curriculum review in marketing, human resources, strategy, accounting, and finance, and by providing funding for faculty and doctoral research on international business issues.

Programs: One of CIBER's most visible programs is the International Management Fellows Program (IMF), which prepares students for executive positions in the global business environment. The twenty-four-month certificate program combines the regular Anderson MBA with ten weeks of intensive business-oriented language instruction abroad in Japanese, French, Spanish, or Chinese; a six-month internship in the target region; attendance at a foreign MBA program for one semester; and continuing language courses emphasizing business and cultural content. CIBER also operates the International Business Roundtable (INTable), a quarterly meeting of international executives who gather to discuss topics of importance to their firms and business in general. The Center funds research, assists with inter-university and corporate contacts, and funds and organizes research conferences and seminars.

Publications: The Center publishes working papers series.

Funding sources: CIBER UCLA is funded in part by grants from the U.S. Department of Education and administered under Title VI, Part B of the Higher Education Act of 1965.

Staffing: No researchers are on staff. Research is done by faculty.

Head of the institution: Dr. Jose de la Torre, Director

Contact officer: Ms. Sara D. Tucker, Associate Director

Center for International Business Education and Research
The Anderson School at UCLA
110 Westwood Plaza
Box 951481
Los Angeles, CA 90095-1481
USA
Tel: (1-310) 206-5317
Fax: (1-310) 825-8098
e-mail • ciber@anderson.ucla.edu
URL • http://www.anderson.ucla.edu/research/ciber/
      hmpg.htm

University of California, Los Angeles

Center for International Relations

Background and objectives: The Center for International Relations (CIR), an interdisciplinary program, grew out of the Center for International and Strategic Affairs, which was established in 1975 to study arms control and international security. The new Center seeks to understand security in the broader context of economic, environmental, and social issues, as well as the traditional military and strategic ones.

Programs: CIR conducts research in five areas: the environment; population and migration; the relationship between economics and security; international political economy; and the link between strategy and cooperation among nations. The CIR also sponsors conferences, seminars, and lectures on these topics ranging from small, informal gatherings to large public addresses delivered by policy makers and specialists. Recent conferences have focused on "Social Science and Environmental Problems," "The Emergence of New Norms in Personal and International Behavior," and "Cooperative Models and International Relations Research." The Center sponsors the annual Bernard Brodie Lecture, now devoted to the "Conditions of Peace." Recent lecturers have included McGeorge Bundy, Carl Kaysen, and Stanley Hoffman. The Center provides several pre-doctoral fellowships for UCLA graduate students working on CIR projects. A post-doctoral fellowship is also offered for a recent Ph.D., and a limited number of senior fellows are invited each year to the CIR to undertake their own research.

Publications: CIR authors publish working papers, books, and articles in the mainstream press.

Funding sources: CIR conferences are frequently co-sponsored by other research centers such as the Institute on Global Conflict and Cooperation, Sandia National and Lawrence Livermore Laboratories, the U.S. Arms Control and Disarmament Agency, Ploughshares, and the Department of Education.

Staffing: The Center has a combination of six part-time and four full-time researchers. Of these there are two full-time administrative staff and one student assistant.

Head of the institution: Dr. Richard Rosecrance, Director

Contact officer: Ms. Becky Carrera, Administrative Analyst and Assistant to the Director

UCLA
Center for International Relations
11381 Bunche Hall
University of California, Los Angeles
405 Hilgard Avenue
Los Angeles, CA 90095-1486
USA
Tel: (1-310) 825-0604
Fax: (1-310) 206-2582

University of California, Los Angeles

Center for Pacific Rim Studies

Background and objectives: The Center for Pacific Rim Studies was founded in 1985 to study the emerging importance of the Pacific Rim and its economic, social, political, and cultural implications.

Programs: The Center's current projects include comparing China's social stratification during the Cultural Revolution and market transition periods; predicting the effects of El Nino conditions in the Pacific on regional water supplies; using Asian-language mass media for tuberculosis education in Los Angeles County and Taiwan; and studying political culture and participation in mainland China, Taiwan, and Hong Kong. The Center also sponsors major public lectures; recent speakers have included former U.S. Ambassador to Korea and China James R. Lilley on "Relations across the Taiwan Strait," former Ambassador to the Philippines Nicholas Platt on "The United States in the Pacific Rim Century," and Professor Lawrence Lau of Stanford University on "Sources and Prospects for Economic Growth in East Asia." As a provider of consulting and training services on contract for businesses throughout the Pacific Rim, the Center has offered programs ranging from technical training on health care reform issues to workshops on finance and accounting for Asian factory managers. The Center also administers four fellowship awards for UCLA students and acts as the UCLA representative to the University of California Pacific Rim Research Program.

Publications: The Center publishes *The Pacific Rim*, a newsletter that is published twice a year and includes a report on the Center's activities and the current research of UCLA faculty. In collaboration with the UCLA Center for Chinese Studies, the Center for Pacific Rim Studies publishes *Chinese Science*, a journal devoted to the scholarship of Chinese science and medicine.

The Center's scholars publish their work in books, journal reprint series, and an occasional monograph series. Recent publications include *Global Production: The Apparel Industry in the Pacific Rim* (1994), *The Role of the State in Taiwan's Development* (1994), and *Migration of Highly Educated Asians and Global Dynamics* (1992).

Funding sources: The Center's activities are funded through grants from such institutions as the Ford Foundation and the Luce Foundation, through the University of California Pacific Rim Research Program, and through contract work for public and private entities.

Staffing: Nearly 120 UCLA faculty members are affiliated with the Center or otherwise involved with Pacific region issues. One faculty member oversees administrative details working with a staff of four.

Notes: Among the Center's current interests is the development of new media applications for Pacific Rim Studies. It is working with the UCLA East Asian Library and other East Asian studies programs to develop a digital library of Chinese-language original source materials on the Internet. Another project under development may involve educational programs offered via new distance learning technologies.

Head of the institution: Prof. Dean T. Jamison, Director

Contact officer: Ms. Sue W. Fan, Assistant Director

Center for Pacific Rim Studies
11282 Bunche Hall
University of California, Los Angeles
Los Angeles, CA 90095-1487
USA
Tel: (1-310) 206-8984
Fax: (1-310) 206-4018
URL • http://isop.sscnet.ucla.edu/pacrim

University of California, Los Angeles

North American Integration and Development Center

Background and objectives: The North American Integration and Development (NAID) Center was established in July 1995 to conduct research concerning North America and to assist communities and governments with policies, investment projects, and Internet tools for sustainable development across borders.

Programs: The NAID Center's research focuses on the dynamic impacts of economic, social, and environmental interdependence between the United States and Mexico. It conducts both macro-level research, including the development of large-scale databases and modeling capacity, and micro-level research consisting of sectoral and regional dynamics needed for the reliable tracking of broader economic, social, and environmental trends in America.

The NAID Center also works directly with communities that have been experiencing adverse economic effects due to NAFTA and helps them to identify solutions at the regional and sectoral level for local communities in both the United States and Mexico.

The NAID Center utilizes a multi-country, sectoral-regional approach, which includes CGE (Computable General Equilibrium) modeling and the creation and maintenance of on-line relational databases that include information on trade, investment, migration, agricultural and industrial production, employment, income demographics, and environmental resources. Current sectoral and regional case studies include glass and garment industries in Los Angeles, sustainable agriculture along the Sonora and Arizona border, and forestry in Southern Mexico and along the U.S.-Canadian border.

The NAID Center has a program to provide Internet connectivity to a wide range of Consortium partners and to develop advanced tools for wide-area database management and interactive communication.

The NAID Center has hosted two major conferences. In September 1996, it hosted a binational conference, "Post-NAFTA Policies and Investment in Mexican Agriculture," examining the impact that NAFTA has had on the agricultural community. In October 1996, the NAID Center hosted "Mitigating the Impacts of NAFTA: Assistance Programs for Southern California Communities."

The NAID Center is a founding member of the NADBank Community Adjustment and Investment Technical Assistance Consortium, which includes two important national Latino organizations—the Southwest Voter Research Institution and the National Council of La Raza.

The NAID Center and the NADBank consortium are working to create partnership and computer-aided linkages with other universities, non-governmental organizations, labor unions, private sector firms, and other agents of community empowerment to assist localities that suffer NAFTA-related job displacement to identify alternative strategies for sustainable economic development and to apply for financing from NADBank and other sources.

Publications: In December 1996 the NAID Center published "North American Integration Three Years after NAFTA," a comprehensive report on NAFTA. The NAID Center has also established a working paper series for NAID-based scholars whose expertise deals with issues of integration within North America, all of which are available on the Internet.

Funding sources: The NAID Center funding has come from several sources including foundations, the private sector, government and international agencies, and the UCLA Vice Chancellor of Research.

Staffing: The NAID Center core professional staff include economists, planners, computer scientists, and community organizers.

Head of the institution: Dr. Raul Hinojosa-Ojeda, Research Director

Contact officer: David Runsten, Office Manager

North American Integration and Development Center
School of Public Policy and Social Research
University of California, Los Angeles
3250 Public Policy Building
BOX 951656
Los Angeles, CA 90095-1656
USA
Tel: (1-310) 206-4609
Fax: (1-310) 825-8574
e-mail • naid@ucla.edu
URL • http://naid.sppsr.ucla.edu

University of California, San Diego

Center for U.S.-Mexican Studies

Background and objectives: The Center, established in 1979, is the largest U.S. program devoted to the study of Mexico and U.S.-Mexican relations. It supports research in the social sciences and history, provides graduate training, and organizes public outreach activities.

Programs: The Center's research areas include the political, social, and economic consequences of North American integration (including the foreign policy implications of regional economic integration for Canada, Mexico, and the United States; the issue of labor rights and free trade in North America; and the impact of market opening and technological change on Mexico's economic competitiveness); Mexico's political transition in comparative perspective (including such topics as the dilemmas of political change in post-revolutionary regimes and the role of conservative political parties in democratization in Mexico and other Latin American countries); Mexican labor migration to the United States in comparative perspective, with special reference to the role of immigrant labor in the U.S. economy; and the political, social, and environmental consequences of economic restructuring in Mexico (including agricultural modernization and the transformation of social relations in the Mexican countryside, the emergence of new patterns of state-society relations, and the relationship between economic restructuring and political liberalization).

The Center's Visiting Fellowship Program supports the research of twenty to twenty-five scholars each year. The annual Summer Seminar in U.S. Studies, offered in collaboration with UCSD's American Political Institutions Program, trains promis-ing young social scientists, public officials, and journalists from Mexico and other Latin American countries.

Publications: The Center's publications include research monographs, the U.S.-Mexico Contemporary Perspectives series, and Current Issues Briefs. The Center's newsletter, *ENFOQUE*, is published biannually and reports on Center activities, economic and political trends in Mexico, and U.S.-Mexico relations.

Funding sources: The Center's main support comes from foundations such as the Hewlett Foundation, the Ford Foundation, the Tinker Foundation, the Irvine Foundation, and the Japan Foundation.

Staffing: In addition to permanent academic personnel, affiliated faculty, and visiting researchers, the Center has six full-time administrative staff members.

Head of the institution: Dr. Kevin J. Middlebrook, Director

Contact officer: Ms. Graciela Platero, Program Officer

Center for U.S.-Mexican Studies
University of California, San Diego
9500 Gilman Drive, 0510
La Jolla, CA 92093-0510
USA
Tel: (1-619) 534-4503
Fax: (1-619) 534-6447
e-mail • usmex@weber.ucsd.edu
URL • http://weber.ucsd.edu/Depts/USMex/welcome.htm

University of California, San Diego

Institute on Global Conflict and Cooperation

Background and objectives: The University of California Institute on Global Conflict and Cooperation, founded in 1983, is a statewide University-based research institute that studies the causes of international conflicts and the opportunities for resolving them through international cooperation. Housed at the University of California at San Diego, the IGCC draws on scholars from the nine campuses of the University of California system, as well as from the Livermore and Los Alamos National Laboratories.

Programs: During the Institute's first five years of operation, research focused largely on averting nuclear war through arms control and confidence-building measures between the superpowers. Since that time, the IGCC has diversified into areas including regional relations, ethnic and internal conflicts, international environmental policy, international relations theory, and the domestic sources of foreign policy.

Research programs and projects include the Northeast Asian cooperation dialogue; the military and the Middle East peace process; the structure of investment in Asia (in cooperation with the Berkeley Roundtable on the International Economy); linkages between security and economics in U.S.-Japan relations since 1960 (in cooperation with the National Security Archive); the impact of China's opening on its economic and political integration; comparative regional approaches to nuclear non-proliferation; and building regional environmental cooperation.

Scholars, researchers, government officials, and journalists from the United States and abroad participate in IGCC projects.

Publications: The IGCC *Newsletter*, published twice per year, informs scholars, policy makers, and the public about IGCC-sponsored research, conferences, publications, grants, and seminars. The Institute also publishes books, policy papers, and policy briefs. Recent publications include *Ethnic Fears and Global Engagement: The International Spread and Management of Ethnic Conflict* (1996); *Preventative Diplomacy and Ethnic Conflict: Possible, Difficult, Necessary* (1996); *The Middle East Arms Control and Regional Security (ACRS) Talks: Progress, Problems, and Prospects* (1996); *Middle East Environmental Cooperation* (1996); *Power and Prosperity: Economics and Security Linkages in Asia-Pacific* (1996); and *Regional Orders: Building Security in a New World* (1996).

Funding sources: IGCC receives support primarily from the Regents of the University of California and the State of California. Additional funding has been provided by the U.S. Department of Energy, the U.S. Institute of Peace, the Japan-U.S. Friendship Commission, and Japan's National Institute for Research Advancement (NIRA). Important foundation support has come from the Ford Foundation, William and Flora Hewlett Foundation, the Japan Foundation Center for Global Partnership, the W. Alton Jones Foundation, the John D. and Catherine T. MacArthur Foundation, the Pew Charitable Trusts, the Ploughshares Fund, the Rockefeller Brothers Fund, the Rockefeller Foundation, and the Smith Richardson Foundation.

Staffing: IGCC has seven research faculty and academic staff, six visiting fellows, and an administrative staff of ten.

Head of the institution: Prof. Stephan Haggard, Director

Contact officer: Mr. Ronald Bee, External Affairs

Institute on Global Conflict and Cooperation
Robinson Building
University of California, San Diego
9500 Gilman Drive
La Jolla, CA 92093-0518
USA
Tel: (1-619) 534-3352 / 534-6429
Fax: (1-619) 534-7655
e-mail • ph13@sdcc12.ucsd.edu
**   rbee@ucsd.edu**
URL • http://www. igcc.ucsd.edu/igcc/igccmenu.html

University of Colorado

Institute for International Business

Background and objectives: The Institute for International Business, founded in 1988, is a center for the advanced study and teaching of international business. It supports faculty members in internationalizing curricula and programs; assists faculty in their globalization efforts; hosts conferences and seminars; develops and implements international programs for business; and impacts hundreds of regional, national, and international companies as well as thousands of students.

Programs: The Institute organizes monthly International Executive Roundtables for CU-Denver faculty; conducts a Faculty Development in International Business Program for faculty across the nation, and carries out seminars and workshops for local business people.

Publications: The Institute publishes *Shinbum*, a periodic newsletter, and proceedings following major conferences.

Funding sources: The Institute is funded through a CIBER grant by the Department of Education, corporate gifts, and by the support of the University of Colorado at Denver.

Staffing: The Institute has several faculty members, researchers, and students assistants. It has three full-time employees.

Head of the institution: Dr. Donald Stevens, Director

Contact officer: Ms. Jana Blakestad, Director of Development

Institute for International Business
University of Colorado
1380 Lawrence Street, Suite 1150
Denver, CO 80202
USA
Tel: (1-303) 556-4738
Fax: (1-303) 556-6276
e-mail • jblakest@carbon.cudenver.edu

University of Hawaii / East-West Center

APEC Study Center

Background and objectives: The APEC Study Center was formed in July 1994 as a joint venture between the University of Hawaii and the East-West Center, and is one of the founding members of the US Consortium of APEC Study Centers. The Center aims to support the APEC Leaders Education Initiative by promoting greater understanding of the APEC region and the economic cooperation process through educational, research, and policy dialogue programs. The Center is an active player in the APEC Study Center movement.

Programs: The East-West Center and University of Hawaii elements of the APEC Study Center engage in separate as well as joint programs. The East-West Center provided the secretariat for the US Consortium during its first two years, and its director is currently the chair of the Consortium.

EWC projects include the New Generation Seminar, an educational program for younger leaders from the region, and an academic research project on institutionalizing Asia-Pacific: Region Formation and the Future of APEC.

It also joined Brandeis University and Keio University in a macroeconomic modeling project on making APEC work.

The University component joined the Pacific Basin Economic Council and the APEC Human Resources Development for Small and Medium Enterprises. In the Cross Cultural Management in APEC project, work is underway on a series of case studies dealing with the special challenges that managers face when working in the diverse APEC region. The APEC Study Center's co-directors have offered a graduate-level course on APEC in the University of Hawaii School of Business.

Publications: *Meeting Minds*, a newsletter for the APEC Study Centers, is published by the Study Center. The program also publishes working papers, and the directors publish widely through other vehicles.

Funding sources: Research and educational programs are funded through private foundations such as the Center for Global Partnership, the Freeman Foundation, and the Ford Foundation. University of Hawaii funds support its component.

Staffing: Approximately four people, aside from the directors, are associated with the APEC Study Center, but they and the directors also work on other activities outside the framework of the Study Center.

Heads of the institution:
Dr. Charles E. Morrison, East-West Center Co-Director

Dr. David McClain, University of Hawaii Co-Director

APEC Study Center
East-West Center
1601 East-West Road
Honolulu, HI 96848
USA
Tel: (1-808) 944-7384
Fax: (1-808) 944-7389
e-mail • morrisoc@ewc.hawaii.edu

APEC Study Center
University of Hawaii
2404 Maile Way
Honolulu, HI 96822
USA
Tel: (1-808) 956-7331
Fax: (1-808) 956-3261
URL • http://www.cba.hawaii.edu/apec

University of Hawaii at Manoa

Center for International Business Education and Research

Background and objectives: The UH Center for International Business Education and Research (CIBER), funded by the U.S. Department of Education under the Omnibus Trade and Competitiveness Act of 1988, is one of twenty-six centers across the U.S. that serve as national resources for improved business techniques, strategies, and methodologies that emphasize the international context in which business is transacted. The UH CIBER also serves as a regional resource to businesses in the Pacific Rim by offering programs and providing research to meet their international needs.

Programs: The CIBER promotes the creation of interdisciplinary business and language courses, Asia-sighted faculty and student development programs, as well as executive development seminars and conferences. Innovative research projects on international business topics such as strategic management, joint ventures, information systems development and technology issues, and global marketing strategies are also funded by the CIBER. Current research projects sponsored by UH CIBER include Application of Cross-Cultural Constructs in Business Relationships; Preparing Managers for International Assignments: Using a Multimedia Individualism/Collectivism Culture Assimilator; Global Strategic Alliances and the Chinese Firm; and Applications of Technology in Distance Education.

The UH CIBER offers a variety of interdisciplinary programs that integrate foreign-language training and international studies into business, finance, management, and other professional curricula. They include degree programs such as the Japan-focused Executive MBA (JEMBA); the China-focused Executive MBA (CHEMBA); and the Executive MBA (EMBA)—Master of Business Administration degree programs scheduled so that working professionals can earn the MBA degree in the shortest amount of time and focus on international and regional business issues. The UH CIBER also sponsors the Pacific-Asian Management Institute (PAMI) Summer Program, which offers extensive courses on the business, cultural, political and economic dimensions of Asia and the Pacific. The UH CIBER is committed to outreach programs for the local business community that provide a two-way dialogue between the University and the private sector. Recent conferences and workshops include Export Opportunities for Hawaii in the Asia-Pacific Region; Venture Capital and Foreign Investments; New Opportunities for Hawaii's Travel Industry in Vietnam; and Advanced Information on Japanese Consumer Trends.

Publications: The UH CIBER sponsors the publication of the Pacific Asian Management Institute International Business Series, which addresses such topics as international management, international marketing, and cross-cultural comparisons of concepts related to business.

Staffing: The UH CIBER's two full-time administrators work with over sixty faculty members who devote 10-15% of their time to CIBER-related research and outreach activities.

Head of the institution: Dr. Shirley J. Daniel, Director

Center for International Business Education and Research
University of Hawaii
College of Business Administration
2404 Maile Way
Honolulu, HI 96822
USA
Tel: (1-808) 956-2875
Fax: (1-808) 956-9685
e-mail • ciber@ciber.cba.hawaii.edu
URL • http://www.cba.hawaii.edu/ciber

University of Hawaii at Manoa

Pacific Asian Management Institute

Background and objectives: The Pacific Asian Management Institute (PAMI), founded in 1977 at the University of Hawaii College of Business Administration, serves as a center for international management research and education. With a focus on the Asia-Pacific region, the goal of the Institute is to foster cross-cultural and transnational management training, and to conduct research for the development of teaching materials and management information useful to business schools and the business community.

Programs: The PAMI International Summer Program was the first University summer session offering to focus exclusively on Asia-Pacific business subjects. The program was initiated in the late 1970s, and has grown to two six-week semesters with over 400 enrollments. The student body is composed of undergraduate and graduate degree students from Hawaii and all over the world, plus others from the middle management ranks of local companies.

An innovative curriculum provides a unique Asia-Pacific comparative focus that mixes core functional courses with topical subjects related to the latest activities in the region. Supplementing the course work is a series of weekly PALS lectures (Pacific Asian Lecture Series), also open to the public, featuring distinguished speakers form the world of business and academia. By successfully completing specified minimum requirements, students may earn a PAMI Certificate. Most students earn credits towards their MBA degree at the University of Hawaii, or the credits are transferable because the University Business School is accredited at the highest level by the American Assembly of Collegiate Schools of Business (AACSB).

PAMI's study abroad programs include the "Field Study Abroad: Industry in Asia," which is offered each summer. This program provides business students the opportunity to observe firsthand the developed and developing economies of Asia: such as China, Japan, Korea, Hong Kong, Malaysia, Singapore, and Thailand. Students visit factories, businesses, embassies, and universities, as well as cultural sites, and are required to complete an in-depth economic analysis of the region.

PAMI is also a founding member and serves as the Secretariat for the "Pacific Asian Consortium for International Business Education and Research" (PACIBER). The PACIBER consortium is composed of prominent business schools (currently twenty-eight members) from around the Pacific Rim. PACIBER has created a network for regular exchange of points of view about business cultures and practices, teaching of management, and development of new business theory.

Publications: PAMI publishes *PACIBER Newsletter* (semiannual), *PACIBER Conference Proceedings, PALS Lecture Series* (in process), *and PAMI Monograph Series* (in process).

Funding sources: The Institute is fully funded by University of Hawaii College of Business Administration.

Staffing: PAMI has three full-time staff.

Head of the institution: Dr. Shirley J. Daniel, Director

Pacific Asian Management Institute (PAMI)
College of Business Administration
University of Hawaii at Manoa
2404 Maile Way
Honolulu, HI 96822-22822
USA
Tel: (1-808) 956-8041
Fax: (1-808) 956-9685
e-mail • pami@pami.cba.hawaii.edu
URL • http://www.cba.hawaii.edu/pami

University of Hawaii at Manoa

School of Hawaiian, Asian and Pacific Studies

Background and objectives: In 1987 the University of Hawaii Board of Regents established the School of Hawaiian, Asian and Pacific Studies (SHAPS) to provide academic leadership, improve administrative support and coordination, and heighten visibility for Hawaiian, Asian, and Pacific studies at the University. The School's objectives are to promote and coordinate resources in Hawaiian, Asian, and Pacific studies throughout the University; support faculty and student development, instruction, research, and publication; and serve the educational and cultural interests of the people of Hawaii by promoting a deeper understanding of the Hawaiian, Asian, and Pacific heritage.

Programs: The School comprises nine area centers, one area program, an Asian Studies academic program, and an active publications program that encompasses several of the centers. The nine area centers promote the School's mission by securing and administering extramural research and instructional and training grants; providing a forum and structure that supports area studies faculty and students across UH Manoa; supporting and staffing the interdisciplinary instructional programs; coordinating scholarly activities; and representing and promoting the broad interests of area studies in the local, national, and world communities.

The area centers are Center for Chinese Studies, Center for Hawaiian Studies, Center for Japanese Studies, Center for Korean Studies, Center for Pacific Islands Studies, Center for Philippine Studies, Center for Russia in Asia, Center for South Asian Studies, and Center for Southeast Asian Studies.

Eight of the area centers are led by a full- or half-time director with support assistance. The SHAPS academic programs offer interdisciplinary instructional programs at the bachelor's and master's levels. Certificate and concurrent programs culminating in dual graduate degrees also exist with other schools and colleges within UH Manoa.

Publications: The School of Hawaiian, Asian and Pacific Studies' publications program include works from all geographic areas encompassed by the School. Some are area-specific. These include the Library of Asian Studies, published in conjunction with the University of Hawaii Press to reflect the School's interest in supporting teaching programs; the SHAPS Library of Translations series, which is published in conjunction with the University of Hawaii Press to make available English translations of works of enduring significance from all parts of Asia and the Pacific; the Pacific Islands Monograph Series and South Sea Books; journals, Occasional Papers series, and newsletters including East Asia, Lei o Ka Lanakila, Pacific News from Manoa, and Southeast Asian & Philippine Studies Monthly Bulletin.

Staffing: Thirty-one faculty and fifteen staff members are associated with the School.

Funding sources: The Center receives funding primarily from the state, Federal Title VI funds, and private sources.

Head of the institution: Dr. Willa J. Tanabe, Dean

Contact officer: Edgar A. Porter, Associate Dean

School of Hawaiian, Asian and Pacific Studies
University of Hawaii at Manoa
Moore Hall 315
1890 East-West Road
Honolulu HI 96822
USA
Tel: (1-808) 956-8922
Fax: (1-808) 956-6345
e-mail • wjtanals@hawaii.edu
URL • http://www2.hawaii.edu.shaps

Programs and Area Centers:
Asian Studies Program
University of Hawaii at Manoa
Moore Hall 320
1890 East-West Road
Honolulu HI 96822
USA
Tel: (1-808) 956-9708
Fax: (1-808) 956-6345
e-mail • rtrimil@hawaii.edu
Chair: Prof. Ricardo Trimillos

Buddhist Studies Program
University of Hawaii at Manoa
Moore Hall 222
1890 East-West Road
Honolulu HI 96822
USA
Tel: (1-808) 956-4728
Fax: (1-808) 956-6345
Director: Prof. Nancy Dowling

Center for Chinese Studies
University of Hawaii at Manoa
Moore Hall 417
1890 East-West Road
Honolulu HI 96822
USA
Tel: (1-808) 956-6083
Fax: (1-808) 956-2682
e-mail • china@hawaii.edu
Director: Prof. Roger Ames

Center for Hawaiian Studies
University of Hawaii at Manoa
Hawaiian Studies Building, Room 209A
2645 Dole St.
Honolulu HI 96822
USA
Tel: (1-808) 973-0989
Fax: (1-808) 973-0988
e-mail • chsuhm@hawaii.edu
Director: Prof. Haunani-Kay Trask

Center for Japanese Studies
University of Hawaii at Manoa
Moore Hall 216
1890 East-West Road
Honolulu HI 96822
USA
Tel: (1-808) 956-2665
Fax: (1-808) 956-2666
e-mail • sharonam@hawaii.edu
Director: Prof. Sharon Minichiello

Center for Korean Studies
1881 East-West Road
Honolulu, HI 96822
USA
Voice: (1-808) 956-7041
Fax: (1-808) 956-2213
e-mail • lchung@hawaii.edu
Director: Prof. Chung H. Lee

Center for Pacific Islands Studies
University of Hawaii at Manoa
Moore Hall 215
1890 East-West Road
Honolulu HI 96822
USA
Tel: (1-808) 956-7700
Fax: (1-808) 956-7053
e-mail • kiste@hawaii.edu
Director: Prof. Robert C. Kiste

Center for Philippine Studies
University of Hawaii at Manoa
Moore Hall 416
1890 East-West Road
Honolulu HI 96822
USA
Tel: (1-808) 956-6085
Fax: (1-808) 956-2682
e-mail • marissa@hawaii.edu
Director: Prof. Belinda Aquino

Center for Russia in Asia
University of Hawaii at Manoa
Moore Hall 416
1890 East-West Road
Honolulu HI 96822
USA
Tel: (1-808) 956-2663
Fax: (1-808) 956-6345
e-mail • valliant@hawaii.edu
Director: Dr. Robert Valliant

Center for South Asian Studies
University of Hawaii at Manoa
Moore Hall 416
1890 East-West Road
Honolulu HI 96822
USA
Tel: (1-808) 956-6277
Fax: (1-808) 956-2682
e-mail • csas@hawaii.edu
Associate Director: Dr. Mary Chin

Center for Southeast Asian Studies
University of Hawaii at Manoa
Moore Hall 412
1890 East-West Road
Honolulu HI 96822
USA
Tel: (1-808) 956-62676
Fax: (1-808) 956-2682
e-mail • cseas@hawaii.edu
Director: Prof. Stephen O'Harrow

University of New Mexico

New Mexico U.S.-Japan Center

Background and objectives: Originally known as the Center for the Study of Japanese Industry & Management of Technology, the Center seeks to enhance U.S. competitiveness and technological leadership through an increased understanding of Japanese management of technology policies and practices, professional exchanges in Japan, and cooperative ventures in research and development with Japanese and U.S. institutions. The Center, established in 1992, has trained over 150 scientists, engineers, and other professionals for future placement in Japanese corporate and government research facilities.

Programs: The Center is one of twelve national participants in the Japan Industry and Technology Management Training Program (JITMT). This training program was established by the federal government in 1991 to provide instruction in such topics as technical Japanese, comparative U.S. and Japanese technology management methods, Japanese public policy, and Japanese culture and history. The Center's programs offer participants from New Mexico's national laboratories (Los Alamos, Sandia, and Phillips Laboratories) and the high-tech business community opportunities to learn to read and analyze Japanese scientific and technical information, live and work in Japan, and learn about Japanese public and private policies and practices to manage technology. In addition to its Technical Japanese Program, the Center has an Internship Preparation and Placement Program that emphasizes the skills necessary to take an internship in a Japanese company or laboratory. The Center also provides funding and collaborates with the Japan Policy Research Institute (San Diego, California), the Japan Information Access Project (Washington, D.C.), and the Microelectronics and Computer Technology Corporation (Austin, Texas) to disseminate important and timely information on Japan and to conduct conferences, workshops, and other public events. The Center's own research focuses on issues such as comparative technology transfer practices in the U.S. and Japan, the post-Cold War security regime in the Asia-Pacific, strategies and methods to access Japanese science and technology information, and Japanese industrial policy. Research results are communicated through conferences, workshops, symposiums, and publications.

Publications: The Center publishes a quarterly newsletter. JPRI and JIAP also have their own extensive publications.

Funding sources: The Center's funding comes from the federal government and the University.

Staffing: The Center has six full-time and four part-time employees, plus a number of graduate students working as research assistants either directly for the Center or on University departmental research projects funded by the Center. Most of the staff is administrative, but two staff members also conduct research.

Notes: There is a related organization called the Asian Technology Information Program (ATIP), which was originally a joint project of the Center and NIST (National Institute for Standards and Technology), but is now a nonprofit organization. ATIP tracks S&T trends and developments across Asia and publishes them in electronic form on its Internet site. Its headquarters are in Tokyo, with local offices in a number of other Asian countries. Wallace Lopez, Director of the Japan Center, is the U.S. contact for ATIP.

Head of the institution: Wallace H. Lopez, Director

New Mexico U.S.-Japan Center
1601 Randolph Road SE
Suite 200 South
Albuquerque, NM 8710
USA
Tel: (1-505) 277-1490
Fax: (1-505) 766-5112
e-mail • info@nmjc.org
URL • http://www.nmjc.org

University of Oregon

Center for Asian and Pacific Studies

Background and objectives: The Center for Asian and Pacific Studies at the University of Oregon was created in 1987 by the Oregon State Legislature to coordinate the activities and research of several academic programs and of more than ninety faculty members concerned with the Asia-Pacific region. The Center aims to produce competent professionals and informed citizens who understand and work effectively in the region. The Center emphasizes the need to understand the cultural foundations as a base for interpreting the changes taking place in the region. The Center emphasizes the combining of area with functional studies, and works very closely with international business and international studies.

Programs: The Center serves the state of Oregon and the Pacific Northwest through academic program development, research, and public service activities. These activities are facilitated by membership in the Northwest Regional Consortium for Southeast Asian Studies.

Academic programs include the Asia Studies Program, East Asian languages and literature, anthropology, history, policy and management, environmental studies, and public planning.

The Center organizes seminars and workshops to inform the community about major trends and developments in the Asia-Pacific region. "Interwoven Identities: Southeast Asia in the Greater Asia-Pacific Community" was the theme of the 7th biennial conference of the Northwest Regional Consortium for Southeast Asian Studies, held in April 1997.

In February 1997, the Center helped develop and host a Portland-based conference for teachers of Japanese immersion programs at the K-12 level. Over seventy-five teachers attended from throughout the U.S. to work together on curriculum development, teaching methodologies, resource identification, and planning for future collaborative projects.

The Freeman Public Lecture Series, in its second year, will focus on "China 2000: Perspectives on a Rising Superpower." In May 1997, the Center hosted a seminar on the political, social, economic, and international relations changes anticipated as Hong Kong again becomes a part of China.

The Center also builds educational connections with institutions in the countries of the region with growing economic and cultural links with Oregon and the Pacific Northwest. The Center is particularly concerned with developing educational opportunities that benefit the state of Oregon and the Pacific Northwest. These opportunities include intensive summer programs in Asian languages and cultural traditions as well as managerial programs. The Center participates annually in the popular Asian Celebration sponsored by Asian American groups in the local community. An annual film festival sponsored by the Center features many of the best recent films from Asian and Pacific countries. A partnership with Lewis and Clark College, a private liberal arts college in Portland, enhances statewide understanding of Asia and the Pacific.

The Center also places a strong emphasis on the innovative teaching of Asian languages, facilitated by the presence of the technologically equipped Yamada Language Center. Japanese, Chinese, Korean, Indonesian, Thai, and Vietnamese are offered. The Yamada Language Center offers professionally developed pedagogical training materials to those interested in self-study in other languages such as Pohnpeian, Kosraen, Yapese, Tagalog, and Burmese.

Publications: The Asian Studies Program has several publications focused on traditional Chinese and Japanese culture, while the Southeast Asian Studies Program published in 1997 a 200-page book of marketing and agribusiness case-studies focused on businesses in Oregon and Thailand. In 1997, the Center will publish a bulletin on the Pacific Islands, focusing on successful efforts in higher education to teach and conduct research about this diverse region. Also in 1997, the Center will begin publishing an academic journal on international collaborative higher education programs, based on the eight-year-old Vietnam-University of Oregon Sister Universities Project.

Staffing: The Center for Asian and Pacific Studies is directed by an eight-member Advisory Board and draws upon more than sixty faculty members. The Center houses approximately twelve visiting scholars per year and also provides office space for the Thai-, Vietnamese-, and Indonesian-language staff. The staff includes assistant director Sandi Leavitt, research coordinator Lori O'Hollaren, outreach coordinator Jon Labrousse, Asian studies/student coordinator Miyuki Taguchi, and office coordinator Steve Crowe.

Funding sources: The center is supported by the state of Oregon and the University of Oregon, primarily through faculty appointments in the various departments and colleges. Some state funding is granted for basic infrastructure, staffing, and small-scale outreach projects. Most projects sponsored by the Center are collaborative, interdisciplinary projects supported through the efforts and funds of many organizations, both on and off campus. Outside funding is generally sought for larger-scale projects for teaching innovations, research, and outreach.

Head of the institution: Dr. Stephen Durrant, Director

Contact officer: Ms. Sandi Leavitt, Assistant Director

Center for Asian and Pacific Studies
University of Oregon
110 Gerlinger Hall
Eugene, OR 97403-1246
USA
Tel: (1-541) 346-5087
Fax: (1-541) 346-0802
e-mail • caps@darkwing.uoregon.edu
URL • http://darkwing.uoregon.edu/~caps

University of San Francisco

Center for the Pacific Rim

Background and objectives: The Center for the Pacific Rim (CPR), founded in 1988, seeks to foster American understanding of the Asian Pacific and promote communication among the nations of the Pacific Rim. The Center is located at the University of San Francisco, a Jesuit institution established in 1855.

Programs: The Center administers interdisciplinary Pacific Rim Studies programs for graduate and undergraduate students; organizes international conferences, lectures, and seminars; and conducts outreach activities for the San Francisco Bay area. The Ricci Institute, a research arm of the Center, was founded by the Society for Jesus in 1984 for the study of Chinese-Western cultural history. Directed by its founder, Edward J. Malatesta , S.J., it houses a 70,000 volume Chinese library. The Institute is currently developing an electronic database on the 21st Century Roundtable for the History of Christianity in China, to include data on all known sources of information regarding the history of Christianity in China. The Center also invites Visiting Fellows each year to participate in research projects. Ongoing projects include "The Greater China Project" and "Computer-Assisted Instruction in Teaching Japanese as a Second Language." The Center also sponsors or co-sponsors ongoing seminars and lectures for the business and civic communities. Recent speakers include Winston Lord, Assistant U.S. Secretary of State for East Asian and Pacific Affairs, on "Asia and the U.S.- A Dynamic Relationship," Tommy Koh, Singapore's Ambassador-at-large and Executive Secretary of the Asia Pacific Economic Cooperation (APEC) Pacific Business Forum, on "The Relevance of APEC to the Business Community," Ambassador Burton Levin on "The China Triangle: Hong Kong, Taiwan and Mainland China: Opportunities and Challenges for the Future," and Chalmers Johnson on "The Empowerment of Asia."

The CPR administers the Master of Arts in Asia Pacific Liberal Studies, the only evening/weekend graduate degree of its kind in the U.S. It is a 23-month interdisciplinary program that places East Asian economics, politics, history, art, religion, and language (Mandarin Chinese, Japanese and Korean) in the context of the Pacific Rim.

Funding sources: The CPR's programs and activities are funded through tuition, grants from foundations such as the Union Bank Foundation, Henry Luce Foundation, and the Japan Foundation, and individual gifts.

Staffing: Including the Ricci Institute, CPR has a total of six full-time staff , two part-time clerical-administrative assistants, one permanent research fellow in residence, and an annual visiting position for teaching and research (The Kiriyama Chair for Pacific Rim Studies). Faculty from various academic departments also teach in the Center.

Notes: The Center and Ricci Institute have two endowed chairs: The Kiriyama Chair for Pacific Rim Studies and a chair in Chinese-Western Cultural History.

Head of the institution: Dr. Barbara K. Bundy, Founding Executive Director

Center for the Pacific Rim
University of San Francisco
2130 Fulton Street, LM 200
San Francisco, CA 94117-1080
USA
Tel: (1-415) 422-6357
Fax: (1-415) 422-5933
e-mail: pacrim@usfca.edu

University of Southern California

Center for International Studies

Background and objectives: The Center for International Studies (CIS), established by the School of International Relations (SIR) at the University of Southern California in 1986, promotes research and critical debate on theoretical questions and policy issues in world affairs. Led by SIR's faculty, the Center also engages faculty and students of political science, economics, history, sociology, business, and law.

Programs: During 1994-96, the Center's programs included a series of seminars on "Rethinking Security" to compare international systems throughout history and lessons from Cold War definitions of "security"; a series of four sessions on International Environmental Policy; seven sessions of the Southern California Workshop on Political and Economic Liberalization in which political scientists, economists, and social scientists from throughout California joined with invited experts from elsewhere in the United States as well as Europe and Latin America to discuss the politics of economic reform and the economics of political transitions; and a major international conference on "George Kennan, the Cold War, and the Future of American Foreign Policy." For the fifth year, the Center hosted *International Organization,* one of the most prestigious academic journals in the field of international relations. During 1995-96, CIS organized an "Editor's Choice" seminar series to bring contributing authors to meet with CIS members and associates and USC graduate students. Scholars spoke on such issues as the future of the welfare state, foreign direct investment and demands for protectionism, and culture's influence on international leaders—issues also being highlighted in *International Organization.*

The Center also conducts its traditional core activities such as providing research assistantship funding and furnishing substantial dissertation fellowship support for International Relations graduate students; funding the research of visiting research scholars at the post-doctoral level; and organizing a variety of research colloquia and special seminars to reflect on emerging trends and major international issues of the day. During 1995-96, some of these academic meetings featured the School of International Relations alumnus Young-Hoon Kang, president of Korea's Red Cross and prime minister of the Republic of Korea from 1988-90, who talked about the future of Korea; former Canadian Consul General to Los Angeles, Dennis Browne, who examined the referendum in Quebec over whether to secede from Canada; and Stephan Haggard of the University of California, San Diego's School of International Relations and Pacific Studies, who discussed the effects of economic conditions on transitions to democracy.

The CIS visiting scholar program brings promising scholars to the USC campus to collaborate with faculty on research projects, assist in teaching and leading discussion sessions with students, and participate in developing the programs of the Center.

Publications: The Center published *Conversations about Democratization and Economic Reform* (1996), a book that highlights the key questions and ideas explored in CIS's year-long workshop on political and economic liberalization. It examines both the tensions and the supportive relationships between capitalist development and democratic politics.

Staffing: The Center's core staff includes a director, assistant director for administration, director of public affairs, coordinator of program and events, coordinator of microcomputer information systems, and an executive assistant.

Funding sources: The Center's main support comes from the Harris Endowment. CIS has also received recent grants from the Ford Foundation, the North-South Center of the University of Miami, and General Service Foundation.

Heads of the institution:
Dr. Abraham F. Lowenthal, 1992-1997, Director

Dr. Laurie Brand, 1997-1998, Director

**Center for International Studies
School of International Relations
University of Southern California
Los Angeles, CA 90089-0037
USA
Tel: (1-213) 740-0800
Fax: (1-213) 740-1070
e-mail • brand@usc.edu**

University of Southern California

The Center for Multiethnic and Transnational Studies

Background and objectives: The Center for Multiethnic and Transnational Studies (CMTS) was founded in 1992 to analyze the social and political impact of the world's changing demographics, especially the patterns of interaction among people of different national, ethnic, racial, gender, and religious backgrounds. In particular, the Center encourages reflection on the role of present-day Los Angeles as a multiethnic city and a player in the transnational communications and commerce network.

Programs: CMTS research explores the connection between the forces of transnationalism, the development of loyalties and allegiances "outside" the traditional nation-state parameters, and multiethnicity, the study of ethnic groups to compare and contrast areas of potential cooperation and conflict management. Recent research has examined the effects of globalization on urban centers, more representative methods of serving the social, economic, spiritual, and political needs of minority groups, and the impact of non-governmental organizations in a diverse world. The Center sponsors both regular meetings and occasional conferences that bring together academic scholars and public figures from large cities from around the world. In a lecture series co-sponsored by USC's Center for Feminist Research and the American Studies Program, CMTS brings notable USC speakers to discuss how multicultural and gender issues can shape the undergraduate curriculum. The first lecture, "Immigration: Curse or Blessing?" was a discussion about the fate of migratory peoples whose movements eschew traditional natural boundaries. This series will also feature "Faculty Roundtables" in which newly hired faculty will present their research and writing. In 1995, together with the Korean Studies Center at California State University, Los Angeles, the CMTS hosted a pre-conference workshop on the trans-Pacific diaspora (e.g., Koreans in Japan and Chinese in Thailand) to analyze the issue from a comparative perspective. The workshop will lead to a scholarly conference in Japan in 1997-98. Another recent public meeting focused on "Rethinking Los Angeles: Can We All Get Along?" and an address by former U.S. Senator Alan Cranston discussing the fate of ethnic minorities in Russia.

Publications: CMTS publishes Occasional Paper Series, which includes "Central Americans in California: Transnational Communities, Economics and Culture," Monograph Paper No. 1 (1996). The Center has also published *Hope and Power In Partnership* (1996), *New Beginning* (1996), and *Community in Crisis: The Korean American Community after the Los Angeles Civil Unrest of April 1992* (1994).

Funding sources: The CMTS is funded through the College of Letters, Arts, and Sciences and through private foundations, such as the Luce Foundation.

Staffing: The Center has a core administrative staff of four. Six full-time resident affiliated scholars work at the Center, along with two to four visiting scholars. In addition, CMTS draws periodically upon USC's rich interdisciplinary faculty and graduate students to conduct research and projects.

Head of the institution: Dr. Michael B. Preston, Director

Contact officer: Dr. H. Eric Schockman, Associate Director

The Center for Multiethnic and Transnational Studies
University of Southern California
Grace Ford Salvatori Hall 344
Los Angeles, CA 90089-1694
USA
Tel: (1-213) 740-1068
Fax: (1-213) 740-5810
e-mail • hschock @mizar.usc.edu
URL • http://www.usc.edu/dept./cmts/cmts-
       homepage.html.

University of Southern California

East Asian Studies Center

Background and objectives: The East Asian Studies Center (EASC), founded in 1975, supports the teaching and research activities of sixty associate faculty members and offers interdisciplinary bachelor's and master's degree programs in East Asian studies.

Programs: The Center sponsors several ongoing research seminars, including the Southern California Japan Seminar, an annual series of five to ten presentations by visiting and local scholars with topics covering a broad range of Japan-related research, as well as conferences on such topics as "Taiwanese Historical and Cultural Studies" and "Continuity and Change: Japan as It Prepares to Enter the 21st Century." The Center also hosts five to ten visiting scholars and associates each year. Its Korean Studies Institute, established in 1995, coordinates the Korean and Korean American Studies Group and hosts annual scholarly conferences on the Korean Diaspora (1995), Korean Literature and Gender (1996), and APEC (1997). EASC also collaborates with its counterpart at UCLA as a Joint National Resource Center funded by the U.S. Department of Education. The Joint Center (JEASC) sponsors a variety of programs about East Asia for the academic community, secondary schools, and the general public, including an annual summer institute for educators and the educational website, "East Asia-On-Line." The USC East Asia library has approximately 70,000 volumes; the Korean Heritage Library, supported by an $820,000 endowment, has the largest annual acquisitions budget of any university-based Korean collection in the United States.

Publications: None.

Funding sources: EASC's programs are supported by University funds and grants from the U.S. Department of Education, the U.S. Institute of Peace, the Social Science Research Council, the Japan Foundation, the Korea Foundation, the Korea Research Foundation, Daesan Foundation, and Asia Society.

Staffing: The Center's staff is made up of two full-time and one part-time professionals, and is supported by four research assistants and two student assistants.

Head of the institution: Dr. Otto Schnepp, Director

Contact officer: Mr. Christopher Evans, Program Coordinator

East Asian Studies Center
Taper Hall of Humanities, Room 331M
University of Southern California
Los Angeles, CA 90089-4351
USA
Tel: (1-213) 740-2991
Fax: (1-213) 740-8409
e-mail • easc@usc.edu
URL • http://www.usc.edu/dept/EASC

University of Southern California

International Business Education and Research Program

Background and objectives: The International Business Education and Research (IBEAR) Program serves as the international business center of the School of Business Administration at the University of Southern California. IBEAR administers an international MBA program, executive programs, a research program, and the University's federally-funded Center for International Business Education and Research (CIBEAR).

Programs: The IBEAR MBA Program is an intensive twelve-month program in international management with an emphasis on Pacific Rim business leading to the USC MBA degree. Participants are mid-career managers with an average of ten years of full-time business, government, and/or post-graduate academic experience. Through the Visiting Expert Seminar Program, IBEAR brings many Pacific Rim experts to campus annually. Recent Visiting Experts include Toyoo Gyohten, Chairman of the Board of Directors, Bank of Tokyo; Cao Yuanzheng, Deputy Director, Research Institute on Economic Systems, State Commission for Restructuring Economic Systems, Beijing; Chavarat Charnvirakul, Chairman, Advisory Board, Sino-Thai Group of Companies and Former Deputy Finance Minister, Ministry of Finance, Thailand; Clyde Prestowitz, President, Economic Strategy Institute; Ronnie Chan, Chairman, Hang Lung Development Co., Hong Kong; Adlai E. Stevenson, President, U.S. National Committee for Pacific Economic Cooperation; Gordon Redding, Director, University of Hong Kong Business School; and Gareth Chang, President, Hughes International.

IBEAR's non-degree Executive Programs provide intensive education on international and Pacific Rim-related issues. The Asia/Pacific Business Outlook is an annual three-day conference co-sponsored by IBEAR and the U.S. Department of Commerce. The ninth annual conference in 1996 attracted over 400 U.S. and foreign executives. Participants choose from 125 country outlooks, country and industry workshops, and functional business seminars, and have the opportunity to interact with over 100 academic, business, and government experts including the Senior Commercial Officers from each U.S. Embassy in Asia.

In its Pacific Rim Management Programs, IBEAR offers three-day seminars on the economic, political, and social environments of selected Pacific Rim countries. Its twelfth annual seminar series in 1996 featured programs on Japan, China, and Southeast Asia. IBEAR's half-day Critical Issues Forums bring together experts and members of the business and academic communities to discuss topics of pressing importance relating to Asia and the Americas. IBEAR also offers custom-designed international executive programs for corporations in the U.S. and abroad.

IBEAR also sponsors occasional research conferences. IBEAR is also responsible for administering the USC Center for International Business Education and Research (CIBEAR), one of twenty-five in the United States funded by the U.S. Department of Education. The Center oversees thirty University-wide teaching and research projects on international business, including MBA courses that have field-study components in Asia and Europe, international internships for MBA students, research on U.S.-China technology transfer, and intensive language programs in Chinese, Japanese, and Korean.

Publications: IBEAR actively sponsors international business research. USC faculty members are currently conducting CIBEAR-funded research on topics such as international communications liberalization, modeling worldwide takeoff and growth of new products, and developing and testing information technology for global operations. The proceedings of three IBEAR Research Conferences have been published by Oxford University Press: *Small Firms in Global Competition* (1994), *Technology Transfer in International Business* (1991), and *Trade Policy and Corporate Business Decisions* (1989).

Funding sources: The IBEAR program is funded through professional program fees, tuition revenues, registration fees, and corporate and alumni donations.

Staffing: IBEAR is staffed by eight full-time employees as well as a number of part-time student workers. Twenty-three faculty members currently head CIBEAR-funded research projects.

Heads of the institution:

Dr. Richard Drobnick, Vice Provost for International Affairs, Executive Director, IBEAR, Director, CIBEAR

Dr. Jack Lewis, Director, IBEAR

Ms. Susan Bradforth, Associate Director, IBEAR Executive Programs

Mr. John Windler, Associate Director, CIBEAR

IBEAR Program
School of Business Administration
University of Southern California
Los Angeles, CA 90089-1421
USA
Tel: (1-213) 740-7140
Fax: (1-213) 740-7559
e-mail • ibear@usc.edu
URL • http://www.usc.edu/dept/IBEAR

University of Southern California

Southern California Studies Center

Background and objectives: The Southern California Studies Center (SC2) was established at the University of Southern California in 1995 as an interdisciplinary initiative to monitor and analyze environmental, political, economic, and cultural changes in Southern California.

Programs: The Center promotes research on Southern California through the construction of a centralized data source that will expand existing campus capacities for information storage and retrieval, and data processing and imaging. The Center is collaborating with the College of Letters, Arts, and Sciences to establish a central Geographical Information Systems (GIS) Laboratory on campus and with the Leavey Library's "Information System for Los Angeles" (ISLA) and with University Computing Services to create a "one-step" data archive for Southern California.

In 1996, SC2 organized the presidential roundtable on "The State of Southern California," the first in an annual series of public events, to provide an overview of Southern Californian society, politics, economy, and culture. As part of its mission to provide a home for advanced urban and regional studies on the USC campus, the Center also organizes a workshop series on the theme of the origins and potential of the "Los Angeles School" to explore the meanings of Southern California's urbanism.

Currently, the Center is working to produce a curriculum development plan for Southern California studies.

Publications: The Center aims to publish a regular series entitled *Metro Trends* (MT), a summary of key indicators of regional "well-being" in Southern California. In September 1996, the Center published *Rethinking Los Angeles*, a compendium of a year-long public lecture series held on campus during 1993-94 in response to the 1992 civil unrest.

Funding sources: The Center's core funding comes from the College of Letters, Arts, and Sciences at USC.

Staffing: SC2 has a director, an assistant director, and a full-time employee.

Head of the institution: Dr. Michael J. Dear, Director

Contact officer: Mr. Richard Parks, Assistant Director

Southern California Studies Center
University of Southern California
Los Angeles, CA 90089-1696
USA
Tel: (1-213) 740-5303
Fax: (1-213) 740-5302

University of Washington

APEC Study Center

Background and objectives: The APEC Study Center at the University of Washington was established in 1994 in response to the APEC Leaders Education Initiative introduced by President Clinton in Seattle during the APEC Summit in November 1993. The mission of the Center is to stimulate, facilitate, and coordinate interdisciplinary, multilateral policy-related research on regional and global issues that affect APEC member nations.

Programs: The APEC Study Center is engaged in three major programs. The APEC Education Network (EduNet), an Internet-based interactive network linking APEC Study Centers, partner institutions, businesses, and governments in the eighteen APEC member economies, is being developed to facilitate and intensify collaborative research and teaching. Former Secretary of State Warren Christopher and Philippine Foreign Minister Domingo Siazon formally inaugurated the EduNet at the Manila APEC Ministerial meeting in November 1996, and launched its first project on Integrated Coastal Management.

Future plans call for extending this network to form the basis for a Trans-Pacific Internet University. The APEC Financial Markets project has produced two conferences and two publications. The most recent meeting generated a proposal to create an Infrastructure Mediation Center, a new international organization to facilitate the transfer of capital to fund Asian infrastructure projects. The project on Leadership and International Institutions: APEC and Its Global Context addresses the interdependence of continuing economic growth and stability and political and security arrangements in the Asia-Pacific region and the world. Proceedings of two conferences organized under this project were published in 1997. This project, which includes the participation of leading scholars and research institutions in Asia and the United States, expanded to include European participants with a conference in Brussels in 1997.

Publications: The APEC Study Center has published *Financial Market Regulation in the Asia-Pacific Region: Legal and Policy Issues* (1995), a report on the first APEC Financial Markets conference, and published *From APEC to Xanadu: Creating a Viable Community in the Post-Cold War Pacific* in 1997. "America, Japan, and APEC: The Challenge of Leadership in the Asia-Pacific" and "Security Regulation in the APEC Countries," two of the Center's research works, have also been published in special issues of the *NBR Analysis* (1995) and *Pacific Rim Law & Policy Journal* (1995), respectively.

Funding sources: Initial funding for the Center is provided by the University of Washington and the Henry M. Jackson Foundation. Specific projects are supported by corporate and foundation sponsorship, including GE Capital and the Ogasawara Foundation.

Staffing: The Center has three full-time researchers and project staff, one administrative staff, and hosts student interns and visiting scholars.

Head of the institution: Prof. Donald C. Hellmann, Director

Contact officers:
Ms. Diane Adachi, Programs

Mr. Chris Coward, APEC Education Network

**APEC Study Center
University of Washington
120 Thomson Hall
Box 353690
Seattle, WA 98195
USA
Tel: (1-206) 543-0663
Fax: (1-206) 616-1978
e-mail • apecctr@u.washington.edu
URL • http://www.apec.org**

University of Washington

Center for International Business Education and Research

Background and objectives: The Center for International Business Education and Research (CIBER) at the University of Washington has focused its educational programs on global competitive issues. CIBER's goals are to become a national and international center for excellence in international business education, and to act as a catalyst for the expansion of international business education and research programs in other colleges and universities in the Northwest.

Programs: CIBER has developed academic, research, and outreach activities to serve both students and businesses, which include the International Management Fellows Program, an intensive twenty-four-month program in which MBA students integrate their graduate courses with advanced language and area studies, foreign study, and an overseas business internship; the Certificate in International Studies in Business, an undergraduate program designed to encourage students to combine foreign language and area studies with their general business courses; the MBA Exchange Programs, through which the Center selects students for the existing foreign exchange programs and develops new exchange relationships with prominent business schools throughout the world such as the Management School, Shanghai Jiao Tong University (People's Republic of China), Hong Kong University of Science and Technology (Hong Kong), International University of Japan (Japan), Instituto Tecnologico y Estudios Superiores de Monterrey (Mexico), etc. CIBER incorporates global competitive issues in the business core curriculum by providing funding for faculty who are involved in developing new international business courses and new materials for existing courses. The Center also hosts speakers who offer critical insights about the changes in the world of international business. The 1996 Global Business Forum has recently discussed such issues as "How to Do a Deal Internationally?" "Doing Business in the Russian Far East," and "Global Expansion Strategies." CIBER's research programs include Research Colloquium on Global Business, an interdisciplinary faculty research seminar that includes participants from business, international studies, law, engineering, and other professional schools, as well as representatives from the business community, and that stimulates applied research on the topics and problems that companies face in a global setting. The Center also provides research and travel grants to faculty and doctoral students whose projects improve the understanding of global competition and foreign business systems. Funding has been provided for research on strategic alliances, Japanese manufacturing practices, and management control systems in international companies, among others. CIBER's outreach programs include the International Business Certificate Program, which is designed to inform and train business managers in the specifics of international competitive environment and foreign business systems and to encourage companies to pursue international business plans and expansion; and the Pacific Northwest International Business Workshops for the international business faculty at other colleges and universities in the Pacific Northwest.

Publications: No information provided.

Funding sources: CIBER is funded by a grant from the United States Department of Education, by the School of Business Administration at the University of Washington, and by private donations.

Staffing: The Center's staff is made up of one executive director, one faculty director, one managing director, and one program assistant.

Head of the institution: Prof. Douglas MacLachlan, Executive Director

Contact officer: Ms. Elizabeth A. C. O'Shea, Managing Director

Center for International Business Education and Research (CIBER)
Business School
P.O. Box 353200
University of Washington
Seattle, WA 98195-353200
USA
Tel: (1-206) 685-3432
Fax: (1-206) 543-6872
e-mail • uwciber@u.washington.edu
URL • http://weber.u.washington.edu/~ciberweb

Washington Council on International Trade

Background and objectives: Founded in 1973, the Washington Council on International Trade is a private, nonprofit association that supports public policies favorable to expanded trade between the United States and its trading partners. With support from Washington State's large international trade sector, the Council strives to illuminate key trade issues affecting the state's businesses and communities.

Programs: The Washington Council analyzes and speaks on major public policy issues affecting international trade and economic affairs, which include NAFTA, GATT, and the MFN status for China, and also such issues as intellectual property piracy, immigration, infrastructure, education, agricultural policy, fast track, protectionism, export bans, and so on. In addition, the Council maintains relations with national organizations, government agencies in trade-policy fields, foreign diplomatic representatives, and counterpart organizations abroad to provide sound trade policy information to the state's trade interests, and to inform decision makers of critical trade sector concerns, based on support for trade liberalization. The organization sponsors meetings for its members with trade and economic specialists and routinely distributes to its members information on major trade policy issues and on bilateral relations with major U.S. trade partners. The Council works with local and national media to promote a balanced view of the trade field. In the summertime, the Council conducts an annual Seminar on International Trade for Teachers to provide deeper understanding of the international economic environment. This Seminar program emphasizes the principles of economics and international trade, brings guest speakers from the international business community, and organizes visits to port facilities and international businesses operating in Washington State.

Publications: The Council publishes *The Washington State Trade Picture*, an annual pamphlet highlighting the year's most important trade facts for the state of Washington, and *Issues Watchlist*, an annual booklet featuring key trade-related issues likely to confront policy makers and public opinion leaders. The Council also publishes *Tools of the Trade*, a directory of international trade organizations in Washington State.

Funding sources: Funding comes primarily from private sector membership dues from corporations such as Boeing Company, SEAFIRST, the Port of Seattle, and Microsoft Corporation.

Staffing: The Council has two researchers and one administrative staff member.

Head of the institution: Ms. Patricia J. Davis, President

Washington Council on International Trade
2615 Fourth Avenue, Suite 350
Seattle, WA 98121-1253
USA
Tel: (1-206) 443-3826
Fax: (1-206) 443-3828
e-mail • wcit@eskimo.com
URL • http://www.eskimo.com/uWCIT

World Affairs Councils

Background and objectives: World Affairs Councils (WACs) are nonprofit, nonpartisan organizations based on the principle of open membership. The national system, started in 1918, currently consists of eighty-five councils and fifteen affiliated organizations. The councils collectively have about 73,000 individual members and are supported by 3,060 companies and organizations. Including the national affiliates in the total, the system has more than 115,000 individual members. WACs aim to improve American awareness and education in international affairs, empower citizens to participate in the national debate on world affairs, stimulate communities to interact effectively in the global economy, enrich people's lives by enhancing their international perspective, develop international awareness among America's young people, and build citizen support for the U.S. role in the world.

Programs: All WACs sponsor speakers' programs on international affairs. Many also sponsor business roundtables, school programs, teachers' workshops, model UN sessions for high school students, a citizens' world affairs discussion series, young professionals programs, international exchanges and festivals, travel programs, international town meetings, local newspaper columns, publications series, and radio and television programs. The national office organizes an annual conference, international study tours for council leaders, Washington tours for members, and national projects.

Funding sources: WACs are supported by dues, corporate sponsorships, grants, in-kind donations, and local fund-raising events.

Los Angeles World Affairs Council

Background and objectives: The Los Angeles World Affairs Council (LAWAC) is a nonprofit, nonpartisan, educational and civic organization. Founded in 1953, the Los Angeles World Affairs Council is an important Southern California forum for major statements by international leaders, policy makers, and experts from the United States and other countries. The Council has more than 9,000 active members.

Programs: The Los Angeles World Affairs Council's main activities are luncheon and dinner meetings, at which speakers share their perspectives on important international issues. The Council presents more than forty of these events annually, each typically involving 100 to 2,000 people. Special programs are also arranged for particular constituencies, such as corporate members, major donors, and participants in the student program.

The Los Angeles World Affairs Council also offers tours that feature private, substantive briefings at U.S. embassies and foreign ministries abroad, typically involving discussion of social, economic, and political issues in the host country.

Publications: The Los Angeles World Affairs Council publishes *The World Affairs Journal*, a monthly journal, and *The World Affairs Journal: A Compendium*, an annual publication featuring transcripts of all speeches held throughout the Council's season.

Mr. J. Curtis Mack II
President
Los Angeles World Affairs Council
911 Wilshire Boulevard, Suite 1730
Los Angeles, CA 90017
USA
Tel: (1-213) 628-2333
Fax: (1-213) 628-1057
e-mail • worldaffairs@lawac.org

World Affairs Council of Northern California

Background and objectives: The World Affairs Council of Northern California, a nonprofit, nonpartisan membership organization, educates and informs citizens of Northern California about the importance and relevance of international affairs. The Council seeks to provoke thought, to elicit opinion, to generate interest in foreign affairs issues, giving voice to its members' opinions, interests and concerns. Founded in 1947, the Council, with over 11,000 members throughout the Bay Area, is now the largest foreign affairs organization in the United States.

Programs: The Council offers some 250 programs a year on important foreign policy issues. The Schools Program serves over 2,500 schoolteachers throughout Northern California by assisting them with resources, curricula, guides, and other materials to use in K-12 classrooms. The Council provides 3,000 schoolteachers each year (reaching over 50,000 students in the region) with information on world events.

The Council's Bay Area International Forum (IF) is a group of Bay Area business executives who convene for private, "off the record" meetings with leaders from around the world. The IF usually sponsors one or two programs per month on topics ranging from a review of the Russian presidential elections to a North Beach Festival Walking Tour.

Ambassador David J. Fischer
President
World Affairs Council of Northern California
312 Sutter Street, Suite 200
San Francisco, CA 94108
USA
Tel: (1-415) 982-2541
Fax: (1-415) 982-5028
e-mail • wacpres@netcom.com

World Affairs Council of Orange County

Background and objectives: The World Affairs Council of Orange County, founded in 1971, is a nonprofit, nonpartisan, educational and civic organization with an active membership of more than 2,000 leading individuals and companies in the Orange County area. The Council serves as an international forum, featuring national leaders, policy makers, and experts from the United States and abroad.

Programs: The Council hosts approximately fourteen dinner meetings annually, featuring notable speakers. Five to six special programs are arranged each year on specific issues of concern to the board, corporate members, and local universities. The Council also offers an annual diplomatic tour featuring private, in-depth briefings at U.S. embassies, foreign ministries, and international business organizations overseas.

Publications: The Council publishes *The Orange County Globe* three to four times a year. Background briefings on international issues are provided to corporate and diplomatic members.

Sir Eldon Griffiths
Executive Director
World Affairs Council of Orange County
P.O. Box 7587
Laguna Niguel, CA 92607
USA
Tel: (1-714) 363-0735
Fax: (1-714) 363-1243

World Affairs Council of San Diego

Background and objectives: The World Affairs Council of San Diego, established in 1954, is a nonprofit, nonpartisan membership organization that provides educational opportunities in international affairs and foreign cultures, and activities that would have an impact on U.S. foreign policy.

Programs: The Council hosts monthly debates, panels, and forums on important international topics. It also conducts two outreach programs. The World Youth Education Program, which principally targets high school and university students, provides information on international affairs for the San Diego school system, hosts workshops for teachers, and sponsors forums for student discussion. The Young Professionals Forum is dedicated to promoting interests in world affairs and provides social and networking events for students and professionals of all ages.

Publications: The Council publishes the *Communiqué*, a monthly newsletter and calendar of events.

Mr. Jim Taft
Executive Director
World Affairs Council of San Diego
1250 Sixth Avenue, Suite 230
San Diego, CA 92101
USA
Tel: (1-619) 235-0111
Fax: (1-619) 235-0204

World Forum of Silicon Valley

Background and objectives: The World Forum of Silicon Valley is a nonprofit, nonpartisan global affairs organization.

The Forum, which began operations in 1987, sponsors lectures and seminars with experts on a wide range of international topics including political, economic, social, environmental, and trade issues. It has over 1,000 individual and more than sixty corporate members.

Programs: Each year the Forum presents twenty-five to thirty programs at breakfast, luncheons, and after-work receptions, as well as the occasional full day or half-day seminars. Programs take place at hotels and community sites in San Jose, Santa Clara, Sunnyvale, and Palo Alto.

Speakers at World Forum events have included former United States Secretary of Defense William Perry; former Secretary of State George Shultz; Malcom S. Forbes, Jr., Editor-In-Chief of *FORBES Magazine* and President & CEO, Forbes, Inc.; Congressman Lee Hamilton, Ranking Minority Member of the House Foreign Affairs Committee; Richard Rosenberg, Chairman, President & CEO, Bank of America; Dr. Andrew Grove, President & CEO, Intel Corporation; and Nobel Peace Prize Winner Oscar Arias, former President of Costa Rica.

Mr. Thomas H. Gewecke
Executive Director
World Forum of Silicon Valley
100 Park Center Plaza, Suite 105
San Jose, CA 95113
USA
Tel: (1-408) 298-8342
Fax: (1-408) 298-0832
e-mail • wldforum@aol.com

Other Western States World Affairs Councils

ARIZONA
Ms. Susan Reiner
Executive Director
World Affairs Council of Arizona
6850 Main Street
Scottsdale, AZ 85251
Tel: (1-602) 945-7750
Fax: (1-602) 970-0294

CALIFORNIA
Mr. Douglas Mooers
President
World Affairs Council of the Monterey Bay Area
P.O. Box 83
Monterey, CA 93942
Tel: (1-408) 626-6213
Fax: (1-408) 643-1846
e-mail • rgrower@edshift.com

Ambassador Frederick Zeder
President
World Affairs Council of the Desert
#2 Stanford Court Drive
Rancho Mirage, CA 92270
Tel: (1-619) 322-7711
Fax: (1-619) 322-7711

Ms. Marylin V. Jacobsen
President
World Affairs Council of Inland Southern California
Riverside Community College
4800 Magnolia Avenue
Riverside, CA 92506
Tel: (1-909) 222-8160
Fax: (1-909) 202-8376
e-mail • marylinj@rccd.cc.ca.us

Ms. Maryl Gray
Acting Executive Director
World Affairs Council of Sacramento
P.O. Box 191046
Sacramento, CA 95819-1046
Tel: (1-916) 278-4570
Fax: (1-916) 641-1281

Ms. Sherri Balsillie
President
World Affairs Council of Sonoma County
P.O. Box 1433
Santa Rosa, CA 95402
Tel: (1-707) 573-6014
Fax: (1-707) 579-2059
e-mail • wacsc@am.net

Ms. Cynthia Cooke
Executive Director
World Affairs Council of Ventura County
3125 Hillcrest Dr.
Westlake Village, CA 91362
Tel: (1-805) 449-9953
Fax: (1-805) 449-9943

COLORADO
Dr. Loren Thompson
Executive Director
Colorado Springs World Affairs Council
P.O. Box 608
Colorado Springs, CO 80906
Tel: (1-719) 579-8443
Fax: (1-719) 579-8443

Ms. Kyle Reno (IIE)/ Executive Director
Mr. Steve Seifert (WAC)/Program Director
IIE/Denver World Affairs Council
700 Broadway, Suite 112
Denver, CO 80203
Tel: (1-303) 837-0788
Fax: (1-303) 837-1409
e-mail • kylereno@iie.org

HAWAII
Ms. Diane Peters-Nguyen
Executive Director
Pacific and Asian Affairs Council
633 East-West Road, Building 96-35
Honolulu, HI 96848-1633
Tel: (1-808) 944-7781
Fax: (1-808) 944-7785
e-mail • paac@aloha.net

OREGON
Mr. Jeffrey A. Merkley
Executive Director
World Affairs Council of Oregon
121 SW Salmon, Suite 320
Portland, OR 97204
Tel: (1-503) 274-7488
Fax: (1-503) 274-7489
e-mail • wacouncil@aol.com

TEXAS
Mr. Stuart Holliday
Executive Director
Dallas Council on World Affairs
P.O. Box 420368
Dallas, TX 75258
Tel: (1-214) 748-5663
Fax: (1-214) 747-5662

Mr. Joseph L. Orr
Vice President
Greater Fort Worth Council on World Affairs
1800 Commerce Building
307 West Seventh Street
Fort Worth, TX 76102
Tel: (1-817) 332-3421
Fax: (1-817) 334-0304
e-mail • rpatton@aol.com

Ms. Linda Wuest
Executive Director
Houston World Affairs Council
P.O. Box 981031
Houston, TX 77098-1031
Tel: (1-713) 522-7811
Fax: (1-713) 522-7812

Ms. Barbara Schneider
Executive Director
World Affairs Council of San Antonio
40 N.E. Loop 410, Suite 608
San Antonio, TX 78216
Tel: (1-210) 308-9494
Fax: (1-210) 308-9497
e-mail • wacofsa@aol.com

Dr. Marcus Stadelmann
President
East Texas Council on World Affairs
3900 University Boulevard, University of Texas
Tyler, TX 75799
Tel: (1-903) 566-7412
Fax: (1-903) 566-7377
e-mail • tyvaill@aol.com

WASHINGTON
Dr. Niels Skov
President
Olympia World Affairs Council
4133 Biscay, NW
Olympia, WA 98502
Tel: (1-360) 866-2326
e-mail • dskov@aol.com

Mr. Robert van Leeuwen
Executive Director
World Affairs Council in Seattle
515 Madison Street, Suite 501
Seattle, WA 98104
Tel: (1-206) 682-6986
Fax: (1-206) 682-0811
e-mail • hworlafrs@aol.com

Barbara Kuhn & Jack Daniels
Co-Presidents
World Affairs Council of Tacoma
Bates Technical College
Tacoma, WA 98402
Tel: (1-206) 596-1765
Fax: (1-206) 596-1775

NATIONAL OFFICE
National Council of World Affairs Organizations
1726 M Street, NW, Suite 800
Washington DC 20036-4502
Tel: (1-202) 785-4703
Fax: (1-202) 833-2369
e-mail • ncwao@aol.com

Head of the institution: Dr. Jerry W. Leach, Executive Director

Contact officer: Ms. Cori L. Welbourn, Assistant Executive Director

World Trade Center Association

Background and objectives: The World Trade Center Association (WTCA), a nonpartisan and nonprofit membership organization, was established in 1970 to encourage the expansion of world trade through providing services needed to compete in global markets. World Trade Centers and affiliated associations are located in many major commercial centers around the world. There are 180 WTCs now operating and over 120 more planned. The Association is dedicated to three goals: encouraging mutual assistance and cooperation among members, promoting international business relationships, and fostering increased participation in world trade by industrializing nations. More than 400,000 companies are affiliated with the WTCA's member organizations. There are twelve WTCA offices in the Western United States.

Programs: WTCA benefits to members include office space and clerical support at a local World Trade Center building, meeting and conference facilities, market research assistance, video conference sites, educational seminars and programs on international business, and participation in trade missions and exhibitions.

Most WTCs organize specialized seminars on request. Sponsored by the World Trade Centers Association in cooperation with over 300 World Trade Centers in more than ninety countries, WTCnet helps companies explore new markets, streamline transactions, promote products, and build global networks.

WTCnet services include U.S. government data on foreign trade flows and prices. In conjunction with Dun & Bradstreet Information Services, the WTCA presents the D&B Exporters' Encyclopedia, a global resource for country, market, transportation, regulation, and contact information.

In cooperation with U.S. Department of Commerce STAT-USA, WTCnet connects its members with new trading partners, and the WTCA with Gale Research Inc. offers the World Trade Centers Association World Business Directory containing more than 140,000 worldwide company listings and contact information including WTC members.

The WTC Virtual Trade Fair serves as a multimedia catalog trading hub, streamlining the buying and selling process by helping WTCNET members build networks, and facilitating transactions.

Funding sources: WTCAs are funded through corporate and individual membership dues.

WTCA Western States' Offices

Arizona
World Trade Center Phoenix
201 N. Central Avenue, Suite 2700
Phoenix, AZ 85073
Tel: (1-602) 495-6480 / 495-2199
Fax: (1-602) 253-9488
e-mail • wtcaz@worldnet.att.net

URL • http://www.banet.com/wtcaz/wtcaz.htm
WTCNETWORK: WTCPH@wtca.geis.com

Head of the institution: Mr. Michael R. Grant, President

Contact officer: Mr. Brad Buchholz, Vice President

California
World Trade Center Irvine
1 Park Plaza, Suite 150
Irvine, CA 92714
Tel: (1-714) 724-9822
Fax: (1-714) 752-8723
WTCNETWORK: WTCOC@wtca.geis.com

Head of the institution: Mr. Donald A. Miller, President

Contact officer: Colleen Costello, Director, Membership Services

Greater Los Angeles World Trade Center Association
350 S. Figueroa Street, Suite 172
Los Angeles, CA 90071
Tel: (1-213) 680-1888
Fax: (1-213) 680-1878
WTCNETWORK: WTCLA@wtca.geis.com
e-mail • enter@glawtca.latrade.org

Head of the institution: Mr. Tom Teofilo, President

Contact officer: Ms. Debbie Palmer, Executive Vice President

Greater Los Angeles World Trade Center - Long Beach
One World Trade Center, Suite 295
Long Beach, CA 90831-0295
Tel: (1-310) 495-7070
Fax: (1-310) 495-7071

Head of the institution: Mr. Tom Teofilo, President

Contact officer: Ms. Debbie Palmer, Executive Vice President

World Trade Center Oxnard
300 Esplanade Drive, Suite 2090
Oxnard, CA 93030
Tel: (1-805) 988-1406
Fax: (1-805) 988-1862
WTCNETWORK: WTCOX@wtca.geis.com

Head of the institution: Mr. Gary R. Snyder, Executive Director

Contact officer: Mr. Scott de Ruyter, Manager

World Trade Center Sacramento
917 7th Street
Sacramento, CA 95814
Tel: (1-916) 552-6800
Fax: (1-916) 443-2672

Head of the institution: Mr. Thomas G. Ferrell, Executive Director

World Trade Center San Diego
1250 6th Avenue, Suite 100
San Diego, CA 92101
Tel: (1-619) 685-1450
Fax: (1-619) 685-1460
WTCNETWORK: WTCSD@wtca.geis.com
WTC URL • http://www.wtcsd.com

Head of the instituion: Mr. Robert Plotkin, President

Contact officer: Mr. Hugh Constant, General Manager

World Trade Center of San Francisco, Inc.
345 California Street, 7th Floor
San Francisco, CA 94104
Tel: (1-415) 392-2705
Fax: (1-415) 392-1710
WTCNETWORK: WTCSF@wtca.geis.com
URL • http://www.wtcsf.org

Head of the institution: Amb. Robert Pastorino

Contact officer: Ms. Lei Na, Chief Operating Officer

Nevada World Trade Center, Las Vegas
901 E. Desert Inn Road
Las Vegas, NV 89109
Tel: (1-702) 387-5581 / 329-0901
Fax: (1-702) 893-2339
WTCNETWORK: WTCLV@wtca.geis.com
e-mail • wtclv@wtca.geis.com

Head of the institution: Mrs. Lucinda Badillo, President & CEO

Contact officer: Mr. Leonard S. Shoen, Owner & Chairman

Oregon
World Trade Center Portland
One World Trade Center
121 SW Salmon Street, Suite 250
Portland, OR 97204
Tel: (1-503) 464-8888
Fax: (1-503) 464-8880
WTCNETWORK: WTCPD@wtca.geis.com
URL • http://www.wtcpd.com

Head of the institution: Mr. Charles Allcock, President

Contact officer: Ms. Catherine DeVaul, Association Manager

Washington
World Trade Center Seattle
1301 Fifth Avenue, Suite 2400
Seattle, WA 98101-2603
Tel: (1-206) 389-7265
Fax: (1-206) 624-5689
WTCNETWORK: WTCSE@wtca.geis.com
URL • http://www.pan.ci.seattle.wa.us/
        business/tda/wtchome.htm

Head of the institution: Ms. Rio Howard, Acting Director

Contact officer: Ms. Ellen Wohl, Program Coordinator

World Trade Center Tacoma
3600 Port of Tacoma Road
Suite 309
Tacoma, WA 98424
Tel: (1-206) 383-9474
Fax: (1-206) 926-0384
WTCNETWORK: WTCTA@wtca.geis.com

Head of the institution: Mrs. Constance Bacon, Executive Director

Index by Institution

Academy of Macroeconomic Research of the State Planning Commission, *China*, 3

Academia Sinica, *Taiwan:* Institute of Economics, 95; Institute of European and American Studies, 96; Sun Yat-Sen Institute for Social Sciences and Philosophy, 97

American Graduate School of International Management/ Thunderbird, Center for International Business Education and Research, *USA*, 223

APEC Study Center, University of Hawaii at Manoa, *USA*, 285

APEC Study Center, University of Washington, *USA*, 298

Area de Relaciones Internacionales, Facultad Latinoamericana de Ciencias Sociales, *Argentina*, 171

Asia 2000 Foundation of New Zealand, *New Zealand*, 129

Asia Foundation, The, *USA*, 224

Asia Institute, *China*, 4

Asian American Studies Center, University of California, Los Angeles, *USA*, 277

Asian Institute for Development Communication, The, *Malaysia*, 65

Asian Institute of Management, Washington SyCip Policy Forum, *Philippines*, 73

Asian Strategy & Leadership Institute, *Malaysia*, 66

Asia Pacific Association of Japan *(Asia Taiheiyo Kenkyukai)*, *Japan*, 40

Asia Pacific Foundation of Canada, *Canada*, 137

Asia/Pacific Research Center, Stanford University, *USA*, 263

Asia-Pacific Research Institute, Macquarie University, *Australia*, 124

Asia Research Centre on Social, Political and Economic Change, Murdoch University, *Australia*, 125

Asia Society, The (Southern California Center), *USA*, 225

Asiatic Research Center, Korea University, *South Korea*, 86

Association for Promotion of International Cooperation *(Kokusai Kyoryoku Suishin Kyokai)*, *Japan*, 41

Australia-Japan Research Centre, Australian National University, Research School of Pacific and Asian Studies, *Australia*, 118

Australian Institute of International Affairs, *Australia*, 117

Australian National University, Research School of Pacific and Asian Studies, *Australia:* Australia-Japan Research Centre, 118; Contemporary China Centre, 119; Department of International Relations, 120; National Centre for Development Studies, 121; Strategic and Defence Studies Centre, 122

Berkeley APEC Study Center, The, University of California, Berkeley, *USA*, 272

Berkeley Roundtable on the International Economy, University of California, Berkeley, *USA*, 273

Better Hong Kong Foundation, The, *Hong Kong*, 26

Brigham Young University and University of Utah, Center for International Business Education and Research, *USA*, 226

British Columbia Chamber of Commerce, *Canada*, 138

Business Council on National Issues, *Canada*, 139

C.D. Howe Institute, *Canada*, 140

Canada-ASEAN Centres, *Canada*, 141

Canadian Consortium on Asia Pacific Security, The, *Canada*, 142

Canadian Council for International Co-operation, *Canada*, 143

Canadian Council for International Peace and Security, *Canada*, 144

Canadian Foundation for the Americas *(Fondation canadienne pour les Amériques)*, *Canada*, 145

Canadian Institute of International Affairs, *Canada*, 146

Canadian Institute of Strategic Studies, The, *Canada*, 147

Carleton University, Centre for Trade Policy and Law, *Canada*, 148

Center for American Studies, Fudan University, *China*, 18

Center for Asian and Pacific Studies, Seikei University *(Seikei Daigaku Asia Taiheiyo Kenkyu Center)*, *Japan*, 60

Center for Asian and Pacific Studies, University of Oregon, *USA*, 291

Center for Continuing Study of the California Economy, *USA*, 227

Center for East Asian Studies, Monterey Institute of International Studies, *USA*, 246

Center for East Asian Studies, Stanford University, *USA*, 264

Center for Environmental Research, Education, and Development, *Vietnam*, 107

Center for Information and Development Studies, *Indonesia*, 35

Center for International Business Education and Research, American Graduate School of International Management/Thunderbird, *USA*, 223

Center for International Business Education and Research, Brigham Young University and University of Utah, *USA*, 226

Center for International Business Education and Research, San Diego State University, *USA*, 260

Center for International Business Education and Research, University of California, Los Angeles, *USA*, 278

Center for International Business Education and Research, University of Hawaii at Manoa, *USA*, 286

Center for International Business Education and Research, University of Washington, *USA*, 299

Center for International Business Studies, Texas A&M University, *USA*, 268

Center for International Economics, Chulalongkorn University, *Thailand*, 103

Center for International Relations, University of California, Los Angeles, *USA*, 279

Center for International Security and Arms Control, Stanford University, *USA*, 265

Center for International Studies, University of Southern California, *USA*, 293

Center for Japanese Studies, Fudan University, *China*, 19

Center for Japanese Studies, National Center for Social Sciences and Humanities, *Vietnam*, 110

Center for Japan-United States Relations, International University of Japan *(Kokusai Daigaku Nichibei Kankei Kenkyujo)*, *Japan*, 48

Center for Latin American Studies, Stanford University, *USA*, 266

Center for Multiethnic and Transnational Studies, The, University of Southern California, *USA*, 294

Center for Nonproliferation Studies, Monterey Institute of International Studies, *USA*, 246

Center for North America Studies, National Center for Social Sciences and Humanities, *Vietnam*, 111

Center for Pacific Basin Monetary and Economic Studies, Federal Reserve Bank of San Francisco, *USA*, 235

Center for Pacific Rim Studies, University of California, Los Angeles, *USA*, 280

Center for Policy and Implementation Studies, *Indonesia*, 36

Center for Political and Regional Studies, Indonesian Institute of Sciences, *Indonesia*, 38

Center for Research and Communication Foundation, *Philippines*, 70

Center for Southeast Asian Studies, The, Kyoto University *(Kyoto Daigaku Tonan-Asia Kenkyu Center)*, *Japan*, 55

Center for Strategic and International Studies, *Indonesia*, 37

Center for the New West, *USA*, 228

Center for the Pacific Rim, University of San Francisco, *USA*, 292

Center for Trade and Diplomatic Commerce, Monterey Institute of International Studies, *USA*, 246

Center for U.S.-Mexican Studies, University of California, San Diego, *USA*, 282

Centre d'études de l'Asie de l'Est, Université de Montréal, *Canada*, 159

Centre for Asian Legal Studies, University of British Columbia, *Canada*, 161

Centre for Asian Studies, University of Adelaide, *Australia*, 126

Centre for Asia-Pacific Initiatives, *Canada*, 149

Centre for Canada-Asia Business Relations, The, Queen's University, *Canada*, 156

Centre for Environmental Studies, Chinese University of Hong Kong, *Hong Kong*, 27

Centre for Policy Research on Science & Technology, Simon Fraser University, *Canada*, 157

Centre for Research on Latin America & the Caribbean, York University, *Canada*, 164

Centre for Research Policy, University of Wollongong, *Australia*, 128

Centre for Strategic Studies, Victoria University of Wellington, *New Zealand*, 132

Centre for the Study of Australia-Asia Relations, Griffith University, *Australia*, 123

Centre for Trade Policy and Law, Carleton University, *Canada*, 148

Centre of Asian Studies, University of Hong Kong, *Hong Kong*, 32

Centre of Urban Planning and Environmental Management, University of Hong Kong, *Hong Kong*, 33

Centro de Economía Internacional y Desarrollo, Universidad de Chile, *Chile*, 192

Centro de Estudios Asiáticos, Universidad de los Andes, *Colombia*, 196

Centro de Estudios del Desarrollo, *Chile*, 185

Centro de Estudios del Pacífico, Universidad de Guadalajara, *Mexico*, 208

Centro de Estudios Internacionales, Universidad de los Andes, *Colombia*, 197

Centro de Estudios Monetarios Latinoamericanos, *Mexico*, 201

Centro de Estudios Públicos, *Chile*, 186

Centro de Estudios y Promoción del Desarrollo, *Peru*, 210

Centro de Estudos Estratégicos, *Brazil*, 176

Centro de Investigación de la Universidad del Pacífico, Universidad del Pacifico, *Peru*, 211

Centro de Investigaciones Europeo-Latinoamericanas, *Argentina*, 169

Centro de Investigaciones sobre América del Norte, Universidad Nacional Autónoma de México, *Mexico*, 204

Centro de Investigación para el Desarrollo, *Mexico*, 202

Centro de Investigación y Docencia Económicas, *Mexico*, 203

Centro de Relaciones Internacionales, Universidad Nacional Autonoma de Mexico, *Mexico*, 209

Centro Peruano de Estudios Internacionales, *Peru*, 212

Centro Universitario de Estudios e Investigaciones sobre la Cuenca del Pacífico, Universidad de Colima, *Mexico*, 207

China Center for International Studies, *China*, 5

China Institute for International Strategic Studies, *China*, 6

China Institute of Contemporary International Relations, *China*, 7

China Institute of International Studies, *China*, 8

Chinese Academy of Social Sciences, *China*: Institute of Asia-Pacific Studies, 9; Institute of Finance and Trade Economics, 10; Institute of Industrial Economics, 11; Institute of Japanese Studies, 12; Institute of Latin American Studies, 13; Institute of World Economics and Politics, 14

Chinese Council of Advanced Policy Studies, *Taiwan*, 98

Chinese People's Institute of Foreign Affairs, *China*, 15

Chinese University of Hong Kong, *Hong Kong*: Centre for Environmental Studies, 27; Hong Kong Institute of Asia-Pacific Studies, 28

Chulalongkorn University, *Thailand*: Center for International Economics, 103; Institute of Asian Studies, 104; Institute of Security and International Studies, 105

Chung-Hua Institution for Economic Research, *Taiwan*, 99

City University of Hong Kong, Contemporary China Research Centre, *Hong Kong*, 29

Claremont Graduate School, Program in Politics and Policy, *USA*, 229

Claremont McKenna College, Keck Center for International and Strategic Studies, *USA*, 230

Comisión Andina de Juristas, *Peru*, 213

Comisión Económica para América Latina y el Caribe, *Chile*, 187

Comision Sudamericana de Paz, *Chile*, 188

Commonwealth Club of California, *USA*, 231

Conference Board of Canada, The, *Canada*, 150

Consejo Argentino para las Relaciones Internacionales, *Argentina*, 170

Contemporary China Centre, Australian National University, Research School of Pacific and Asian Studies, *Australia*, 119

Contemporary China Research Centre, City University of Hong Kong, *Hong Kong*, 29

Corporación de Estudios para el Desarrollo, *Ecuador*, 200

Corporación de Investigaciones Económicas para Latinoamerica, *Chile*, 189

David Lam Centre for International Communication, Simon Fraser University, *Canada*, 158 Departamento do Relações Internacionais, University of Brasília, Instituto de Ciencia Politica e Relações Internacionais, *Brazil*, 184

Department of International Politics, Fudan University, *China*, 20

Department of International Relations, Australian National University, Research School of Pacific and Asian Studies, *Australia*, 120

Development Research Center of the State Council, *China*, 16

Discovery Institute, *USA*, 232

East Asian Studies Center, University of Southern California, *USA*, 295

East-West Center, *USA*, 233

Economic Development Corporation of Los Angeles County, *USA*, 234

El Colegio de la Frontera Norte, Tijuana, *Mexico*, 205

El Colegio de México, *Mexico*, 206

Facultad de Ciencias Sociales, Universidad de Buenos Aires, *Argentina*, 175

Facultad de Finanzas, Gobierno y Relaciones Internacionales, Universidad Externado de Colombia, *Colombia*, 198

Facultad Latinoamericana de Ciencias Sociales, Área de Relaciones Internacionales, *Argentina*, 171

Federation of Industries of the State of São Paulo, *Brazil*, 180

Foundation for Advanced Information and Research *(Kenkyu Joho Kikin)*, *Japan*, 42

Foundation for International and Strategic Studies, *China*, 17

Fraser Institute, The, *Canada*, 151

Fudan University, *China:* Center for American Studies, 18; Center for Japanese Studies, 19; Department of International Politics, 20

Fundação Getúlio Vargas, *Brazil*, 181

Fundación Chilena del Pacífico, *Chile*, 190

Fundación de Investigaciones Económicas Latinoamericanas, *Argentina*, 172

Fundación para la Educación Superior y el Desarrollo, *Colombia*, 195

Global Peace and Conflict Studies, University of California, Irvine, *USA*, 276

Gobierno y Relaciones Internacionales, Facultad de Finanzas, Universidad Externado de Colombia, *Colombia*, 198

Griffith University, Centre for the Study of Australia-Asia Relations, *Australia*, 123

Groupe d'études et de recherche sur l'Asie contemporaine, Laval University, *Canada*, 153

Grupo APOYO, *Peru*, 214

Grupo de Análisis para el Desarrollo, *Peru*, 215

Hong Kong Centre for Economic Research, The, *Hong Kong*, 30

Hong Kong Institute of Asia-Pacific Studies, Chinese University of Hong Kong, *Hong Kong*, 28

Hong Kong Institute of Business Studies, Lingnan College, *Hong Kong*, 31

Hoover Institution, *USA*, 236

Human Rights Watch, California, *USA*, 237

Ilmin International Relations Institute, Korea University, *South Korea*, 87

Indonesian Institute of Sciences, Center for Political and Regional Studies, *Indonesia*, 38

International University of Japan, Center for Japan-United States Relations *(Kokusai Daigaku Nichibei Kankei Kenkyujo)*, *Japan*, 48

Institute for Contemporary Studies, *USA*, 238

Institute for Asian Research, University of British Columbia, *Canada*, 162

Institute for Economic and Social Research, Education and Information, *Indonesia*, 39

Institute for Economic Research of Ho Chi Minh City, *Vietnam*, 108

Institute for Far Eastern Studies, Kyungnam University, *South Korea*, 89

Institute for Global Economics, *South Korea*, 78

Institute for International Business, University of Colorado at Denver, *USA*, 284

Institute for International Policy Studies *(Sekai Heiwa Kenkyujo)*, *Japan*, 43

Institute for International Relations, University of British Columbia, *Canada*, 163

Institute for International Relations, *Vietnam*, 109

Institute for National Policy Research, *Taiwan*, 100

Institute for Southeast Asian Studies, National Center for Social Sciences and Humanities, *Vietnam*, 112

Institute for Strategic and Development Studies, *Philippines*, 71

Institute of Asia and Pacific Studies, Shanghai Academy of Social Sciences, *China*, 22

Institute of Asian Studies, Chulalongkorn University, *Thailand*, 104

Institute of Asia-Pacific Studies, Chinese Academy of Social Sciences, *China*, 9

Institute of Asia-Pacific Studies, Kyung Hee University, *South Korea*, 88

Institute of Developing Economies *(Ajia Keizai Kenkyusho)*, *Japan*, 44

Institute of East and West Studies, Yonsei Universtiy, *South Korea*, 94

Institute of East Asian Political Economy, *Singapore*, 74

Institute of East Asian Studies, University of California, Berkeley, *USA*, 274

Institute of Economics, Academia Sinica, *Taiwan*, 95

Institute of European and American Studies, Academia Sinica, *Taiwan*, 96

Institute of European and Asian Studies, Shanghai Academy of Social Sciences, *China*, 23

Institute of Finance and Trade Economics, Chinese Academy of Social Sciences, *China*, 10

Institute of Foreign Affairs and National Security, The, *South Korea*, 79

Institute of Industrial Economics, Chinese Academy of Social Sciences, *China*, 11

Institute of International Relations, National Chengchi University, *Taiwan*, 101

Institute of International Relations for Advanced Studies on Peace and Development in Asia, Sophia University *(Johchi Daigaku Kokusai Kankei Kenkyujo)*, *Japan*, 61

Institute of International Studies, University of California, Berkeley, *USA*, 275

Institute of Japanese Studies, Chinese Academy of Social Sciences, *China*, 12

Institute of Latin American Studies, Chinese Academy of Social Sciences, *China*, 13

Institute of Oriental Culture, University of Tokyo *(Tokyo Daigaku Toyo Bunka Kenkyujo)*, *Japan*, 64

Institute of Policy Studies, The, *Singapore,* 75

Institute of Policy Studies, Victoria University of Wellington, *New Zealand,* 133

Institute of Security and International Studies, Chulalongkorn University, *Thailand,* 105

Institute of Southeast Asian Studies, *Singapore,* 76

Institute of Strategic and International Studies, *Malaysia,* 67

Institute of the Americas, *USA,* 239

Institute of World Economics and Politics, Chinese Academy of Social Sciences, *China,* 14

Institute on Global Conflict and Cooperation, University of California, San Diego, *USA,* 283

Instituto de Ciência Política e Relações Internacionais, University of Brasília, Departmento do Relações Internacionais, *Brazil,* 184

Instituto de Estudios del Pacífico, Universidad Gabriela Mistral, *Chile,* 194

Instituto de Estudios Internacionales, Universidad de Chile, *Chile,* 193

Instituto de Estudios Peruanos, *Peru,* 216

Instituto de Estudios Políticos y Relaciones Internacionales, Universidad Nacional de Colombia, *Colombia,* 199

Instituto de Estudos Econômicos, Sociais e Políticos de São Paulo, *Brazil,* 177

Instituto de Estudos Políticos e Sociais, *Brazil,* 178

Instituto de Relaciones Internacionales de Asia-Pacífico, *Argentina,* 173

Instituto de Relações Internacionais, Pontificia Universidade Catolica, *Brazil,* 182

Instituto Libertad y Democracia, *Peru,* 217

Instituto para la Integración de América Latina y el Caribe, *Argentina,* 174

Instituto Universitario de Pesquisas do Rio de Janeiro, *Brazil,* 179

Instituto Venezolano de Estudios Sociales y Políticos, *Venezuela,* 218

International Business Education and Research Program, University of Southern California, *USA,* 296

International Center for the Study of East Asian Development, The *(Kitakyushu Kokusai Higashi-Asia Kenkyu Center), Japan,* 45

International Development Center of Japan *(Kokusai Kaihatsu Center), Japan,* 46

International House of Japan *(Kokusai Bunka Kaikan), Japan,* 47

James A. Baker III Institute for Public Policy, The, Rice University, *USA,* 259

Japan America Society of Southern California, National Association of Japan-America Societies, *USA,* 247

Japan Center for Economic Research *(Nihon Keizai Kenkyu Center), Japan,* 49

Japan Center for International Exchange *(Nihon Kokusai Koryu Center), Japan,* 50

Japan Economic Foundation *(Kokusai Keizai Koryu Zaidan), Japan,* 51

Japanese American Citizens League, *USA,* 241

Japan Forum on International Relations, The *(Nihon Kokusai Forum), Japan,* 52

Japan Institute of International Affairs *(Nihon Kokusai Mondai Kenkyujo), Japan,* 53

Japan Policy Research Institute, *USA,* 240

Joint Centre for Asia-Pacific Communication Research/Centre conjoint de Recherche en Communication sur l'Asie Pacifique, Université du Québec á Montréal and Concordia University, *Canada,* 160

Joint Centre for Asia Pacific Studies, *Canada,* 152

Keck Center for International and Strategic Studies, Claremont McKenna College, *USA,* 230

Keidanren (Japan Federation of Economic Organizations), *Japan,* 54

Kim Dae-jung Peace Foundation for the Asia-Pacific Region, *South Korea,* 80

Korea Development Institute, *South Korea,* 81

Korea Economic Research Institute, *South Korea,* 82

Korea Institute for Industrial Economics and Trade, *South Korea,* 83

Korea Institute for International Economic Policy, *South Korea,* 84

Korea Institute for National Reunification, *South Korea,* 85

Korea University, *South Korea:* Asiatic Research Center, 86; Ilmin International Relations Institute, 87

Kyoto University, Center for Southeast Asian Studies, The *(Kyoto Daigaku Tonan-Asia Kenkyu Center), Japan,* 55

Kyung Hee University, Institute of Asia-Pacific Studies, *South Korea,* 88

Kyungnam University, Institute for Far Eastern Studies, *South Korea,* 89

Laval University, Groupe d'études et de recherche sur l'Asie contemporaine, *Canada,* 153

Leadership Education for Asian Pacifics, Inc., *USA,* 242

Liberdad y Desarrollo, *Chile,* 191

Lingnan College, Hong Kong Institute of Business Studies, *Hong Kong,* 31

Los Angeles Urban League, *USA,* 243

Macquarie University, Asia-Pacific Research Institute, *Australia,* 124

Malaysian Institute of Economic Research, *Malaysia,* 68

Malaysian Strategic Research Centre, *Malaysia,* 69

Mansfield Center for Pacific Affairs, The, *USA,* 244

Massey University, New Zealand Centre for Japanese Studies, *New Zealand,* 130

Mexican-American Legal Defense & Educational Fund, *USA,* 245

Monterey Institute of International Studies, *USA:* Center for East Asian Studies, 246; Center for Trade and Diplomatic Commerce, 246

Murdoch University, Asia Research Centre on Social, Political and Economic Change, *Australia,* 125

National Association of Japan-America Societies, Japan America Society of Southern California, *USA,* 247

National Bureau of Asian Research, *USA,* 248

National Center for APEC, *USA,* 249

National Centre for Development Studies, Australian National University, Research School of Pacific and Asian Studies, *Australia,* 121

National Center for Social Sciences and Humanities, *Vietnam:* Center for Japanese Studies, 110; Center for North American Studies; Institute for Southeast Asian Studies, 112

National Chengchi University, Institute of International Relations, *Taiwan,* 101

National Institute for Defense Studies *(Bouei Kenkyujo), Japan,* 56

National Institute for Research Advancement *(Sohgo Kenkyu Kaihatsu Kikoh), Japan,* 57

Nautilus Institute for Security and Sustainable Development, *USA,* 250

New Mexico U.S.-Japan Center, University of New Mexico, *USA,* 290

New Zealand Centre for Japanese Studies, Massey University, *New Zealand,* 130

New Zealand Institute of Economic Research, *New Zealand,* 131

New Zealand Institute of International Affairs, Victoria University of Wellington, *New Zealand,* 134

Niagara Institute of International Affairs, *Canada,* 154

Nomura Research Institute *(Nomura Sohgo Kenkyujo), Japan,* 58

North America Forum, Stanford University, *USA,* 267

North America Institute, The, *USA,* 251

North American Integration and Development Center, University of California, Los Angeles, *USA,* 281

North-South Institute, *Canada,* 155

Núcleo de Pesquisa em Relações Internacionais, Universidade de São Paulo, *Brazil,* 183

Pacific Asian Management Institute, University of Hawaii at Manoa, *USA,* 287

Pacific Asia Society, *South Korea,* 90

Pacific Basin Economic Council, *USA,* 252

Pacific Basin Institute, *USA,* 253

Pacific Council on International Policy, *USA,* 254

Pacific Forum CSIS, *USA,* 255

Pacific Institute for Women's Health, *USA,* 256

Peking University, School of International Relations, *China,* 21

Philippine Institute for Development Studies, *Philippines,* 72

Pontifícia Universidade Católica, Instituto de Relações Internacionais, *Brazil,* 182

Program in Politics and Policy, Claremont Graduate School, *USA,* 229

Public Policy Institute of California, *USA,* 257

Queen's University, Centre for Canada-Asia Business Relations, The, *Canada,* 156

RAND, *USA,* 258

Research Institute for Asia and the Pacific, University of Sydney, *Australia,* 127

Research Institute for International Affairs, The, *South Korea,* 91

Research Institute for Peace and Security *(Heiwa Anzen Hosho Kenkyujo), Japan,* 59

Research School of Pacific and Asian Studies, Australian National University, *Australia:* Contemporary China Centre, 119; Department of International Relations, 120; National Centre for Development Studies, 121; Strategic and Defence Studies Centre, 122

Rice University, James A. Baker III Institute for Public Policy, The, *USA,* 259

San Diego State University, Center for International Business Education and Research, *USA,* 260

School of Hawaiian, Asian and Pacific Studies, University of Hawaii at Manoa, *USA,* 288

School of International Relations, Peking University, *China,* 21

Seikei University, Center for Asian and Pacific Studies *(Seikei Daigaku Asia Taiheiyo Kenkyu Center), Japan,* 60

Sejong Institute, The, *South Korea,* 92

Seoul Forum for International Affairs, *South Korea,* 93

Shanghai Academy of Social Sciences, *China:* Institute of Asia and Pacific Studies, 22; Institute of European and Asian Studies, 23

Shanghai Center of International Studies, *China,* 24

Shanghai Institute for International Studies, *China,* 25

Simon Fraser University, *Canada:* Centre for Policy Research on Science & Technology, 157; David Lam Centre for International Communication, 158

Singapore Institute of International Affairs, *Singapore,* 77

Sistema Económico Latinoamericano, *Venezuela,* 219

Southern California Association of Governments, *USA,* 261

Southern California Studies Center, University of Southern California, *USA,* 297

Southwest Voter Research Institute, *USA,* 262

Stanford University, *USA:* Asia/Pacific Research Center, 263; Center for East Asian Studies, 264; Center for International Security and Arms Control, 265; Center for Latin American Studies, 266; North America Forum, 267

Strategic and Defence Studies Centre, Australian National University, Research School of Pacific and Asian Studies, *Australia,* 122

Sun Yat-Sen Institute for Social Sciences and Philosophy, Academia Sinica, *Taiwan,* 97

Taiwan Institute of Economic Research, *Taiwan,* 102

Texas A&M University, Center for International Business Studies, *USA,* 268

Thailand Development Research Institute, *Thailand,* 106

Tokyo Club Foundation for Global Studies *(Tokyo Kokusai Kenkyu Club), Japan,* 62

Tomás Rivera Policy Institute, The, *USA,* 269

Town Hall Los Angeles, *USA,* 270

United Nations University, The *(Kokusai Rengoh Daigaku), Japan,* 63

United States-Mexico Border Progress Foundation, *USA,* 271

Universidad de Buenos Aires, Facultad de Ciencias Sociales, *Argentina,* 175

Universidad de Chile, *Chile:* Centro de Economía Internacional y Desarrollo, 192; Instituto de Estudios Internacionales, 193

Universidad de Colima, Centro Universitario de Estudios e Investigaciones sobre la Cuenca del Pacífico, *Mexico,* 207

Universidad de Guadalajara, Centro de Estudios del Pacífico, *Mexico,* 208

Universidad de los Andes, *Colombia:* Centro de Estudios Asiáticos, 196; Centro de Estudios Internacionales, 197

Universidad del Pacifico, Centro de Investigacion de la Universidad del Pacifico, *Peru,* 211

Universidade de São Paulo, Núcleo de Pesquisa em Relações Internacionais, *Brazil,* 183

Universidad Externado de Colombia, Facultad de Finanzas, Gobierno y Relaciones Internacionales, *Colombia,* 198

Universidad Gabriela Mistral, Instituto de Estudios del Pacífico, *Chile,* 194

Universidad Nacional Autónoma de México, *Mexico:* Centro de Investigaciones sobre América del Norte, 204; Centro de Relaciones Internacionales, 209

Universidad Nacional de Colombia, Instituto de Estudios Políticos y Relaciones Internacionales, *Colombia,* 199

Université de Montréal, Centre d'études de l'Asie de l'Est, *Canada,* 159

Université du Québec á Montréal and Concordia University, Joint Centre for Asia-Pacific Communication Research/Centre conjoint de Recherche en Communication sur l'Asie Pacifique, *Canada,* 160

University of Adelaide, Centre for Asian Studies, *Australia,* 126

University of Brasília, Instituto de Ciência Política e Relações Internacionais, Departamento do Relações Internacionais, *Brazil,* 184

University of British Columbia, *Canada:* Centre for Asian Legal Studies, 161; Institute for Asian Research, 162; Institute for International Relations, 163

University of California, Berkeley, *USA:* Berkeley APEC Study Center, 272; Berkeley Roundtable on the International Economy, 273; Institute of East Asian Studies, 274; Institute of International Studies, 275

University of California, Irvine, Global Peace and Conflict Studies, *USA,* 276

University of California, Los Angeles, *USA:* Asian American Studies Center, 277; Center for International Business Education and Research, 278; Center for International Relations, 279; Center for Pacific Rim Studies, 280; North American Integration and Development Center, 281

University of California, San Diego, *USA:* Center for U.S.-Mexican Studies, 282; Institute on Global Conflict and Cooperation, 283

University of Colorado at Denver, Institute for International Business, *USA,* 284

University of Hawaii at Manoa, *USA:* APEC Study Center, 285; Center for International Business Education and Research, 286; Pacific Asian Management Institute, 287; School of Hawaiian, Asian and Pacific Studies, 288

University of Hong Kong, *Hong Kong:* Centre of Asian Studies, 32; Centre of Urban Planning and Environmental Management, 33

University of New Mexico, New Mexico U.S.-Japan Center, *USA,* 290

University of Oregon, Center for Asian and Pacific Studies, *USA,* 291

University of San Francisco, Center for the Pacific Rim, *USA,* 292

University of Southern California, *USA:* Center for International Studies, 293; The Center for Multiethnic and Transnational Studies, 294; East Asian Studies Center, 295; International Business Education and Research Program, 296; Southern California Studies Center, 297

University of Sydney, Research Institute for Asia and the Pacific, *Australia,* 127 University of Tokyo, Institute of Oriental Culture *(Tokyo Daigaku Toyo Bunka Kenkyujo), Japan,* 64

University of Washington, *USA:* APEC Study Center, 298; Center for International Business Education and Research, 299

University of Wollongong, Centre for Research Policy, *Australia,* 128

Victoria University of Wellington, *New Zealand:* Centre for Strategic Studies, 132; Institute of Policy Studies, 133; New Zealand Institute of International Affairs, 134

Vietnam Asia-Pacific Economic Center, *Vietnam,* 113

Vision 2047 Foundation, *Hong Kong,* 34

Washington Council on International Trade, *USA,* 300

Washington SyCip Policy Forum, Asian Institute of Management, *Philippines,* 73

World Affairs Councils, *USA,* 301

World Trade Center Association, *USA,* 305

York Centre for International and Security Studies, York University, *Canada,* 165

York University, *Canada:* Centre for Research on Latin America and the Caribbean, 164; York Centre for International and Security Studies, 165

Index by Head of Institution

Aggarwal, Vinod K., The Berkeley APEC Study Center, University of California, Berkely, *USA,* 272

Agosin, Manuel R., Centro de Economia Internacional y Desarrollo, Universidad de Chile, *Chile,* 192

Albuquerque, Jose Augusto Guilhon, Núcleo de Pesquisa em Relações Internacionais, Universidade de São Paulo, *Brazil,* 183

Anderson, Peter, Centre for Policy Research on Science and Technology, Simon Fraser University, *Canada,* 157

Archdeacon, Maurice, Canadian Council for International Peace and Security, *Canada,* 144

Arregui, Patricia McLauchlan de, Grupo de Análisis para el Desarrollo, *Peru,* 215

Bach, Bay Van, Institute for Economic Research of Ho Chi Minh City, *Vietnam,* 108

Baginda, Abdul Razak Abdullah, Malaysian Strategic Research Centre, *Malaysia,* 69

Barrett, Charles, Niagara Institute of International Affairs, *Canada,* 154

Barros, Sergio Miceli Pessoa de, Instituto de Estudos Econômicos, Sociais e Políticos de São Paulo, *Brazil,* 177

Boeker, Paul H., Institute of the Americas, *USA,* 239

Boeninger, Edgardo, Fundación Chilena del Pacífico, *Chile,* 190

Boron, Atilio, Centro de Investigaciones Europeo-Latinoamericanas, *Argentina,* 169

Borrus, Michael, Berkeley Roundtable on the International Economy, University of California, Berkeley, *USA,* 273

Braddock, Richard, Asia-Pacific Research Institute, Macquarie University, *Australia,* 124

Branan, Alvord G., Center for International Business Education and Research, San Diego State University, *USA,* 260

Browne, Dean J., Canadian Foundation for the Americas, *Canada,* 145

Browne, Dennis, Center for Trade Policy and Law, Carleton University, *Canada,* 148

Bundy, Barbara K., Center for the Pacific Rim, University of San Francisco, *USA,* 292

Burdon, Philip, Asia 2000 Foundation of New Zealand, *New Zealand,* 129

Burgess, Phillip M., Center for the New West, *USA,* 228

Bustamante, Jorge A., El Colegio de la Frontera Norte, *Mexico,* 205

Caceres C., Carlos F., Libertad y Desarrollo, *Chile,* 191

Camargo, Sania de, Instituto de Relações Internacionais, Pontifíícia Universidade Católica do Rio de Janeiro, *Brazil,* 182

Campos, Monica Verea, Centro de Investigaciones sobre América del Norte, *Mexico,* 204

Cao, Peilin, Department of International Politics, Fudan University, *China,* 20

Cardenas S., Mauricio, Fundación para la Educación Superior y el Desarrollo, *Colombia,* 195

Cha, Dong-Se, Korea Development Institute, *South Korea,* 81

Chapman, Bruce, Discovery Institute, *USA,* 232

Charron, Claude-Yves, Joint Centre for Asia-Pacific Communication Research, Université du Québec á Montréal and Concordia University, *Canada,* 160

Chen, Jiagui, Institute of Industrial Economics, Chinese Academy of Social Sciences, *China,* 11

Chen, Peiyao, Shanghai Institute for International Studies, *China,* 25

Chen, Qiwei, Asia Institute, *China,* 4

Cheng, Joseph Y. S., Contemporary China Research Centre, City University of Hong Kong, *Hong Kong,* 29

Chengxu, Yang, China Institute of International Studies, *China,* 8

Chirathivat, Suthiphand, Center for International Economics, Chulalongkorn University, *Thailand,* 103

Cho, Suck-Rai, Korea Economic Research Institute, *South Korea,* 82

Choue, Chungwon, Institute of Asia-Pacific Studies, Kyung Hee University, *South Korea,* 88

Chu, Yun-peng, Sun Yat-Sen Institute for Social Sciences and Philosophy, Academia Sinica, *Taiwan,* 97

Coeytaux, Francine, Pacific Institute for Women's Health, *USA,* 256

Cohen, Stephen S., Berkeley Roundtable on the International Economy, University of California, Berkeley, *USA,* 273

Contreras, Carlos, Comisión Sudamericana de Paz, *Chile,* 188

Cooper, Kerry, Center for International Business Studies, Texas A&M University, *USA,* 268

Costa, Eduardo Ferrero, Centro Peruano de Estudios Internacionales, *Peru,* 212

Crysler, Lindsay, Joint Centre for Asia-Pacific Communication Research, Université du Quebéc á Montréal and Concordia Univerity, *Canada,* 160

Culpepper, Roy, North-South Institute, *Canada,* 155

Daniel, Shirley, Center for International Business Education and Research and Pacific Asian Management Institute, University of Hawaii at Manoa, *USA,* 286

Dao, Ngoc Huy, Institute for International Relations, *Vietnam,* 109

Davidson, Giff, New Zealand Institute of International Affairs, Victoria University of Wellington, *New Zealand,* 134

Davila, Consuelo, Centro de Relaciones Internacionales, Universidad Nacional Autónoma de México, *Mexico,* 209

Davis, Patricia J., Washington Council on International Trade, *USA,* 300

Dear, Michael J., Southern California Studies Center, University of Southern California, *USA,* 297

Derr, C. Brooklyn, Center for International Business Education and Research, Brigham Young University/University of Utah, *USA*, 226

Dewitt, David, The Canadian Consortium on Asia Pacific Security, *Canada*, 142; York Centre for International and Security Studies, York University, *Canada*, 165

Dibb, Paul, Strategic and Defence Studies Centre, Australian National University, *Australia*, 122

Djerejian, Edward P., The James A. Baker III Institute for Public Policy, Rice University, *USA*, 259

Do, Diep Loc, Center for North America Studies, National Center for Social Sciences and Humanities, *Vietnam*, 111

Doung, Hiep Phu, Center for Japanese Studies, National Center for Social Sciences and Humanities, *Vietnam*, 110

Drobnick, Richard, International Business Education and Research Program, University of Southern California, *USA*, 296

Drysdale, Peter, Australia-Japan Research Centre, Australian National University, *Australia*, 118

Duffy, Gloria, The Commonwealth Club of California, *USA*, 231

Duncan, Ron, National Centre for Development Studies, Australian National University, *Australia*, 121

Durrant, Stephen, Center for Asian and Pacific Studies, University of Oregon, *USA*, 291

Duus, Peter, Center for East Asian Studies, Stanford University, *USA*, 264

Ellings, Richard, The National Bureau of Asian Research, *USA*, 248

Esteban, Enrique, Center for Research and Communication Foundation, *Philippines*, 70

Fernandez-Baca, Jorge, Centro de Investigación de la Universidad del Pacífico, *Peru*, 211

Ferreira, Carlos Eduardo Moreira, FIESP/CIESP, *Brazil*, 180

Fischer, David J., World Affairs Council of Northern California, *USA*, 301

Frolic, B. Michael, Joint Centre for Asia Pacific Studies, *Canada*, 152

Fuller, William P., The Asia Foundation, *USA*, 224

Fugita, Edmundo Sussumu, Centro de Estudos Estratégicos, *Brazil*, 176

García Sayán, Diego, Comisión Andina de Juristas, *Peru*, 213

Gard, Jr., Robert G., Monterey Institute of International Studies, *USA*, 246

Gewecke, Thomas H., World Forum of Silicon Valley, *USA*, 302

Ghigliazza, Sergio, Centro de Estudios Monetarios Latinoamericanos, *Mexico*, 201

Gibney, Frank B., The Pacific Basin Institute, *USA*, 253

Glick, Reuven, Center for Pacific Basin Monetary and Economic Studies, Federal Reserve Bank of San Francisco, *USA*, 235

Gonzales, Antonio, Southwest Voter Research Institute, *USA*, 262

Griffiths, Eldon, World Affairs Council of Orange County, *USA*, 301

Grinspun, Ricardo, Centre for Research on Latin America & the Caribbean, York University, *Canada*, 164

Grosse, Robert, Center for International Business Education and Research, The American Graduate School of International Management/Thunderbird, *USA*, 223

Gu, Yuanyang, Institute of World Economics and Politics, Chinese Academy of Social Sciences, *China*, 14

Guan, Kwa Chong, Singapore Institute of International Affairs, *Singapore*, 77

Guizado, Alvaro Camacho, Instituto de Estudios Políticos y Relaciones Internacionales, Universidad Nacional de Colombia, *Colombia*, 199

Hadad, Ismid, Institute for Economic and Social Research, Education and Information, *Indonesia*, 39

Hadisumaro, Djunaedi, Center for Policy and Implementation Studies, *Indonesia*, 36

Hahn, Bae Ho, The Sejong Institute, *South Korea*, 92

Hamashita, Takeshi, Institute of Oriental Culture, University of Tokyo, *Japan*, 64

Han, Sung-Joo, Ilmin International Relations Institute, Korea University, *South Korea*, 87

Harrington, Lee K., Economic Development Corporation of Los Angeles County, *USA*, 234

Hashimoto, Shozo, Nomura Research Institute, *Japan*, 58; Tokyo Club Foundation for Global Studies, *Japan*, 62

Hawke, Gary, Institute of Policy Studies, Victoria University of Wellington, *New Zealand*, 133

Hawkins, Jr., Robert B., Institute for Contemporary Studies, *USA*, 238

Hayes, Peter, Nautilus Institute for Security and Sustainable Development, *USA*, 250

Hellmann, Donald C., APEC Study Center, University of Washington, *USA*, 298

Hergert, Michael L., Center for International Business Education and Research, San Diego State University, *USA*, 260

Hernandez, Antonia, Mexican American Legal Defense and Educational Fund, *USA*, 245

Hernandez, Carolina G., Institute for Strategic and Development Studies, *Philippines*, 71

Hidayat, Moh Jumhur, Center for Information and Development Studies, *Indonesia*, 35

Hills, Peter, Centre of Urban Planning and Environmental Management, University of Hong Kong, *Hong Kong*, 33

Hinertrosa, Roberto, Facultad de Finanzas, Gobierno y Relaciones Internacionales, Universidad Externado de Colombia, *Colombia*, 198

Hinojosa-Ojeda, Raul, North American Integration and Development Center, University of California, Los Angeles, *USA*, 281

Hokoyama, J. D., Leadership Education for Asian Pacifics, Inc., *USA*, 242

Holloway, David, Center for International Security and Arms Control, Stanford University, *USA*, 265

Hoshiono, Shinyasu, National Institute for Research Advancement, *Japan*, 57

Hu, Sheng-Cheng, Institute of Economics, Academia Sinica, *Taiwan*, 95

Hurtado L., Osvaldo, Corporación de Estudios para el Desarrollo, *Ecuador*, 200

Hwang, Kyu Woong, The Research Institute for International Affairs, *South Korea*, 91

Intal Jr., Ponciano S., Philippine Institute for Development Studies, *Philippines*, 72

Ishihara, Takashi, National Institute for Research Advancement, *Japan*, 57

Ismail, Haji Basir bin, Malaysian Institute of Economic Research, *Malaysia*, 68

Ito, Kenichi, The Japan Forum on International Relations, *Japan*, 52

Jackman, Lesley, Australian Institute of International Affairs, *Australia,* 117

Jacome, Francine, Instituto Venezolano de Estudios Sociales y Políticos, *Venezuela,* 218

Jain, P. C., Centre for Asian Studies, University of Adelaide, *Australia,* 126

Jamison, Dean T., Center for Pacific Rim Studies, University of California, Los Angeles, *USA,* 280

Jeong, Se Hyun, Korea Institute for National Unification, *South Korea,* 85

Job, Brian, Institute for International Relations, University of British Columbia, *Canada,* 163

Joesoef, Daoed, Center for Strategic and International Studies, *Indonesia,* 37

Johnson, Chalmers, Japan Policy Research Institute, *USA,* 240

Jung, Ku-Hyun, Institute of East and West Studies, Yonsei University, *South Korea,* 94

Kaji, Motoo, International House of Japan, *Japan,* 47

Karl, Terry L., Center for Latin American Studies, Stanford University, *USA,* 266

Kawai, Saburo, International Development Center of Japan, *Japan,* 46

Kehn, E. B., Japan-America Society of Southern California, National Association of Japan-America Societies, *USA,* 247

Kelly, James A., Pacific Forum CSIS, *USA,* 255

Kersten, Rikki, Research Institute for Asia and the Pacific, University of Sydney, *Australia,* 127

Kierans, Thomas E., C.D. Howe Institute, *Canada,* 140

Kim, Dae-jung, Kim Dae-jung Peace Foundation for the Asia-Pacific Region, *South Korea,* 80

Kim, Kyung-Won, Seoul Forum for International Affairs, *South Korea,* 93

Kim, Suk-Kyu, The Institute of Foreign Affairs and National Security, *South Korea,* 79

Klabin, Israel, Instituto de Estudos Políticos e Sociais, *Brazil,* 178

Klaveren, Alberto van, Instituto de Estudios Internacionales, Universidad de Chile, *Chile,* 193

KOH, Tommy Thong-Bee, The Institute of Policy Studies, *Singapore,* 75

Komura, Chikara, Center for Asian and Pacific Studies, Seikei University, *Japan,* 60

Kosai, Yutaka, Japan Center for Economic Research, *Japan,* 49

LaDier, Tovah, The Mansfield Center for Pacific Affairs, *USA,* 244

Larsen, Gary, The Asia Society/California Center, *USA,* 225

Le Blanc, Charles, Centre d'études de l'Asie de l'Est, Université de Montréal, *Canada,* 159

Lee, Chae-Jin, Keck Center for International and Strategic Studies, Claremont McKenna College, *USA,* 230

Lee, Kyu Uck, Korea Institute for Industrial Economics and Trade, *South Korea,* 83

Lee, Su-Hoon, Institute for Far Eastern Studies, Kyungnam University, *South Korea,* 89

Leonie, Ki, The Better Hong Kong Foundation, *Hong Kong,* 26

Lessa, Renato, Instituto Universitario de Pesquisas do Rio de Janeiro, *Brazil,* 179

Leung, Yee, Centre for Environmental Studies, Chinese University of Hong Kong, *Hong Kong,* 27

Levy, Stephen, Center for Continuing Study of the California Economy, *USA,* 227

Lewis, Jack, International Business Education and Research Program, University of Southern California, *USA,* 296

Li, Luye, China Center for International Studies, *China,* 5

Liang, Shoude, School of International Relations, Peking University, *China,* 21

Lira, Andres, El Colegio de México, *Mexico,* 206

Liu, Shuqing, Chinese People's Institute of Foreign Affairs, *China,* 15

Lopez, Wallace H., New Mexico U.S.-Japan Center, University of New Mexico, *USA,* 290

Lowenthal, Abraham F., Pacific Council on International Policy, *USA,* 254

Lyon, David W., Public Policy Institute of California, *USA,* 257

Mack, Andrew, Department of International Relations, Australian National University, *Australia,* 120

Mack, John W., Los Angeles Urban League, *USA,* 243

Mack II, J. Curtis, Los Angeles World Affairs Council, *USA,* 301

Maguire, John, Program in Politics and Policy, Claremont Graduate School, *USA,* 229

Mahathir, Mirzan, Asian Strategy & Leadership Institute, *Malaysia,* 66

Mahbob, Sulaiman bin, Malaysian Institute of Economic Research, *Malaysia,* 68

Mai, Chao-cheng, Chung-Hua Institution for Economic Research, *Taiwan,* 99

Masuda, Minoru, Japan Economic Foundation, *Japan,* 51

Matsunaga, Nobuo, Japan Institute of International Affairs, *Japan,* 53

Mayer-Serra, Carlos Elizondo, Centro de Investigación y Docencia Económicas, A.C., *Mexico,* 203

McClain, David, APEC Study Center, East-West Center/University of Hawaii, *USA,* 285

McGee, Terry D., Institute for Asian Research, University of British Columbia, *Canada,* 162

Medawar, Adrienne, Town Hall Los Angeles, *USA,* 270

Mee-kau, Nyaw, Hong Kong Institute of Business Studies, Lingan College, *Hong Kong,* 31

Middlebrook, Kevin J., Center for U.S.-Mexican Studies, University of California, San Diego, *USA,* 282

Miller, William F., North America Forum, Stanford University, *USA,* 267

Mira, Fernando A. Rivas, Centro Universitario de Estudios e Investigaciones sobre la Cuenca del Pacífico, Universidad de Colima, *Mexico,* 207

Miyoshi, Masaya, Keidanren, *Japan,* 54

Moneta, Carlos Juan, Instituto de Relaciones Internacionales de Asia-Pacífico, *Argentina,* 173; Sistema Económico Latinoamericano, *Venezuela,* 219

Montalvo, Juanita, Canadian Foundation for the Americas, *Canada,* 145

Montero, Cecilia Blondet, Instituto de Estudios Peruanos, *Peru,* 216

Morgan, Patrick M., Global Peace and Conflict Studies, University of California, Irvine, *USA,* 276

Morrison, Alex, Canadian Institute of Strategic Studies, *Canada,* 147

Morrison, Charles E., APEC Study Center, East-West Center/University of Hawaii, *USA,* 285

Moxon, Richard W., Center for International Business Education and Research, University of Washington, *USA,* 299

Mullen, Michael C., National Center for APEC, *USA,* 249

Muniz, Carlos Manuel, Consejo Argentino para las Relaciones Internacionales, *Argentina,* 170

Nakanishi, Don T., Asian American Studies Center, University of California, Los Angeles, *USA,* 277

Naya, Masatsugu, Institute of International Relations for Advanced Studies on Peace and Development in Asia, Sophia University, *Japan,* 61

Neilson, William A. W., Centre for Asia-Pacific Initiatives, *Canada,* 149

Nguyen, Ninh Huu, Center for Environmental Research, Education, and Development, *Vietnam,* 107

Nininger, James R., The Conference Board of Canada, *Canada,* 150

Nordin, Haji Mazlan, Asian Institute for Development Communication, *Malaysia,* 65

O'Brien, Terence, Centre for Strategic Studies, Victoria University of Wellington, *New Zealand,* 132

Ogasawara, Toshiaki, Asia Pacific Association of Japan, *Japan,* 40

Ohta, Hirotsugu, National Institute for Defense Studies, *Japan,* 56

Okawara, Yoshio, Association for Promotion of International Cooperation, *Japan,* 41

Okimoto, Daniel I., Asia/Pacific Research Center, Stanford University, *USA,* 263

Oliveira, Henrique Altemani de, Nucleo de Pesquisa em Relações Internacionais, Universidade de São Paulo, *Brazil,* 183

Pabottingi, Mochtar, Center for Political and Regional Studies, Indonesian Institute of Sciences, *Indonesia,* 38

Pachón, Harry P., The Tomás Rivera Policy Institute, *USA,* 269

Packard, George R., Center for Japan-United States Relations, International University of Japan, *Japan,* 48

Palacios, Juan Jose, Departmento de Estudios del Pacífico, Universidad de Guadalajara, *Mexico,* 208

Pan, Guang, Institute of European and Asian Studies, Shanghai Academy of Social Sciences, *China,* 23; Shanghai Center of International Studies, *China,* 24

Parra, Jaime Barrera, Centro de Estudios Asiáticos, Universidad de los Andes, *Colombia,* 196

Peixoto, Celina Vargas do Amaral, Fundação Getúlio Vargas, *Brazil,* 181

Peren, Roger, New Zealand Centre for Japanese Studies, Massey University, *New Zealand,* 130

Pham, Thanh Duc, Institute for Southeast Asian Studies, National Center for Social Sciences and Humanities, *Vietnam,* 112

Pierano, Luis, Centro de Estudios y Promoción del Desarrollo, *Peru,* 210

Pisano, Mark, Southern California Association of Governments, *USA,* 261

Plewes, Betty, Canadian Council for International Co-operation, *Canada,* 143

Portantiero, Juan Carlos, Facultad de Ciencias Sociales, Universidad de Buenos Aires, *Argentina,* 175

Posada, Rafael Rivas, Centro de Estudios Internacionales, Universidad de los Andes, *Colombia,* 197

Potter, Pittman, Centre for Asian Legal Studies, University of British Columbia, *Canada,* 161

Preston, Michael B., The Center for Multiethnic and Transnational Studies, University of Southern California, *USA,* 294

Radebaugh, Lee H., Center for International Business Education and Research, Brigham Young University/University of Utah, *USA,* 226

Raisian, John, The Hoover Institution, *USA,* 236

Ramon, Francisco L., Washington SyCip Policy Forum, Asian Institute of Management, *Philippines,* 73

Robertson, Ian B., Canada-ASEAN Centre, *Canada,* 141

Robison, Richard, Asia Research Centre on Social, Political and Economic Change, Murdoch University, *Australia,* 125

Rocha, Antonio Jorge Ramalho da, Instituto de Ciência Política e Relações Internacionais, Departmento do Relações Internacionais, University of Brasília, *Brazil,* 184

Rodriguez-Trias, Helen, Pacific Institute for Women's Health, *USA,* 256

Romo, Alicia, Instituto de Estudios del Pacífico, Universidad Gabriela Mistral, *Chile,* 194

Rosecrance, Richard, Center for International Relations, University of California, Los Angeles, *USA,* 279

Rosenthal, Gert, Comisión Económica para América Latina y el Caribe, *Chile,* 187

Roth, Kenneth, Human Rights Watch/California, *USA,* 237

Rubio, Luis F., Centro de Investigación para el Desarrollo, *Mexico,* 202

Saint-Pierre, Guy, Business Council on National Issues, *Canada,* 139

Saito, Jiro, Foundation for Advanced Information and Research, *Japan,* 42

SaKong, Il, Institute for Global Economics, *South Korea,* 78

Sanf-Chul, Kim, Pacific Asia Society, *South Korea,* 90

Sang-Yong, Choi, Asiatic Research Center, Korea University, *South Korea,* 86

Sasono, Adi, Center for Information and Development Studies, *Indonesia,* 35

Sato, Seizaburo, Institute for International Policy Studies, *Japan,* 43

Savanti, Victor L., Fundación de Investigaciones Económicas Latinoamericanas, *Argentina,* 172

Saxod, Elsa R., United States-Mexico Border Progress Foundation, *USA,* 271

Saywell, William, Asia Pacific Foundation of Canada, *Canada,* 137

Schnepp, Otto, East Asian Studies Center, University of Southern California, *USA,* 295

Searby, Richard, Australian Institute of International Affairs, *Australia,* 117

Shaw, Yu-ming, Institute of International Relations, National Chengchi University, *Taiwan,* 101

She, Jianming, Academy of Macroeconomic Research of the State Planning Commission, *China,* 4

Shen, Qurong, China Institute of Contemporary International Relations, *China,* 7

Sheu, Jia-You, Institute of European and American Studies, Academia Sinica, *Taiwan,* 96

Shirk, Susan, Institute on Global Conflict and Cooperation, University of California, San Diego, *USA,* 283

Silva, Patricio, Centro de Estudios del Desarrollo, *Chile,* 185

Siu-lun, Wong, Centre of Asian Studies, University of Hong Kong, *Hong Kong,* 32

Smith, Darrel, British Columbia Chamber of Commerce, *Canada,* 138

Snitwongse, Kusuma, Institute of Security and International Studies, Chulalongkorn University, *Thailand,* 105

Sohmen, Helmut, Pacific Basin Economic Council, *USA,* 252

Somavia V., Juan, Comisión Sudamericana de Paz, *Chile,* 188

Sopiee, Noordin, Institute of Strategic and International Studies, *Malaysia,* 67

Soto, Hernando de, Instituto Libertad y Democracia, *Peru,* 217

Souza, Heitor Gurgulino, The United Nations University, *Japan,* 63

Stevens, Donald, Institute for International Business, University of Colorado, *USA,* 284

Su, Zhenxing, Institute of Latin American Studies, Chinese Academy of Social Sciences, *China,* 13

Sucharithanarugse, Withaya, Institute of Asian Studies, Chulalongkorn University, *Thailand,* 104

Sumida, Kenji, East-West Center, *USA,* 233

Sussangkarn, Chalongphob, Thailand Development Research Institute, *Thailand,* 106

Taccone, Juan Jose, Instituto para la Integración de América Latina y el Caribe, *Argentina,* 174

Taft, Jim, World Affairs Council of San Diego, *USA,* 302

Talavera, Arturo Fontaine, Centro de Estudios Públicos, *Chile,* 186

Tanabe, Willa J., School of Hawaiian, Asian and Pacific Studies, University of Hawaii at Manoa, *USA,* 288

Tanaka, Kenzo, The International Center for the Study of East Asian Development, Kitakyushu, *Japan,* 45

Thomson, James A., RAND, *USA,* 258

Tien, Hung-mao, Institute for National Policy Research, *Taiwan,* 100

Tooker, Gary L., Pacific Basin Economic Council, *USA,* 252

Torre, Jose de la, Center for International Business Education and Research, University of California, Los Angeles, *USA,* 278

Toyoda, Shoichiro, Keidanren, *Japan,* 54

Trood, Russell, Centre for the Study of Australia-Asia Relations, Griffith University, *Australia,* 123

Tsubouchi, Yoshihiro, Center for Southeast Asian Studies, Kyoto University, *Japan,* 55

Turpin, Tim, Centre for Research Policy, University of Wollongong, *Australia,* 128

Tussie, Diana, Facultad Latinoamericana de Ciencias Sociales, Área de Relaciones Internacionales, *Argentina,* 171

Unger, Jonathan, Contemporary China Centre, Australian National University, *Australia,* 119

Vautier, Kerrin M., New Zealand Institute of Economic Research, *New Zealand,* 131

Vial R-T, Joaquin, Corporación de Investigaciones Económicas para Latinoamerica, *Chile,* 189

Vu, Tuyen Quang, Vietnam Asia-Pacific Economic Center, *Vietnam,* 113

Wakeman, Frederic E., Institute of East Asian Studies, University of California, Berkeley, *USA,* 274

Walker, Michael, Fraser Institute, *Canada,* 151

Walls, Jan W., David Lam Centre for International Communication, Simon Fraser University, *Canada,* 158

Wanandi, Jusuf, Center for Strategic and International Studies, *Indonesia,* 37

Watts, Michael J., Institute of International Studies, University of California, Berkeley, *USA,* 275

White, Peter G., Canadian Institute of International Affairs, *Canada,* 146

Wirth, John D., The North America Institute, *USA,* 251

Wong, Y. C. Richard, The Hong Kong Centre for Economic Research, *Hong Kong,* 30

Wright, Lorna, The Centre for Canada-Asia Business Relations, Queen's University, *Canada,* 156

Wu, Rong-I, Taiwan Institute of Economic Research, *Taiwan,* 102

Wu, Wong Gung, Institute of East Asian Political Economy, *Singapore,* 74

Xie, Xide, Center for American Studies, Fudan University, *China,* 18

Xu, Xin, China Institute for International Strategic Studies, *China,* 6

Yamada, Katsuhisa, Institute of Developing Economies, *Japan,* 44

Yamamoto, Tadashi, Japan Center for International Exchange, *Japan,* 50

Yamamoto, Takuma, Research Institute for Peace and Security, *Japan,* 59

Yamanishi, Herbert, Japanese American Citizens Leauge, *USA,* 241

Yang, Richard H., Chinese Council of Advanced Policy Studies, *Taiwan,* 98

Yang, Shengming, Institute of Finance and Trade Economics, Chinese Academy of Social Sciences, *China,* 10

Yoo, Jang Hee, Korea Institute for International Economic Policy, *South Korea,* 84

Yu, Zhengliang, Department of International Politics, Fudan University, *China,* 20

Yuan, Lee Tsao, The Institute of Policy Studies, *Singapore,* 75

Yue, Chia Siow, Institute of Southeast Asian Studies, *Singapore,* 76

Yue-man, Yeung, Hong Kong Institute of Asia-Pacific Studies, The Chinese University of Hong Kong, *Hong Kong,* 28

Zevallos M., Felipe Ortiz de, Grupo APOYO, *Peru,* 214

Zhang, Yunling, Chinese Academy of Social Sciences, *China:* Institute of Asia-Pacific Studies, 9; Institute of Japanese Studies, 12

Zheng, Lizhi, Center for Japanese Studies, Fudan University, *China,* 19

Zhou, Jianming, Institute of Asia and Pacific Studies, Shanghai Academy of Social Sciences, *China,* 22

Zysman, John, Berkeley Roundtable on the International Economy, University of California, Berkeley, *USA,* 273